NAZIS IN NEWARK

NAZIS IN NEWARK

WARREN GROVER

TRANSACTION PUBLISHERS
NEW BRUNSWICK (U.S.A.) AND LONDON (U.K.)

Library of Congress Number: 2003050772
ISBN: 0-7658-0193-0 (cloth); 0-7658-0516-2 (paper)
Printed in the United States of America

Library of Congress Cataloging-in-Publication Data

Grover, Warren.
    Nazis in Newark / Warren Grover.
        p. cm.
    Includes bibliographical references (p.) and index.
    ISBN 0-7658-0193-0 (alk. paper) ; ISBN 0-7658-0516-2 (paper: alk. paper)
    1. Newark (N. J.)—Ethnic relations.   2. Newark (N. J.)—History—20th
century.   3. Nazis—New Jersey—Newark—History—20th century.   4. Na-
tional socialism—New Jersey—Newark—History—20th century.   5. German
American Bund—History.   6. Anti-Nazi movement—New Jersey—Newark—
History—20th century.   7. Jews—New Jersey—Newark—Politics and govern-
ment—20th century.   8. Jews—New Jersey—Newark—Biography.   9.
Minorities—New Jersey—Newark—Political activity—History—20th century.
I. Title.

F144.N69 G76 2003
974.9'3200431—dc21   2003050772

For My Son
Owen Peck Grover
and
To the Enduring Memory of My Son
Daniel Charles Grover
(1966-1997)

Contents

Illustrations follow page 173

Acknowledgements

Without my supportive family the writing of this book would have been much more difficult. I thank my wife Andrea for her patience and her editorial skills, my brother Dr. Stuart Grover for serving as a sounding board for many of the ideas in this work as well as for editing the first draft of the manuscript, and my son Owen for good-naturedly enduring endless calls about computer problems.

I thank the United Jewish Communities of MetroWest New Jersey and its executive vice president, Max Kleinman, for their support of this project.

Irving Louis Horowitz, Chairman of Transaction Publishers, made valuable suggestions for *Nazis in Newark.*

For early and consistent advice and encouragement, I am grateful to Franco Zerlenga and Myron Sugarman. Myron was also instrumental in helping me obtain interviews with some of the surviving Minutemen.

Dr. Edward Shapiro read the manuscript and provided insightful historical and editorial suggestions. Dr. John Earl Haynes, 20th Century Political Historian of the Library of Congress, was helpful with the chapters involving the American Communist Party. Jon Zonderman edited an early draft of the manuscript, and my editor at Transaction Publishers, Laurence Mintz, applied his fine skills to the final manuscript.

Jennifer Lenkiewicz provided valuable research and clerical assistance.

Throughout the research and writing of the book, I received assistance from many archival and library institutions. I wish to express special gratitude to the Jewish Historical Society of MetroWest, repository of the community records that were invaluable in the writing of this book, and its archivist, Joseph Settanni. Archivists Marek Web and Fruma Mohrer and library directors Zachary Baker and the late Dina Abramowitz at the YIVO Institute were unstinting in their help. Charles Cummings, director of the New Jersey Division of the

Newark Public Library, was a font of information on that collection and offered much useful advice. Principal librarian Robert Blackwell was unflappable during six years of requests for sources and information. Staff members James Stuart Osbourn, Valerie Austin, Willis Taylor, and April Kane were always gracious with their assistance.

Other archivists who facilitated my research include Timothy Driscoll, Andover Harvard Theological Library; Linda Colton, FBI; the late Monsigneur William Field, Seton Hall; Father Ed Leahy, St. Benedicts; Tom Frusciano, Rutgers University; Kenneth Myers, New Jersey Historical Society; Kevin Proffitt, American Jewish Archives; Ronald L. Bulatoff, Hoover Archive; Ruth Grant, Steven Wise Free Synagogue; Wayne De Caesar and Fred Romansky, National Archives College Park Maryland; Marilyn Ibach, Library of Congress; Jeff Cohen, Jewish War Veteran's Archive; and Bette Epstein, New Jersey Archives.

I am grateful to the many people who provided information and leads, including Judy Amsterdam, Frank Askin, Ruth Bardach, Jack Behrle, Steven M. Bergson, Burton Bleakney, Ed Brody, Bernard Bush, Emma Byrne, the late Nat Dunetz, Jack Fischer, Bernard Forgang, Martin Fox, Loretta Freeman, Martin Gen, Miriam Gittelson, the late David Goldfarb, Pam Goldstein, Melissa Fay Green, Dr.Irena Gross, Seymour Graifman, Doris Harlan, Henry Hascup, Dr. William Helmreich, Isidor Hirschhorn, Russell Hollister, Joseph Horowitz, Martin Horowitz, Michael Howard, Donald Karp, Drs.Alan and Deborah Kraut, the late Jerry Kugel, Phil Lax, the late Jerry Lehman, Roberta Levine, Mac Lohman, Janet Lowenstein, Dr. Robert and Zelda Lowenstein, Mark Lowenthal, Maurice Malamuth, Seymour Malamuth, David Margolick, Tina Marzell, the late Miriam Melrod, Bruce Miller, Jon Miller, Dr. Barbara Mitnick, Emmanuel Nathan, Jack Oelbaum, Laurissa Owen, Sarah Owen, Dr. Victor Parsonnet, Rose Peck, James Patuto, Benjamin Perlmutter, Dr. Clement Alexander Price, the late Lucille Procida, Sid Rosenkrantz, Akiva Roth, Dr. Donald Rothfeld, Dr. Albert Rothseid, Doris Rothseid, Paula Sandfelder, Bernard Schneiderman, Martin Schwartz, Fran and Clark Silver, the late Hope Shapiro, Seymour Sperling, Daniel Stacher, Harry Starrett, John Steinbach, Barbara Steiner, Ned Steiner, the late Harry Stevenson, the late Allie Stoltz, Elliot Sudler, Barry Taub, the late Hank Veillette, Paula Warhaftig, Ray Weckstein, Dr. Robert Weinmann, Dr. Jay Weiss, and Dr. Stephen Whitfield.

My maternal grandfather, Rabbi Simon Glazer (1879-1938), author of *The Jews of Iowa* (1905), provided the genetic component of my interest in local history.

I am indebted to the late Pinnie Josephson and the late Mickey Fischer for providing the inspiration to write *Nazis in Newark*. A few weeks before leaving a thirty-year business career, I was swapping Newark stories with Pinnie. He mentioned an event about which I had heard many versions over the preceding forty years—the night Abner "Longie" Zwillman and his gang beat up a group of local Nazis. The next day I was with Mickey Fischer, a top-ranked amateur boxer in the late 1930s. When I asked if he remembered the incident, he related that Zwilllman, Newark's Jewish crime boss, had formed an anti-Nazi group in the 1930s called the Minutemen and that Nat Arno, an ex-boxer and member of Zwillman's gang, had been its leader. I decided that I would write an article on the Minutemen for the local press. After some initial research, I realized that this incident was only one part—and a fascinating part, at that—of a larger story. A month later I began writing this book.

Without the help of those acknowledged, this book could not have become a reality. However, I take sole responsibility for the book's contents.

Abbreviations

ACLU	American Civil Liberties Union
AFC	America First Committee
AFF	American Fellowship Forum
AJC	American Jewish Congress
ALAWF	American League Against War and Fascism
ALPD	American League for Peace and Democracy
AYC	American Youth Congress
BPWC	Business and Professional Women's Club
CDA	Committee to Defend America by Aiding the Allies
CIO	Congress of Industrial Organizations
FFF	Fight for Freedom
Friends	Friends of the New Germany
HUAC	House Un-American Activities Committee
IWO	International Workers' Order
JBC	Joint Boycott Council
JDC	Joint Distribution Committee
JLC	Joint Labor Committee
JWV	Jewish War Veterans
LWV	League of Women Voters
NSANL	Non-Sectarian Anti-Nazi League
NSDAP	National Socialist German Worker's Party (Nazi Party)
OD	Uniformed Service of the Friends and the Bund
WILPF	Women's International League for Peace and Freedom
WPU	Women's Political Union
Y	YM&YWHA

List of Illustrations and Maps

Introduction

An insignificant-looking building stands on Springfield Avenue, less than a mile from downtown Newark. Its ground floor is occupied by a bar; on the second and third floors are meeting halls for African-American Masonic orders. Long forgotten, this building was once the center of the fierce anti-Nazi struggle that took place in Newark from 1933 until 1941.

Then called Schwabenhalle, it was the scene of two major riots five years apart, as well as numerous lesser conflicts over an eight-year period. The combatants were the same each time—Newark's Nazis and its anti-Nazis. From Hitler's ascension to power in January 1933 until the attack on Pearl Harbor in December 1941, Newark was the center of a battle that pitted the Nazi movement and its supporters against those who believed in freedom and democracy.

What makes Newark unique in this struggle is that two anti-Nazi groups, the Minutemen[1] and the Newark division of the Non-Sectarian Anti-Nazi League (NSANL), combined to attack two domestic Nazi organizations, first the Friends of the New Germany and later its successor the German-American Bund. The struggle extended to efforts against neo-Nazi groups such as the Silver Shirts and the Christian Front, as well as the potentially Nazi America First.

The Minutemen was a group made up of prizefighters and gangsters who fought against domestic Nazis and their sympathizers with physical confrontation and intimidation. The NSANL, on the other hand, used protests and a boycott against German goods as its weapons of choice.

As in other American cities with large Jewish and German populations, Newark in the 1930s had both Nazi activities and Jewish opposition. Many works on the Jewish history of American cities include the period 1933-1941, but few mention Jewish physical and political resistance to domestic Nazism.[2] Only in Newark was there an anti-Nazi fighting force that remained active from Hitler's rise in 1933 to American entrance into World War II. Additionally, in works

1

on Jewish boxers and gangsters who fought Nazis, there are no groups mentioned with the longevity of the Minutemen or a leader who remained as committed to the battle as Nat Arno.[3]

Arno was a minor prizefighter in the 1920s, and an enforcer for Newark's preeminent Jewish gangster, Abner "Longie" Zwillman, a role he continued to play throughout his time as the Minutemen's "commander." Dr. S. William Kalb, leader of Newark's anti-Nazi boycott effort, could not have been more different. A physician by training, Kalb essentially gave up his medical practice in the 1930s to make anti-Nazism his life's work.

Close coordination between Arno and Kalb, based both on personal feelings and ideology, made it possible for the Minutemen and the anti-Nazi boycott activists to consistently aid each other and to create an anti-Nazi force in Newark that held at bay German-American Nazis and other anti-Semitic groups while at the same time giving a sense of purpose to those Newark Jews who wanted to inflict damage on Germany.

Newark, New Jersey was one of the nation's most prominent cities. Strong leadership kept Newark from becoming a suburb of New York City. Newark's large industrial and commercial base produced enough jobs to employ its workforce. By the close of World War I in 1919, Newark was one of America's largest industrial producers. But beginning in the 1920s the city entered a long era of decline during which its industrial base steadily shrunk.

The city's inability to expand by absorbing adjoining suburbs, along with zoning policies that allowed manufacturing and commercial use close to or within residential areas led to an exodus of many of the city's business and cultural leaders. By 1929, over 60 percent of the board members of Newark's influential Chamber of Commerce lived in Newark's suburbs while keeping their businesses in the city.[4] The Great Depression and attendant social problems led to the city's further decline. Newark's employed population of almost 200,000 in 1930 dropped 20 percent to 159,000 in 1940, while the population also declined from 442,337 to 429,760.[5]

Founded in 1666 by Puritans from Connecticut, Newark remained a fundamentally conservative city. The waves of German, Irish, Jewish, and Italian immigrants who populated the city throughout the nineteenth and early twentieth centuries created vibrant working and middle classes, but did little to change the city's underlying conservatism. Throughout the period studied in this work, effective anti-

Nazi responses came from conservative rather than liberal sources.

Those Newark liberals who were also anti-Nazi were few in number and unable to transmit their values to the public at large. The small liberal community found itself co-opted during the late 1930s by the American Communist Party, and thus tied up in that organization's internecine strife around the Nazi-Soviet Pact of 1939 and Hitler's subsequent march east into the Soviet Union in 1941.

The Newark chapter of the Communist Party was organized in July 1932,[6] and became the city's first organized opponent of Nazism immediately after Hitler came to power six months later. By seizing on the issues of Nazism, as well as pacifism, unionism, and racism, Newark communists were able to influence many of the city's liberals. Although they had no influence on the socially conservative Minutemen and NSANL, there were times when these two groups cooperated with the communists in anti-Nazi actions.

Ethnic groups made up much of Newark's population. It is estimated that in 1930 the city included 85,000 Italians, 65,000 Jews, 47,000 Germans, and 38,000 Irish. According to the 1930 census, there were also 39,000 African Americans in Newark.[7]

Newark's ethnic groups often battled each other for political, social, and economic power. In the nineteenth and early twentieth centuries, descendants of the city's Puritan founders vied with both German Lutherans and Irish Catholics for religious and political pre-eminence. In the 1920s and 1930s, Italians and Jews battled the Irish for political power. The emergence of Mussolini and Hitler caused distrust between the Jews and their Italian and German neighbors. Irish Catholics' latent anti-Semitism was piqued both by European events and such homegrown anti-Semites as Father Charles E. Coughlin. Newark's Irish Catholics especially resented Jewish radicals, although they made up only a small fraction of Newark's Jewish population.

Within the Jewish community itself, the split between Eastern European and German Jews made matters worse. German Jews had settled in Newark as early as the middle of the nineteenth century, part of a larger wave of liberal Germans who had fled the reactionary regimes that came to power after the failure of democratic revolution throughout Europe in 1848. By the 1930s, the German Jews had established themselves economically as well as socially. They had their own liberal synagogues, a business club, and a country club. They were the powerful voices on the Conference of Jewish

Charities, which provided economic and social aid to the city's needy Jews, mostly Eastern Europeans who had come to America in the 1880s after Polish and Russian pogroms. At first resentful of these Yiddish-speaking Eastern European Jews, the German Jews soon saw that it was in their interest to help assimilate these newcomers and provide them with charitable assistance. The Young Men's/Young Women's Hebrew Association (YM&YWHA) and Jewish settlement houses sprouted up in Newark, as they did in other Eastern and Midwestern cities during the early decades of the twentieth century.

The two factions in the Jewish community had different responses to Nazism. The prosperous German Jews held political and economic views similar to those of other businessmen—they were anti-union and anti-radical, and they saw Nazism as a temporary phenomenon. They felt they were "100 percent American" and should attend to their businesses and families, leaving God and government to attend to Hitler.

They took no action against Newark's Nazis and for the most part were unenthusiastic about the boycott Kalb and the NSANL organized against German goods and services. And they would never think of mixing it up in the streets of Newark alongside Arno and his Minutemen. Their activities were focused on supporting relief efforts for both Jews in Germany and those who had emigrated to other countries, particulary America.

Many in Newark's German Jewish community belonged to Temple B'Nai Jeshurun, a synagogue in the liberal Reform movement of Judaism. They followed the political and religious lead of their rabbi, Solomon Foster, the first rabbi in America with two American-born parents. An anti-unionist, Foster was hostile to Eastern European Jews, whom he said were more active in unionism than Christians. Foster's involvement on the boards of the Salvation Army and the University of Newark, and his frequent participation in interfaith events, made him the Christian clergy's favorite Newark Jew.

Large numbers of Eastern European Jews arrived in Newark in the 1880s through the early 1920s. Most worked as laborers and craftsmen in the trades they brought with them from their homelands. Some opened small retail businesses. Their children learned English in Newark's schools and tried to achieve the American dream.

Whether they remained in the working class or became professionals, small business owners, or white-collar workers, Jews shared a fear of anti-Semitism instilled in them by their parents and grandparents, who had faced it personally in Europe. It was from these roots that Newark's particular brand of anti-Nazism was born.

Jews in Newark enjoyed a rich organizational life. A series of studies conducted in the late 1930s identified 140 Jewish fraternal and family associations providing welfare, charitable, social, and cultural services. In addition there were local branches of sixteen national organizations, plus eight athletic and three political clubs.[8]

There were approximately 65,000 Jews in Newark during the 1930s.[9] The only English-language Jewish newspaper in the city (or in the state for that matter) was the weekly *Jewish Chronicle*, founded in 1921 by Anton Kaufman, who was still the publisher. The paper was tightly aligned with the organized Jewish community, and reported on the charitable, social, and religious activities of the Newark area's major Jewish institutions. During the 1930s, the *Chronicle* increasingly covered the activities of Newark's Eastern European Jews.

Through the early 1930s Rabbi Solomon Foster wrote a weekly editorial for the *Chronicle,* which reflected the assimilationist ideology of his congregation. He was a strong proponent of the maintenance of good relations with the Christian community. During the 1930s, the *Chronicle* reflected the internal conflicts of much of the Jewish community, trying to maintain a middle course. Fearing the Nazis, the *Chronicle* endorsed the anti-Nazi boycott, yet remained aloof from the street brawls and other violent tactics the Minutemen used against the Nazis.

Germans first arrived in Newark in the 1830s. In 1833 the first German church and aid society were founded and by 1835 there were approximately 300 Germans in the city.[10] The 1848 German revolution brought substantial numbers of Germans to Newark. By 1879, the community had become influential enough to produce a German-born mayor, William H. Fiedler.

With their industriousness, thrift, and focus on education, Newark's Germans established an economically thriving community. Their many singing societies and *turnvereins* (sports clubs) encouraged the city's educational system to adopt compulsory music and gym classes. Additionally, Newark's first opera house and the Academy of Newark were the products of German initiative.

Germans were the first to challenge Newark's Puritan hegemony. The major battle was over Sunday Sabbath observance, which most German-Americans eschewed in favor of a day of family relaxation and beer and wine drinking. The issue came to a head in 1879 when

William H. Fiedler was elected on a platform of non-enforcement of the Sunday laws prohibiting alcohol. His opponent, Theodore Macknet, on the other hand, was committed to strict enforcement of the Sunday laws.[11]

World War I brought a halt to the German community's ascendancy in Newark. Anti-German hysteria affected the entire country and in Newark, streets with German names were changed and Germans were discriminated against in employment and housing.[12] This hysteria had a permanent effect on many Germans, who dropped out of German-American organizations and sought to completely integrate themselves into American life.

Another wave of German immigrants came to Newark in the wake of World War I. While they helped maintain and invigorate the German community, they also brought a heightened nationalistic identity. Simultaneously, the German population spread from its traditional neighborhoods, moving west up Springfield Avenue and into the suburb of Irvington.[13] While Germans who arrived in the nineteenth century were escaping undemocratic regimes, those who immigrated in the 1920s were fleeing a German economy decimated by war, reparations to the victorious allies, and hyperinflation. Many were resentful of Jews and angry at the communists. They would prove to be fertile ground for Nazi provocateurs.

Newark's Third Ward working class and small-business owners were the first Jews to encounter Nazism, in 1933. The Third Ward had once been home of much of the city's German population, but Jews gradually replaced the Germans starting in the 1880s. And African Americans were a significant minority in the area by the 1930s. Springfield Avenue ran through the Third Ward. It was one of Newark's main retail shopping streets and a mixed Jewish/German area. Many Jews and Germans lived in adjacent neighborhoods along Springfield Avenue in Newark and Irvington. Their relations were generally cordial. They shopped in each other's stores, lived with each other in multiple-family homes, and went to the same schools. Relations between the older German settlers and the German Jews, communities that had come to America at the same time, were even closer. The Essex County branch of the German-Austrian War Veterans, the largest German-American veteran organization, had Jewish members. However, once Hitler came to power in January 1933 and persecution against Jews in Germany began, relations between Jews and Germans in Newark deteriorated.

The Minutemen came from the large Eastern European working class. They perceived the essence of Nazism and acted accordingly. They did not trust the government to protect the Jews. Indeed, they believed that Nazism in Newark could only be defeated with iron pipes and fists. No rallies, resolutions, picketing, or words of any kind would stop the Nazi's lethal hatred of Jews—only force. From 1933 to 1940 they fought the Nazis in the streets.

The majority of the German-American population in the Newark area avoided Nazism and its bellicose anti-Semitism. However, a minority composed mainly of post-World War I immigrants—many of whom remained resident aliens and had not sought American citizenship—actively engaged in pro-Nazi activities. They were encouraged by a small group of German nationals planted in Newark—some as early as the 1920s—as agent provocateurs by the German Nazi Party (NSDAP) to set up an American Nazi party.

These men worked to win over elements of the Newark area's German-American community, using ceaseless propaganda, consisting mainly of charges that a Jewish-Communist cabal was running the Unites States. Hundreds of agents were sent to cities with large German populations to convert the local German Americans to the Nazi cause and set up a "fifth column." The German government assumed responsibility for this effort in 1933.

The Friends of the New Germany (Friends) was established to further this cause. Newark was one of the Friends' first targets, both because of its large German-American population and its proximity to New York City, the center of Nazi activity in the United States. When the Friends began operating in Newark in the spring of 1933, it openly advertised its meetings and anti-Semitic message, a provocation that led to the creation of the Minutemen.

Although a few German Americans denounced the Nazis, most simply did not want to get involved. But Newark and Irvington's Eastern European Jews lived cheek-by-jowl with the German community. They felt threatened by the Nazi presence in their neighborhoods and with the unchecked violence against Jews in Germany.

They felt even more threatened after learning that the Friends were distributing anti-Semitic literature and holding meetings of brown-shirted men. Unreported by the press, these manifestations elicited neither governmental denunciation nor police action. Consequently, the Jews determined to protect themselves. Longie Zwillman, Newark's most feared Jew, picked the toughest members of his gang for an anti-Nazi organization, the Minutemen. When the Friends of the New Germany held its first public meetings in Newark in the fall of 1933, the Minutemen attacked them with a fury that was noted throughout America.

An anti-Nazi boycott group, led first by Newark Post 34 of the Jewish War Veterans, then by the city's Young Men's Hebrew Club, and finally by the NSANL, soon joined Zwillman's anti-Nazi effort. Dr. S. William Kalb became boycott chairman of Post 34 in April 1933. By early 1934, Kalb had formed a personal and organizational alliance with Nat Arno, Zwillman's designated Minutemen commander. Arno and Kalb's organizations proceeded to battle Nazism in Newark until 1941.

The alliance between criminals and aspiring middle-class sons of Eastern European immigrants was a remarkable seven-year partnership. It demonstrates once again how America's immigrants are willing to fight against those who threaten the ideals of freedom and democracy.

Notes

1.   Elements of Longie Zwillman's Third Ward Gang merged with and then assumed control of the Minutemen in 1934. The Minutemen emanated from Newark Post 34, Jewish War Veterans, and the Young Men's Hebrew Club (see chapter 2).

2.   See Endleman, Judith E., *The Jewish Community of Indianapolis*, Bloomington, IN, 1984, pp. 172-178 (resistance to the German-American Bund through violence and education); Swichkow, Louis J. And Lloyd Gartner, *The History of the Jews of Milwaukee*, Philadelphia, 1963, pp. 304-307 (resistance to domestic anti-Semitism by education); Sarna, Jonathan D. and Nancy Klein, *The Jews of Cincinnati*, 1989, pp. 139-146 (resistance to domestic anti-Semitism by education); *Jewish Life in Philadelphia, 1830-1940*, Murray Friedman, ed., Philadelphia, 1983, pp. 20, 21 (resistance to the German-American Bund through education); Gartner, Lloyd P., *History of the Jews of Cleveland*, Cleveland, OH, 1978, pp. 300-302 (resistance to Nazism and anti-Semitism through education and the anti-Nazi boycott); Gordon, Rabbi Albert I., *Jews in Transition (Minneapolis)*, Minneapolis, MN, 1949, pp. 50-53 (mention of anti-Semitism but not of resistance); Vorspan, Max, and Lloyd P. Gartner, *History of the Jews of Los Angeles*, Philadelphia, 1970, pp. 205-207 (resistance to Nazism and anti-Semitism through education); Cutler, Irving, *The Jews of Chicago, From Shtetl to Suburb*, Urbana, 1996, p. 128 (resistance to Nazism through anti-Nazi boycott); Klinger, Maurice, A. Abbot Rosen and Dr. Walter Zand, "Jewish Defense Agencies," pp. 175-178 as published in Sentinel Publishing Co.'s *History of Chicago's Jewry, 1911-1961*, Chicago, 1961 (resistance to Nazism through anti-Nazi boycott and education); Adler, Selig and Thomas E. Connolly, *The History of the Jewish Community of Buffalo*, Philadelphia, 1960, p. 383 (mention of Nazi activity but no resistance); Raphael, Marc Lee, *Jews and Judaism in a Midwestern Community: Columbus, Ohio, 1840-1975*, Columbus, OH, 1979 (no mention of Nazism or anti-Semitism); Helmreich, William B., *The Enduring Community: The Jews of Newark and MetroWest*, New Brunswick, NJ, 1999, pp. 29, 172 (resistance to Nazism through violence and education); Burton Alan Boxerman, "Rise of Anti-Semitism in St. Louis, 1933-1945," pp. 251-269, as published in *YIVO Annual*, XIV, New York, 1969 (demonstrations against Nazis in St. Louis in 1938).

3. See Teller, Judd, *Scapegoat of Revolution*, New York, 1954, pp. 183,184 (attacks by Murder Incorporated against Nazis in metropolitan New York); Berman, Susan, *Easy Street*, New York, 1981, pp. 144-146 (David Berman —father of Susan— a gangster, fought Nazis in Minneapolis); Eisenberg, Dennis, Uri Dan, and Eli Landau, *Meyer Lansky: Mogul of the Mob*, New York, 1979, pp. 184-186 (Rabbi Stephen Wise asked Lansky to stop the German-American Bund in New York. After several years of success, adverse publicity caused Wise to tell Lansky to halt the operation.); Rockaway, Robert A., *But He Was Good to His Mother*, Jerusalem, 1993, pp. 225-233 (Jewish gangsters in New York, Newark, Minneapolis, Chicago, and Los Angeles fought Nazis); Levitt, Cyril H. And William Shaffir, *The Riot at Christie Pits*, Toronto, 1987 (a riot between Toronto anti-Semites, many of whom supported the Nazis, and Jewish youths, some of whom were boxers).

4. Stellhorn, Paul Anthony, *Depression and Decline: Newark, New Jersey: 1929-1941*, pp. 26,27; PH.D. Dissertation, University Microfilms International. By the onset of World War II over 85 percent of the Chamber's board lived outside of Newark. In 1916 all members of the Chamber's predecessor, the Newark Board of Trade, lived in the city.

5. U. S. Bureau of the Census, *Fifteenth Census of the United States: 1930, New Jersey Abstract*, New Jersey Division, Newark Public Library, pp. 191, 213; *Sixteenth Census of the United States: 1940*, Population, Vol. II, Part 4, Washington, DC, 1943, pp. 928, 930.

6. CPUSA, Reel 225, Delo 2919, Report on the New Jersey District-District 14, 7/18/32, p. 1.

7. U. S. Bureau of the Census, *Sixteenth Census of the United States: 1940*, op. cit., p. 930.

8. WPA New Jersey Writer's Project, Ethnological Survey, Box 2, Folder 25, Jews in New Jersey- Notes, Mazie Berse, "List of Newark Organizations," 13 pages, undated circa late 1939, early 1940.

9. Ibid., Box 2, Folder 28, Letter from H.S. Linfield, director, Jewish Statistical Bureau to Dr. G.Y. Rusk, 4/14/37.

    A Newark YMHA flier from 1939 estimates the Jewish population of Newark as 70,000 (see Box 2, Folder 4). Linfield estimates the Jewish population of Newark's suburbs as:

Irvington	1,295
East Orange	2,000
South Orange	1,000
West Orange	500
Orange	1,000
Montclair	450

10. *A History of Newark*, Newark, 1911, vol. 2, William Von Katzler, "The Germans of Newark," pp. 1048,1049.

11. Cunningham, John T., *Newark*, Newark, 1988, pp. 199, 200.

12. Ibid., pp. 259, 260.

13. Irvington was a total suburb of Newark—it had neither a hotel nor a railroad station, depending on Newark for both. For purpose of this study, events in Irvington are construed as part and parcel of the struggle between Newark's Nazis and anti-Nazis.

1

Responses to Nazism

On January 30, 1933 Adolf Hitler became the chancellor of Germany. The next evening, Rabbi Jonah P. Wise, national chairman of the Joint Distribution Committee (JDC),[1] appeared in Newark to plead for funds for Eastern European Jews who faced "starvation conditions and economic pressure [which were reducing them] to an animal level." Wise made his plea at a regularly scheduled meeting of the Board of Directors of the Newark Conference of Jewish Charities.[2] To meet the crisis, the JDC hoped to raise $1.5 million from American Jewish communities. Although he mentioned no quota for Newark, Wise asked the board to sponsor fund-raising activities to help the effort. The board's response was to appoint a committee of five, to formulate plans and to "cooperate fully" with the JDC.[3]

Rabbi Solomon Foster of Temple B'Nai Jeshurun, Newark's oldest, wealthiest, and most prestigious congregation, was chosen to chair the committee.[4] The Newark Conference of Jewish Charities was dominated by wealthy, relatively assimilated Jews whose families had emigrated from German states, including Moravia and Bohemia (now the Czech Republic), in the nineteenth century.[5] Many belonged to Temple B'Nai Jeshurun.

The fund-raising campaign for Eastern European Jewry never got off the ground because events in Germany turned Jewish attention from Eastern to Western Europe. By February, newspapers were reporting that an ugly tide of anti-Semitism was sweeping Germany. Across the United States, Jews and Christians, collectively and individually, voiced solidarity with German Jewry. In Newark, the City Commission passed a resolution calling on the German government to desist from attacks on Jews. The North Jersey Region of the American Jewish Congress (AJC) and the New Jersey Federation of YM & YWHAs (the "Y") sent a resolution to President Franklin Roosevelt protesting Nazi excesses.[6]

Newark's English-language Jewish weekly, the *Jewish Chronicle*, on February 17 (in its first editorial notice of Hitler's ascension to power), took German Jews to task for "smoothing the road" for Hitler by treating his predecessors Heinrich Bruening, Franz von Papen, and Kurt von Schleicher with tolerance "and even flattery."[7] In the same issue, the *Chronicle* reported that at an event honoring Meyer Ellenstein, a newly appointed Newark commissioner, Rabbi Julius Silberfeld of Temple B'Nai Abraham lauded Ellenstein's rise to prominence from humble beginnings as a tribute to democracy and contrasted it with a recent speech by Hitler condemning democracy.[8]

Across the nation, Jewish groups discussed how to respond to Nazi actions. The AJC called a March 19 meeting, which was attended by 1,500 delegates from national and local Jewish organizations. It was decided to hold anti-Nazi protest rallies in Jewish communities throughout the country on Monday, March 27. In Newark, Samuel I. Kessler, a prominent attorney and president of the Newark Y, called a meeting to discuss the city's participation. He appointed a committee, composed mainly of Conference of Jewish Charities board members, to organize the rally. The committee added representatives from Newark Jewish groups to ensure that the rally committee represented a cross-section of the Jewish community.[9] However, it soon became apparent that some Newark Jewish constituencies were either excluded or under-represented.

The rally was scheduled for the 1,800-seat Fuld Hall at the Newark Y, located near the city's center. Participants would include not only Jewish groups but also Protestant and Catholic representatives. William Untermann, president of Newark's Ezekiel Lodge of B'Nai Brith, said that his group was generally opposed to mass meetings, preferring that "responsible Jewish leaders" meet with representatives of the German and American governments. He was, however, in favor of the rally. [10] The position of national B'Nai Brith mirrored that of the American Jewish Committee in its preference for behind-the-scenes diplomacy. Neither group supported the March 27 rallies.

Uninvited, Newark's Communist Party organization, a group with many Jewish members, decided to stage its own protest rally on April 2 at Newark's Krueger Auditorium, a popular venue for Jewish and left-wing meetings. Other participants in this event were Communist- affiliated groups such as the Russian Mutual Aid Society, the Slovak Worker's Society, the Unemployed Council, the International Workers Society, International Labor Defense, and the Jack London Society.[11]

Representatives of twelve Newark-area Jewish youth groups, feeling excluded from the March 27 event, met at the office of Assemblyman Herman Blank and made plans for their own anti-Nazi rally on April 2. This would protest the treatment of German Jewish students and young professionals. This was unacceptable to the organizers of the Y rally, since it would nullify their objective of a unified Jewish response. Assemblyman Blank was called to a meeting with Joseph Kraemer, the North Jersey AJC president and chairman of the Y rally committee. Under pressure, Blank agreed to cancel the youth rally. He told the press that the youth groups would take part in the Y rally because "I believe the demonstration will be more effective if young and old hold hands."[12]

The rally was taken seriously by all segments of Newark's Jewish population. *Schochtim*, who slaughter animals in accordance with the Jewish laws of *kashrut,* vowed to fast all day on March 27, to stop work at 4 PM, and to attend a special service at Adas Israel Synagogue on Prince Street. Newark Post 34 of the Jewish War Veterans of America (JWV) said it would forward to the British Embassy in Washington a resolution asking that Great Britain temporarily set aside the quota restriction on immigration to Palestine. Edward Fenias, a Newark lawyer and president of the New Jersey Institute of Social Research, called upon members of Kappa Delta legal fraternity at Mercer Beasley Law School (which became part of Rutgers Newark Law School in 1937) to support the rally and described the "present orgy of Hitlerism as a moral pagan reversion."[13]

The day of the rally, many Jews fasted and attended prayer services. That evening over 2,000 people filled Fuld Hall, with another 1,000 outside listening on loudspeakers. Mayor Jerome T. Congleton declared that as the "chief executive of Newark, I wish to add my protest to yours. Reports from Germany fill our souls with indignation. We not only protest but revolt against such deeds." Rev. Dr. Benjamin Washburn, Episcopal bishop of Newark, added his protest and praised "the tremendous power of such protest meetings" held throughout the country. Eugene Kinkead, a former congressman and Catholic lay leader, pledged the Catholic Church's support for Germany's beleaguered Jews. The two congressmen representing the Newark area, Frederick R. Lehlbach and Fred Hartley, also decried Nazi persecution.

Michael A. Stavitsky, vice president of the Conference of Jewish Charities, emphasized that Jews had survived "many Hitlers" and would again. In attendance were the rabbis from Newark's three non-Orthodox synagogues, Rabbi Foster of B'Nai Jeshurun, Rabbi Silberfeld of B'Nai Abraham, and Rabbi Leo Lang of Oheb Sholem. The sole representative of the over thirty Orthodox synagogues was Rabbi Joseph Konvitz, of Congregation Anshe Russia, who spoke to the crowd in Yiddish.[14]

The rally resulted in a resolution demanding cessation of anti-Semitic propaganda; abandonment of the Nazi policy of discrimination and economic exclusion of Jews from German life; proper protection of Jewish life and property by the German government; and protection for the 200,000 Eastern European Jews who had fled to Germany to escape persecution and starvation. President Roosevelt was asked to place the resolution before the German government.

Other rallies took place on March 27 in Chicago, Paris, and in New York City, where over 22,000 filled Madison Square Garden while 25,000 more outside listened to Governor Alfred E. Smith and Senator Robert Wagner.[15] The *Newark Star Eagle* editorialized that the rallies in Newark, New York, and elsewhere were part of a moral duty "to protest against brutality and stupid hatred."[16]

The sudden and intense Nazi persecution of Jews in Germany evoked the reaction that culminated in the March 27 rallies. But over the next five-and-a-half years, until Kristallnacht in November 1938, there would be no other such interdenominational mass action in Newark on behalf of German Jewry. Throughout America, the Depression, isolationism, latent anti-Semitism, and fear of communism, muted Christian opposition to atrocities against Jews. Thus, with few exceptions, the burden of the anti-Nazi struggle, both in Newark and across America, was borne by Jews.

By the end of the first year of Nazi rule in Germany, Newark's Jews had countered with five responses: commitment by Jewish organizations to a boycott against German goods; financial support from Jewish groups to help impoverished German Jews either live in Germany or emigrate; rallies and petitions to influence the American government to act against Nazi persecution of Jews; agitation to allow persecuted Jews unrestricted access to Palestine; and violence against the Friends of the New Germany, an American Nazi organization.

The boycott against German goods enabled Newark's Jews to strike a direct blow at Nazi Germany. Since the boycott campaign was international, it had the potential to promote solidarity among

Jews throughout America and all over the world. Indeed, the participation of all Jewish organizations in Newark could bridge the gulf
separating "establishment" Jews from first-and second-generation
Eastern European Jews. By the end of 1933 the boycott effort in
Newark was well underway, as it was in other American cities.

Fundraising for endangered Jews in Europe was another important response. The Newark Conference of Jewish Charities was a
leader in this regard, raising tens of thousands of dollars. Since an-
cestors and relatives of many conference board members came from
German-speaking lands, they had a familial sympathy for their brethren in Germany. Eastern European Jews also participated in
fundraising, often through *landsmanshaftn* and other benevolent and
fraternal orders. *Landsmanshaftn*, sometimes called KUVs, were
immigrant hometown associations that provided health and death
benefits to members and their families, financed by monthly dues.[17]

Rallies, mass meetings, and petitions were outlets for the anger
and frustration of Newark's Jews and had the potential to influence
public opinion against Nazism. They generated press coverage in
Newark's two dailies, both of which had a predominantly Christian
readership. The participation of political leaders could influence government policy against the Nazis. Also, some of these rallies and mass
meetings enlisted the aid of sympathetic Christian clergy and lay leaders who had access to large and/or influential Christian audiences.

Physical violence against Nazi events in Newark and its suburbs
had positive effects on the struggle against domestic Nazism. To
first and second-generation Jews in Newark's Third Ward,[18] attacks
on Nazis were a morale booster. Impotent in the face of the Depression
and anti-Semitism abroad, these residents were elated that Jewish men
from their neighborhood, frequently relatives or friends, were confronting the Friends of the New Germany. This was particularly so since the
Friends were staging anti-Semitic rallies adjacent to Jewish homes
and businesses. Other Jews in the Newark area were proud of the
fighters and viewed them as embodying Jewish manhood.

Violence against the Friends and their sympathizers had a salu-
tary effect. Nazis in Newark and Irvington, a city adjacent to Newark, were less likely to hold events close to the Third Ward. The
threat of violence discouraged active membership in the Friends and
later in the German-American Bund. Additionally, the fear of violence prevented the Friends from engaging in hostile incursions
against Jewish businesses in the Third Ward.

The sum total of these responses was impressive. The Jewish community of Newark, from the establishment (living in upper Clinton Hill, southern Weequahic, or in the suburbs of South Orange and East Orange) to the working-class residents of Prince Street, recognized the threat of Nazism. The establishment, secure in its financial and social positions, was dismissive of the Friends of the New Germany, viewing them as a small group of crackpots. Most were concerned about the fate of European Jews, especially those in Germany. Newark's Eastern European Jews worried about friends and relatives abroad, but were equally concerned with domestic Nazism. They had less faith than their wealthy co-religionists in the willingness of the police and government to prevent anti-Semitic outbreaks.

* * *

The spring of 1933 saw a spate of repressive measures against German Jews: on April 1 a one-day, nationwide boycott against Jewish businesses occurred; April 7 saw quotas applied to the number of Jewish students allowed in institutions of higher learning and laws prohibiting Jews from working in government offices; on April 21 ritual slaughter was prohibited; and on May 10 books by Jewish authors were publicly burned.

The American Jewish response to these outrages was a boycott against German goods, shipping, and services. The first call for the boycott was made on March 19, 1933 by the national JWV.[19] The New Jersey JWV endorsed the boycott on April 23 at its annual convention in Atlantic City.[20] Newark Post 34, of the JWV acted immediately and appointed Dr. S. William Kalb, a popular activist physician, its boycott chairman.[21]

In May, Dr. Abraham Coralnik, an editor of the Yiddish language daily *Der Tog* (the Day), founded the American League for the Defense of Jewish Rights. A national organization, it was established to pursue the boycott. Congressman— and soon-to-be New York City mayor— Fiorello LaGuardia, and Samuel Untermyer, an international lawyer and former advisor to President Woodrow Wilson,[22] addressed its organizational meeting. The league's formation was well publicized and received a prompt offer of help from the Young Men's Hebrew Club of Newark.

The Hebrew Club was one of the founding organizations (in 1924) of the Y. It had originally been a sports club but then became a social club as well, as the popularity and prowess of its basketball team attracted youngsters of both sexes. The Hebrew Club left the Y in 1933 for its own location on Clinton Avenue. In a May 17, 1933 letter to the league, the club described itself as an organization of more than 400 young men and women over twenty-one. The letter included the text of a resolution passed the previous night pledging to be "100 percent behind the league" in its struggle to take effective measures against Hitler, and promising to establish a committee to cooperate fully with the league "to help enforce the boycott in Newark." The league wrote back two weeks later that it would send a representative to Newark to organize a branch there.[23]

The Hebrew Club invited more than fifty Jewish fraternal organizations to its facility to meet with Coralnik to create a Newark chapter of the league. In addition to pursuing the boycott, the new group agreed to petition England and the League of Nations to allow unimpeded Jewish immigration to Palestine. The president of the Hebrew Club, the Newark Zionist leader Sholem Lipis, announced that it was contributing $25 to meet the league's expenses and would solicit other organizations.[24]

Meanwhile the league sent its secretary, Maurice Firth, to Newark to meet with "prominent and not so prominent leaders" to enlist financial support and membership for the league's Newark chapter. One of those contacted was Kessler, who supported the league boycott but objected to fundraising on the grounds that it would divert funds from other Jewish charitable campaigns. Firth also contacted the Y's executive director, Dr. Aaron G. Robison, who promised to acquaint Louis Bamberger, Newark's outstanding philanthropist and merchant, with "what is being done." A meeting was scheduled for October 23 at the Y. Firth asserted that "boycott sentiment is very strong here and a powerful body of young men have been doing a lot of effective work. They are rather tired of the local stand-pat leaders."[25]

In October there were meetings between national league leaders and the JWV. But J. George Fredman, the JWV's National Commander and a member of the league's national board, despaired that individual and class antipathies would make such cooperation difficult. [26] Fredman actively sought both JWV and general support for the October 23 meeting. Kalb, speaking for the Newark JWV, went even further, calling for the creation of a Central Jewish Committee:

> The time has come when all Jewish forces must combine their actions in all Jewish critical activities in order to cope with the boycott movement in a more systematic

manner. The amalgamation of such organizations as the American Jewish Congress, the League for the Defense of Jewish Rights and the American Jewish Committee is imperative.[27]

Kalb and other members of an organizational sub-committee prepared a report describing the boycott as the only weapon that could restore the rights of those who could not defend themselves from the Nazi government's oppression. The new committee would include men and women who were "motivated by American traditions and ideals" and desired to help carry out the boycott.[28]

It is significant that one of the three paragraphs describing the "purpose of the committee" was concerned that "no innocent German-American storekeeper or manufacturer" should suffer from the boycott.[29] Eastern-European Jews and Gentile German-Americans in the Third Ward and in Irvington lived in the same neighborhoods and often shopped in each other's stores. In 1933, relations between the two groups were still correct, if not friendly, and a boycott against German-American concerns could have resulted in a counter-boycott of Jewish stores by German-Americans. Indeed, within a year this scenario was realized.

Kalb's hope for a Central Jewish Committee was not realized at the October 23 meeting. According to Firth's notes, the meeting "was extremely fine and enthusiastic and some of the leading Jews in Newark were there." Fredman spoke on the league's aims, but because of his preliminary meetings he thought it inadvisable to mention a campaign or funds. A special committee, which included Rabbi Foster and Kessler, was appointed to make "Christian contacts." Local leaders promised to cover set-up expenses. Kalb was appointed secretary,[30] and Michael A. Stavitsky,[31] newly elected president of the Newark Conference of Jewish Charities, agreed to chair the league's Newark chapter.

League headquarters in New York pressed Stavitsky to delineate how his chapter would interact with New York and how much money Newark could supply the national group. The enormous responsibilities of the Conference of Jewish Charities compelled Stavitsky to resign the presidency of the league by the end of 1933, however, before he could address these issues. Kalb assumed leadership of it, without the title of president, and led the Newark boycott movement until 1940, when the group disbanded. The end of 1933 also saw changes at the national level, with Untermyer succeeding Coralnik as president. Untermyer changed the group's name to the Non Sectarian Anti-Nazi League (NSANL).

The AJC joined the American boycott in retaliation for an April 1 Nazi boycott of German Jewish businesses. Rabbi Stephen S. Wise, a founder and leader of the AJC from 1923 to his death in 1949, assumed a leading role in the American effort.[32] The World Jewish Conference (forerunner to the World Jewish Congress), of which Wise was also leader, endorsed the boycott at its annual convention in Zurich in September 1933 (by that time, boycott committees had already been organized in Great Britain, France, Poland, Belgium, Mexico, and Canada).[33] Wise bitterly criticized Jews who made commercial arrangements with the Nazi government.[34] In Newark, the New Jersey AJC endorsed the boycott at its state convention in late November.[35]

Newark's almost forty *landsmanshaftn* were ardent supporters of the boycott. The largest two were the Israel KUV and the Erste Bershader KUV, and both supplied leaders of Newark's chapter of the League for the Defense of Human Rights and its successor, the NSANL. In response to a request from the league's national office, the Israel KUV—at its June 15, 1933 meeting—appointed a three-man coordinating committee to work with the league. Five months later, the KUV committee reported back to its membership that the boycott in Newark was underway and that funds were needed. A $50 donation was made to the league's Newark chapter, the first of many contributions that the Israel KUV made to the boycott effort.[36]

Adherence to the boycott was a theme of a September 24 memorial service for victims of Nazi persecution sponsored by the Erste Bershader KUV and Newark Post 34 of the JWV. Kalb was the event's organizer and chair. Several thousand came to the Mosque Theater to hear acting New Jersey Governor Emerson L. Richards, Congressman Peter Cavicchia, and Rabbis Foster and Joseph Konvitz, among others. Fredman predicted that German industry would be paralyzed within a year "if the boycott remained as operative as it is now."[37]

Newark's Universalist Church of the Redeemer [38] also supported the boycott. Dr. Sherwood Eddy, a nationally known author and lecturer, encouraged such support at the Church's Community Forum, a venue for lectures and debates on contemporary subjects. The Forum's organizer was the minister of the church, Rev. L. Hamilton Garner, who also endorsed the boycott. Garner, very popular in the Jewish community, was well known for his liberal views and for inviting controversial speakers to the Forum.[39]

* * *

Another early response to Nazism was to give material aid to threatened European Jews, and, when possible, help them emigrate. By May 1933, the Newark Conference of Jewish Charities abandoned its plans for a fund-raising effort for Eastern European Jews because of the greater peril faced by Jews in Germany. The conference's decision to mount a fundraising campaign for German Jewry came after hearing a report from Jonah B. Wise, chairman of the JDC, who had just returned from a fact-finding trip to Germany.

The campaign's opening rally took place on June 12, 1933 at the Y. Louis Bamberger, founder of L. Bamberger, Newark's largest department store, and Newark's foremost Jewish philanthropist, was chairman of the event, and Kessler and Stavitsky were on the committee.[40] Endorsements came from the American Jewish Committee, B'Nai Brith, and the Union of American Hebrew Congregations (the umbrella organization of Reform synagogues). Protestant clergy, including Dean Arthur Dumper of Trinity Cathedral (Episcopalian), one of Newark's most historic and influential Protestant churches, also joined in planning the event.[41]

Soon after, the fundraising leadership met at the Progress Club, a private Jewish businessman's club favored by members of Newark's Jewish establishment. Stavitsky set a campaign goal of $200,000. Bamberger immediately contributed $25,000. The campaign's opening dinner at the Essex House, Newark's premier hotel and catering facility, raised another $20,000. Rabbi Jonah Wise reported that on his trip to Germany he had seen one million people assemble on May Day to hear Nazi speeches. He added that most Jewish children did not go to school, and the few who did were so harassed that they could not learn. He was pessimistic about the possibility of eradicating anti-Semitism in Germany in the near future and felt that money raised by the campaign should be used to help Jews leave Germany.[42]

The campaign was to have ended on June 22, but it was extended another few days because only $47,500 had been raised. New York City had already raised $600,000 out of its goal of $1,000,000. The final figure for Newark was approximately $50,000,[43] only a quarter of the goal set. Nevertheless, it was a respectable sum, exceeding the amount raised by the Newark Conference of Jewish Charities for 1933.

Other groups also raised funds and held rallies for German Jews. The "United Front Conference Against German Fascism," a Communist group, met on April 30 to plan such an event.[44] Dr. Frank

Kingdon of Calvary Methodist Episcopal Church in East Orange was the speaker at a rally for German Jews sponsored by the Workman's Circle and other Zionist, Socialist and Jewish labor groups at the Workmen's Circle Lyceum in Newark. Kingdon said fascism was an "outgrowth of unfair terms of the Versailles Treaty." He deplored attacks on Jews and condemned racial, religious, and national prejudice.[45] Stavitsky, concerned about duplication of effort, recommended that organizations and individuals planning relief drives for German Jews unite "for greater efficiency and less confusion."[46]

Jewish organizations formed or expanded in response to Nazism. They hoped a stronger Jewish voice in America would influence Washington to put pressure on Germany to ease its persecution of Jews. The AJC, which had functioned through regional groups, now sought to organize in every Jewish community in the country. Newark had one of the first city chapters. On May 11, over 1,000 people came to the Newark School for Fine and Industrial Arts for the first meeting of the Newark District Office of the AJC, at which Judge Joseph Siegler, president of the New Jersey AJC, presided.[47] Siegler was soon elected president of the Newark district. Two months later a Newark Women's Division of the congress was organized. Its first meeting, on July 11, was a rally in defense of Jewish rights abroad, with Judge Siegler the speaker.[48]

In early July, Abraham Silverstein, a writer for the *Jewish Chronicle* and correspondent for the Jewish Telegraphic Agency, formed the Newark Commencement in Absentia League. The purpose of this organization was to hold commencement exercises "in absentia" for German-Jewish students who had not been permitted to receive their diplomas or degrees. The committee's first graduation was held at the "Y" on July 12, 1933. The event's theme was Nazi persecution in the fields of culture, science, and education. A resolution was passed: "To assail vigorously the spread to these shores of the vicious and poisonous propaganda of Nazism." It was sent to the State Department, the German Student Federation, AJC, American Jewish Committee, and B'Nai Brith.[49] These graduations would be held every year throughout the 1930s.

* * *

Zionism was an important factor in Newark's response to Nazism. From 1933 until 1940, Zionists argued for the unrestricted immigration to Palestine of persecuted European Jews. The Order of the Sons of Zion, a national fraternal Zionist organization, was the strongest Zionist group in Newark. At the national convention in Long Branch in July 1933, members voted to support the boycott of German goods by the American League for the Defense of Jewish Rights and to establish a Jewish commonwealth in Palestine.[50]

Liberal Christian clergy participated in the debate on Zionism, as they had in the boycott. Kingdon organized an October 19 interfaith seminar of Catholics, Protestants, and Jews at which Rev. Dr. John Hayes Holmes, a well- known New York liberal, advised all Jews to leave Germany because its youth were being taught hatred of Jews. Rabbi Stephen Wise advised Jews to remain rather than forsake a heritage of centuries because of the "present regime of hatred and hysteria."

Although Catholic clergy were invited to the seminar, none appeared, causing Bishop Washburn of the Episcopal Diocese of Newark to remark: "I am sorry there is no one speaking at this luncheon representing the Catholic communion."[51] The absence of Catholics at the seminar is not surprising. The ambivalent papal attitude toward Nazism and Judaism, as compared to its attitude of hatred of communism, was shared by the predominantly Irish clergy of Newark.[52] Throughout the pre-war period, with few notable exceptions, Catholic clergy were loathe and, in some cases, forbidden to appear at Newark interfaith gatherings where Nazism, Judaism, or religious pluralism was to be discussed.

* * *

Among the African-American community of Newark there was little if any response to either the plight of German Jews or the appearance in Newark of the Friends of the New Germany. Although 12,000 African Americans lived in the Third Ward along with 15,000 Jews, the two communities lived in separate worlds.

Until World War I there were fewer than 10,000 African Americans in Newark. Employment was plentiful, although mostly in the personal service sphere. World War I brought demand for labor in Newark and African Americans migrated there from the South to find jobs in manufacturing and industry. From 1915 to 1920 the number of African Americans in Newark increased from 9,400 to 16,997. During the 1920s, African Americans continued to migrate to Newark to both escape oppression in the South and to find jobs in Newark's expanding economy. Housing discrimination forced African Americans to cluster in a few of the worst areas in Newark, particularly the Third Ward. They moved into dilapidated tenements in the ward that had been abandoned first by the Germans and then by the Jews. Much of this housing lacked electricity, running water, and indoor toilets.[53]

Similar to the German Jews, attitudes towards their Eastern European brethren, older Newark African-American residents resented the influx of their southern brethren, complaining that the new arrivals "didn't know how to act." Lacking the resources of the German-Jews, the older African Americans made little effort to aid new arrivals. African-American churches, traditionally providers of social services, could not keep up with the needs of their poor.[54]

Dr. Clement A. Price, Newark's scholar on the African-American experience, states that Newark was in many respects a "Jim Crow City" during the 1930s. Downtown theaters had special African-American sections; private clubs had white only policies; stores refused to hire African-American personnel; city pools run with taxpayers dollars were closed to African Americans except on a segregated basis, and African-American children were refused admission to camps run by the Community Chest.[55]

Despite the poverty of many Third Ward Eastern European Jews, they faced few of the economic, social, and political liabilities of their African-American neighbors. For most of these Jews, the African Americans could be customers in their stores or tenants in their buildings, but not equals in any sense of the word. For their part, African Americans viewed the Jews as part of a system that exploited them.

* * *

Emboldened by Hitler's early success, Nazis and their sympathizers began to congregate in public in large American cities with German-American populations. Organized by agents sent from Germany, and operating with the support of the German Consulate in New York City, the Friends of the New Germany (Friends) appeared in cities throughout America. An Associated Press dispatch from Detroit on March 22, 1933 reported that Hans Spanknoebel, the Friends leader, was Hitler's personal propagandist in America. His title was "Leader of the Hitler Movement in the United States."[56] Spanknoebel called himself Führer and instructed his followers to do the same. He would soon be famous in Newark. The Newark branch of the Friends became one of the largest in the country.

The first meeting of the Newark Friends took place on April 16, 1933 at Schwabenhalle, a meeting hall for German-American societies on Springfield Avenue, one mile west of the heart of the Third Ward. The approximately 100 people in attendance heard Frederick Weigand, who had recently returned from Germany, speak glowingly of the Hitler movement. Plans were made to hold monthly meetings.[57]

An anti-Semitic incident had occurred a month earlier at an unlikely venue, the Y, during a symposium organized by youth groups to discuss the status of Jews under the Nazi government. After Harry Jacobs, national quartermaster of the JWV, urged the young people to cooperate in the boycott against German-made goods, Richard Krueger, former commander of the German-Austrian War Veterans and an invited guest, replied that the boycott might injure Jewish interests and, in any event, would not force Hitler out of office. Further, he advised the Jews "to draw a sharp line of distinction between themselves and the Communists," which he said had many Jewish leaders. "The present situation came about because Germany had to choose between Bolshevism and Nationalism," Krueger said.

When Krueger sat down, a dozen people sprang to their feet. Dr. Jacob Polevski, a Labor Zionist, asserted "taken individually and collectively the Fatherland never had a more devoted body of citizens, in peace or war, than the Jews." Benjamin Epstein, [58] who had recently abandoned his medical studies at the University of Goettingen because of anti-Semitism, pointed out that about 600,000 Jews lived in Germany, whereas the German Communist party had a membership of 14 million, all of voting age. Krueger did not reply.[59]

Soon after Krueger's remarks at the Y, posters in Newark and Irvington announced a Friends rally for Hitler on May 28 at Montgomery Hall (a common meeting place in Irvington for German groups). This advance notice, unlike the April 16 Friends meeting in Newark, provided opportunity for planning an anti-Nazi action.

On the evening of May 28, 400 people gathered in Irvington to hear Nazi speakers. Forty-five uniformed Nazi sailors from the crew of the Hamburg-American liner *Hamburg* were present. At 8:30, a fleet of taxis arrived with more than forty members of Newark's Young Communist League and their supporters. Some of them unfurled banners denouncing Hitler. Others threw rocks at the hall. There were shouts of "Down with Hitler!" When a group of the Friends went outside to see what was happening, they were attacked. Not expecting trouble, the Irvington Police had assigned only one patrolman to the event, and when violence erupted the patrolman called headquarters for reinforcements. Thirty-five police were soon at the scene with riot guns and tear gas. They arrived too late for Hans Dreher of Newark and Albert Kappler of Union. It took five stitches to close Dreher's facial cut and Kappler suffered nose and lip contusions.[60]

The police reinforcements broke up the melee, menacing the crowd with nightsticks and ordering them to "keep moving!" Order was quickly restored. There were only two arrests: Albert Woods (a pseudonym), the action's organizer, who gave the Newark Unemployment League (a communist organization) as his address,[61] and Ruth Miller, who protested Woods' arrest. After the two were booked and released on $100 bail, Ruth Miller said, "I was there protesting against fascism in Germany and protesting against the birth of fascism in America."[62] At their trial a week later in Irvington Police Court, Woods and Miller were found guilty of disorderly conduct. The judge, however, suspended their sentences, telling them they were misguided and unwise to stage the demonstration.[63]

After this conflict, Newark's communists established the German Worker's Club, an organization composed of German-American communists and Jews. The group picketed and passed out anti-Nazi literature at Friends meetings. However, the club soon dissolved as Nazis threatened violence against the German-Americans in their neighborhoods and workplaces.[64]

Although the communists were the first Newark group to use violence against the Nazis, after this early encounter, the Minutemen assumed the role of intimidators of local Nazis.

* * *

The Friends announced a celebration on September 31 at Schwabenhalle marking the eighty-fifth birthday of German President Paul von Hindenburg, commander in chief of the German armies in World War I. The Friends local leader, Albert Schley, and national leader Fritz Gissibl were to speak, and the German Consul General in New York, Dr. Hans Borchers, was to be a guest of honor. To stress the non-confrontational nature of the event, a memorial service for the war dead of all nations and musical entertainment were to follow the speeches.[65]

Third Ward Jewish residents and merchants were nervous. Signs in German with swastikas on them had been tacked on trees in German areas adjacent to Springfield Avenue, a thoroughfare lined with Jewish businesses. Rumors of late-night meetings of men in Nazi uniforms proliferated. The constant outrages against Jews in Germany were given prominence in the Newark dailies, the *Newark Evening News* and the *Newark Star Eagle*, as well as the weekly *Jewish Chronicle*. For the many Yiddish-speaking Newarkers, the *Daily Forward* and *Der Tog* delivered the same sad news. First- and second-generation Eastern European Jews envisioned imminent threats to their lives and property.

It is not known whether Abner "Longie" Zwillman was approached by others to intervene against the Friends of the New Germany or undertook the responsibility on his own. Prior to the Hindenburg celebration at Schwabenhalle, Zwillman called a meeting of about a dozen of the toughest members of his Third Ward Gang, including Hymie "The Weasel" Kugel, Julius "Skinny" Markowitz, Harry Green, Harry Sanders, Max Leipzig, "Primo" Weiner, and the ex-boxers Nat Arno and Abie Bain.[66] A plan was devised to halt the upcoming Nazi celebration by attacking the attendees.

Prior to the rally members of the gang wrapped iron pipes in newspapers and hid them in a dark alley adjacent to Schwabenhalle. A guard watched the cache as 300 Friends of the New Germany, many in Nazi uniforms, filed into the hall. Zwillman's men did not arrive until the program had started. They picked up their weapons from the alley, being careful to conceal them from the small contingent of police guarding the front door.

Nat Arno went to the back of Schwabenhalle and tossed stench bombs through a second-floor window into the auditorium where the meeting was taking place. Pandemonium broke loose. As some of the Friends rushed down the stairway into the street, Hymie Kugel, screamed "Look what they did to me!" While the police ran to his aid, the other gang members rushed the hall and attacked the Nazis. Having created the necessary diversion, Kugel escaped by outrunning the police. By the time the police returned to the hall, all of Zwillman's men had fled the scene.[67]

Three Nazis were injured—Fred Riddel and Joseph Hamann of Newark and William Van Der Heide of Union. A reporter from the

Newark Star Eagle asked Albert Schley why the young men were wearing Hitler uniforms with swastikas on them. Schley replied that the uniforms were "sports" costumes and that the swastikas were the wearers' choice. He told the reporter that the goal of the Friends was "to promote friendly relations between the United States and Germany," and that the Nazi salute was only a "gesture."[68]

The Friends attracted Congressional scrutiny on October 10 when Rep.Samuel Dickstein, a New York Democrat and chairman of the House Immigration Committee, said the Friends and Hans Spanknoebel were spreading Nazi propaganda. 300 German nationals had recently arrived to work in German consulates supposedly as servants and aides, said Dickstein, but they really worked for the German propaganda ministry. The congressman said he would begin an unofficial investigation of the Friends.[69]

The next day Spanknoebel strenuously objected to the Congressional investigation. He announced a meeting of the Friends on Monday night, October 16th, at Schwabenhalle to further protest Dickstein's proposal. The Newark police said they were prepared for any trouble and would deploy a full contingent of men to prevent a repeat of the melee at the Hindenburg event. The Friends said they would have their own guard unit at Schwabenhalle.[70]

The relationship between Spanknoebel and the Newark Friends was problematic. In July, a Newark Friends' official, R. Stollberg, wrote to Walter Kappe, a well-known Nazi propagandist, proposing that Spanknoebel be replaced. Stollberg said that Spanknoebel "seems to be an inflated, notorious swindler." He also claimed that the Newark Friends had manifested little respect for Spanknoebel during the "Führer's visit to Newark on the previous day.[71] The negative feelings of the Newark Friends would not deter Spanknoebel from appearing at the meeting.

Three communist affiliates—the United Front Conference Against German Fascism, the German Anti-Fascist Conference of Newark,[72] and the Newark Anti-War Committee—lodged the only recorded protest against the October 16 meeting. The day before the event was to take place, representatives of the three groups asked to appear before Mayor Meyer Ellenstein[73] to protest the city's grant of a permit to the Friends on the grounds that the gathering would incite racial hatred. When the mayor refused the request, one of the groups, the United Front Against German Fascism scheduled a rally for October 17, the day after the Spanknoebel appearance.[74]

Both Newark dailies ran articles on October 16. The morning *Star Eagle* reported that Hans Spanknoebel would be at Schwabenhalle, and that Schley had assured the paper "there will be sufficient police protection to avoid any disturbances." The afternoon *Newark News* stressed that Bernard Ridder, publisher of the New York *Staats Zeitung* (the largest circulation German-language paper in America), claimed Spanknoebel had been ordered by the German government to form a pro-Nazi organization in the United States.[75]

The publicity surrounding the October 16 event was more extensive than for any previous German-American gathering held in Newark in 1933. The impending Congressional inquiry into the Friends, press reports of Nazis drilling in storm trooper uniforms near Union City, New Jersey, and the recent attack by Longie Zwillman's contingent at the Hindenburg birthday celebration at Schwabenhalle had unnerved Jewish residents of the Third Ward. Coupled with the almost daily newspaper accounts of the Nazi onslaught against Jews in Germany, Spanknoebel's expected appearance with uniformed guards at Schwabenhalle produced anger and consternation among these Jews.[76] The stage was set for Newark to become the first major battleground in America in the struggle against domestic Nazism.

* * *

Longie Zwillman's men were poised and ready for a reprise of their September 31 victory. This time the rumor of an impending face off attracted more anti-Nazi activists, including JWV and Young Men's Hebrew Club members, who wanted to get their own licks in against the Nazis. In addition, a steady stream of onlookers arrived at Schwabenhalle, anxious to see the altercation.

True to their promise, the Newark Police were prepared. They stationed two patrolmen at the entrance of Schwabenhalle prior to the rally's 8:30 start, with reserves at the ready nearby. Initially the fifty men sent by Zwillman stood across the street from the hall and did not interfere with the crowd as it filed in. A ten-cent admission charge did not deter attendees, and soon there was standing room only as an overflow crowd of 800 people filled the hall. Swastika lapel pins were on sale for ten cents, and books in German and English on Hitler were available for from ten cents to three dollars. The American and German flags on the speaker's platform seemed dwarfed by a swastika banner between them.[77]

Outside the crowd swelled. Several men the police identified as "obviously belligerent" were prevented from entering the building by a detail of plainclothesmen who had joined the two patrolmen at the door. At 9:00 a wagonload of uniformed officers arrived, along with a squad car of detectives from headquarters to direct police activities.[78]

By the time the anti-Nazis numbered 200, they began to get unruly. Police were ordered to use their nightsticks. The commotion attracted a constant stream of onlookers. Fearing that the situation had gotten out of hand, police called for reinforcements from seven precincts. Soon motorcycle officers were driving onto the sidewalks to help their nightstick-wielding colleagues disperse the protestors. When a car carrying five men parked a block away from the scene, the police determined that "these were characters who were best out of the neighborhood" and ordered them to leave. The occupants groused vociferously. Soon hundreds of people were milling about the car. Someone dropped a stench bomb and the car took off. Another car, which a witness referred to as "expensive," cruised the streets behind Schwabenhalle slashing the tires of cars belonging to Nazi sympathizers.[79]

By 10:00, 2,000 people clogged the area around Schwabenhalle. To make matters worse, Springfield Avenue was choked with sightseers driving up and down the street. The air was filled with the sound of police sirens, as squad cars fighting the traffic tried to get to the scene. Over 200 police were now there.

The meeting had started at about the same time the police reserves arrived. Speaking in German, Schley opened the meeting and introduced Spanknoebel. Brown-shirted men gave him the Nazi salute. Spanknoebel spoke in German. He tried to draw a parallel between Hitler and President Roosevelt: they both faced difficulties in getting their programs enacted. Wasn't Roosevelt's National Recovery Act (NRA) meeting the same type of opposition that Hitler's recovery plan had engendered in Germany? Spanknoebel denounced liberalism and communism and warned against the continuation of the boycott of German goods. Germany's imports from America had twice the value of its exports to the United States, he noted. He claimed that Jews had been socialist and communist leaders in Germany and "now must take their place with other enemies of the state." Spanknoebel said that the purpose of the Friends was to stem anti-Nazi propaganda, and that American citizens of German origin were

100 percent behind President Roosevelt. "We do not need to fear any investigation of our activities," he said. He finished his speech and received another Nazi salute from the brown shirts. Since he had another meeting to attend, he prepared to leave.[80]

The next speaker was Fritz Griebl, head of the New York City Friends. He was blaming an influx of Jews from Eastern Europe for communist disorders in Germany when Zwillman's men attacked. Using similar tactics to those at the Hindenburg event, Nat Arno and an accomplice went to the rear of Schwabenhalle, where they had previously stored a ladder. They climbed the ladder and tossed stench bombs and rocks through the second story windows that faced the auditorium. A man opened a window in the front of the building screaming, "Help police!"

The police rushed into the building. Several of them sprinted to the backyard and discovered only the ladder, as Arno and his associate had already fled the scene. The attack's timing was perfect, occurring at the very moment Griebl was spewing out anti-Semitic rhetoric. The stench in the hall forced a halt to the proceedings as both the speaker and Nazi guards pleaded for calm. Police found the Friends no longer in the mood for speeches and advised them to leave the building.[81]

By this time, Spanknoebel and his bodyguards had left the hall and were headed toward a waiting car. Zwillman's men were waiting. The sight of Spanknoebel and his men was incendiary. A crowd surged toward the Nazis, and Leo Bateman, thirty-four, the proprietor of Leo's Delicatessen on West Runyon Street in Newark, charged Spanknoebel. Before Bateman could reach his target, Walter Kauf, thirty-one, one of Spanknoebel's bodyguards, hit him in the jaw, knocking him to the pavement. The police rushed in as the crowd was attempting to get at Kauf and his cohorts. During the melee Spanknoebel escaped. Kauf, a German citizen living in Newark, drew a blackjack and was immediately arrested by the police. The audience poured into the street and found themselves in the middle of bodyguards, protestors, and police. These "involuntary" reinforcements turned the tide of battle temporarily, allowing many of the Friends to escape.[82]

The fight spread to twelve square blocks around Schwabenhalle, and at 11:30 the conflict raged on. Police estimated there were about 200 anti-Nazis engaged in fighting the men who had attended the meeting. Police cars with their sirens blaring tried to be everywhere at once but the police were so out manned that only the most persistent belligerents were arrested. The police used tear gas when a crowd threatened to engulf them during one skirmish. The smoke and confusion led combatants and onlookers to flee the scene, giving rise to a rumor that a nearby house was on fire.[83]

A majority of the injured were Friends and their sympathizers. For the most part, the Nazis refused medical attention, wishing no publicity. Exceptions included Oscar Haerle, thirty-one, and his brother William, thirty-four, who were seriously beaten when their car was surrounded and their windshield smashed by an iron pipe. They were taken to Irvington General Hospital for treatment. Frank F. Ritger, twenty-five, another Nazi, was taken to Newark City Hospital.

The riot ended after midnight. Seven people were arrested, including five anti-Nazis charged with disorderly conduct: Reuben Wilensky, twenty-three; Harry Green, nineteen; Harry Sanders, twenty; Morris Mandelstein, forty; and Julius Markowitz, twenty-three.[84] All but Mandelstein were part of Zwillman's Third Ward group. The five were taken to night court and released in the custody of their counsel, William Untermann and William Fogel. Walter Kauf and Frank Ritger were the other two arrested. After being treated at the hospital, Ritger was held as a material witness. Kauf was held overnight for carrying a concealed weapon.[85]

The Schwabenhalle riot was reported in most New York metropolitan area newspapers on October 17 and produced banner headlines in several. Longie Zwillman and the Third Ward fighters were given prominent mention. The *New York Times* reported that some witnesses at the scene claimed "a group of anti-Nazi followers had hired a group of gangsters in the Third Ward in Newark to break up the meeting. The police were forewarned, however."[86] The *New York Herald Tribune* reported that the Friends belittled Longie Zwillman and his gang for egging on other assailants while keeping out of danger themselves.[87]

The *New York Journal* featured a boldface headline above its masthead proclaiming "1,000 fight in Newark Nazi Riot; 20 Hurt." It reported that the Newark Police suspected that Longie Zwillman had instigated the attack.[88] The *New York Evening Journal* described the riot on page one: "Last night's outbreak came after weeks of increased activity on the part of Hitlerites in the New York area." A caption for a picture in the same paper read, "The Nazi issue came right smack over to these United States and resulted in a good many bruised heads and knuckles as a result of a battle in Newark last night."[89]

The Yiddish dailies the *Forward* and *Der Tog* reported the riot. The *Forward* noted that protestors chanted (presumably in English) "Chase away the Nazi spies!" and "Down with Hitler's gang!" The socialist daily denied that any gangsters were present at the riot, but rather "men, women, Jews and Christians, and also children," who fought the hated Nazis. *Der Tog* claimed that the riot was spontaneous, the Nazis were the ones with clubs, and the anti-Nazis were very careful not to attack women![90]

The most imaginative coverage was the first edition of the tabloid, *New York Daily Mirror.* Its story pictured Longie Zwillman in an armored car near Schwabenhalle directing his men in the assault on the Friends. After Zwillman called the *Mirror*, this story did not appear in later editions. In fact the *Mirror* printed a retraction two days later, explaining that its "informant" admitted his error.[91] Zwillman called reporters at Newark police headquarters the morning of October 17 and denied that he had any part in the riot: "I have checked and learned that all Newark newspapers had reporters at this meeting and certainly if I had been there these reporters would have carried the story to their offices. Nothing of the sort was published in Newark and now I must rely on the fairness of Newark editors to assist me in refuting the story carried by the New York tabloid. From 6 PM until midnight Monday I was in Dinty Moores in New York, seventeen miles from Schwabenhalle."[92]

The day after the riot, the defendants appeared before Judge Ralph Villani in Newark's Fourth Precinct Court. Villani was a close associate of Zwillman, and it was rumored that he received his judgeship through Zwillman's influence. Zwillman asked Essex County Assemblyman Herman Blank to represent his defendants.

Sanders was found not guilty of interfering with a police officer, and decision was reserved on Markowitz (disorderly conduct), Green and Mandelstein (loitering), and Wilensky (interfering with a police officer). The Nazi, Walter Kauf, was held on $1,000 bail for a grand jury hearing. The judge raised it to $2,500 after Assemblyman Blank objected that $1,000 was too low because Kauf was an alien and might jump bail. In passing judgement, Villani said, "These fights must be cut out. If there are any more such disturbances here and they are brought before me, I shall deal severely with them, regardless of which side they represent."[93]

The riot elicited little public reaction in Newark. A *Newark News* editorial lauded Germans for their contributions to Newark, but admonished their descendants and recent German immigrants to cherish that contribution: "We want no Nazi cells, no fascist or royalist or any other organizations predicated on European politics and perpetuating European prejudices." The *News* condemned the riot at the Friends' meeting, calling it "cowardly" and the crowd's tactics "contemptible." However, the paper allowed that none of this would have occurred if "there had been no initial incitement by displays of swastikas and brown-sleeved salutes."[94]

As a result of the riot, the rally organized by the United Front Conference Against German Fascism scheduled for October 17 at Krueger Auditorium was canceled. Krueger's manager claimed he was forced to cancel because of threats to avenge the Schwabenhalle attacks. However, Jack David, a leader of Newark's Unemployed Council, a communist group, accused Mayor Meyer Ellenstein and Public Safety Commissioner Michael Duffy of pressuring Krueger's manager to cancel the meeting.[95] Both the mayor and the commissioner denied the charges. Ellenstein said: "I am too busy with other city business to bother with anything like that."[96]

The meeting was moved to Sokol Hall, a block away from the Third Ward, and it drew over 500 people. The police were out in full force, and no disturbance took place. At the rally, David accused Newark's five city commissioners of a pattern of denying permission to anti-Nazis to hold parades and rallies, whereas "the Nazis receive every possible protection for their propaganda here." David particularly chastised Mayor Ellenstein for allowing Nazis to parade in the German Day Parade in August. "And our Mayor is a Jew!" he added.[97]

Charles Blohm, representing the German anti-Fascist League, was the evening's main speaker. He declared that a majority of Germans in America were against fascism, and that fascism abroad could only be defeated by the overthrow of capitalism. Other speakers noted that the Nazis were so overwhelmed by negative public opinion in New York that they might move their headquarters to Newark.[98]

The events in Newark may have been on his mind when Rep. Samuel Dickstein spoke on "the Nazi Movement in the United States" on the NBC network the day after the riot. He said that the Hitler government was financing and directing Nazi propaganda in the United States: "They have already established an official newspaper, they are importing and flooding sections of the country with booklets, pamphlets and leaflets, they are holding public meetings in public halls, they are actually drilling their storm troopers on American soil." Dickstein indicated that he would hold hearings on the Nazis sponsored by a subcommittee of the House Committee on Immigration and Naturalization, and that over 300 witnesses would be called.[99]

Before Dickstein could start his investigation, the United States Secret Service of the Department of Justice came to Irvington on October 28 to question Schley, the Friends' former leader and a speaker at the October 16 meeting. The Secret Service, which had been ordered to investigate the Friends in the aftermath of the riot, was unsuccessful in locating Schley and in obtaining information on Spanknoebel's whereabouts.[100]

Dickstein asked Essex County Prosecutor William Wachenfeld to keep him apprised of the case of Walter Kauf, whose trial for carrying a concealed weapon was soon to be held. Wachenfeld informed him when Kauf pleaded "non vult" (a guilty plea according to Wachenfeld). Sentencing, however, was held off until the county completed a background check on the defendant.[101]

It took until October 30 for a mainstream Jewish group in Newark to issue a statement on the Friends. At a dinner meeting at the Progress Club, the Ezekiel Lodge of B'Nai Brith announced a campaign to attract 1,500 new members. Mayor Ellenstein was named honorary chairman of the drive and Judge Joseph Siegler chairman. In his remarks, Siegler said there was a great need "for some agency to watch against the many manifestations of anti-Jewish propaganda which is being promulgated throughout the United States. The movement of the Friends of the New Germany is becoming a distinct menace and is striking a blow to American free institutions." No mention was made of the riot at Schwabenhalle.[102]

Two German-American groups took positions against local Nazis. Delegates of the German-Austrian War Veterans of Newark reiterated their loyalty to the United States and denounced those with Hitlerite leanings. Nine members were forced to resign, including the former president of the veteran's group, George Ganss; two participants in the Schwabenhalle riot, Walter Kauf and Fred Ritter; and two former presidents of the Friends, Matthias Kohler and Schley. [103]

At a meeting of the German-American League of Essex County at Schwabenhalle, the group's president, John Koerber, urged the organization to rally against further inroads by Nazism. "We are

American citizens and our duties lie with America first," he said, referring to recent attempts by Hitler sympathizers to gain control of German-American organizations in Essex County.[104]

In a November 3 editorial, "Nazis and Free Speech," The *Jewish Chronicle* was hopeful that the upcoming Congressional investigation sponsored by Samuel Dickstein would drive Nazi agitators out of the country. Without mentioning the Schwabenhalle riot, the *Chronicle* lobbied to prohibit Nazi meetings in America: "Free speech is important but not at the expense of racial and religious hatred." The paper criticized two Jews, who had appeared at a New York City hearing to protest barring a Nazi meeting, for having "incomprehensible" and "indefensible" attitudes. These Jews "would be the first to find themselves in concentration camps if they were in Germany," said the paper.[105]

Perhaps Arthur Garfield Hays, a Jew and counsel to the American Civil Liberties Union (ACLU), was thinking of the *Chronicle* editorial when he spoke two weeks later at Dana College in Newark. He opined that American Nazi sympathizers should not be barred from speaking and assembling, and related his experiences in Germany trying to defend four Communists on trial before the Supreme Court for the Reichstag building arson.[106]

The New Jersey Division of the AJC took its first official action against domestic Nazism under Judge Siegler's leadership. Siegler called for a conference in Newark to discuss Hitlerism in Germany and Nazi-paid propagandists in America. He declared that New Jersey was "one of the greatest strongholds of Nazi propaganda and this imposes upon us a special duty." On November 26 delegates from more than fifty organizations met at the Y to discuss the threat of local Nazism and the usefulness of the boycott against Germany.[107]

1933 closed with the discovery in late December of an apartment filled with large quantities of Nazi literature, pictures of area bridges, and printing and developing equipment. Firemen fighting a blaze in a four-story house on Gillette Place, in the Ironbound section of Newark, found the cache. The occupants of the apartment were Oscar Schilling, twenty-eight, a former secretary of the Newark Friends, and his brother Frank Schilling, twenty-four, a Friends member as well. Both had been in the country since 1928 and neither had taken out citizenship papers.

Fire officials called the Secret Service, who had agents question the brothers. They told federal investigators they had recently resigned from the Friends because of that group's reorganization, which allowed only American citizens to be members. Files found in the apartment contained letters from the Shillings to Spanknoebel, Schley, and other high-ranking Friends. Hundreds of letters requesting funds to fight the boycott against German goods and member questionnaires bore the signature of Fritz Gissibl, Spanknoebel's successor. They were ready for mailing.

Among the papers was Oscar Schilling's membership card in the National Socialist German Workers Party (NSDAP), the Nazi party of Germany, issued April 1, 1932, four years after his entry into the United States.[108] Rep. Dickstein said he would subpoena the brothers to appear before his committee in the following weeks. He also requested the Department of Labor to have immigration authorities initiate an investigation.[109]

Having the most to fear from the Nazis, the Jews were more aware than other Newarkers of people like the Schillings. Some Jews realized that indifference would aid the Friends, and that neither good will nor exposure of the Friends' ideology would be sufficient to weaken them. Longie Zwillman's Third Ward gang—transformed from criminals and boxers into "Minutemen"—provided the strongest response to the Nazi threat in Newark.

Notes

1. The Joint Distribution Committee was founded in America in 1914 to aid Jews in Palestine and Europe from the ravages of World War I. Since then it has helped Jews in need all over the world. In the early 1930s its major focus was on Eastern European Jews. However, after Hitler's accession to power in 1933, aid to German Jews became its main priority.

2. The Newark Conference of Jewish Charities was created in 1923 as a clearing house for the financial affairs of thirteen Jewish charitable institutions in the city. Up to that time, the Newark Community Chest allocated funds to these and most Newark charitable institutions from their annual Community Chest campaign. Individuals and companies in Newark's Jewish community were substantial supporters of the Community Chest. After 1923, it was the Conference that decided how much funds each agency would receive. Within several years the Conference also conducted an annual campaign to supplement the amounts the agencies received through the allocation of Chest funds.

3. Board of Directors Minutes, Conference of Jewish Charities of Newark, 1/31/33, p. 1.

4. Rabbi Foster (1878-1966), in reporting back to the executive committee of the board, said that the fundraising for Eastern European Jews would interfere with the fundraising for the Conference of Jewish Charities, Beth Israel Hospital, and the YM&YWHA. Instead, he recommended a special committee to be organized to solicit wealthier Jews through individual organizational members, congregations, etc. Executive Committee Minutes of the Conference of Jewish Charities of Newark, 2/27/33, p. 3.

5. Although German Jews dominated the Conference of Jewish Charities, the Depression caused some of the Conference's leaders to retire from the field. This proved an opportunity for Michael A. Stavitsky and Samuel I. Kessler, two Jews with Eastern

European roots, to assume top leadership positions in the Conference, which they maintained into the 1950s. See William B. Helmreich, *The Enduring Community, The Jews of Newark and MetroWest*, New Brunswick, 1999, pp. 185, 186.

6.   N.N., 3/22/34, p. 4; 3/24/33, p. 21; 4/5/33, p. 4. Joining in the protests were such diverse groups as the Newark Optimist Club and the Essex County Medical Society.

7.   J.C., 2/17/33, p. 7.

8.   Ibid., p. 1.

9.   N.N., 3/21/33, p. 2; 3/22/33, p. 2.

10.   Ibid., 3/27/33, p. 2.

11.   Ibid., 4/1/33, p. 2. The Jack London Society, a literary discussion group, was very popular in Newark with the young Jewish intelligentsia. The political milieu of the society was leftist, and its sponsor was the Newark Communist Party. However, many of its members were not Communists. Interviews, Saul Schwarz, 9/7/98; Lilly Lowenthal, 2/27/98.

12.   N.N., 3/24/33, p. 21; 3/27/33, p. 2. The youth leaders included Joseph Braff, Erwin I. Meyer, Fred Frankel, Emanuel Millman, Louis Winard, Louis B. Englander, Lawrence B. Weisberg, and Dr. Sidney H. Blumberg.

13.   Ibid., 3/25/33, p. 3; 3/24/33, pp. 11, 21.

14.   Joseph Konvitz (1878-1944) was elected president of the Union of Orthodox Rabbis of the United States and Canada in November 1933.

15.   N.N., 3/28/33, p. 1. An interesting sidelight of the rally was the withdrawal from the program of Bishop John J. Dunn of the Catholic Archdiocese of New York. This followed Secretary of State Cordell Hull's announcement of an official communication from Germany that physical mistreatment of Jews in Germany was "virtually eliminated." At the chancery it was said that the bishop had withdrawn from the protest rally "in deference to the State Department." See, N.N., 3/27/33, p. 2.

16.   S.E., 3/28/33, pp. 1,2; N.N., 3/28/33, p.1; S.E., 3/28/33, p.10.

17.   Soyer, Daniel, *Jewish Immigrant Associations and American in New York, 1890-1939*, Cambridge, MA, 1997, pp. 1, 6. Landsmanshaftn served as important Americanizing institutions for the newly arrived immigrants, as well as a source of material benefits. In Newark as well as elsewhere in America, landsmanshaftn used as part of their names "K.U.V." (Sick and benevolent societies) See pp. 3,4, 54.

18.   The Third Ward stretched along Springfield Avenue, Newark's main east-west artery. It was also Newark's main retail area and home to the majority of Newark's Eastern European Jewish proletariat.

19.   JWV Archives, J. George Fredman Collection, Box 2; Gottlieb, Moshe, *American Anti-Nazi Resistance, 1933-1941*, New York, 1982, p 45 . Gottlieb's book is the most comprehensive work available on the boycott movement.

20.   N.N., 4/24/33, p.17.

21.   Dr. S. William Kalb (1897-1992) was known as "Sam" to his friends.

22.   Moshe Gottlieb, "In the Shadow of War: The American Anti-Nazi Boycott Movement in 1939-1941," *American Jewish Historical Quarterly* 1972 62 (2), p. 146.

23.   NSANL, Geographic Files, Box #11, Folder 1, 5/17/33 letter from the Young Men's Hebrew Club to American League for the Defense of Jewish Rights; 5/30/33 letter from American League for the Defense of Jewish Rights to the Young Men's Hebrew Club.

24.   N.N., 6/23/33, p. 9.

25.   NSANL, op. cit, Report from Maurice Firth, 10/14/33.

26.   Fredman Collection, memo 10/21/33; letter from Fredman to Samuel Untermyer, 12/19/33, Box 2.

27.   S.C., 10/22/33, p. 6; J.C., 10/20/33, p. 1.

28.   Ibid.

29.   Papers of Dr. S. William Kalb, "Report of the Organization Committee," undated.

30.   NSANL, op. cit., Report from Maurice Firth, 10/23/33.

31.   Michael Aaron Stavitsky (1895-1967) was Newark's outstanding Jewish leader from the 1920s through the 1950s. He influenced some of the city's wealthiest Jewish businessmen to support the Jewish community's projects. A successful real estate operator, Stavitsky's background was as a Jewish communal worker. Interview, Alan V. Lowenstein, 6/9/98.

32. NSANL, op. cit. Letter from Michael A. Stavitsky to the League, 6/5/33; Urofsky, Melvin I., *A Voice that Spoke for Justice the Life and Times of Stephen S. Wise*, Albany, NY, 1982, p. 264.
33. Urofsky, op cit.
34. N.N., 9/8/33, p. 5.
35. J.C., 11/24/33, p. 2.
36. Israel Sick Benefits Society Archives (IKUV), Box 2, Minutebook of the Israel Kranken Untersteutzung Verein, pp. 184, 199. The three committee members were Charles Grossman, Donald Gilson, and Louis J. Platt.
37. N.N., 9/25/33, p. 13.
38. Ibid., 10/16/33, p. 2.
39. J.C., 11/24/33, p. 3.
40. N.N., 6/10/33, p.9.
41. Ibid. 6/3/33, p. 3.
42. Ibid., 6/7/33, p. 6; 6/13/33, p. 5.
43. Ibid., 6/23/33, p. 6; 9/8/33, p. 20.
44. Ibid., 5/1/33, p. 15. The "United Front" was completely controlled by the Communist Party. Interview, Jack Gipfel, 7/22/97.
45. N. N., 5/23/33, p. 13; 5/29/33, p. 13.
46. Executive Committee Minutes, Conference of Jewish Charities of Newark, 6/5/33, p. 1.
47. N.N., 5/12/33, p. 2.
48. Ibid., 7/12/33, p. 11. The speakers included the President of Upsala College, Carl G. Erickson and the Dean of the Seth Boyden School, Herbert C. Hunsaker.
49. Ibid. 7/11/33, p. 9; 7/13/33, p. 7.
50. Ibid. 7/26/33, p. 9; 7/27/33, p. 4.
51. Ibid., 10/20/33, p. 26.
52. For recent works on the Vatican's views and policies on Judaism, Communism, and Nazism, see: Kertzer, David I., *The Popes Against the Jews: The Vatican's Role in the Rise of Modern Anti-Semitism*, New York, 2001; Phayer, Michael, *The Catholic Church and the Holocaust, 1930-1965*, Bloomington, IN, 2000; Cornwell, John, *Hitler's Pope: the Secret History of Pius XII,* New York, 2000; Zuccotti, Susan, *Under His Very Windows: The Vatican and the Holocaust in Italy*, New Haven, CT, 2000; Passelecq, Georges and Bernard Suchecky, *The Hidden Encyclical of Pius XI*, New York, 1997; Carroll, James, *Constantine's Sword*, Boston, 2001; Wills, Gary, *Papal Sin: Structures of Deceit*, New York, 1999.
53. Price, Clement Alexander, "The Beleaguered City as a Promised Land: Blacks in Newark, 1917-1947," as published in *Urban New Jersey Since 1870*, edited by William C. Wright, Trenton, NJ, 1975, pp. 19, 23.
54. Ibid., p. 24.
55. Price, Clement Alexander, *Freedom Not Far Distant: A Documentary History of Afro-Americans in New Jersey*, Newark, NJ, 1980, p. 141.
56. N.N., 3/22/33, p. 4.
57. Ibid., 4/18/33, p. 11.
58. Dr. Benjamin Epstein (1912-2000) was a science teacher and then principal of Newark's Weequahic High School. He was also a leader in the American Jewish Congress.
59. N.N.4/24/33, p. 15; Interview, Dr. Benjamin Epstein, 6/19/98.
60. N.N., 5/29/33, p. 13.
61. Interview, Jack Gipfel, 7/22/97.
62. N.N., 5/29/33, p.13; I.H., 6/2/33, p. 5.
63. N.N., 6/5/33, p. 6.
64. Interview, Jack Gipfel and Lucille Friedman, 6/24/97. Gipfel remembers participating with the club in picketing Newark's Schwabenhalle.
65. N.N., 9/27/33, p. 8.
66. Interview, Heshie Weiner, 6/29/96.
67. S.C., 10/1/33, p. 1; Interviews, Itzig Goldstein, 6/14/96; Heshie Weiner, 6/29/96.
68. S.C., Ibid.
69. N.N., 10/10/33, p. 28.

70. Ibid., 10/11/33, p. 9; S.E., 10/13/33, p. 3.
71. National Archives, RG 233, Box 379, Letter from R. Stollberg to Walter Kappe, June 22, 1933.
72. The German-American Anti-Fascist Conference of Newark was founded 9/22/33 at the Labor Lyceum, a half block from Schwabenhalle, ostensibly to protest against "the Hitler regime in Germany and its terror." Four hundred attended this first meeting. N.N., 9/23/33, p. 4.
73. Ellenstein, after reelection as city commissioner with the highest vote total in May 1933, was selected as mayor by his four fellow commissioners. See, Paul Stellhorn's Depression and Decline, PHD Dissertation, 1982, p. 155 and his "Champion of the City: Reflections on the Political Career of Meyer C. Ellenstein," unpublished manuscript based upon a presentation made before the Jewish Historical Society of MetroWest, 6/9/97, pp. 24, 25.
74. S.C., 10/15/33, p. 7; N.N., 10/16/33, p. 7.
75. S.E., 10/16/33, p. 15; N.N., 10/16/33, p. 17.
76. J.C., 10/12/33, p. 1; S.E., 10/13/33, p. 3.
77. N.N., 10/17/33, p. 1.
78. Ibid.
79. Ibid.
80. Ibid; NYHT, 10/17/33, p. 3.
81. NYHT, ibid.; S.E., 10/17/33, p.1.
82. NYHT, 10/17/33, p. 3.
83. Ibid.
84. Julius "Skinny" Markowitz, at this and subsequent conflicts, got under the skin of the Nazis by taunting them as cowards—afraid to fight. Interview, Alex Portnoff, 6/25/96.
85. N.N., 10/17/33, p. 1.
86. NYT, 10/17/33, p. 18.
87. NYHT, 10/17/33, p. 3.
88. *NY Journal*, 10/17/33, p.1.
89. *NY Evening Journal*, 10/17/33, p. 1.
90. *Der Tog*, 10/17/33, p. 1; *Forward*, 10/17/33, p.1, translated from Yiddish by Nikolai Borodulin.
91. *NY Daily Mirror*, 10/19/33, p. 7.
92. S.E., 10/18/33, p. 3; N.N., 10/18/33, p.1.
93. N.N., 10/17/33, p.5.
94. Ibid., 10/18/33, p.14.
95. Ibid.., 10/19/33, p. 9.
96. S.E., 10/19/33, p. 2. Jewish communists often used aliases to conceal Jewish-sounding surnames. "Jack David" was the alias used by Jack Gipfel in his party work.
97. N.N., 10/19/33, p. 9. Sixty-four years later, during an interview, Jack David regrets making the remark about Ellenstein claiming it was made in the heat of the moment. He cited several instances where Ellenstein was fair to his group. Interview, Jack Gipfel, 7/22/97.
98. N.N., 10/19/33.
99. NYT, 10/18/33, p. 3.
100. S.C., 10/29/33, p. 1.
101. Papers of Samuel Dickstein, Box 5, folder 7, Letter from William Wachenfeld to Samuel Dickstein, 11/14/33.
102. N.N., 10/31/33, p. 36.
103. Ibid., 11/2/33, p. 22; 11/25/33, p. 23.
104. Ibid. 11/3/33, p. 14.
105. J.C., 11/3/33, p. 4.
106. N.N., 11/14/33, p. 34.
107. Ibid., 11/20/33, p. 9; J.C., 11/24/33, pp. 1,.2
108. N.N., 12/22/33, p. 1; 12/23/33, p. 3; S.E., 12/27/33, p. 13.
109. N.N., 12/28/33, p. 22.

2

The New Minutemen

Throughout the 1930s the "Minutemen" consistently and effectively opposed Nazi activities in Newark and northern New Jersey. This fighting force included criminals and boxers who used fists, clubs, and baseball bats to counter the Nazi threat. Often just a rumor that the Minuteman had been sighted was enough to deter Newark's Nazis from holding events. The Minutemen were from Newark's Third Ward and possessed the means to stand up to the Nazis—a group of boxers and a tightly controlled criminal enterprise that relied on violence. Abner "Longie" Zwillman, Newark's criminal czar, used his Third Ward Gang to oppose the Friends of the New Germany and its successor, the German-American Bund. Zwillman backed the struggle with men, money, and political influence from 1933 until the Bund's demise in 1940.

Starting in 1934, what had previously been spontaneous responses to Nazi provocations, evolved into a well-organized operation, employing public relations as well as violence. Nat Arno, appointed by Zwillman as Minuteman commander, led the group, which was an ongoing anti-Nazi presence in Newark through 1940.

Zwillman was Newark's most powerful Prohibition (1920-1933) era bootlegger. After repeal, although active in several legitimate businesses, he was the dominant crime boss in the city and its suburbs. He was involved in gambling, the protection racket, and labor-union extortion. Zwillman also had substantial political influence in Newark, Essex County, and at the state level. He used his political clout—seldom publicized—primarily to extend and protect his criminal enterprises. But from 1933 through 1940 he also used it to aid the Minutemen.

Why would a hardened criminal get involved in an eight-year struggle against Newark-area Nazis? They didn't interfere with his

illegal enterprises or his legitimate businesses, and his political connections rendered him immune from threats. Confrontations and riots generated publicity and curiosity, which Zwillman shunned as-
siduously. Zwillman was used to acting in his own self-interest and
the anti-Nazi struggle he undertook in many ways ran contrary to
this self-interest.

For the answers to this question we need to explore Zwillman's
Third Ward working-class roots. Zwillman identified with the poverty and discrimination Eastern European immigrants suffered. He
had witnessed anti-Semitic gang violence in his neighborhood as a
child, and when he was barely out of his teens he organized a gang
that fought anti-Semites in the streets. Along with most second-generation Jews, he heard stories of anti-Semitic pogroms in Eastern
Europe, from which his parents' generation had fled.

With Hitler's rise to power, Third Ward residents saw newsreels
and heard radio reports of atrocities committed against Jews in Germany. Within a few months, Nazis appeared in their neighborhood,
some attending meetings in Nazi uniforms. With his large, violent
gang, Zwillman saw it as his responsibility to protect his neighbors,
friends, and co-religionists against this threat. He mobilized his gang
for action.

New York newspaper accounts of the October 16, 1933 riot at
Schwabenhalle mentioned Zwillman's name prominently as the leader
of the gang that provoked the battle. Thereafter, however, he was
not mentioned in articles about anti-Nazi violence. There was good
reason for this. In denying any role in the riot, Zwillman was announcing that to link him to the rioters would be "bad for business."
Over the years he had given gifts to reporters and helped newsmen
in financial trouble. They sympathized with his desire to avoid publicity. After his complaints about reportage on the Schwabenhalle
riot, reporters from Newark's two dailies were careful not to mention Zwillman's name in connection with anti-Nazi violence for the
duration of the interwar period.

Newspaper reporters, as well as police, politicians, and informed
citizens knew that after the repeal of Prohibition, Zwillman continued to operate his criminal network throughout northern New Jersey under the cover of his legitimate businesses. There were peri-
odic investigations or publicity involving his activities. But not until
1951, when federal authorities moved against him, was there a con-
certed effort to prosecute him.

Early in his career in the 1920s, Zwillman learned how to deal with police and politicians—a prerequisite for a gambling operator and bootlegger. A street-level bookie in his teens, Zwillman learned to pay off police for protection, and when he became one of the most powerful bootleggers on the East Coast, he befriended many officeholders eager to share in the profits of the illegal liquor trade. These men owed Zwillman, and they in turn provided protection for his illegal enterprises and jobs for his cronies. Judges and prosecutors were generally lenient with Zwillman and his men whenever criminal charges were brought against them.

Another aspect of Zwillman's power was his control over north Jersey labor unions, including movie-house projectionists, retail clerks, and liquor salesmen. Through his henchmen, who ran the day-to-day operations of the locals, money flowed in from union dues and extortion. Zwillman also had influence over the competing American Federation of Labor (AFL) and Congress of Industrial Organizations (CIO) at both the county and state levels. The labor union connection garnered him money, votes for political candidates he backed and, once again, jobs for his cronies.

By the early 1930s, Zwillman was a major figure in Newark's political life, actively backing candidates for the city commission. When a vacancy occurred on the five-person commission in 1932, Zwillman and the Third Ward political leader Joseph Heimberg secured the spot for Meyer C. Ellenstein. With the help of Heimberg's large political association and Zwillman's financial aid, Ellenstein was elected to a full commission term in 1933. His fellow commissioners then chose him mayor, a position he held for eight years. Ellenstein was Newark's only Jewish mayor.[1]

Zwillman's long-time friendship with William Egan, an important Essex County Democratic leader and one-time Newark commissioner and assistant state attorney general, gave him access to the county government.[2] At the state level, his alliance with Frank Hague, Hudson County's boss and New Jersey's dominant Democratic Party leader from the 1920s to 1949, provided him with favors and protection, particularly when Hague's hand picked governor, A. Harry Moore, was in power.[3]

* * *

Abner "Longie" Zwillman was born in 1904 in Newark's Third Ward. His parents had emigrated from Russia in the 1890s. His father sold chickens in a public market on Prince Street, Jewish Newark's most colorful street, from the late 1880s to the 1940s, eking out a meager living to support his wife and six children. By the time Zwillman was fourteen, he had a reputation as a fearless fighter, who was also the best athlete in his teenage gang. He was already six-foot-one at a time when the average man was about five-foot-six. One account of Zwillman's boyhood claims that whenever Irish gangs attacked the pushcart peddlers on Prince Street the cry would go out "Reef der Langer!" (Yiddish for "get the long 'tall' one!") Zwillman and his gang would come to the rescue. The Americanization of "Langer" produced the nickname "Longie," which remained with Zwillman throughout his life.[4] Another account posits that the name Longie came from an alias that Zwillman used early in his career, George Long.[5]

Zwillman dropped out of school in the eighth grade when his father died. To help support his family, he started selling fruit and vegetables from a truck. He soon began taking numbers from his customers for a Third Ward gambling operator. Zwillman eventually gained a piece of the operator's business and began to expand to other Newark neighborhoods by employing friends from the Third Ward.

With the advent of Prohibition, Zwillman saw an opportunity to get rich. He was not alone. Newark had a score of enterprising criminals who were looking to get a foothold in the nascent bootleg business. Competition was savage, both for products and outlets, and violence, including murder, was not uncommon. Though still in his late teens, Zwillman prevailed over his older rivals. His physical strength and courage intimidated many opponents. His quick mind grasped new ideas and he recognized an opportunity when it presented itself. When many were still using horses and wagons to transport bootleg liquor, Zwillman had already bought trucks.

Zwillman's first foray into bootlegging was as a provider of transportation and protection for other bootleggers' shipments. Zwillman's men proved to be the best protection available; the only attempt to hijack a shipment they were transporting was met with a fusillade of bullets. Word spread that Zwillman's crew would protect their shipments with guns, and thereafter no one attacked his convoys.[6]

Zwillman's reputation was enhanced in 1923 when he shot Leo Kaplus, a well-known Newark bootlegger and tough who was harassing some of Zwillman's employees. That Zwillman was only nineteen at the time and Kaplus was already an established criminal made the shooting even more notable. The FBI said that Kaplus was shot in the leg,[7] but another source claims the bullet was aimed at and hit Kaplus in the testicles.[8] Kaplus did not report the shooting to the police, either because he was afraid of Zwillman or because he was paid off.

Even after Zwillman had a gang of two-fisted brawlers at his disposal, he still enjoyed dishing out punishment himself. His first arrest, in 1926, was for disorderly conduct, for which he received a suspended sentence. From March 1927 to June 1928, he was arrested five times for atrocious assault and battery. In the first four incidents, the victims, Leo Kaplus, Jacob Rosen, Meyer Satsky, and Jacob Kleinman, withdrew their complaints. However, the fifth complainant, Preston Buzzard, an African-American numbers banker, refused to withdraw the charge and Zwillman was sentenced to six months in jail and a $1,000 fine.[9] Sergeant James Conlon and Detective Louis Thomas testified that when they asked Zwillman why he had beaten Buzzard with a blackjack, Zwillman replied he was sorry he hadn't killed him.[10] Zwillman served the sentence, less one month for good behavior. This was the only time Zwillman went to jail. He had learned his lesson; from then on gang members administered the beatings.

* * *

Joseph Reinfeld was an entrepreneurial and well-connected businessman whose tavern in the First Ward, Newark's Italian neighborhood, was a meeting place for Italian gangsters. With the advent of Prohibition, he turned to bootlegging and was one of the first operators to make a deal with a Canadian distillery (Seagrams) to import liquor to the East Coast. Initially, bootleg liquor was produced either in distilleries—which were to have suspended production in January 1920—or in hastily assembled production facilities. The product from these sources was uneven and, when manufactured by the unscrupulous, sometimes lethal. The liquor from Seagrams was of good quality, even when cut—which it often was. Although Canada—under pressure from the American government—had passed a law prohibiting direct sales of liquor to the United States, bootleggers and Seagram's owners, the Bronfman family of Montreal, had devised a plan that would not violate Canada's statutes. Liquor would be consigned to St. Pierre and Miquelon, two French islands, and then transported to the New Jersey coast.[11]

The Canadian liquor arrived via large ships at Sandy Hook, at that time an isolated New Jersey area with calm waters. Smaller boats transported the liquor to various New Jersey ports. Most docked at Port Newark, the gateway to the New York metropolitan area. From there it was transported to warehouses and on to speakeasies. Most hijackings took place at Port Newark and during transport to the cities. Zwillman became Reinfeld's security agent, protecting his shipments from hijackings.[12]

Reinfeld had the connections and experience, Zwillman the muscle and ambition. While still working as security for Reinfeld, Zwillman and his men began their own small bootleg operation centered in the Third Ward. Zwillman became the prime distributor of bootleg alcohol in the Third Ward and neighboring areas. He and his gang were successful in persuading bootleg outlets to distribute the liquor he bought on the docks of Port Newark. Zwillman maintained speedboats that trafficked as much as fifty truckloads a night from Port Newark.[13] At this time, Zwillman's numbers game was the largest in Newark and he was also active in the slot machine racket. Zwillman had a number of advantages over his rivals, including an organization of loyal numbers runners who had been his companions in the playgrounds and streets of the Third Ward. He provided competent legal assistance for arrested employees, and, when possible, "fixed" the case through political contacts.

Reinfeld realized the obvious—Zwillman was now his chief rival as well as his employee. Thus he acquiesced when Zwillman and several of his associates demanded 50 percent of Reinfeld's sizeable bootlegging enterprise.[14] The older man needed Zwillman and his organization for protection. Together they became the dominant bootlegging combine in New Jersey and one of the largest on the East Coast.

Zwillman's bootlegging and gambling activities put him in touch with other leading criminals in New Jersey, including Willie Moretti and Albert Anastasia. They in turn introduced him to New York gangsters Meyer Lansky, Lucky Luciano, Joe Adonis, Frank Costello, and Bugsy Siegel. By 1925 Zwillman often did business with these men. A product of their association was the creation of the "Big Six " or the "Broadway Gang," consisting of Zwillman, Luciano, Costello, Siegel, Lepke Buchalter, and Gurrah Shapiro (another source has Meyer Lansky and Joe Adonis rather than Buchalter and Shapiro). They established territories in the New York metropolitan area within which one member controlled both gambling and bootlegging. In

1929, the top bootleggers in the country met at an Atlantic City gathering—allegedly suggested by Zwillman—to determine regions and validate territories. The "Big Six" were in charge of the largest region, New York and New Jersey. Only twenty-four, Longie Zwillman was one of the most powerful crime bosses in the country.[15]

* * *

Zwillman rose to power at an early age because of intelligence, business acumen, and physical courage. Years later Zwillman explained why he went into crime:

> Sure I was a bootlegger, and I'd be one again given the same setup—kid brothers and sisters hungry, no food, bills. I was the oldest boy. There were four boys and three girls. The youngest was six months old when my father died. We didn't have enough money to bury him. I was just a kid—twelve. I had to get money somehow. I got it bootlegging.[16]

There were many such stories of poverty in the Third Ward. Zwillman never had trouble filling the ranks of his gambling and bootlegging operations with friends from his childhood. His group became the Third Ward Gang, and some of the original members remained with Zwillman until his death forty years later.

Throughout his career Zwillman was generous to the poor. When the Depression started in 1929, Zwillman was already a wealthy and influential man. Primarily because of his sympathy for the underdog—but partly out of self-interest—he began subsidizing soup kitchens run by the Mount Carmel Guild of the Catholic Charities in Newark's Military Park in 1932. One source claims that Zwillman provided the kitchen with $1,000 a week until it closed in 1939. Prior to the Depression, Zwillman provided a yearly Christmas carnival at Laurel Gardens for orphans of all colors and creeds through the Third Ward Political Club. For the youngsters at the Daughters of Israel Hebrew Orphanage, Zwillman supplied clothing and gifts each year.[17] These and many other charitable contributions brought Zwillman respect and admiration.

When necessary, Zwillman used his philanthropy as a public relations tool. In 1935, after being named number thirty-three on the U.S. Department of Justice's public enemy list, he gave an interview to the press. Admitting that some members of his "club" were "not exactly Sunday School boys" Zwillman insisted that the "club" had committed no serious crimes. He said

At the same time there are thousands of poor persons who have reason to remember the club, especially during the Depression winters. The good that the club did was plenty and its members never went around town carrying banners or shouting about it.

When reminded by a reporter that those in the know attributed much of the club's income to slot machines and the numbers racket, Zwillman said there was nothing to the rumor.[18]

Zwillman's luck ran out in 1951 when he appeared before the televised Kefauver Committee hearings on organized crime in the United States. Photogenic and well-spoken, Zwillman attempted to portray himself as a businessman with several legitimate companies. His testimony before the committee was polite and intelligent, and despite taking the Fifth Amendment against self-incrimination forty-seven times, his demeanor was hardly that of a gangster. He even managed to impress some of the senators, but ultimately the hearings succeeded in exposing Zwillman's enormous power in New Jersey and his influence in the nationwide crime syndicate. From then until his suicide in 1959, Zwillman was dogged by legal problems and unwelcome publicity. Before 1951, Zwillman had portrayed himself as a former bootlegger gone legitimate. After 1951, such an image was no longer possible. In an editorial after his testimony before the Kefauver Committee, the *Newark News* observed that Zwillman was "a sympathetic witness for himself. He was a man trying to escape from his past. He wants a respectable status in the community. But he cannot have it both ways. He never accepted Senator Tobey's invitation to 'come clean.' So Zwillman the man did nothing to dissipate Zwillman the myth, which will live on."[19]

Over forty years after his death, Zwillman remains a mythic personality in the annals of Newark Jewish history. Today many people who knew him in any of his guises—businessman, gangster, family man, benefactor or friend—speak of him with respect. He fought hard to straddle two worlds. His acquaintances included lawyers, doctors, office holders, and legitimate businessmen as well as a spectrum of criminals ranging from the most notorious in the country to the lowest-level bookmakers and strong-arm men.

Popular lore holds that if Zwillman had pursued an honest career after Prohibition, he would have been a greater success than Joseph Reinfeld, his bootlegging partner. Reinfeld left the rackets and built a very profitable liquor distributing company, Renfield Importers. By the time of his death, Reinfeld was a respected member of the community. Zwillman, on the other hand, loved the life of a crime boss—the power, the money, the action, and the relationships with other criminals.

* * *

Whereas Zwillman nourished Newark's anti-Nazi movement financially, Nat Arno commanded[20] the Minutemen as they fought the Nazis in the streets and meeting halls. A former boxer and member of Zwillman's security force protecting shipments of bootleg liquor, Arno was employed by Zwillman in a variety of jobs after Prohibition's repeal. Above all, Arno's job from 1933 to 1940 was fighting Nazis, a cause he believed in and performed with skill and zeal.

Nat Arno was born Sidney Abramowitz on April 1, 1910 in Newark. He was the middle child in a family of five, two girls and three boys, all born in Newark. His parents, Bertha and Harry Abramowitz, were Romanians who came to America in 1903. Bertha came first, found work, and saved enough money to send for Harry. The family lived on the Lower East Side of Manhattan until 1905, when they married and moved to Newark. Harry's Newark relatives told him that he would find work as a carpenter in that expanding city. The Lower East Side was already built up and carpentry jobs were not plentiful. For the rest of his career, Harry worked for construction bosses in the Newark area.[21]

According to Rose Abramowitz Yannick, Arno's older sister, "Nat was a mischievous kid." The neighbors would holler from downstairs, 'Mrs. Abramowitz, come take Sidney upstairs, he's fighting again.' My mother would dress us up to go visit someone, and by the time we were ready to leave, he was rolling in the ice wagon. He was filthy. Or he would be climbing up on an electric pole to save a kitten. He didn't care whether he could fall down or electrocute himself, but he went up there to save the kitten. And then one night he came home with a little puppy that he said was all alone and people were throwing him around. He was very good with animals, and always fought for the person who was right."

Arno was enrolled at Charlton Street School, where he got into trouble. When his father came home from work his mother would immediately tell him how Nat had misbehaved and his father "would beat the hell out of him." Afterward she would often remonstrate with her husband, "Why did you hit him?" Nat's father had a short temper and was extremely strong. Because of these frequent beatings Nat learned early on to take a punch, a prerequisite for becoming a successful boxer.

When Nat wasn't in school his grandfather, who was also a carpenter, would take him to work to keep him out of trouble. "Papa had a crew of men working for him, so what Nat used to do—he always liked to box. What happened was he was getting the men to stop working and he was teaching them how to box, and my grandfather was hitting him all the time saying, 'They're at work. Leave the men alone. Don't teach them to box. I want them to use a hammer and a nail— not their hands for boxing!'"

Arno had his Bar Mitzvah at the *Roumanian Shul* on Prince Street. Rose remembers it: "In those days, they didn't make big Bar Mitzvahs. The women sat upstairs and the men downstairs (in the shul), and when he (Nat) was through reading, women threw down nuts and raisins, and that was it." One year later, Arno dropped out of school. His father was terribly disappointed (one of his two other sons became a doctor and the other a pharmacist). As punishment, Harry wouldn't let his father take the boy to work anymore. Arno didn't mind. He spent his days in downtown Newark gyms with other Third Ward youths learning how to box, and his evenings in the streets getting into mischief. His father, struggling to make a living for his family, could no longer impose his will on Nat with his fists.

When he was fourteen, Arno had two idols: Benny Leonard, the world's lightweight champion, and the Third Ward's most famous boxing fan, Longie Zwillman. Aggressive and undisciplined, Arno got into many street fights. With his physique and strength, which he inherited from his father, and a hard punch, he usually came out on top. Arno, who had been sparring and fighting amateur bouts since he was fourteen, was waiting until he could turn professional at fifteen.

Nat Arno had his first boxing match on April 1, 1925, his fifteenth birthday, winning a four-round decision against Sheik Hanson in Newark. In the next eight months Arno had six bouts, winning them all, four by knockout.[22] According to Rose: "My father didn't know he was boxing. Nobody knew until a friend of my father's said, 'I saw your son boxing on this-and-this date,' and my father was furious. So he went down and he brought him [Nat] home and wouldn't let him go anymore."[23]

Unable to fight in New Jersey without his parents' permission, Arno hitchhiked alone to Florida in January 1926. Rose said: "My mother was wringing her hands and crying every day. She didn't know whether he was alive or dead. Finally, when he got to Florida he called up, he told us where he was."[24] He had forty-one fights in thirteen months in Florida, winning thirty-six and drawing five. He returned to Newark in February 1927, undefeated in forty-eight bouts[25] and aspiring to become a champion. Arno moved back to his parents' apartment and reconciled with his father. Soon afterward Harry began attending his son's fights.[26]

In the late 1920s, other well-known Jewish boxers from the Third Ward included Abie Bain, Sollie Castellane, Lou Halper, Moe Fischer, and Benny Levine. They were all born about the same time to immigrant parents. These Newark fighters were not an isolated phenomenon. In urban ghettos throughout the country, second-generation Italians and Irish, as well as Jews, pursued boxing as an escape from poverty. From 1928 Jews were the dominant nationality in professional boxing, followed by Italians and Irish.

The interwar years, 1919-1939, were the golden age of boxing in America, and Jews figured prominently in it. Prior to World War II, Jews held twenty-six world titles, slightly over 16 percent of the total. None of Newark's Jewish boxers ever wore a championship belt, and only Abie Bain had a championship fight. On October 22, 1930, Bain was knocked out in the eleventh round by another Jew, the world light heavyweight champion, Maxie Rosenbloom.

The most famous Jewish boxer was Benny Leonard, who held the world lightweight championship from 1917 to 1924. According to boxing authority Nat Fleischer, Leonard was the second greatest lightweight fighter of all time. He retired undefeated in January 1925. After he lost all his money in the 1929 stock market crash, Leonard made a comeback as a welterweight in 1931. This second career, although successful, did not lead to a championship. He was a well-known Jewish personality in America during the 1920s and 1930s.[27]

According to a 1928 news account: "When Benny Levine [another well known Jewish boxer] was an 8-year-old kid up in Newark's Ghetto section, his father took him to see Champion Benny Leonard fight Willie Ritchie at the Newark Armory. That was the biggest sight of Benny's boyhood. He gasped with admiration at the champ—then made a decision. 'Some day' he confided to his dad, 'I'm gonna be just like that guy.'[28]

Jewish boxers fought because they loved it, hoped to become champions, and needed to make money. They didn't fight to prove

Jewish masculinity or to defend their heritage, despite the romantic notion of the Jewish boxer as a fighter against anti-Semitism. Yet these boxers did not retreat from their Jewish identity. They considered themselves part of the Jewish community and participated in Jewish holidays and rituals.[29] In the Third Ward they attended Prince Street-area synagogues. Most wore the Star of David on their trunks. Although this was often for the benefit of the fans, men like Arno were proud of the symbol. These fighters lived at home until they married and helped support their families. Like 95 percent of Jews at that time, they married Jewish women and did not divorce.

Boxing was acceptable in Newark's Jewish community. The YMHA, part of the Conference of Jewish Charities, had a boxing club, which was seen as one way to keep the more aggressive boys and young men off the streets. The YMHA of Elizabeth, a town adjoining Newark, also sponsored a team, whose members often boxed against their Newark Y rivals.[30] The situation was similar in large urban areas throughout the East Coast, where both Christian and Jewish Y's sponsored amateur boxers.

As the amateurs turned fifteen, the Newark Y team transformed itself into a professional boxing club with Al Thoma as its coach and trainer. The sport was very popular with both longtime Americans and immigrants. The rules were simple, and theaters or meeting halls that had been turned into a boxing site were in easy walking distance. Club-fighting cards were numerous and the entrance fee was minimal. Boxers not skilled enough for the big arenas plied their trade at these venues along with newcomers.

All the Third Ward fighters began their professional careers fighting in small smoke-filled venues run by such groups as the Newark Athletic Club, the Lyric Theatre Boxing Club, and the Olympic A.C. Some later fought at the three large arenas that flourished in the city in the inter-war period—Laurel Gardens, Dreamland Arena, and the Velidrome. Pay for the boxers could be as little as an inexpensive gold watch (to be immediately sold at a pawn shop), or as much as $200. In the late 1920s, the going rate for a four-round bout at Laurel Gardens was $10. When Lou Halper and Benny Levine fought their second fight, a feature event at an outdoor arena on Halsey Street, each man received $125.[31]

In Newark, Jews constituted the largest group of fans among ethnic groups. The size of the Jewish boxing audience led fight promoters to match Jewish lightweights against each other. Although they were used to sparring and had personal rivalries, meeting in a professional bout before their friends and neighbors was difficult for some. Arno and Levine were extremely close and had vowed never to meet in the ring. However, finances forced them into two fights in 1929, and the action was so fierce that no one could claim collusion. Levine had previously had been matched against Lou Halper, in two 1926 fights, and both had won once. All three—Arno, Halper and Levine—beat their fellow Third Ward lightweight, Moe Fischer. [32] The Third Ward fighters fought too frequently and were burnt out by their early and mid-20s. This was the case with most boxers of the era, since there were no safeguards to protect them.

There were two other well-known lightweight Jewish boxers from Newark, Maxie Fisher from the Third Ward and Allie Stolz from the more prosperous Clinton Hill. Fisher had a long career, from 1930 to 1940, and was a Third Ward favorite, fighting the best lightweights in the area. When he started his professional career in 1937, Stolz was hailed as a possible champion. However, he lost both of his title matches, one in a split decision to Sammy Angott and the other by knockout to Bob Montgomery.

Arno continued his boxing career from 1927 to 1932 in and around Newark. In an additional seventy-one fights he won forty-nine, lost thirteen and drew nine. Never a classic boxer, Arno was a brawler unafraid to take punishment. Newspaper accounts of the time said he was willing to take two punches in order to land one. By the end of 1932, it was clear to Arno he would not be a champion. In his last fight, on September 30, 1932, he defeated Lope Tenorio in a ten-round decision in Passaic, New Jersey.[33] At age twenty-two, he retired from the ring to become a full-time member of Longie Zwillman's Third Ward Gang. In his eight-year career, Arno had fought 121 matches in scores of arenas. Not once had he suffered a knock down.

From the time he returned to Newark from Florida in 1927, Arno—in addition to boxing—worked for Zwillman transporting bootleg alcohol, and as an enforcer in Zwillman's other criminal dealings. In this latter capacity, Arno paid unannounced visits to men who owed the Third Ward Gang money, weren't buying the gang's liquor, or were resisting the gang's dictates. If Arno didn't get his way with verbal persuasion, he used his fists.

* * *

The boxers, the Third Ward Gang, Longie Zwillman, and the fight against the Friends of the New Germany are closely connected. The boxers of the Third Ward remained, for the most part, life-long friends. They had played and fought together. None retired from boxing wealthy. Zwillman never became a boxer, although he was a supporter of Newark's Jewish boxers and for a time under the aegis of the Third Ward Political Club, an arm of his gang used for political and charitable activities, Zwillman sponsored several boxing matches. In one event, held at Laurel Gardens, Benny Levine fought his first ten-round fight. Two other Third Ward Jewish lightweights were on the card: Sollie Castellane in a ten-round co-feature and Norman Wolfe in a six-round bout.[34]

Political relationships were also solidified by boxing backgrounds. When Zwillman helped make Meyer Ellenstein a city commissioner in 1932 and mayor of Newark in 1933, one of their common interests was boxing. Ellenstein had been a successful amateur boxer under the name "Kid Meyer." He became a dentist rather than turn professional, thus sparing his patients from visiting a dentist without teeth. Mickey Breitkopf, one of Ellenstein's advisors, also had a close relationship with Zwillman. He fought sixty-three professional bouts under the name Mickey Fox prior to World War I.[35] Breitkopf was also associated with Nat Arno and Dr. S. William Kalb.

Nearly all of the Third Ward boxers helped Zwillman protect his bootleg shipments. The $25 pay per trip was easy money and more than most made for a boxing match. Zwillman also supplied them with corned beef or pastrami sandwiches from a nearby Prince Street delicatessen. Nat Arno, Benny Levine, Lou Halper, Abie Bain, Al Fisher, Puddy Hinkes, and Moe Fischer were among the boxers who served in Zwillman's security force and later became Minutemen. Hymie "The Weasel" Kugel, the most popular boxing referee in Newark in the 1920s and 1930s, also served in both capacities. Zwillman gave the boxers' relatives jobs with the security force, including Arno's brother-in-law and Benny Levine's father.[36] Some of these men worked for Zwillman until after World War II.

With the end of Prohibition, Zwillman's need for muscle was reduced. Hitler's rise, and the advent of the Friends of the New Germany provided the group of former boxers with an outlet for their skills. When Zwillman called them into action as fighters for a Jewish cause, they responded. The former boxers were used to adulation from their Third Ward friends and neighbors. Now that many of their boxing careers were over, or in their waning years, fighting Nazis would again gain them recognition and self-esteem.

***

When Zwillman opposed the Friends of the New Germany with his Third Ward Gang in 1933, he had no idea how long the struggle would take. As the months passed and the Friends continued their meetings and propaganda, Zwillman determined that a more autonomous group, less associated with his gang, would be necessary to fight the Nazis. Zwillman turned to Nat Arno to lead such a group. Arno had the requisite ingenuity, toughness, and leadership ability. From 1934 until 1940, when he was inducted into the U.S. Army, Arno was the organizer, field commander, and strategist in the fight against Newark-area Nazi groups.

Although Arno ran the day-to-day operations of the Minutemen, much of his strength derived from the fact that public officials, the police, and the press knew that he was Longie Zwillman's man. From 1933 to 1940, Zwillman stood behind Arno and his anti-Nazi group. He paid the legal and medical bills for the jailed or injured[37] and provided jobs. The advance notice of Nazi gatherings that Arno sometimes got, as well as the lenient treatment often accorded the anti-Nazis by police and the judiciary, were due to Zwillman's influence. However, Zwillman stayed in the background. Nat Arno did the recruiting, led the confrontations, and acted as group spokesman. Arno's status among Newark's working-class Jews reached skyward.[38]

Other organizations played supporting roles in the struggle with the Friends of the New Germany. Both the Young Men's Hebrew Club and Newark Post 34 of the Jewish Veterans (JWV) actively opposed Nazi meetings. Indeed, it was the JWV that gave the anti-Nazi fighters of Newark the name Minutemen.

Minuteman was the name used for the armed civilians who before and during America's Revolutionary War were ready to fight the British at a minute's notice. During 1775, Minuteman companies were organized in all New Jersey counties, including six in Essex County. Serving four-month terms, they "were held in constant readiness, on the shortest notice, to march any place where their assistance might be required."[39] Minutemen is a name many American groups have wrapped themselves in since, all of them seeking to associate themselves with patriotic endeavors. It is not surprising that Newark's anti-Nazi fighters, mainly second generation American Jews concerned about their status as Americans in an increasing anti-Semitic atmosphere, proudly adopted the name Minutemen. The Minutemen became synonymous with the anti-Nazi struggle in Newark from 1934 to World War II.

The first mention of the Newark Minutemen was in the *Jewish Chronicle* of February 2, 1934. The weekly announced a movement to organize young men opposed to Nazism into a group effort to press the boycott against German-made goods. The group was sponsored by the National Boycott Committee of the JWV and would cover Newark and its suburbs. The group was called the Minutemen. Those interested were told to call either the *Chronicle* or Irving Piltch of the Young Men's Hebrew Club.[40] Another aim of the local group, not publicized in the *Chronicle*, was to oppose Nazi meetings in Newark and the vicinity.

The Minutemen also organized in New York City. According to Judd Teller, a Jewish journalist of the time, the JWV formed the Minutemen to raid Nazi meetings, but they "were no match for the trained storm troopers guarding these meetings." Teller says that because the New York Minutemen needed added muscle against the Nazis, he became an intermediary between Jewish leaders and men who identified themselves as being from Murder Incorporated. The gangsters coordinated attacks that for a time successfully prevented Nazi meetings.[41] Another source claims that it was Rabbi Stephen Wise who sent a messenger (unnamed) to Meyer Lansky to do something about the Nazis. Lansky then had young men trained in street fighting so they could successfully fight the Nazis.[42]

The National JWV soon regretted its creation of the Minutemen. In April, Jewish war veterans in New York and "Blue Shirt Minutemen" demonstrated at a Nazi meeting in Manhattan. A minor riot occurred, apparently begun by the Minutemen.[43] The Minutemen volunteers in New York City, as in Newark, often had criminal backgrounds and were more interested in beating up Nazis than in peaceful picketing in front of meeting halls. Gangsters and violence were not in keeping with the JWV's image. In May the national organization repudiated the Minutemen and adopted a resolution declaring no further connection between the groups. The JWV specifically denounced Minutemen groups for their violent activities.[44] Louis Freeman, a tavern owner and Third Ward politician, led Newark's Post 34 of the JWV. The membership of Post 34 was sympathetic to the Newark Minutemen's objectives but, because of the national organization's policy, could no longer sponsor the group. Informally, however, Post 34 remained active in the anti-Nazi struggle supporting the Minutemen and the anti-German boycott.

The Young Men's Hebrew Club assumed sponsorship of the Minutemen in May 1934. The Club included among its members some of Newark's top Jewish athletes. The group's leader was Louis Slott, who had starred on both the YMHA and Hebrew Club's basketball teams. The Hebrew Club wanted to prevent the Friends of the New Germany from meeting in Newark and Irvington and from spreading anti-Semitic propaganda. Many of them were not averse to using violence.

When rumors of an impending meeting of the Friends of the New Germany at a meeting hall in Irvington reached the anti-Nazi groups, Slott and Arno, old friends from the Third Ward, met and decided on a joint action. Although Slott and the Young Men's Hebrew Club were not connected to Zwillman's Third Ward Gang, they had participated in the 1933 anti-Nazi demonstrations and fights. Arno welcomed the Hebrew Club as an ally.

* * *

The Minutemen's first organized effort against the Nazis occurred on May 21,1934 in response to a public meeting held by a front for the Friends at the Irvington YMCA. Both components of the Minutemen, the Third Ward Gang and the Young Men's Hebrew Club, were made up of second-generation Eastern European Jews who recognized the dangers of domestic Nazism and were willing to fight in the streets against the Friends and its supporters. Many of these men were veterans of 1933 skirmishes including the October 16 Schwabenhalle riot. The combination of crime toughened gang members and the middle-class aspiring athletes of the Hebrew Club made for an uneasy alliance.

That spring the Friends had passed out circulars, some with swastikas, throughout Irvington urging voters not to vote for Jewish candidates in the upcoming municipal election. When the results were in, Jewish candidates had run uncharacteristically far behind their opponents.

Immediately following the election, publicity printed in German announced a meeting under the auspices of the German Cultural Society, an *ad hoc* group controlled by the Friends, to be held on

May 21 at the Irvington YMCA adjacent to an area that had Jewish as well as German-American residents. The event's purpose was to protest the anti-German boycott and to sponsor a counter boycott against Jewish businesses. The Friends were attempting to get support among German-Americans who would not join the Friends but who might be sympathetic to its cause.

The Third Ward Gang and the Hebrew Club informed Jewish neighborhoods in Newark and Irvington that there would be an anti-Nazi demonstration at the YMCA. [45] Alexander Portnoff, a former football star at Newark's Central High School (the high school for those in the Third Ward who made it through grammar school) heard about the demonstration. He liked to box, and although he had not turned professional he had sparred with many of the fighters from the Third Ward and became one of Longie Zwillman's security guards for bootleg shipments. He remembers being approached by Zwillman one day and being asked to participate in a confrontation with the Nazis in Irvington. Portnoff agreed and was told to wait for a call from Nat Arno.[46]

Emboldened by the 1933 riots and confrontations, the anti-Nazis prepared for May 21st. Al Gorlin's father, owner of a pharmacy, manufactured stench bombs. Others wrapped steel pipes in rubber. Arno, Slott, and Puddy Hinkes scouted out the meeting hall, paying particular attention to rear windows and access to the back of the building. Slott and Arno discussed the deployment of their men and where to set up the caches of clubs.[47]

The Newark Friends were not negligent in their preparations for the rally. Positive they would face opposition from the anti-Nazis, they called on their colleagues in New York for protection. They were promised several busloads of the elite uniformed Ordnungs-Dienst (O.D.) guards, the American equivalent of the German Nazi S.A. The guards had been much in evidence at a Madison Square Garden Friends' rally the week before. The stage was set for the Newark area's second major encounter between the Nazis and their foes.

The day of the event saw a flurry of activity in the Third Ward. Arno made calls to all his men, telling them where to pick up their clubs and to arrive near the meeting hall on Lyons Avenue by 8 PM. Alex Portnoff remembers driving to the site with Al Gorlin and Elliot Sherman. They were eager to attack the Nazis.[48]

By 8:00 sixty men lined the sidewalk across the street from the hall. Twenty Irvington police guarded the entrance. Patrol cars roamed the neighborhood to make sure no attendees would be attacked on their way to the meeting. As the audience filed in, they were greeted by catcalls and curses. Two buses pulled up to the curb and discharged fifty uniformed O.D. guards. Some of the anti-Nazis charged the guards but a police cordon repelled the attack, allowing the guards to safely file up the stairs to the meeting.

The first attack took place when three of the guards returned to their bus to get their coats. Police rushed to their aid. One of the guards, Robert Michaelis of Manhattan, was taken to a hospital with a black eye, a gash on his head, and injuries to his right arm. Unnoticed by the police, several of the anti-Nazis approached the two bus drivers and told them if they did not return to New York immediately both their buses and they would be in danger. The buses left.

The brief altercation with the three guards served as a call for a full-scale attack on the meeting. The Minutemen and others began throwing rocks and stench bombs through the second-story windows. The crowd had grown by this time. Most came prepared for a fight, dressed in shirt sleeves or polo shirts. Police found bats, clubs and iron pipes in the trunk of one car. Lou Halper, a boxer, was the first arrested, charged with disorderly conduct.[49]

About 9:30 Arno ordered an assault on the hall. Outnumbered by the onrushing crowd, police drew their guns and the front rank of attackers halted. Arno and others yelled for a retreat. A tragedy was averted.

Many in the crowd now took positions in the courtyards of apartments opposite the hall, shouting challenges and taunts at those inside. The police set off tear gas bombs when the crowd, swollen by newcomers, again advanced toward the hall. Groups rushed down the street in an attempt to divert the police away from the front of the building. This ruse met with little success.[50]

Meanwhile, the Nazi meeting continued. Police were stationed at the doors of the second-floor auditorium. Seeking to end the confrontation, the Irvington police told the guards they would escort them back to their buses. When the police learned that the buses had gone back to New York, they told the guards to stay away from the windows so as not to infuriate the mob outside.

By 10:00 the crowd outside had expanded to over 2,000. The Irvington Police made an emergency call to Chief James A. McRell of Newark to send help. McRell sent eight motorcycle policemen. When the crowd began an attack on the rear of the building, Newark police sent over fifty more men from three precincts and headquarters.[51]

The screeching of sirens resounded through both cities, and their police headquarters were flooded with calls. Police said they were particularly troubled by the curious who came out "to see the fun." Many explained that they had heard of the fighting and had traveled from downtown Newark to Irvington to see the action. The spectators paid a price for their curiosity when police used tear gas to disband both participants and onlookers.

Police had a problem getting the audience and uniformed guards safely out of the hall. They decided to use a convoy of over thirty police cars and patrol wagons to take the audience of 200, including thirty women, to their homes and cars. They would then take the O.D. guards to police precinct stations in Newark, from where they could safely reach the Hudson Tube station for their trip back to New York. The police used most of their manpower to transport the audience. When guards came down the stairs, there weren't enough police to protect them from the anti-Nazis, who were more interested in confronting them than the audience. The lucky ones were escorted to Newark. But many guards, once in the street, were attacked.

At 11:00, Louis Slott approached the police. He said he would advise his followers not to make further trouble if the police would promise that no such assembly would be permitted again in Irvington. Speaking for the Irvington department, Lieutenant William Graef agreed to Slott's request. Immediately after this conference, a brick hit Newark patrolman Frank Dwyer on the head. He reeled and almost fell. Police ordered the crowd moved back with clubs, which provoked new hostilities, despite the Slott-Graef agreement.

When the riot ended at 2 AM, it was estimated that sixty people had been injured, some seriously. Three hospitals, Newark Beth Israel, Irvington General, and Newark City had admitted twelve patients: six Friends, three anti-Nazis, two police officers, and one newspaper reporter. As with the October 1933 Schwabenhalle riot in Newark, most of the injured had their wounds nursed at home or at their doctor's, eschewing the publicity of a hospital visit. The great majority of the injuries inflicted on the anti-Nazis were from police clubs rather than from the O.D. guards. Five O.D. guards and four anti-Nazis were arrested. The number of arrests would have been greater, but the police were mainly concerned with avoiding violence and escorting the Nazis to safety.[52]

Mayor Percy Miller of Irvington denounced the rioters to the press, saying "mob violence and gangster methods will not be tolerated regardless of irritations that may be engendered from any source." Public Safety Director Edward D. Balentine said "in the future we won't stand for outsiders coming to Irvington and creating such disturbances. Next time we shall go further and if necessary use a fire hose. Innocent bystanders who come out of curiosity will receive the same treatment. We can't pick the wheat from the chaff."

When events in Irvington ended new rioting broke out in Newark, where the O.D. guards had been taken first to precinct stations and then to the Hudson Tubes for their trip home. Arno and his men followed police to where the guards were deposited. At the Sixth Precinct police station, where six of the Nazis were brought, a crowd of hundreds gathered. Police used clubs to disperse them. Jack Aronowicz, an anti-Nazi, was clubbed with sufficient force to suffer a concussion. He was first arrested on disorderly conduct charges and then taken to Beth Israel Hospital.

Reserves from the First Precinct were summoned when twenty-five anti-Nazis attacked four of the uniformed guards at the St. Regis Restaurant on Park Place, opposite the Hudson Tubes. The hapless guards had missed a train and decided to have coffee at the restaurant while waiting for the next train. While they were sipping their coffee, a group of shouting men surged through the front door and charged them. Scooping up tableware as they advanced, the intruders aimed a fusillade at the Nazis. The barrage narrowly missed fifty innocent diners, who either fled into the street or ducked under tables. Tables, chairs and crockery were demolished. The Nazis retreated to the rear door. Two escaped but the other two were caught, floored by brass knuckles and given a severe beating.[53]

By the time police arrived, both the Nazis and their assailants had disappeared. Four persons were picked up nearby and brought back to the restaurant. They were O.D. guards Walter Plath of Yonkers and Paul C. Johannsenn of Manhattan, and anti-Nazis Al Gorlin and Alex Portnoff. A large crowd gathered outside the restaurant, and the police had difficulty keeping order. The standoff ended when police cars took the four men to the First Precinct Court on Washington Street. Anti-Nazis got into cars and followed the police vehicles to the court.

The throng gathered outside the court while the arraignment was taking place before Judge Carl Duveneck. Plath and Johannsenn appeared before the judge with bloodied heads and shirts. They accused Portnoff and Gorlin of assault. Zwillman sent a lawyer, Herman

Fast, to represent Portnoff and Gorlin. The two Nazis protested to no avail that they too wanted a lawyer. Portnoff claimed the guards had assaulted him. The judge charged all four with disorderly conduct. Al Gorlin was held on $1,000 bail on the additional charge of carrying a concealed weapon—a rubber-coated lead pipe blackjack. Judge Duveneck warned the four: "We're not going to have any racial disturbance in this city and that goes for both sides. Confine your troubles to Europe and keep them out of here."[54]

Duveneck ordered a sizeable escort for the two Nazis as the impatient crowd began surging up the steps toward the courtroom. A dozen policemen went outside with their clubs and chased the men down the stairs and into the street. A moment later someone yelled, "Lets get them!" and the crowd surged forward again. The police pushed the crowd back for the second and final time. Meanwhile a dozen cars circled the block. The two Nazis were hustled out the back door and placed into a car. Escorted by two other cars and three motorcycles, they sped toward New York. Everyone then went home. It was 4 AM.[55]

Several hours earlier, a group of six anti-Nazis had appeared at the offices of Newark Police Chief James McRell and urged him to refuse permits for Nazi demonstrations in Newark. Louis Rosenbaum, spokesman for the six, said: "There's no reason for Nazi demonstrations here." McRell told the committee he would comply with their request.[56] Thus, within four hours, the acting police chief in Irvington and the police chief in Newark unequivocally promised that there would be no more Nazi meetings held in the two cities.

The next morning nine anti-Nazis appeared before McRell with swollen eyes and bruised heads to protest rough police tactics. When they could give no satisfactory reason for their presence at the riot scene, he said, "You men were there to cause trouble. You got what you deserved. I sent my men to Irvington to end the riot. They had tear gas guns and clubs and I told them not to use them as ornaments. After this stay in Newark and mind your own business."[57]

Heavy rains allowed the remaining Nazi guards to leave the next day. Police in Irvington placed guards at German halls and clubs. Irvington's director of public safety, Edward Balentine, banned all Nazi and anti-Nazi meetings.[58] He also made extensive preparations to guard against new riots. After an inspection of riot supplies, he ordered more tear gas bombs and other equipment, including 115 clubs—one for each of the sixty-five members of the department and fifty for deputies. Veterans groups were contacted for possible hasty deputization.[59] Newark's commissioner for public safety, Michael P. Duffy, reaffirmed Chief McRell's ban on pro-Nazi meetings, and added anti-Nazi meetings to the edict.[60]

In its editorial "Riot," the *Newark Sunday Call* supported the Newark and Irvington bans on Nazi meetings but also criticized the rioters: "There should be no compunction about denying permits for such riot-provoking gatherings. The constitutional guarantee of the right of free assemblage was to give the American people protection against tyranny and oppression by insuring their right to gather in protest. It was not intended to give alien-minded mobs an opportunity to nourish old-world quarrels and dramatize old-world racial antagonisms. Irvington's director of Public Safety, Edward Balentine, has the right idea. The fire hose is the thing to use on those alien spirits who can't act like gentlemen."[61]

Other than the *Call's* editorial there was no public comment on the riot, with the exception of one letter to the editor of the *Newark News*. Justin Reiss condemned the Nazis, but said they should be allowed to meet in peace. In an attitude typical of those who eschewed confrontation, Reiss said, "Educate and agitate against it (Nazism). Employ not the sanguinary and bellicose methods which characterize the Nazis. Only persuasion, logic, education and peaceful agitation can have permanent results and rid America of the Hitler menace."[62]

In an investigative report, the *Star Eagle* made the correct assertion that there was a well- directed organization behind anti-Nazi attacks in Essex. Its evidence included eyewitness reports of caches of lead, iron, and cable-wire bludgeons placed at pre-designated stations near 717 Lyons Avenue an hour before the riot. Also, according to the *Eagle* there was

> apparently a bare nucleus of the mob of more than 1,000 which gathered much of its strength from free lance opposition to Nazi thought. Many were members of Communist and anti-fascist organizations on hand to distribute circulars. Witnesses to the disturbance remarked today on the similarity of movement apparent in Irvington with that of the Springfield Avenue riot in Newark several months prior. The same tactics of creating a slight disturbance at a street corner to bring police on the rush, and leave an opening elsewhere were used in both riots.[63]

Never mentioned in any press reports was the content of the literature distributed at the meeting hall the night of the riot. The material was in German but was translated into English for the McCormick-Dickstein Committee six days after the riot. One circular read:

Red friends, we swear vengeance to you. Every pawnbroker is a Jew. Fifty percent of all Jews are criminals. Every Communist leader is Jewish. Most counterfeiters are Jews, white slavers, dope peddlers, atheists, and so forth. We demand a Gentile government for America. Who will blame us for that? America, awake. Destroy your vermin, the Jews.[64]

Over the next weeks the Irvington Police Court became a legal battleground as attorneys for both sides filed charges and counter-charges. Ultimately, Police Magistrate Thomas J. Holleran ordered fifteen men, ten Nazis and five anti-Nazis (Louis Slott, Jerome Rodburg, Harry Schwartz, Lou Halper, and Irvington dentist Harry H. Hermann), held on $500 cash bail or $1,000 property bond for Essex County Grand Jury action.

The Irvington riot became an international incident when the German government complained to Secretary of State Cordell Hull that Albert Jung, a German national, had been beaten on a trolley car in Irvington after leaving the event. Hull sent a message to the New Jersey Governor, A. Harry Moore, asking him to investigate.[65] Immediate action was taken and the next day a state detective reported that Irvington police had no record of the incident. The German embassy countered by asserting that Jung had been at both the Irvington and Newark police stations and Newark City Hospital. At this point Governor Moore turned the investigation over to Essex County Prosecutor William Wachenfeld.

In September, an Essex County Grand Jury was empanelled, whose most important task, according to New Jersey Supreme Court Justice Charles W. Parker, was to investigate complaints arising from the anti-Nazi riot.[66] Cases of the fifteen men on bail from Holleran's court were also forwarded to the panel for possible indictments. The jury issued its findings a month later. In a presentment to Common Pleas Judge William Brennan,[67] the jury condemned the riot but issued no indictments. The evidence proved that many people were assaulted, but the seventy-four witnesses could not identify any assailants because of the "extreme confusion." The panel noted that many in the audience were alien residents and non-residents. It also condemned the "vile" racist literature distributed at the meeting and the uniforms worn by the guards that gave the appearance of a military organization. Nevertheless, the jury strongly denounced the riot and urged police to use strong measures to prevent any reoccurrence.[68]

On May 21, Judge Duveneck gave suspended sentences and three years probation to both Al Gorlin and Alex Portnoff for assaulting the two Nazi guards at the Newark restaurant. Portnoff later felt that this conviction was the reason he was not admitted to the FBI a few years later.[69] Gorlin was worried that the three years probation would hurt his employment possibilities.[70]

* * *

The federal government reacted quickly to the riot. The next morning, F.W. Morris, divisional operative of the Secret Service office in Newark, conferred with Balentine. He wanted to know whether there was any policy in place to address the fact that fifty uniformed men came from New York to participate in the Irvington meeting.[71] Morris also wanted to determine the extent of Nazi involvement in the meeting. He noted that Walter Kauf, Spanknoebel's former bodyguard, participated in the Irvington riot. Morris also spoke with McRell.[72]

The riot in Irvington coincided with the start up of activities of the McCormick-Dickstein Congressional Committee, which had been established to examine the Friends of the New Germany. Five days after the riot, Dickstein held a hearing in Newark (see Chapter Three).

For the next few weeks Friends' meetings were cancelled under Minutemen pressure. The Minutemen were so successful that John V. Laddey, a Newark lawyer who represented some of the riot's Nazi defendants, complained that three meetings were canceled "when hoodlum elements threatened to cause disturbances." Two meetings were to be in Irvington, one at Montgomery Hall and the other at the YMCA, and one in Newark at Schabenhalle.[73]

After the Irvington riot, Arno merged the Third Ward Gang's anti-Nazi fighters with like-minded members of the Young Men's Hebrew Club into the Minutemen. Initially, Slott remained commander and Arno assumed the post of vice commander. The gentlemanly Slott, a Nazi fighter when he had to be, was increasingly uncomfortable in the role of strong-arm man. Arno's aggressive demeanor and reputation as a boxer made him more suitable.

Arno liked his new publicity as a fighter for the Jews.[74] The *Jewish Chronicle* ran a picture of him in August 1934 describing him as the Senior Vice-Commander of the Minutemen and one of its founders "who is engaged in combatting Nazi propaganda."[75] The Erste Bershader KUV hosted the Minutemen and the JWV at a meeting to hear about anti-Nazi activities in the Newark area. Arno appeared at the meeting and received congratulations from the crowd. Morris

Mason, "judge advocate" of the Minutemen, reported on the group's activities rather than Arno, who did not enjoy public speaking.[76]

The Friends were relatively quiet in Newark and Irvington during the summer of 1934. Meanwhile, the Minutemen moved into Hudson County and successfully broke up Nazi meetings there. Two such incidents occurred in Union City. After the second, during which Minutemen chased Friends out of the hall and down a street, no landlords would rent property to the Nazis.[77]

At about this time Max Feilshuss was shot in both legs while he was walking with Arno on South Orange Avenue. Feilshuss, a member of Zwillman's Third Ward Gang and Minutemen "chaplain," [78] had participated in the Irvington riot. According to Arno, a black sedan pulled up, a man got out, yelled "Hey you Jew!" and shot Feilshuss. Arno made a dramatic statement to the press: "For more than a year Max and I have conducted investigations into Nazi movements in Newark and Essex County. We have done a lot to fight Hitlerism in this country and will continue to do so, even if they use guns against us." The Minutemen executive board asked for a police probe. The police were skeptical about the alleged motive behind the shooting and suspected the real target was Arno. They never found the culprit.[79]

The next incident between the Friends and the Minutemen occurred in October, 1934 at Montgomery Hall in Irvington. The Friends had been gathering there twice a month since June, despite the promise the police had made to Louis Slott that no more Nazi meetings would be permitted in the city. Approximately 100 Friends and sympathizers attended each event. The Minutemen sent observers to Montgomery Hall to verify the rumored meetings. When an informant told them that a Friends meeting would be held on October 18, they decided to stop it. The Irvington police called Newark for help. The afternoon of the meeting, Slott visited Irvington Police Lieutenant William Graef and reminded him of Graef's May promise. Graef told Slott that the matter was not in his hands and the meeting would take place. Slott said he had no choice but to call the Minutemen.

By 7 PM everyone was ready. Irvington and Newark police were at Montgomery Hall with riot guns and tear-gas bombs. The Irvington Fire Department stood ready with fire hoses. A crowd of several hundred Minutemen and supporters gathered across the street, barred from inching closer by the police. The Friends knew there would be a confrontation and fewer than fifty assembled that evening. Before the meeting was to begin, Nat Arno, along with fellow Minuteman Benjamin Hirsch, appeared at the office of Irvington Commissioner of Public Safety Edward Balentine to tell him that the Friends meeting was "an incitement to riot." Balentine urged restraint, asserting that to avoid any problems the Friends would not be in uniform and would behave "in an orderly fashion." He then asked Hirsch to accompany him to the meeting as an observer. Hirsch agreed and the two drove to Montgomery Hall, passed through the police cordon and entered the meeting room.

Arno drove to the hall to confer with Slott, who was already meeting with Balentine and Graef. It was in Balentine's interest as an elected official to keep the peace, but he was loath to give in to the Minutemen. After the May riot his department had come under criticism from the Nazis, the Minutemen, and law-and-order citizens. Unwilling to make a difficult decision, he left it to the Friends. He climbed onto the stage and asked for permission to speak from Matthias Kohler, president of the Newark Friends. He told the audience that they had the constitutional right to meet, and guaranteed them police protection if they wanted to continue. However, because of the size and temper of the crowd outside, estimated at 400, he recommended that the Friends leave the hall and return home. Kohler agreed to cancel the meeting. Hirsch promised Balentine that the Friends would not be assaulted once outside. Hirsch left the hall and delivered the news to the crowd. Many cheered the victory, but Arno and his men knew that this was not to be the end of the Friends' meetings in Irvington.[81]

* * *

The Minutemen's success did not garner them kudos from any mainstream Jewish organizations. Minutemen exploits embarrassed those Jews who felt their respectability tarnished by Jewish hooligans. The fact that a Nazi meeting had been cancelled and bloodshed averted was beside the point. An exception to this tendency occurred two weeks later when the Knights of the Round Table, a small Jewish civic group, invited Louis Slott to speak at Krueger Hall on Minutemen activities in and around Newark.[82]

Balentine soon regretted giving in to the Minutemen's pressure. The Friends' attorney, Frank D. Van Sickle, criticized him for having made "a tactical error in asking the group to adjourn."[83] There were many more German Americans in Irvington than Jews. Town officials were predominantly German American, as was the police force. Few German Americans were either Nazis or Nazi sympathizers, but many resented the fact that Jewish toughs from Newark were travelling to Irvington to beat up Germans and German Americans who were meeting peacefully. After the May riot and the cancelled meeting in October, much of Irvington's German-American community wanted their police department to be firmer against the Newarkers. On the other hand, some policemen and public officials were in cahoots with Zwillman and his operatives in slot machine and other gambling enterprises. It was alleged at the time that Balentine himself was "friendly with Zwillman."[84] There was no question that Irvington officialdom knew from whom the Minutemen had sprung.

Wishing to resume their public activities, and with the tacit support of influential public officials, the Friends scheduled a meeting for November 21 at the Irvington YMCA on Clinton Avenue. These officials, particularly Balentine and Holleran, were eager to demonstrate that they were masters of their own turf. They Nazis were promised maximum security for the event. Irvington superior officers were instructed to contact their Newark counterparts to prevent the Minutemen from appearing in Irvington. A challenge had been laid down to the anti-Nazis.

The Minutemen soon heard that they were not welcome in Irvington. Arno and Slott argued over the appropriate Minuteman response. Slott urged restraint and said he would fight the Nazis but not the police. Arno said he wanted to stop the meeting whatever the cost. He reasoned that if the police protected the Nazis and the Minutemen stayed away, there would be greater attendance at future meetings. A compromise was reached. There would be a small demonstration and Minutemen cars would circle the YMCA, letting both the Friends and the police know the meeting was being watched.

Under the watchful eyes of the police, over 200 Friends and sympathizers filed into the YMCA. A dozen Minutemen marched across the street while sixty cars filled with Minutemen reconnoitered. The Irvington police were out in full force, but they did not see two men hiding behind the Y carrying stench bombs and bricks wrapped in a message, "Warning! Nazis Keep Out! Stop Meeting!" As soon as the meeting was underway, Nat Arno and George Hirsch hurled the bombs and the bricks through the building's rear windows into the hall where the Friends were assembled. Many trying to escape the onslaught huddled in the corridors.

Against the odds, Arno was determined to break up the meeting. He failed. The police quickly gave chase to the two Minutemen, immediately catching Hirsch. Arno was sprinting to safety when Officer George Krasle fired several warning shots over his head. He halted and was arrested. The meeting resumed. Hirsch and Arno were booked, held without bail, and charged with loitering. Asked by newsmen why he allowed the Nazis to meet in Irvington, Balentine said he had no right to cancel any meeting as long as the participants were orderly.[85]

Two days later Arno pleaded guilty and admitted throwing two stench bombs into the meeting hall. Irving Piltch, attorney for Arno and Hirsch, pleaded for leniency, but Holleran said he had warned Arno to stay out of Irvington after the May riot. He fined him $25 and sentenced him to thirty days in jail. Holleran said he would "not tolerate mob rule in Irvington." In conclusion, he remarked

> These outsiders, or rowdies, had no right in this community on the purposes they had in mind. They do not represent the true Jewish attitude.

Hirsch was also fined $25 and placed on probation for six months rather than jailed. He escaped incarceration because he had a good record, was a sergeant in the Newark Junior Police, and "had saved three women from a maniac in Newark."[86]

The incident resulted in Slott's resignation as Minutemen commander and Arno's assumption of that position. Slott was angered at Arno's attack on the YMCA meeting contrary to their agreement, and he was uncomfortable with the freelance tendencies of Arno. From then on Slott and the Young Men's Hebrew Club participated in Minutemen activities on an *ad hoc* basis.

There was a rapid response to Irvington's crackdown on the Minutemen. Newark Post 34 of the JWV, in a four-page supplement to the *Jewish Chronicle*, castigated Irvington's actions. In an editorial titled "Balentine and Holleran a la Hitler," the veteran's group pointed out that Nazi meetings were banned in Newark and eight other New Jersey cities. They were allowed only in Irvington and Guttenberg.[87]

During 1935, the Minutemen kept a close watch on all Friends activities. They avoided violence but picketed all Nazi events. Even the *Newark Evening News*, which had previously criticized the Minutemen, now spoke of their reasonableness. After Arno charged that un-American activities occurred at the October, 1935 German Day in Springfield, the *News* pointed out that the Minutemen make "it a point to confer with police authority before every German affair and ask prohibition of Nazi propaganda."[88] The Friends avoided any public meetings in Newark for the entire year, preferring to hold their meetings in Irvington under Balentine's protective eye, or in Springfield, where the police also protected them.

* * *

Until 1940, the Minutemen and the Nazis fought each other in the Newark area. The struggle, however, had different meanings for the two groups. The aim of the Friends and its successor, the German-American Bund, was to spread their ideology to the tens of thousands of German-Americans in the Newark area. The Friends firmly believed Arno's group was just one more manifestation of the world Jewish conspiracy. Like the McCormick-Dickstein and Dies committees at the federal level, and the Anti-Nazi Law at the state level, the Minutemen were a hindrance to be overcome in due time when Americans of Aryan stock would take over the country.

For the Minutemen, the struggle was not about ideology or politics. Rather it was a battle for Jewish survival. Members believed that American Nazis and their Newark affiliate were out to destroy Jews, and they responded with violence. They believed violence against Nazis was an effective tool. Arno's aim was not only to confront the Nazis on their own turf, but also to deter them from any verbal or physical assaults on Newark's Jews. If this was done peacefully— all the better. He dissuaded hall owners from renting to Nazis. Arno visited public officials, often with one of Zwillman's lawyers, to ask them not to issue parade or meeting permits. They noted that rioting could harm the reputations of those permitting open Nazi activities. Persuasion when possible, violence when necessary, was Arno's *modus operandi* for the duration of the Minutemen's fight against the Nazis.

The Jews of the Third Ward and Irvington were fortunate to have the Minutemen, as the Friends could become violent when left unchecked. Across the river in Manhattan, Friends in Yorkville (a German-American area on the Upper East Side and center of American Nazi activities) went on a rampage in 1934 during the High Holy Days, defacing the windows of over fifty Jewish-owned stores. [89] Later, fifteen uniformed O.D. guards broke up a peaceful meeting of the German-American League for Culture, an anti-Nazi group. Using blackjacks, the guards assaulted members of the audience.[90]

Throughout the rest of the 1930s Arno directed the Minutemen, comprised of a small cadre of regulars and a large bloc of volunteers who were "ready when needed." Always in the background was Longie Zwillman, watching over both his criminal empire and his anti-Nazi force. The Arno-Zwillman team shouldered an important responsibility for Newark's Jewish community.

Newark's first- and second-generation working-class Eastern European Jews were the Minutemen's chief boosters. Most other Jews did not support them, citing the group's violence and the criminal backgrounds of many of its members. But years later, with the Holocaust in mind, some of these Jews admitted that in retrospect the Minutemen had performed a needed service.[91]

Notes

1.   For additional information on Ellenstein, see Paul Stellhorn, "Champion of the City: Reflections on the Career of Meyer C. Ellenstein," unpublished manuscript based upon a presentation made before the Jewish Historical Society of MetroWest, 6/9/97. Meyer Ellenstein (1889-1967), born in Paterson, was, in turn, a boxer, dentist, lawyer, politician, and publicist. Stellhorn considers Ellenstein a populist mayor. During his two terms as mayor—served during the Depression—Ellenstein was sympathetic to the unemployed and opposed big business interests that wanted lower taxes at the expense of Newark homeowners. Loyal to a fault to friends and supporters, Ellenstein's association with Zwillman, along with the allegedly dishonest transactions it entailed, tarnished his reputation.
2.   Abner Zwillman, FBI File 92-3105-29, p. 6.
3.   At the time, New Jersey Governors could not succeed themselves. Moore's gubernatorial terms were 1926-1929, 1932-1935, and 1938-1941.
4.   Mark A. Stuart, *Gangster # 2 The Man who Invented Organized Crime Longy Zwillman*, Secaucus, New Jersey, 1985. This is the only full-length work on Zwillman. Stuart was a journalist who had a long time interest in both Longie Zwillman and New Jersey crime. Information on Zwillman's early life is taken from his book.
5.   *Collier's*: "From Rags to Riches," Lester Velie, 9/1/51, p. 48.
6.   Stuart, *Gangster # 2*, p. 34.
7.   Zwillman, FBI File 92-3105-3, p. 36.
8.   Stuart, *Gangster # 2*, p. 42.
9.   N.N. Morgue: Newark Department of Police, Detective Bureau: Criminal Record Form-undated; Zwillman, FBI File 62-36085-23, p. 22.
10.   Ibid. N.N 12/1/30.
11.   Ibid. N.N. 8/16/51; Stuart op. cit. pp. 32, 33.
12.   Stuart, ibid.
13.   Zwillman, FBI File 62-36085-92-3105-3, p. 36.
14.   Zwillman, FBI File 92-3105-13, p. 26; Stuart, op. cit., pp. 45, 46.
15.   Zwillman, FBI File 62-36085-23 p. 2; Stuart op. cit., pp. 73-77.
16.   *Newsweek*, "Longie Zwillman: Big Businessman and/or Gangster," 8/27/51, p. 23.
17.   Stuart, *Gangster # 2*, pp. 107-109.
18.   N.N. Morgue, N.N., 5/21/35.
19.   N.N. Morgue: Editorials, 3/28/51.
20.   Zwillman dubbed Arno with the sobriquet of "Commander" early in the Minutemen's existence. See, Interview, Anne Arno, 8/6/97.

21. Interview, Rose Abramowitz Yannick, 8/7/97. The paragraphs on Arno's early life are from this interview.
22. Papers of Nat Arno, "Fight Record of Nat Arno," undated, in possession of author
23. Interview, Yannick, 8/6/97.
24. Ibid.
25. Papers of Nat Arno, "Fight Record of Nat Arno."
26. Interview, Yannick, 8/6/97.
27. Robert Slater, *Great Jews in Sports*, Middle Village, NY, 1983, pp. 132-134.
28. Scrapbook of Bennie Levine, in possession of daughter Fran Schneiderman.
29. Bodner, Allen, *When Boxing Was a Jewish Sport*, Westport, CT, 1997, p. 4.
30. Scrapbook of Bennie Levine.
31. Ibid.
32. Ibid.; Papers of Nat Arno.
33. Papers of Nat Arno.
34. Scrapbook of Bennie Levine.
35. Ibid., *American Jewish Ledger*, July 13, 1973, p. 7.
36. Interview, Mickey Fisher, 5/11/96; Interview, Bernard Schneiderman 10/4/98; Interview, Rose Yannick, 8/6/97.
37. Interviews, Alex Portnoff, 1/11/97; Faye Skuratovsky, 4/5/97.
38. Interview, Phil Konvitz, 11/21/96 Konvitz is the brother of Milton Konvitz and the son of Rabbi Joseph Konvitz.
39. Frank John Urquhart, *A History of the City of Newark*, Vol. 1, Newark, 1913, p. 282.
40. J.C., 2/2/34, p. 3.
41. Judd Teller, *Strangers and Natives, The Evolution of the American Jew from 1921 to the Present*, New York 1968, pp. 183-4.
42. Dennis Eisenberg, Uri Dan, Eli Landau, *Meyer Lansky Mogul of the Mob*, New York, 1979, pp. 184,185.
43. J.C. 4/13/34, p. 1.
44. Ibid. 5/4/34, p.1.
45. N.N., 5/22/34, p. 22.
46. Interview, Alexander Portnoff, 6/25/96. Portnoff knocked down a highly regarded boxer while sparring. Reporters who were watching the professional told the famous promoter Jack Kearns about the "kid." According to Portnoff, "He came up to the house to talk my mother into signing permission for me to become a boxer. She was no fool. She let him talk and she let him talk and she let him talk. Then she excused herself, went into the laundry room, picked up a broom and started swinging it saying, "Get out of here, you bums! Get out of here. You're not going to make a bum out of my son! Get out of here!" He said, "But he'll become a millionaire." I said to my mother: "You're ruining my future!"
47. Ibid.
48. Ibid.
49. N.N., 5/22/34, p. 22; S.E., 5/22/34, p. 1.
50. Interview, Portnoff; S.E., 5/22/34, p.1.
51. S.E., 5/22/34, p. 1; N.N., 5/22/34, p.1.
52. Ibid. The four anti-Nazis arrested were Lou Halper, Frank Plentick, Jerome Rodburg, and Harry Schwartz.
53. S.E., 5/22/34, p. 2.
54. S.E., 5/22/34, p. 1; Interview, Alex Portnoff.
55. S.E., 5/22/34, p.1.
56. Ibid., p. 2.
57. Ibid., 5/23/34, p. 1.
58. I.H., 5/25/34, p. 1.
59. S.E., 5/24/34, p. 1.
60. N.N. 5/24/34, p.10.
61. S.C., 5/27/34, Part III, p.1.
62. N.N., 6/2/34, p. 6.
63. S.E., 5/23/34, p.1.

64.   U.S. Congressional Committee Hearings, A Subcommittee of the Special Committee on Un-American Activities, Investigation of Nazi Propaganda Activities and Investigation of Certain Other Propaganda Activities, 73rd Congress, 2nd Session, Confidential Committee Print, at Newark, N.J., May 26, 1934, Hearing No. 73-N.J.-1, p. 4.

65.   N.N., 6/13/34, p. 1.

66.   Ibid., 9/19/34, p. 6.

67.   Justice William Brennan was to later serve on both the New Jersey and the United States Supreme Courts.

68.   N.N. 10/26/34, p. 23.

69.   Interview, Alex Portnoff, 6/25/96.

70.   Gorlin appealed to Dr. Kalb to intervene with the court to have the sentence either reduced or nullified. Kalb called his JWV comrade, Herman Weckstein, an attorney, asking for help. Weckstein was not enthusiastic about the task, and said if Gorlin waited nine months, he "might" see the judge and ask for a reduction. Kalb replied to Weckstein that since the JWV was cooperating with the Minutemen, it was the responsibility of the JWV to help Gorlin, who had joined in the action at the Doctor's behest. Kalb Papers, Letters, Weckstein to Kalb, 2/25/35; Kalb to Weckstein, 2/26/35.

71.   S.E., 5/23/34, p. 1.

72.   National Archives, RG 87, T 915, Daily Reports of the US Secret Service, 1875-1936, Roll   629.   Interesting are the expenses that Morris detailed in this report: " transportation to Irvington and return to Newark by bus, twenty cents, telephone call five cents." Unfortunately, no copy of Morris's investigation could be found.

73.   S.E., 5/29/34, p. 4.

74.   Arno recognized and enjoyed his elevated in status among Newark's Eastern European Jews because of his leadership of the Minutemen. Interview, Phillip Konvitz, 11/21/96.

75.   J.C., 8/10/34, p. 3.

76.   Ibid., 7/13/34, p. 2.

77.   Interview, Alex Portnoff, 6/25/96.

78.   Letterhead of the Minutemen, undated, in author's possession. Arno had many laughs with titles such as "chaplain" and "judge advocate" sarcastically awarded to his strong-arm Minutemen cohorts.

79.   N.N. 7/5/34, p. 7: ibid. 7/6/34, p. 13.

80.   N.N., 10/19/34, p. 25.

81.   Ibid.

82.   J.C., 11/9/34, p. 2.

83.   N.N., 10/19/34, p. 25.

84.   Interview, Harry Stevenson, 4/3/99.

85.   N.N. 11/22/34, p. 22; S.E., 11/22/34, p. 1; I.H., 11/23/34, p. 1.

86.   N.N., 11/23/34, p. 26; ibid., 11/30/34, p. 25.

87.   *Jewish Chronicle*, Jewish War Veterans' Supplement, 12/7/34, p.1. The editorial continues: "In Irvington, Police told the Minutemen to stay out, but they didn't tell the Nazis to stay out." Balentine gives police protection to the Nazis while "Holleran says the boys from Newark are strangers and he doesn't want them in Irvington. How about the people who come to Nazi meetings? Have Holleran or Balentine ever checked the attendance at these meetings? From seventy-five to eighty-five percent are from outside cities where they cannot hold meetings. But Balentine gives them police protection and in effect says "its okay boys you can meet here as long as you don't cause any disturbance. The Nazis themselves don't want a disturbance because it would interfere with their plans.... Do Balentine and Holleran expect to show leniency and offer protection to people who are not residents of Irvington—most of them not even citizens—that come here to spread anti-Semitic and anti-American propaganda and then expect Jewish, Italian and Irish boys and men to sit by and twiddle their thumbs? Fortunately, this is still America and Americans as such retain some rights."

88.   N.N., 8/6/35, p. 14.

89.   NYT, 9/20/34, p. 2.

90.   Papers of J.X. (Jacob) Cohen, Series 111, Folder 103, Letter from I.B. to J.X. Cohen, 12/30/35.

91.   Interview, Joseph Lerner, 2/8/97.

3

The Friends: Supporters and Enemies

The Friends of the New Germany was established in April-May 1933 with support from Berlin, and ceased operations in December 1935 when that support was withdrawn. The group operated in American cities with large German populations such as New York, Chicago, Detroit, Cincinnati, Philadelphia, and Newark. In its two-and-a-half years of existence, it has been estimated that membership ranged from 1,500 to 15,000, probably never exceeding 10,000. About 60 percent of the group was made up of aliens, with most of the rest recent emigrés to America. The Friends' ideology was copied from that of the Nazi party, which it adapted to conditions in America. Its long-range plan was to unify German Americans in the struggle against Jews and communists who, it felt, ran America. Its immediate goal was to combat anti-Nazi propaganda in the United States.[1]

In Newark, the Friends had about 100 members in its first year of existence, including approximately sixty-five aliens and a smaller number of recent American citizens.[2] Observers at its first-year events estimated that there were no more than 500 open sympathizers, whereas those sympathetic to the Friends' program but who were afraid to appear at public events can be estimated at a few thousand. When these figures are compared either to the 200,000 residents of German ancestry in Essex County or to the 1930 United States Census, which put the figure at 150,000,[3] it is obvious that the Friends represented a very small percentage of those residents. Despite its failure to convert more people to its cause, the Newark Friends was successful in infiltrating some of the mainline German-American organizations in Essex County. Sympathizers as well as active Friends were used to spread Nazi propaganda.

Newark was an important location for the Friends because of its geographic proximity to New York and its large and well-organized

German-American community, which contained thousands of post-World War I immigrants. The latter were the most susceptible to Nazi propaganda because they had witnessed the instability of the Weimar Republic, Germany's deteriorating economic situation, and the constant drumbeat of anti-Semitic agitation. Although not numerous, the Newark Friends' core of members and supporters was dangerous. Members were fanatical in their anti-Semitism and obedience to Hitler and the American *bundesleiter*, Hans Spanknoebel. Some were later recruited as spies for Nazi Germany.

The Friends were accepted as a part of the German-American scene in Newark by the end of 1935. Disliked by many, ignored by the vast majority, and embraced by only a few, the group had made its voice heard in the community. The Friends was truly representative of the New Germany, and for better or worse could not be ignored by those who still regarded Germany as their patrimony.

In the 1933-1935 period, most German Americans viewed the group as an alien organization that could stir up trouble. The great majority of German Americans were thoroughly assimilated, and Nazi brutality and suppression of basic liberties had no more appeal for them than it did for other Americans.[4] Many remembered the World War I anti-German hysteria that had pervaded much of America. In Newark, streets that had been named for German Americans had been renamed; German-language instruction in public schools had been suspended; and there had been incidents of unprovoked harassment against German Americans. Few cared to revisit that period. That is not to say that these citizens did not sympathize with some of Hitler's aims, particularly his desire to reverse of some of the more onerous terms of the Versailles Treaty that ended World War I. German Americans in Irvington and Newark were not happy to see conflicts between their brethren and the anti-Nazis. However, a few years later Hitler's continuing successes in Europe led many more Americans of German descent to support a Nazi movement.

Within the German-American population, there were conflicts between those who had left in the wake of the 1848 revolution and those who had left Germany after World War I to escape the uncertainties of the Weimar Republic. The latter were more likely to support Nazism; many of them saw Hitler as a hero who was transforming Germany after its defeat in World War I. This struggle for the minds of German Americans can be illustrated by two speeches that occurred one week apart in Newark and Irvington in 1934.

At the New Jersey convention of *Turnverein* (sports organizations) at Turnverein Hall in Newark, education director Marie B. McDonald told the delegates that German Turners joined Union forces during the American Civil War to help keep America united and free. She urged a return to the liberal principles of 1848, when liberal Germans had been forced to leave their country.[5] Four days later, Reverend Heinrich Manrodt, pastor of Newark's German Lutheran Zion's Church, spoke before the Technischer Verein (Skilled Worker's Club) at Montgomery Hall in Irvington. He praised Hitler's social revolution and claimed that the Führer was on the road to creating "a true people's church" for Germany.[6]

Meetings of Newark's Friends of the New Germany were held twice a month. Originally they were held at Schwabenhalle, but after the riot in October 1933 Newark officials barred Friends meetings and the group moved to the YMCA on Clinton Avenue in Irvington. The meeting format was always the same. The Friends' president began with organizational matters, and then introduced a guest speaker. Speakers were often from national headquarters in New York and included such Friends' leaders such as Fritz Gissibl and Ignatz Griebl. These men eschewed honorariums, whereas lesser lights were paid from $3 to $5. The speeches focused on Nazi Germany's progress and greatness and the perfidy of the Jews. The audience would interrupt, when appropriate, with the Nazi salute and shouts of "Heil Hitler." After the speech, the attendees would sing "Horst Wessel" or "Deutschland Uber Alles," the Nazi anthem, among other songs.[7]

Many of the recent immigrants who joined the Friends had been anti-Semitic in Germany, and it was easy for them to sign the oath required to join the organization:

> I hereby declare my entry into the association of the Friends of the New Germany: the purpose and aims of the association are known to me, and pledge myself to support them unequivocally. I recognize the principle of leadership according to which the association is conducted. I am not a member of any secret organization of any kind, Freemasons and so forth. I am of Aryan extraction, free from Jewish or colored racial admixture.[8]

***

Nazism in America began after the November 8, 1923 failure of Hitler's beer hall Putsch, when a handful of Nazis fled to the United States. One of them, Fritz Gissibl, organized the first Nazi group in America, the National Socialist Association of Teutonia in October

1924. This group, which lasted until 1932, contained aliens and American citizens, some who belonged to the Nazi party in Detroit, where many Germans had immigrated to take jobs in the expanding auto industry, and some who did not.[9] Some of the immigrants who belonged to Teutonia believed that Germany had lost World War I because of the treason of Jews and communists. They arrived in the United States believing that the Nazi party—the National Socialist German Workers Party (NSDAP)—would gain power in Germany and expel both groups of traitors. After this was accomplished, they planned to return to Germany and participate in the Nazi regime. When Hitler came to power in 1933, several of Teutonia's leaders, including Gissibl, returned to Germany and received party posts. [10]

Teutonia gained members at the onset of the Depression in 1929 when many of the new German employees in the auto industry were laid off. Some believed their layoffs were due to a Jewish-capitalist plot. By 1932, Teutonia claimed a membership of over 500, and had branches in Chicago, Los Angeles, New York City, and Cincinnati.

During the same period, small cells of Nazi party members were scattered throughout America, particularly in cities with large German-American populations. By 1932 the total membership was about 200. Cell leaders claimed they, rather than Teutonia, which had a large percentage of non-party members, were the true representatives of the NSDAP in America. In May 1931, the New York cell wrote to the newly created Nazi foreign section in Hamburg that it, not Teutonia, should be empowered to organize a Nazi party in the United States. A positive answer came quickly. The New York Nazi cell was put under the control of NSDAP's foreign section and designated the National Socialist German Workers' Party, New York Unit, or Gau-USA.[11] By June 1931 Gau-USA had branches in Seattle, Detroit, Chicago, and Milwaukee.[12]

It is very possible a NSDAP cell had been operating in Newark before the establishment of Gau-USA. Many early members of the Newark branch of the Friends of the New Germany, such as Walter Kauf and the brothers Oscar and Frank Schilling, had immigrated to the United States in the late 1920s and were active in Nazi affairs before the Friends' creation.

The decision to establish Gau-USA as the official American Nazi party entailed a relocation of American Nazism's base from the Midwest to New York City. New York was already the home to over 100 German immigrant associations, including the American branch of

Germany's largest group of World War I veterans, the Stahlhelm. There was also the well established and prestigious United German Societies of Greater New York (UGS), which included almost all the pre-World War I German-American organizations.[13] The UGS had over 10,000 members, some of whom were German Jews. Many of the societies were concentrated in Yorkville, a Manhattan neighborhood with a predominantly German population, [14] which would be the center of the Nazi movement in America from 1932 to World War II.

Teutonia disintegrated when its Nazi party members joined Gau-USA. Gissibl formally dissolved it when he merged its membership into Gau-USA in October 1932.[15] A friend and fellow Teutonia leader, Hans Spanknoebel, became the first Führer of the American Nazi movement.

* * *

Hans Spanknoebel immigrated to the United States in 1929 at the age of 36.[16] He came to Detroit and worked for Ford Motor Company until he was laid off in 1930 because of the Depression. He had already joined Teutonia and the NSDAP, and when he lost his job he started working full time for Teutonia. After Gissibl dissolved Teutonia, Spanknoebel attempted to take over the American Nazi movement, and Hitler's ascension to power in January 1933 gave him the chance to achieve his objective.[17]

Spanknoebel traveled to Germany and inveigled his way into the inner circle of Rudolf Hess, Hitler's deputy chancellor. He exaggerated the number of German-Americans ready to join an American Nazi party and said it was now up to Berlin to authorize it. Without substantiating this information, Hess gave Spanknoebel a document authorizing him to form a new organization. Armed with this paper, Spanknoebel returned to New York in May 1933 ready to become the American Führer.

The establishment of a Nazi government in Germany caused yet another internecine battle within Gau-USA because leadership in the American Nazi party would now wield much more power. Newspapers carried frequent stories of the intra-party struggles. Two groups broke away from the Gau-USA and formed their own Nazi parties. In April 1933, the NSDAP foreign section, fearing a continuation of negative and unwanted publicity about its squabbling American proteges, cabled the leadership of Gau-USA and told them to disband.

Spanknoebel had his opportunity. Armed with the Hess authorization, he set up headquarters in Yorkville and visited NSDAP members. He told them he was establishing a new organization of German nationals and German Americans that would be secretly controlled by the Nazi party. With the help of Fritz Gissibl and others from Detroit, plus personnel from the New York German consulate, Spanknoebel created the Friends of the New Germany in the spring of 1933.

Arrogant and impetuous, Spanknoebel alienated many of those he sought to influence. But because he obviously had the backing of the NSDAP most fell in line and joined the new group. Despite this, there were still fragments of former Nazi organizations that would not accept the Friends' hegemony. To counter this— and to enforce intraparty discipline—Spanknoebel created a fighting force modeled after Hitler's SS called the Ordnungs-Dienst (OD) Uniformed Service. The organizational setup, uniforms and songs were all imitative of Hitler's storm troopers. Spanknoebel's trusted allies traveled all over the country converting Nazi groups into Friends' units. Spanknoebel's success with the Friends was due partly to his coercive tactics, but mostly to the fact that he had Hess's authorization. By July all dissidents were in line and Spanknoebel felt confident enough to call a two-day convention in Chicago on July 28.

At the convention, Spanknoebel announced that the Nazi movement in America had officially begun. He relinquished his title of Führer, since that belonged only to Hitler, and named himself bundesleiter (organizational leader). Gissibl was his deputy. The Friends was a party created in the image of the Nazi party and administered according to the *führerprinzip* (the unquestioned authority of the leader). Within six months of Hitler's appointment as Germany's chancellor, there existed a Nazi group in the United States under Spanknoebel's control.

After the convention, the bundesleiter brought his message to German-American communities throughout the country and reorganized Nazi press efforts in America. Soon there were two weekly Friends' newspapers in Yorkville. By October, Friends newspapers also existed in Philadelphia, Cincinnati, Detroit, and Chicago.

Over the summer, Spanknoebel successfully courted influential members of the German-American community in New York City, including those of the United German Societies. He felt he could gain a mass following in Yorkville by seizing control of the UGS with its seventy organizations and over 10,000 members.

Spanknoebel's attempt to control the German-American community of New York was a disaster both for himself and the Friends. He failed in his attempt to coerce Victor and Paul Ridder, editors of the *Staats-Zeitung*—the largest German-language paper in the United States (circulation 50,000)—to publish articles favorable to Hitler. At a September 18 UGS meeting to plan the annual German Day parade marking the 250th anniversary of the first German settlers in America, Spanknoebel packed the house with O.D. men. During the proceedings the O.D. started chanting, "Out with the Jews, out with the Jews!" Spanknoebel threatened to use the blackjack on anyone who disagreed. Representatives of four Jewish groups walked out. Representatives of the remaining sixty-six groups voted to add Spanknoebel to the UGS Board of Directors and to permit German ambassador Hans Luther to speak at German Day. However, they voted down Spanknoebel's suggestion that the German flag with its swastika be displayed at the event. This was an important issue because if the flag were flown the UGS would be endorsing the Nazi government, and, since German Day was to conclude at the Manhattan Armory, the Nazi flag would be flown at a United States government building. Another meeting to further discuss the flag issue was scheduled for September 25.[18]

The Bundsleiter's partial coup of the UGS received widespread negative coverage. Three days before the next meeting, six non-Jewish groups resigned from UGS, as did the Societies' entire board of directors,with the exception of Spanknoebel. On the 25th, the meeting was packed with Spanknoebel's men. To everyone's surprise the Ridder brothers and representatives of two Jewish groups appeared. The Ridders were jeered out of the hall after they announced that the UGS was being used for Nazi purposes. One Jewish representative, the treasurer of UGS, resigned, and the other Jew was ejected from the hall. The vote against flying the Nazi flag was reversed. Once again there was negative press.

Spanknoebel continued on his path of self-destruction. In early October, during the Jewish High Holy Days of Rosh Hoshana and Yom Kippur, Spanknoebel was said to be responsible for ordering his men to paint swastikas on the doors of Manhattan synagogues, among them Temple Emanuel, New York's most prominent Jewish house of worship. Complaints about Spanknoebel's behavior were made to many officials, including New York mayor, John Patrick O'Brien. Among the complainants was an advisor to the Mayor,

Samuel Untermyer, a well-known international lawyer and soon to-be founder and president of the Non-Sectarian Anti-Nazi League (NSANL). At a conference with a UGS representative, the mayor said that the German Day event had to be cancelled or he would stop it. At a meeting later in mid-October, Spanknoebel appeared with other members of the UGS and told O'Brien their constitutional rights would be violated if the parade were canceled.[19]

During this period of tension, the Schwabenhalle riot in Newark took place. It was reported on the radio, in all New York daily news-papers, and in national news magazines. A pitched battle just ten miles from Manhattan between Nazis and their foes made a strong impression on the public. Spanknoebel and the Friends were viewed as a threat to America's democratic society. Among those seeking to stop Spanknoebel were members of the United States Congress, par-ticularly Representative Samuel Dickstein of Brooklyn.

Dickstein, chairman of the House Committee on Immigration and Naturalization, had kept abreast of the Spanknoebel-UGS affair, and after the Schwabenhalle riot asked the labor department to deport Spanknoebel on the grounds that he had not registered as a foreign agent with the state department. When the bundesleiter failed to show up at another meeting with Mayor O'Brien, it may have been be-cause he had learned of Dickstein's request. At that October 25 meet-ing a representative of the UGS said Spanknoebel could not be lo-cated and that in any case he had been expelled from the UGS. The next day the UGS cancelled its parade. Spanknoebel went into hid-ing and on October 29 secretly left the country for Germany. He escaped just in time. The Justice Department had just issued an ar-rest warrant charging him with being an unregistered foreign agent.

Spanknoebel's reign as bundesleiter was brief but significant. In less than three months he organized a Nazi party in America with a military arm, filled the leadership ranks of the party with loyal NSDAP members, and established a Nazi press in five important American cities. On the other hand, he had antagonized many influential lead-ers in New York's German-American community, exposed the Friends to an enormous amount of negative publicity, and awakened the United States government to the threat of a militant foreign-backed force in its midst. Spanknoebel not only started the Friends, but planted the seeds for its end as well.

* * *

The House Special Committee on Un-American Activities was the crucial element in the demise of the Friends of the New Germany.[20] The driving force behind the committee was Samuel Dickstein, a controversial public figure during and after his lifetime. In a 1968 account of the House Committee on Un-American Activities, Walter Goodman, in an oft-quoted passage, said of Dickstein's twenty-two-year House career (1922-1944), "during that time no cause took more of his energies or his passions than the creation of a committee to investigate subversive activities. He deserves the title of Father of the Committee. He earned the distinction by relentlessly trying from 1933-1938 and had the rest of his life to regret it."[21] Goodman also claims that Dickstein was a glory seeker and had "inquisitorial passions."[22] Thus Dickstein was set up by Goodman as the prototype for future "witch-hunting" leaders of the House Un-American Activities Committee.

Sander A. Diamond, in his 1974 work on the Nazi movement in the United States, calls Samuel Dickstein Congress's number one anti-Nazi. Diamond asserts that despite the congressman's exaggerations and sensationalism, he had the public's support—much to the chagrin of the Nazis, who considered Dickstein the "incarnation of evil." Dickstein proved Germany was supplying financial and ideological resources to American Nazis.[23]

Twenty-five years later, Allen Weinstein devotes a chapter to Dickstein in a 1999 book on Soviet espionage in America. Weinstein documents Soviet payments made to Dickstein over a two-year period, beginning in July 1937, for materials on Nazi activities and stresses Dickstein's extreme venality.[24]

Samuel Dickstein was born in Vilna, Lithuania in 1885 and arrived in America with his parents in 1887. They settled on the Lower East Side, the area he eventually represented in the United States House of Representatives. He graduated law school and was admitted to the New York bar in 1908. His interest in politics started in high school and while still in law school he became affiliated with Tammany Hall. After graduation, he honed his political skills as deputy attorney general for the state of New York, New York City alderman, and New York State assemblyman.

Dickstein established himself as an accomplished legislator. He authored New York's kosher food law, which became a standard for similar legislation in other states, and initiated New York's sabbath law, which permitted Jewish merchants to be open on Sunday. Throughout his four-year tenure as assemblyman he fought for improved housing and rent regulations to benefit his constituents on the Lower East Side.[25]

In 1922 Dickstein was elected to Congress. He was assigned to the House Committee on Naturalization and Immigration and soon became an invaluable asset to the many Eastern European immigrants in his district. Dickstein was one of only two house members who voted against a clause in the 1924 Immigration Act that limited immigration on the basis of national origin.[26] By the time he assumed chairmanship of the committee in 1931, Dickstein was an expert on immigration law and policy. As committee chairman he became aware of the link between illegal immigration from Germany and the distribution of anti-Semitic and anti-American literature in the United States. There were verified reports as early as March 1933 that over 1,000 Nazis had immigrated to the United States to spread Nazi propaganda.[27]

Dickstein launched an independent investigation of Nazi and other fascist groups in the country in mid-1933. He later claimed that he spent over $6,000 from his congressional salary to finance this probe.[28] The *New York Times* of October 10 reported on its front page that Dickstein had uncovered evidence that "the Nazi government has reached into this country." He claimed that aliens entering America from Germany had as their purpose " the formation of a Hitler-like government, replete with racial and religious hatred and bigotry." This material was sufficient for the congressman to set up a subcommittee of the House Committee on Naturalization and Immigration to probe pro-Nazi activities.

Although Congress was in recess, Dickstein had the House Speaker's approval to pursue the investigation.[29] Dickstein announced that his first target was Hans Spanknoebel and the Friends of the New Germany. It was to denounce this investigation that Spanknoebel came to Newark on October 16, 1933, precipitating the Schwabenhalle riot.

The subcommittee for the investigation was composed of nine congressmen, including Martin Dies of Texas, who would eventually chair the House Un-American Activities Committee (HUAC). Dickstein said his committee would use voluntary witnesses to open the nation's eyes to Nazi machinations, despite lacking the power to subpoena witnesses.

For the remainder of the year, Dickstein made speeches and spoke on national radio outlining the Nazi threat.[30] The committee held informal congressional hearings beginning in mid-November. They discovered that the German government, through its consular staff, was financing a widespread effort to promote Nazism among German-Americans and others. With each charge against the Nazis, Dr. Hans Luther, German ambassador to the United States, issued a denial.[31] When Luther complained to Secretary of State Cordell Hull about being called a propaganda agent for the Nazis, Hull apologized.[32] Samuel Untermyer publicly excoriated Hull and told him that he would live to regret his apology.[33]

Congress reconvened on January 20, 1934 and received a report from the Committee on Immigration and Naturalization that included substantial documentary evidence against the Nazis. The report said that "only the surface has been scratched," and urged passage of Dickstein's resolution for a full-scale congressional investigation of Nazi propaganda.[34] This resolution was transmitted to the House Rules Committee for approval. Two weeks later U.S. Customs officials seized 300 pounds of pamphlets and circulars from a German freighter docked in New York Harbor. The material, described as Nazi propaganda, was destined for distribution to Nazis in New York, Chicago, Detroit, and Cincinnati. Some of the booklets were anti-Semitic. It was the largest seizure of Nazi propaganda ever made in New York.[35] News of this incident flooded the media at a crucial time during the debate over Dickstein's resolution.

The seizure of Nazi propaganda, the publicity Dickstein generated on the Nazi menace, and the findings of his committee all combined to create a climate favorable to the passage of his resolution in early March by the Rules committee and two weeks later by the full House. Speaker of the House Henry T. Rainey asked Dickstein to chair the new Special Committee on Un-American Activities. Dickstein declined and asked that "an outstanding member of this House be appointed so there can be no doubt that this is an American issue of primary importance."[36] Dickstein, a Jew, felt the committee would have less credibility with him as chairman. Deferring to Dickstein, Rainey appointed as chairman John McCormack of Massachusetts, an early proponent of a Congressional investigation of Nazism. McCormack, a Catholic, was familiar with nativist movements that were anti-Catholic as well as anti-Semitic. Dickstein was named vice chairman.

Over the next year, the impatient and impetuous Dickstein and the calm and reserved McCormack became a potent combination.[37] The McCormack-Dickstein committee conducted hearings during 1934 that were broadcast on several radio stations.[38] Most of the important fascists in the United States, including Fritz Gissibl and Dr. Ignatz Griebl, leaders of the Friends of the New Germany, appeared before the committee. Dickstein said he hoped the hearings would rid the country of all traces of fascism. Dickstein had a flair for the dramatic and sensational, and constantly kept the committee's findings in the headlines. With McCormack's approval, he continued his own radio broadcasts to educate the public about the Nazi menace.[39]

A recent assessment of the hearings concludes, "Americans turned on their radios and bought papers to receive detailed accounts of the hearings, and generally condoned the proceedings."[40] The committee adopted a prudent procedure. All witnesses were first examined in executive session, and only if it were deemed necessary were public hearings held. This eliminated much useless publicity and prevented the committee from becoming a sounding board for fanatics, as often happened in similar investigations. The committee heard several hundred witnesses during seven public hearings and twenty-four executive sessions in major American cities.[41] Even Goodman conceded that the hearings "for the most part were based on competent investigation and were fairly respectful of witnesses."[42]

When the committee report was issued in February 1935, many Americans already knew its conclusions: Germany was giving direct financial aid to the Friends of the New Germany; there was "irrefutable evidence" that German diplomatic personnel were "engaged in vicious and un-American propaganda activities, paying for it in cash in the hope that it could not be traced;" American public relations firms ostensibly hired to promote trade had in reality "dealt with public and political questions" and prepared reports "intended to be relayed to the German Government;" and youth camps were pro-Hitler and anti-American.[43] Two of the committee's recommendations were passed into law: compulsory registration of foreign agents distributing propaganda in the United States, and an extension of subpoena powers to congressional committees holding hearings outside the District of Columbia.[44]

The May 21, 1934 clash between the Friends and the Minutemen in Irvington occurred a day after Dickstein had completed a two-day hearing in New York City. He immediately sent an investigator

to Newark and Irvington and announced a hearing in the Newark
Post Office on May 26. Dickstein was familiar with Nazi activities in
the area. He had appeared in Newark a month before to speak before 200 at a B'Nai Brith Anti-Defamation League dinner at the
Progress Club, charging that North Jersey was a "hotbed of Nazism,"
and that Nazi agents were smuggling spies and arms into the United
States from German ships.[45] There had also been previous correspondence between Newark anti-Nazis and Dickstein. A March letter from
Irving Piltch, a Newark attorney and member of the Young Men's Hebrew Club, requested an investigation of the anti-Semitic *Liberator*, the
Silver Shirt magazine.[46] Later (probably April), Dr. S. William Kalb
wrote to Dickstein asking for an investigation of an Irvington candidate
for the city commission who had posted anti-Semitic flyers.[47]

Dickstein conducted the May 26 House Committee on Un-American Activities executive hearing in Newark. The proceedings were
held on a Saturday and he was the only committee member present.
During the five-hour hearing, the congressman questioned seven
witnesses, including the Nazis who had the most prominent roles in
the May riot.

Dickstein's objective at the Newark hearing was to demonstrate
that the Friends of the New Germany was an un-American group
that owed its allegiance to Germany. He attempted to do this in several ways. First he tried to get the Friends to admit that they signed a
membership oath attesting that they were not Jews, Masons, or of
"colored" blood, and that the oath was the same one used for entrance into the German Nazi party. Since the American Constitution
provides freedom of religion and of worship, the oath was not consonant with the Constitution, and therefore the Friends was an un-
American group. Dickstein also attempted to get the Friends to admit that their oath stressed the absolute obedience to Hitler, and that
since Hitler was a foreign leader, their group was un-American.

Witnesses readily admitted that they had signed the oath, and that it
was the same oath that was required for the German Nazi party. However, except for Carl Jaeger, both citizens and non-citizens alike argued
that the provisions of the oath were not un-American, and furthermore
that they were not illegal under United States law. They had been
well coached for the hearings by their attorneys, who were present.

One of the witnesses questioned was Reverend Edward J. Paetzold,
pastor of Irvington's Emanuel Evangelical Lutheran Church.
Dickstein had information that the church was a center of Friends'

activities, and that its pastor was a sympathizer. The congregation included a number of recent immigrants and had services in both German and English. Carl Jaeger was an active member and was friendly with Paetzold. Under questioning by Dickstein, Paetzold denied any pro-Nazi activities, supporting his contention by pointing out that he was a member of the town's board of education. When Dickstein asked him if he ever discussed the Friends with Jaeger, he replied that his interest in the Friends was from a "psychological" and "academic" point of view. Paetzold claimed his conversations were on "the movement of Hitler to unify the churches of Germany" and that at no time was politics mentioned.[48]

Under further questioning, the cleric said he had no knowledge of any friction between groups in Irvington and was not aware of any incidents other than the May riot at the YMCA at which there was hostility between ethnic groups. When Dickstein showed him anti-Semitic pamphlets and handbills that had been circulated in Irvington, Paetzold said they were wrong. He admitted knowledge of the German-American Business League Deutschamerikanischer Wirtschaftsausschuss (DAWA), which opposed the anti-Nazi boycott and had organized an anti-Jewish boycott. In Newark, Irvington, and other areas, German-American merchants displayed DAWA cards in their windows to let sympathizers know they should shop there. Paetzold, however, denied ever seeing such cards in Irvington. Finally, he said he did not subscribe to anti-Semitic or other Nazi doctrines because among other things he was president of the Irvington Rotary Club.[49]

Carl Jaeger, vice president of the Newark Friends and an Irvington resident, was the next witness. Although he held the second position in the group, Jaeger was the real leader, acting as the contact between New York headquarters and Irvington. The president, Ludwig Gruenwald, took his orders from Jaeger and served in the top post only because he was an American citizen. Jaeger testified that he had come to the United States in 1926 but never became a citizen. Dickstein closely questioned him on his relationship with Reverend Paetzold and on the cleric's connection to the Friends. Jaeger admitted that he was close to Paetzold but denied that his pastor had any link to the Friends.[50]

When Dickstein asked him about the purpose of the Friends, Jaeger said it was "to unite the German element here in the United States." He claimed that the Friends were an American organization that sought to promote friendship between the American and German peoples. When confronted by the Friends application form, which prohibited Jews, Masons, and "Coloreds" from joining, and asked how that promoted friendship between Germans and Jews, Jaeger replied, "I am not against the Jewish people." After Dickstein demonstrated that the Friend's membership oath was identical with that of the German Nazi Party, he asked Jaeger if he subscribed to the principles in it. He responded, "Not as an American." Dickstein immediately rejoined, "Are you willing to subscribe as a German living in the United States?" Jaeger made the same reply, "No, I am living here." Jaeger's response was almost certainly predicated on a fear of deportation. Earlier Dickstein had earlier asked Jaeger if he wanted to return to Germany, and Jaeger, a non-citizen, had said he wanted to remain in the United States.[51]

Ludwig Gruenwald, president of the Newark Friends, had, like Jaeger, come to the United States in 1926 and lived in Irvington. Unlike his fellow Nazi, Gruenwald was a United States citizen who worked as a mechanical engineer. Other than financial questions on the income and expenditures of the Newark Friends, Dickstein's line of questioning was similar to that employed with Jaeger. Gruenwald was a more secure witness than Jaeger and was unyielding under questioning. For ninety minutes he refused to admit to Dickstein that the Friends' oath was un-American. Although he understood that it was similar to that of the Nazi party of Germany, Gruenwald insisted that the meaning of the oath in the two countries was different. A frustrated Dickstein finally got an admission from the Nazi that he entirely subscribed to the oath.[52]

The next witness was Joseph Haubner, a Yorkville resident and commander of the O.D. troops brought to Irvington the night of the May riot. When asked if the Friends' attorneys were being paid, Haubner replied that they were not. The witness claimed to be an unemployed waiter who arrived in America from Germany in 1927. He was not a United States citizen. According to his testimony, Jaeger called him and invited him to participate in the May 21 Irvington meeting with his "friends." Apparently Haubner had enough friends to fill two buses. The men wore uniforms because they were "ushers," and they had to pay seventy-five cents fare for the round-trip to Irvington. Dickstein asked why it took so many ushers to handle an audience of from 200 to 300. Haubner replied that since they wanted to "come along" he would not refuse his friends.

Haubner's benign explanation of the O.D. mission to Irvington was soon contradicted by a former Friend, Friederich K. Kruppa. He testified before Dickstein in New York that O.D. troops traveled to Irvington not as ushers but as potential combatants since that city was considered a "danger spot."[53] However, at the Newark hearing, Dickstein did not question Haubner's response. The congressman asked Haubner why the "ushers" wore swastikas on their arms as in Germany. The Nazi denied any special significance to the swastika, saying that the same symbol was also used in India and Arabia.[54]

Haubner said he subscribed to the Friends' membership oath and that it was indeed the same as the one for the Nazi party in Germany. He testified that the Friends were an American organization. He also claimed that he disapproved of racial bigotry and discrimination in the United States. When he was asked how he could justify the oath, he maintained that the Friends "want to be amongst themselves." Pressed further, Haubner said he subscribed to the oath because "I saw everybody hollering and kicking against Germany, and I wanted to defend my homeland."[55]

Dickstein explored the format of Friends meetings, particularly the raising of the arm and the simultaneous shouting of "Heil Hitler!" The purpose of this, according to Haubner, was to "greet members of the Friends of the New Germany." He stated that the Friends also "heiled" Hindenburg and Roosevelt. Dickstein then produced correspondence from the Friends pointing out that all letters "heiled" Hitler but did not do the same for Roosevelt or Hindenburg. The witness said that was because Hitler was the spiritual leader of the Germans and "he brought Germany out of things." When asked why an American group would hail a foreign leader, Haubner said that "as long as we are Germans we go after the German customs" and that he was still not an American citizen. Dickstein then asked if he intended to become one. Haubner said yes. Dickstein rejoined, "If you intend to be, I will give you a friendly tip: You had better stop heiling so much."[56]

Dickstein elicited testimony proving that the Friends accepted only non-Masonic Aryans into the group, and it recognized as its leader not the president of the United States but Adolph Hitler. The argument that such beliefs were not illegal was true but irrelevant— a majority of American citizens and their Congress felt that the Friends were un-American. This, combined with the fact that the German government gave financial and propaganda aid to the Friends made a shambles of the Friends' claims that it was an American group.

After the Newark hearing, Dickstein received an anonymous letter alleging that Edward Balentine, Irvington's public safety director, was anti-Semitic. A committee investigator reported to Dickstein that he did not believe Balentine to be an anti-Semite "as he is helpful in all our work" in Irvington.[57] When the Nazis held a rally in Springfield in October, the congressman requested a report from the town's police chief, Albert Sorge. Dickstein received a detailed description of the event but it added nothing to newspaper accounts already published.[58]

* * *

The Friends also came under attack in the New Jersey legislature, which was being pressured by veterans and Jewish groups to combat the Nazi presence in the state. Although official units of the Friends were in urban areas such as Newark, Trenton, and Hudson County, they also operated in many rural and suburban areas where pockets of German-Americans were to be found. During its three-year existence, Friends' meetings took place in Griggstown, Boonton, Kinnelon, Mountain Lakes, Guttenberg, and Springfield. Thus, many state legislators knew of Friends activities in their districts.[59]

Soon after the McCormack-Dickstein committee was created, John J. Rafferty, the Assembly minority leader, introduced a bill to prohibit the spread of propaganda inciting religious or racial hatred. Any person who printed, wrote, or had such materials in his possession would be charged with a misdemeanor. The bill also provided fines and jail sentences for building owners who rented space to groups or individuals where speakers made such statements.[60] Popularly called the "Anti-Nazi Act," it went through committee and passed the Assembly on April 16.

The American Civil Liberties Union (ACLU) attacked the legislation on the grounds that it was so vague that any group engaging in political or economic propaganda could be prosecuted, even the Nazis' opponents.[61] In the event the bill became law, the ACLU promised to go to court to test its constitutionality.[62] Several days later, 200 communists demonstrated against the bill on the steps of the state capitol because it "named no names and can be used as a further instrument against the working class."[63]

The ACLU's campaign against the bill included a letter-writing campaign to all twenty-one state senators, led by Roger Baldwin, the group's director.[64]   This lobbying and newspaper editorials against the bill were successful, and the measure died in committee.

Assemblyman Rafferty reintroduced the Anti-Nazi Act at the start of the 1935 legislative session. One year had made a difference. The publicity surrounding the McCormack-Dickstein committee's revelations of Nazi activity in the country and the establishment of three Nazi camps in New Jersey made the state's lawmakers more sensitive to the issue. This did not deter the ACLU. It waged another lobbying campaign, but this time to no avail. During the debate in the lower house, Assemblyman Morris Pesin of Hudson County spoke for the measure, claiming that Nazi propaganda agents operating out of his county were encouraging Christians not to vote for Jewish candidates and to demand non-Jewish judges. He urged unanimous approval of the bill.

Assemblyman Theron McCampbell of Monmouth County, said the bill would not have his support because it "is designed to prevent free criticism of the conditions in New Jersey. We have a rotten government in New Jersey, one of the worst governments there is." Sidney Goldberg,[65] Newark and Essex County's sole Jewish legislator, argued for the legislation, saying, "If anyone would have told me five years ago that such a bill would some day be necessary in New Jersey I would have laughed in his face. But today we have such a condition." He called McCampbell a hypocrite because the previous month he had voted for a bill requiring New Jersey teachers to take an oath of allegiance to the government.[66] The bill passed the Assembly on March 17 and was again sent to the Senate, where senators were fearful that a negative vote on the bill would label them as pro-Nazi.[67] Opposition to the bill still existed. Professor John Bebout of Newark's Dana College lobbied Essex County Senator John Wolber, head of the committee deciding the legislation's fate, claiming that the measure was unconstitutional and too broad.

Bebout organized a public debate on the topic: "Does the so-called anti-Nazi bill violate freedom of speech of the person and of the assembly?" Rev. L. Hamilton Garner, the liberal pastor of Newark's Universalist Church, would preside. Arthur Garfield Hays, general counsel of the ACLU, would speak against the bill, and Assemblyman Rafferty in its favor.[68] The Minutemen and the NSANL threatened to picket the debate, scheduled for mid-April, which was to be held at the YMCA–YWCA in Newark.[69]

On April 9, the New Jersey Senate approved the Anti-Nazi Act with only one dissenting vote.[70] Bebout cancelled the debate and characterized the new law as "a menace to Jews and all other minority groups," adding that he was not opposed to the legislation because he had any sympathy with the Nazis, whom he detested. Roger Baldwin claimed that it was the harshest measure ever passed by a state against free speech.[71] Herman von Busch, future leader of Newark's German-American Bund, agreed with Baldwin and petitioned Governor Moore to veto the bill because it was "palpably unconstitutional and infringing upon the inherent right of free speech and assemblage."[72]

After the governor signed the bill, the ACLU went to court to test its constitutionality. An ACLU memo four years later, in 1939, asserted that no Nazi was ever brought to trial under the law.[73] Indeed, it took until July 4, 1940 for the first Nazis to be arrested under the statute. On December 5, 1941, the New Jersey Supreme Court agreed with the ACLU and voided the law on the grounds that it violated both the State Constitution and the Fourteenth Amendment of the United States Constitution.[74]

There were severe restrictions on the New Jersey Friends' freedom of assembly even before enactment of the Anti-Nazi Act. By the end of 1934 the group had been banned from holding meetings in many of its Hudson County strongholds, such as Union City, West New York, Hoboken, and North Bergen. The Friends could meet only in Guttenberg, one of the smallest Hudson County communities, with a mainly German population of less than 7,000. Mayor Paul Schnyder refused to ban the meetings on the grounds that no "overt acts" had taken place. According to the *New York Times,* the meetings consisted of anti-Semitic speeches against New York Governor Herbert Lehman, NSANL president Samuel Untermyer, and the American Jewish Congress (AJC) leader Rabbi Stephen Wise, among others. Books for sale included "Ritual Murders by the Jews." A mimeographed handout listed the names of Jews and of those allegedly under Jewish control in the Roosevelt administration, purporting to show a growing Jewish domination of the American government. [75]

The Newark Friends, banned from that city, met regularly in Irvington. However, even Irvington officials discouraged the Friends from holding large rallies, fearing a disturbance they couldn't control. For such events the Friends met in Springfield, a rural area five miles from Newark. German-Americans controlled the town, and the police were not pressured to tolerate the Minutemen. In addition, there was a tradition of holding German-American events in the town. Indeed, several of the parks were named for Germans and their activities, such as Singer's Park, where German choral groups often performed. In October 1934, the Friends held a rally and parade in Springfield attended by several thousand, some of whom came from as far away as Pennsylvania. Marchers wore uniforms with swastikas on their arms. Speakers assailed the anti-Nazi boycott and the "slander and calumny" heaped on them. Although some Minutemen traveled to the rally, they remained in their cars because of the heavy police presence.[76]

As Nazi activities intensified, the American Legion of Springfield asked the Township Committee to investigate, claiming that an affiliate of the Friends, Der Platt Deutsche Verein of Newark, was scheduled to meet at Singer's Park.[77] The committee contacted Walter Rayelt, president of the Verein, who admitted that the purpose of the gathering was to dedicate a swastika flag. He claimed that his group consisted of veterans and musicians who were not interested in politics but only in providing a home for aged veterans in North Bergen.[78] Sixty-two years later, in an interview in his living room in Union, Walter Rayelt said of his role in German-American affairs in the 1930s, "Politics, ach! I was only interested in a home for the aged." To prove his point, he went to a drawer and took out numerous awards he had received for having helped build and maintain the home, which still stands in North Bergen.[79]

The Friends' most consistent defender was the ACLU. In June 1934, the ACLU went to court in a test case to uphold the Friends' constitutional right to hold meetings. In seeking an injunction to prevent Union City and its mayor, Lewis B. Eastmead, from banning Friends' meetings, the ACLU said it was protecting the Bill of Rights.[80] At the hearing, Arthur Garfield Hays, arguing for the right of free speech, said that as a Jew he recognized the right of the Friends to express its animosity toward Jews. He asserted that it was far better to have the group give anti-Semitic speeches in public than to suppress it and force "underground developments."[81]

John Drewen, the attorney representing Union City, said that it was the Friends' meetings that violated free speech and its activities that violated the peace. In explaining why Friends' speeches were dangerous, Drewen said, "These attacks upon the Jews and this encouragement of a boycott against Jewish merchants are inflammatory and a violation of the peace, and therefore, of the common law." Reading from an affidavit, Drewen quoted from a song that was said to be sung at the beginning of each Friends'meeting, "Our greatest joy will come when Jewish blood flows through the streets."[82]

During testimony before Judge John A. Bigelow, the 150 spectators representing both sides held their emotions in check. However, when the judge adjourned the proceedings and said he would reserve decision, tempers flared. As soon as Bigelow left the bench, about twenty members of each group got into a heated debate. Free speech was not enough for the participants. Angry words turned into a free-for-all. Court officers stepped in and restored peace, marching the two sides to separate elevators.[83]

Judge Bigelow rendered his decision a short time later. He ruled that the right of free speech and assembly did not apply to corporations (the Friends had previously registered in New Jersey as a nonprofit corporation), and furthermore since it was the Friends'policy to foment illegal acts, it had forfeited the right to seek court relief on the ban of its meetings.[84] The Eastmead decision (as Bigelow's ruling was called) gave New Jersey towns the discretion to ban all Friends' meetings.

* * *

One answer to the ban on Nazi meetings was the establishment of camps in rural Griggstown, Parsippany, and Mountain Lakes in the summer of 1934. These camps had four main purposes: to inculcate young people with the German language and Nazi ideology; to drill and train young men as future Nazi soldiers in America; to enable the Friends to relax away from the pressure of surveillance and possible harassment; and to raise funds by charging from the sale of admission tickets and food.

In 1934 Friends camps were small and used primarily for the indoctrination of young men. The Griggstown and Parsippany camps did not reopen in 1935 due to negative publicity, the McCormack-Dickstein committee, and pressure from local officials. However, one new camp opened in Kinnelon in the summer of 1935, the first permitted to sell beer.[85] New Jersey Nazi camps would become an important factor during the period between 1937 and 1940.[86]

The Eastmead decision, New Jersey's Anti-Nazi Act, and the McCormack-Dickstein committee never slowed down the Newark Friends' activities. Soon after the congressional report appeared in May 1935, the Nazi group organized a rally in Linden that was to include speeches and military music. The Minutemen and JWV members visited Mayor Myles McManus to protest. The two groups applied for a permit to hold a rally in a park across the street from where the Friends' rally was being held.

On the day of the rallies, McManus barred the Friends from entering the park on the grounds that the permit issued to them was for a concert and not speeches. He said the meeting was in violation of Linden's "vice and immorality act."[87] Thirty policemen ringed the park, turning back automobiles and buses from northern New Jersey and New York. Undeterred, over 1,000 relocated to Singer's Park in Springfield, where officials permitted several hundred men wearing Nazi uniforms with swastika armbands to march. As in the previous event at Singer's Park, Springfield police did not allow Minutemen who had followed the Friends from Linden to leave their cars.[88]

* * *

Infiltration of mainline German-American organizations was an important Friends objective. The success of Nazism in America depended upon building a mass movement. Since many Americans of German descent were already integrated into American society, it was imperative to convert to the Nazi cause those German Americans who still kept ties to their heritage through membership in German-American organizations. This effort went on unabated despite judicial, legislative, and physical attacks.

The responses to Friends' propagandizing initiatives were varied. Some groups rebuffed all Friends' attempts; others waited for events to dictate their position; and still others embraced Nazism and helped the Friends. The two largest German-American groups in Essex County were the German-American League and the German-Austrian War Veterans.

The German-American League was non-political and consisted of twenty-four welfare, athletic, and singing groups. In October 1933, the Friends applied for membership. The league's president, John C. Koerber, had been criticized in August for not letting the Friends display its swastika flags at an automobile parade for German Day. A committee of the league formed to investigate the matter gave him a vote of confidence. At the October meeting, Koerber stated his objections to the Friends' membership application on the grounds that it was a political group. Albert Frosch and Herrman Dittler of Newark's United Singers Society supported him. Dittler said, "Americans of

German birth and origin will not tolerate dictation or interference in their actions and opinions by any self-styled savior of the Fatherland." Dr. Francis Just and Karl Geiger argued for the Friends' admission on the basis of preserving local German unity. No decision was reached and the application was tabled until a copy of the Friends' constitution was supplied.[89]

Koerber, representing over twenty organizations—some dating from the nineteenth century—strove to accommodate both American patriotism and German nationalism. It was a difficult task. In a speech at Newark's Schwabenhalle before the German-American Political Club, he opposed further Nazi inroads into Essex County German-American groups. In January 1934, the German-American League pledged support for Roosevelt's newly enacted NRA. Three months later, Koerber did not oppose his organization's endorsement of the Irvington German-American Campaign Committee's decision to work only for candidates in the upcoming municipal elections who supported German-American interests. Consequently, several Jewish candidates who ran for the Irvington commission finished last.[90]

During 1934, the Friends was successful in infiltrating small German-American societies that were members of the league. The Nazis joined them pretending they were interested in sports, music, or other activities. The Friends then propagandized society members with the alleged injustices perpetrated against German Americans. In short order they controlled over a half-dozen groups. However, they did not control a majority of the twenty-four league organizations. With the help of the league's vice-president, Dr. Francis Just, a German-born Newark physician, the Nazis hoped to stage a coup at the September 1934 meeting.

The monthly league meetings usually had from thirty to forty attendees, representing about fifteen of the twenty-four constituent societies. Koerber, its anti-Nazi president, was on vacation until mid-September. The Friends sought to have five small societies in Newark and Irvington over which it maintained either partial or full control, but which were not league members, vote at the September 10 Schwabenhalle meeting. The Friends also made sure the six league members they controlled attended the meeting. If successful in having the five new societies vote, the Friends would control a majority of the societies in attendance, and would be able to dictate the league's policies.

In Koerber's absence, Just presided at the meeting. As the first order of business, Just demanded a vote on accepting the five organizations for membership despite the fact that the groups' constitutions had not been submitted to the executive board, as the league's bylaws required. Representatives of anti-Nazi societies protested vehemently. Cries of "schiebung" (fake) pierced Schwabenhalle. Richard Krueger, commander of the Essex German-Austrian War Veterans, protested that the vote was unconstitutional and denounced some of the five groups as sympathetic to the Nazis. He accused Just of employing "Spanknoebel methods." By a margin of one vote, four of the five societies were voted into membership.

Koerber was infuriated when he learned of the events at Schwabenhalle, and he determined to reverse the results. At the league's October meeting, at which fifteen written protests against admission of the four groups were presented, the challengers accused Just of employing unconstitutional procedures in forcing the vote. Koerber made sure that representatives of all the league's societies were present. Another vote was taken, and September's vote was rescinded.[91]

Despite this defeat, the Friends continued to gain sympathizers from among local German Americans. The continuous negative publicity generated by the McCormack-Dickstein committee, and other legal and judicial attacks on Nazi Germany and its American agents conferred victim status upon the Friends. German-American groups, even the anti-Nazi ones, protested the anti-Nazi boycott because they understood that it could harm even non-Hitlerite Germans. These factors produced a siege mentality. Thus it was no surprise that there was substantial support for the German-American Business League (DAWA), which had been founded in New York City by German-American businessmen to counter the boycott of German-made goods.

DAWA sought to discourage shopping in Jewish-owned stores and to promote it in German-owned stores. Establishments supporting DAWA carried the DAWA insignia in their windows and were listed in a directory. Individuals were encouraged to wear DAWA lapel pins. In April 1934 Dr. Francis Just and the Reverend Carl Krepper organized an Essex County DAWA branch.[92] By the end of the month, DAWA stickers appeared in Newark and Irvington businesses. By August the German-American Economic Alliance, located in Irvington, had published two directories of approved DAWA enterprises: the one for New Jersey had almost 300 listings, mainly in Essex and Hudson Counties; the one for "Newark and Vicinity" had fifty listings.[93]

By taking a leading role in promoting DAWA, the Friends ingratiated themselves with those who now felt that all German Americans—Nazi or otherwise—were under attack. Just was active in promoting both DAWA and the Friends. He had survived his role in the September meeting of the German-American League with no apparent handicap. During 1935, he worked with moderate league members to gain acceptance of the Friends. German unity became a rallying cry, and it reached such a crescendo that many anti-Nazi Germans were loathe to denounce the Friends. Under pressure, Koerber retired as president of the league and Just replaced him. The Friends of the New Germany was voted into the German-American League of Essex County at the December 1935 meeting with little ado. The Friends' leaders, Gruenwald and Jaeger, were selected as their group's delegates.[94]

Another group the Friends targeted was the Newark branch of the German-Austrian War Veterans. This group provided members with insurance and health benefits and instilled pride in the military accomplishments of their mother countries. The group sometimes cooperated with mainline veterans' groups in celebrating American patriotic holidays. By mid-1933, many leaders of the Newark Friends, including its president, Albert Schley; future presidents Ludwig Gruenwald and Matthias Kohler, and veterans of the Schwabenhalle riot Walter Kauf, Karl Kauf, and Fred Ritter, belonged to the group. The national commander of the veterans' group, George Ganss, was also a member of the Newark Friends. Ganss openly touted his allegiances, allowing the swastika flag to be flown at German-Austrian War Veterans' events, and permitting Bundsleiter Hans Spanknoebel to speak before the group.

The negative publicity generated by Ganss' Nazism reflected badly on the German-Austrian society. Previously it had participated in joint events with the American Legion, the JWV, and other veterans' groups. As in some other Newark German-American organizations, the German-Austrian War Veterans included Jews among its members. The fall-out from Ganss' Nazi policies caused the Armistice Day Committee in Newark to bar his unit from participating in its 1933 parade, though purportedly the decision was based on the group's resolution condemning the "war guilt" clause of the Versailles Peace Treaty.

Richard Krueger, commander of the group's Newark unit, claimed that the German-Austrian war veterans had always opposed this clause, and to penalize it now was unfair. However, he knew that the passage of this resolution was just a convenient excuse. The real reason for barring his group was Ganss' Nazism. Krueger did not appeal the committee's decision, but he and the majority of his unit decided they could no longer tolerate the Friends' influence.[95]

Other units of the German-Austrian War Veterans, especially New York, were also under siege by the Friends. Two weeks after the parade ban on the Newark unit a national meeting of the veterans' group took place in Union City. Its purpose was to pick a new national commander to replace George Ganss, who had been forced to resign because of his pro-Nazis views. The group reiterated its loyalty to the United States and denounced Nazi leanings within its ranks. Krueger called the swastika a political and anti-Semitic symbol. Fred Obermueller of Elizabeth, the new national commander, vowed to fight un-American tendencies.[96]

At an executive committee meeting two weeks later, discussion of ways to improve relations with other veterans' groups took place. Obermueller admitted that Nazi sympathizers comprised up to 20 percent of the group's membership, and that widespread "reforms" would have to take place to counter Nazi encroachments. Krueger's Newark unit immediately enacted "reforms" forcing the nine members of the veterans group that also belonged to the Friends to resign. Krueger was reelected commander and promised to rebut any efforts to use his group as a "cat's paw."[97]

Although the veterans' group was serious about ridding itself of Nazi influence, it was also sensitive to what it perceived as anti-German measures. In December 1933, Obermueller sent a resolution to President Roosevelt that criticized the boycott of German goods, claiming it discriminated against Americans of German origin. The Newark unit endorsed the resolution.[98] Facing criticism from American veterans' group, Obermueller soon issued a statement denying that Nazi sympathies had led him to oppose the boycott.[99]

The same pattern was repeated in 1934. At a state convention of the veterans' group, Krueger urged support for two resolutions. The first stated that the boycott harmed America because Germany was one of America's best trade partners. The second was in support of

DAWA's hope that Americans of German origin "and other right-thinking Americans" would patronize only firms that rejected the anti-Nazi boycott. Obermueller continued that the resolutions should not be considered pro-Nazi. They passed unanimously.[100]

As a result of the May 21 anti-Nazi Irvington riot, Newark Public Safety Director Michael P. Duffy banned a German-Austrian War Veterans national convention, scheduled for late May 1934. Instead, the group met in Elizabeth, where it denied any Nazi tendencies and reiterated its neutrality on all political and religious matters. To further accentuate its independence from German politics, it inserted in the first article of its constitution that the group was a "national American organization."

On January 13, 1935 Germany retook the Saarland in violation of the Versailles Treaty. The German-American League of Essex County held a celebration at Singer's Park in Springfield. Dr. Just, presided and proclaimed, "The Saar region will always remain an integral part of the German Reich."[101] Krueger said that the German-Austrian War Veterans participated because it was given assurances that the swastika would not be displayed. Fritz Winterscheid, a Friends national official, was a speaker, as was Ernest H. Hausemann of the moderate Steuben Society. Winterscheid's inclusion at this event was significant. It proved that less than two years after its formation, the Newark Friends had become an integral part of the area's German-American social, cultural, and political structure.

* * *

The next struggle over Nazism within Newark's German-American community came in May 1935. Although the Friends were not the leading element in the controversy, the Nazi ideology it had spread was at the root of the problem.

A singing festival might seem an unlikely arena for a conflict over Nazism. However, given the historic role of singing societies in American Germania, the display of the swastika at the festival was a potent catalyst for confrontation. The Northeast Saengerbund (singing organization) had been in existence for eighty-seven years. The triennial Northeast Saengerfest (singing festival) was to be held over a four-day period at Newark's Sussex Avenue Armory. Two hundred and eighty singing societies and over 5,000 singers would compete for prizes. The Saengerfest had last been held in Newark in

1906, when over 100,000 attended. Many more were expected in 1935, and the city was looking forward to the economic boon such a large number of visitors would provide. The honorary chairman of the reception committee was Mayor Meyer Ellenstein, and Governor Harold Hoffman was expected to speak.[102]

Albert Frosch was general chairman of the Saengerfest and also headed its arrangements committee. He was the president of the United Singers of Newark, the umbrella group for the five singing societies from Newark that would take part in the festival. More importantly, he was perhaps the most respected figure in Newark's German-American community life, and his anti-Nazi views were influential. Frosch was also a voice of anti-Nazism within the singing societies and the German-American League.

Just, who was also on the arrangements committee, pressed Frosch and other Saengerbund officials to have the swastika displayed at the armory and at a June 1 Saengerfest parade in Newark.[103] Frosch was adamantly opposed, claiming the swastika was un-American and anti-Semitic. Without Frosch's knowledge, Just, who was also on the executive board of the Northeast Saengerbund, invited German Ambassador Hans Luther and New York Consul General Dr. Hans Borchers to the Saengerfest. Both men had been accused during the McCormack-Dickstein committee hearings of spreading Nazi propaganda in America. These invitations became a point of contention between Just and Frosch and the dispute became public.[104]

The singing societies' origins were cultural and social rather than political. The several thousand members in the Newark groups represented a wide spectrum of political ideology. Once the Nazis began their propaganda efforts in 1933 the atmosphere in the clubs began to change and politics became more important. Several singing society members, who also belonged to the American League Against War and Fascism (ALAWF), an organization that included communists as well as liberals, decided to challenge the pro-Nazi tilt of the upcoming Saengerfest.

The group sent a telegram to Frosch asking whether Ambassador Luther would attend the festival. A copy of the telegram was sent to both Newark dailies. The *Newark News* called Frosch for his response. He said he was ignoring the telegram because no one had signed it, and he declined to reveal if Luther had been invited to the festival. When the *News* queried the ALAWF as to why it had sent the telegram to Frosch, it replied that Nazi influences were trying to make the Saengerfest a pro-Hitler demonstration.[105]

The evening of the *News* story, an emergency meeting of the arrangements committee took place. Frosch and former Essex County Freeholder William C. Fiedler argued against displaying the swastika, but to no avail. After two hours no compromise could be reached and the parade was cancelled. To preserve a vestige of German-American unity, the next day Fiedler told the press that the parade was cancelled because there was concern that not enough marchers would participate. Frosch joined Fiedler in denying that the festival would have any "political tinge." He also denied that the parade cancellation was caused by the "Nazi question." Fiedler said that the scheduled march of visiting societies from Pennsylvania Station to Newark's City Hall would still take place.[106]

Only one week remained before the Saengerfest was to open on Memorial Day. The bitter dispute could not be solved locally. Members of the Northeast Saengerbund executive committee from Pennsylvania, Massachusetts, and New York made an emergency trip to Newark. At the quickly arranged meeting, the anti-Nazi forces prevailed and the swastika was barred at all locations of the four-day Saengerfest. Albert Frosch wrote a letter to the editor of the *Newark Sunday Call* to reiterate that the Saengerfest was about music, not politics. In keeping with a show of unity, he ignored the Nazi debate. Instead, without mentioning names, he criticized both the Friends and the ALAWF: "Now, with the advent of new forms of government, there also has been brought into existence certain groups who in their anxiety to keep their pots boiling will even go so far as to insinuate political significance to a celebration which is purely musical."[107]

Minutemen Commander Nat Arno said he would not call his men to action because of the decision to bar the swastika. In a letter to the Newark City Commission, he stated that his group had determined that the four-day festival would not be a pro-Nazi affair. This was a relief to those who feared that Arno's men would disrupt Saengerfest activities.[108]

Everything now seemed in order. The parade was reinstated, and there no longer seemed to be any doubt that enough marchers would take part. But on Wednesday May 28, everything changed. Dr. Gotthardt E. Seyfarth, president of the Northeast Saengerbund, telephoned Frosch to demand the display of the swastika at the armory. Frosch told him that in light of the fact that both Ambassador Luther and Consul Borchers had declined invitations to the Saengerfest, there was no need to display the Nazi emblem. Seyfarth then issued an ultimatum: he would not attend if the swastika was not displayed and would not allow the Saengerbund's official banner to be flown. Frosch called another emergency meeting that evening at Schwabenhalle.

Francis Just successfully fought for the inclusion of the swastika. Rather than see this happen, Frosch resigned as event chairman, saying, "I do not want to go back on my word, which I have given the city authorities, that there would be no political tinge to our affair." Frank Fechner, vice chairman, assumed Frosch's duties and announced the Saengerfest would be held, replete with swastikas.

When this turn of events became known on Thursday morning, Mayor Ellenstein cancelled both the June 1 parade and the march from Pennsylvania Station to City Hall. Additionally, there would be no official welcome for the visiting singing societies. Rabbi Julius Silberfeld of Temple B'Nai Abraham resigned from the reception committee.[109] More ominously, anti-Nazi groups, including the Minutemen, JWV, ALAWF, and the American Youth Congress (a communist-dominated organization),[110] threatened to demonstrate. Alarmed by this possibility and with thousands of visitors in the city, Ellenstein asked the governor to call out the New Jersey National Guard. Over 200 Guardsmen were ready for action by early Thursday evening. Colonel Edward Winterton, commander of the troops, told the press that Ellenstein informed him that communists would attempt to invade the armory and tear the swastikas down. Since the armory was federal property, Winterton said it was his duty to prevent rioting. The Newark police were also out in force.

Because the opening festivities had been cancelled, visiting singers walked Broad Street, Newark's main artery, and Springfield Avenue, where stores displayed signs in German and English welcoming them. Many walked to City Hall, where the official welcome was to have taken place. In place of official greetings they were welcomed by over 100 members of the Newark branch of the American Youth Congress, marching and shouting, "Keep the Nazis out of Newark" and "down with fascism." Some singers were no doubt pleased when the marchers were dispersed and four youths were arrested for disturbing the peace, creating a disturbance, and interfering with a police officer.[111]

By 8:30 that evening over 4,000 people were in Sussex Armory for the first night's program. According to one account, the scene resembled an armed camp rather than a peaceful singing festival.

Over 200 uniformed Newark police[112] and an equal number of national guardsmen patrolled the streets around the armory, the walls
of which had been painted over with three-foot- high signs that read
"Down with Hitler!" The opening speaker was Frank Fechner. He
apologized to his audience for their reception in Newark that "had
fallen somewhat short of expectations." Seven hundred singers from
the Newark area gave a recital, which the audience appreciated "despite the tense political atmosphere."[113] The swastika was displayed
along with other flags and banners.

The ALAWF immediately blamed Ellenstein for not heeding its
warning that the Nazis would control the Saengerfest. At a meeting
at the YMHA, the group censured the mayor for allowing the police
to break up the American Youth Congress parade protesting Nazi
control of the event. Amelia B. Moorefield, state chair of the Women's
International League for Peace and Freedom (WILPF), spoke about
the Nazis' warlike intentions and the need to stop them before it was
too late. Always quotable, she said, "The next war won't be a tea
party. Let women stop discussing the subject politely at afternoon
teas. Let us handle the subject with naked hands."[114]

The situation changed again on Friday. Swastikas were removed
from the Sussex Avenue Armory where an evening concert of over
3,000 voices was held, with 7,500 in attendance. There were no dis-
ruptions. Saengerfest and Saengerbund officials, most of whom had
opposed the swastika display, had reversed themselves in the face of
both internal pressures and external public relations considerations.

The removal of the swastikas angered Seyfarth, and on Saturday
he called an executive board meeting of the Northeast Saengerbund
at the Hotel Douglas. Rather than resign, Seyfarth asked his board
for a vote of confidence, defending his decision on the grounds that
the U.S. State Department recognized the swastika in the same way
that it recognized the star as the symbol of the Soviet Union. He also
said that the Nazi symbol had no racial or party significance. Just
blamed the entire affair on Frosch, claiming that Frosch had promised to display the swastika if German officials came to the festival
and then changed his mind.[115] In rebutting Seyfarth and Just, Frosch
called Newark "a hotbed of demonstrations against us" because of
the mishandling of the Saengerfest.

Frosch also defended Ellenstein's cancellation of the parade by
pointing out that the large Jewish population of Newark who would
be offended if some young members of a singing society "bubbling

over with enthusiasm for the New Germany" had paraded past city hall with swastika banners. Seyfarth said he wasn't in complete agreement with the Nazi regime and suggested that no German government officials be invited to future Saengerbund affairs so that the swastika would not have to be displayed. The meeting ended with a resolution praising both Seyfarth and Frosch.[116]

Saturday evening's competition was held without incident. Again no swastikas were displayed. The last Saengerfest event was a Sunday picnic celebration at Singer's Park in Springfield where the winners of the singing contests were announced. A special detail of thirty Newark police patrolled the park to insure that there would be no disturbances. The peaceful crowd of 10,000 gathered around refreshment stands and listened to the music. A show of unity was made when Seyfarth, Frosch, Just, and other officials mounted the platform to conduct a flag investment ceremony that had been omitted on Thursday night because of the swastika controversy.[117]

* * *

Newark's Nazis were more successful in their last public controversy of 1935, the flying of the swastika at the annual German Day festivities at Singer's Park. The German-American League of Essex County sponsored this event yearly. In 1934, before the Friends were voted into the league, Richard Krueger and John Koerber had prevented the Nazi symbol from being flown. With the league under Just's control in 1935, another attempt was made to display the Nazi symbol.

A crowd of 200 attended the organizing meeting for German Day at Schwabenhalle. Only fifty-two were eligible to vote, while Nazi sympathizers comprised the balance. Krueger again called the swastika "the symbol of anti-Semitism and race hatred." William Heuer, president of the German-American Non-Partisan League, urged the Nazis not to antagonize the old-line German residents of Newark. He stressed that since its inception, German Day was for all German Americans, regardless of political or religious creed. The Nazi audience booed Krueger and Heuer's remarks. Those speaking for the swastika included Ludwig Gruenwald, president of the Friends, and Just. The delegates voted 26 to 18, with 8 abstentions, to fly the swastika.[118]

Over 1,500 were in attendance at German Day as swastikas flew in Singer's Park. Nazi songs, including "Das Horst Wessel Lied," were sung, and Otto Stiefel,[119] an American-born Newark lawyer and Friends' sympathizer, was the speaker. The Friends were in evidence everywhere, enjoying their increased respectability in the German-American community. They even invited a large contingent of uniformed O.D. troops from New York. Twenty-eight came by bus and eighteen by truck, but they were not needed for protection.[120] Nat Arno claimed that Springfield authorities had promised him there would be no swastikas or Nazi songs at the event so he stayed away. In light of what really transpired, he threatened to retaliate at the next Nazi gathering.[121]

The anti-Nazi leaders of Essex County's German-American organizations announced that they would hold their own rally at Singer's Park on October 6. Albert Frosch, William Heuer, and William Fiedler were among the organizers. All ninety German-American organizations in Essex County were invited. The purpose of the event was to demonstrate American patriotism and it was open to all, regardless of "creed, race, or color."[122]

The rally drew 2,000 people, 500 more than the Nazi-dominated German Day two months before. Alfred Frosch was the master of ceremonies. The principal speaker was again Otto Stiefel. He recalled the tradition of political liberty and tolerance brought to America by the emigres of 1848.[123] Stiefel was the only person to speak at both events. Able to play both sides with great skill, he was both a Friends ally and a respected lawyer.

Attempts by the Friends to infiltrate Newark-area German-American organizations in its year-and-a-half of existence had mixed results. Despite strenuous efforts, they failed with the German-Austrian War Veterans, whereas they succeeded with the German-American League of Essex County, at whose November 1935 annual meeting Just was re-elected president, and Ludwig Gruenwald and Walter Rayelt were elected to the board of directors.[124]

* * *

The increase in the Friends' membership and its successful infiltration of German-American groups in New York, Newark, and other cities did not escape Samuel Dickstein's notice. When the final report of the McCormack-Dickstein committee was issued in February 1935, anti-German sentiment became even more pronounced. The Friends became synonymous with German treachery and intrigue. Thus it remained an obstacle to better relations between Germany and America.

By the time the committee report was issued, Berlin had long since tired of the problems with the Friends. Officials in Germany pointed out that the Friends were "a nuisance" because of the negative publicity it received in America. An internal schism gained further unfavorable publicity for the Friends during 1935.[125] In that year, Hitler was still interested in appearing reasonable in the world. The Friends was running amok, jeopardizing his respectability in America.

On October 11, 1935 the German Foreign Ministry ordered all German citizens living in the United States, including those already with first papers, to resign from the Friends of the New Germany by December 31, 1935. The Friends would not give up and in early November dispatched Fritz Gissibl to Berlin to meet with Nazi officials. When Gissibl arrived he was told the order would be enforced by the end of the year. He argued that the Friends would lose 60 percent of its membership and most of its leadership if German citizens left the movement. Even after Gissibl returned to America with the news, there were still many members who refused to believe that Berlin was ordering the virtual dissolution of their group. Berlin released the order to the Associated Press on December 24, so there would be no question of the Nazi decision.[126]

The NSDAP was satisfied with this situation since the Friends could no longer be viewed as a branch of a foreign political party operating in America. Friends' membership would now be limited to American citizens who believed that National Socialism should be adopted in the United States. A new "Friends" would emerge in 1936, renamed the German-American Bund, with many of the same members and the same ideology as the original Friends. The old organization changed, "chameleon-like, to suit the new demands made of it."[127]

After 1935, the Newark Friends continued to operate but lost a good portion of its members because they were German citizens. It quickly, however, made up the lost membership during 1936 and emerged stronger. The more fanatical former members, such as the Kaufs, returned to Germany to continue their Nazi careers. Others, like Carl Jaeger, stayed active behind the scenes. The Newark German-American Bund would be an active force for Nazism during the next five years.

Notes

1.   Diamond, Sander A., *The Nazi Movement in the United States, 1924-1941*, Ithaca, NY, 1974, pp. 141,142. This remains the best account of the Friends of the New Germany and the German American Bund and was used for much of the background and history of the Friends in this chapter. Other accounts used for the Friends and the Bund are Susan Canedy's *America's Nazis, A Democratic Dilemna, A History of the German American Bund,* Menlo Park, CA, 1990 (the most recent work in the field); Donald S. Strong's *Organized Anti-Semitism in America, The Rise of Group Prejudice During the Decade 1930-1940,* New York, 1941; Leland V. Bell's *In Hitler's Shadow, The Anatomy of American Nazism,* Port Washington, NY, 1973; John O. Rogge's *The Official German Report on Nazi Penetration 1924-1942 Pan-Arabism 1939-Today,* New York, 1961; and, Alton Frye's *Nazi Germany and the American Hemisphere 1933-1941,* New Haven, CT, 1967. For activities of the Friends and the Bund in New Jersey, see Martha Glaser's "The German-American Bund in New Jersey," New Jersey History, vol. XCII, no.I, Spring 1974. For an account of the Bund in Greater New York City, see Evelyn Katherine Knobloch's "The Nazi Bund Movement in Metropolitan New York," M.A. Dissertation, Columbia University.

      The estimates for Friends membership are: Rogge, 1,500 (p. 17); Frye, 10,000 (p. 58); Hanighen, 15,000 (p. 10); Diamond, 5,000 to 6,000 (p. 146).
2.   U.S. Congressional Hearings, Investigation of Nazi Propaganda Activities and Investigation of Certain Other Propaganda Activities, Subcommittee of the Special Committee on Un-American Activities, Hearing No. 73-N.J.-1, p. 21.
3.   N.N., 8/21/34, p. 2.
4.   Remak, Joachim, "'Friends of the New Germany': The Bund and German-American Relations," *Journal of Modern History,* vol. XXIX, March-December, 1957, p. 41.
5.   N.N., 1/15/34, p. 8.
6.   Ibid., 1/19/34, p. 21.
7.   U.S. Congressional Hearings, pp. 11, 24, 25.
8.   Ibid., p. 12.
9.   Rogge, *Official German Report,* pp. 16, 17.
10.   Diamond, *The Nazi Movement in the United States,* pp. 93-96.
11.   Gau-USA was an abbreviation for Gauleitung-USA See Diamond, p. 21.
12.   Ibid., pp. 97-99.
13.   Ibid., pp. 101, 102.
14.   Yorkville is the northeastern quadrant of the Upper East Side—bounded by 77th Street, Lexington Avenue, 96th Street and the East River.
15.   Diamond, *The Nazi Movement in the United States,* pp. 100-102.
16.   Hanighen, Frank C., "Foreign Political Movements in the United States," *Foreign Affairs,* October 1937, vol. 16, no. 1, p. 5.
17.   Diamond, *The Nazi Movement in the United States,* p. 102.
18.   Rogge, *The Official German Report on Nazi Penetration,* p. 18.
19.   Ibid., pp. 18-20; Diamond, *The Nazi Movement in the United States,* pp. 121-123.
20.   Canedy, Susan, *America's Nazis, A Democratic Dilemma,* Menlo Park CA., 1990, p. 64.
21.   Goodman, Walter, *The Committee—The Extraordinary Career of the House Committee on Un-American Activities,* New York, 1968, p. 3.
22.   Ibid., pp. 13, 15.
23.   Diamond, *The Nazi Movement in the United States,* pp. 158, 162, 190, 257, footnote 141.
24.   Weinstein, Allen, *The Haunted Wood,* New York, 1999, pp. 140-150.
25.   Samuel Dickstein Papers, An Inventory to the Samuel Dickstein Papers (1923-1944), Biographical Sketch, pp. 3, 4.
26.   Belth, Nathan C., *A Promise to Keep, A Narrative of the American Encounter with Anti-Semitism,* New York, 1979, p. 94.
27.   NYT, 3/23/33, p. 11.

28. Reminiscences of Samuel Dickstein, Columbia University Oral History Project, p. 29.
29. NYT, 10/10/33, p. 1.
30. Reminiscences of Samuel Dickstein, p. 30.
     Dickstein asserts that he spoke on both CBS and NBC several times a week during this period.
31. NYT, 10/13/33, p15; 10/27/33, p. 11.
32. Ibid. 11/3/33, p. 10.
33. Ibid., 11/4/33, p. 8.
34. Ibid. 1/21/34, p. 12.
35. Ibid., 2/7/34, p. 5.
36. Dickstein Papers, Series A Box 4, Folder 5, Letter from Dickstein to Henry T. Rainey, 4/2/34.
37. Dickstein Papers, Box 3, Folder 7. This folder contains McCormack-Dickstein correspondence. See particularly, Letters from McCormack to Dickstein, 11/3/34 and 11/8/34.
38. Reminiscences of Samuel Dickstein, p. 35.
39. Dickstein Papers, ibid., Letter from McCormack to Dickstein, 11/3/34.
40. Canedy, *America's Nazis*, p. 63.
41. Ogden, August Raymond, *The Dies Committee-A Study of the Special House Committee for the Investigation of Un-American Activities 1938-1949*, Washington, DC, 1945, p. 34; Belth, *A Promise to Keep*, p. 121.
42. Goodman, *The Committee*, p. 10.
43. Belth, *A Promise to Keep*, p. 121; Ogden, *The Dies Committee*, p. 35.
44. Goodman, *The Committee*, p. 11.
45. N.N., 4/24/34, p. 2; J.C., 4/27/34, p. 27.
46. National Archives, Records of the United States House of Representatives, 73rd Congress, Committee Papers of the Special Committee on Un-American Activities, Box 372, Letter from Irving Piltch to Samuel Dickstein, 3/5/34.
47. Ibid., Box 370, Letter from Dr. S. William Kalb to Samuel Dickstein, undated.
48. U.S. Congressional Hearings, pp. 4-7.
49. Ibid., pp. 7, 8. Rev. Paetzold at a 1937 Irvington Rotary meeting introduced Rev. Heinz Kuebler (Pastor St. John's Church, Newark) who spoke on Germany's stand to exclude communism from the country and its attitude toward the Jewish race. Kuebler was a member of the German military forces under Hitler. See *Irvington Herald*, 6/23/37, p. 23.
50. U.S. Congressional Hearings, pp. 8,19.
51. Ibid., pp. 9, 12, 13, 17,18.
52. Ibid., pp. 20, 32-34.
53. Ibid., Hearing No. 73-NY-12, p. 39.
54. Ibid., Hearing No. 73-N.J.-1, pp. 34-41.
55. Ibid., pp. 42-47.
56. Ibid., pp. 48,49.
57. Dickstein Papers, Box 1, Folder 3, Letter from "a Catholic" to Samuel Dickstein, 6/6/34; Memo "Investigation and Report," "S.W.B." to Samuel Dickstein, 6/18/34.
58. Ibid., Box 5, Folder 2, Letter from Chief Albert Sorge to Samuel Dickstein, 10/30/34
59. N.N., 8/24/34, p. 7; 8/30/34, p. 13; 10/15/34, p. 9; 6/18/35, p. 6; S.C., 9/2/34, Sec. II, p. 6
60. NYT, 4/18/34, p.10.
61. For a discussion on the internal debate within the ACLU over defense of Nazi civil liberties, see Samuel Walker, *In Defense of American Civil Liberties*, New York, 1990, pp. 115-118.
62. NYT, 4/22/34, p. 20; N.N., 4/21/34, p. 12.
63. N.N., 4/24/34, p. 1.
64. Glaser, "The German-American Bund," pp. 34, 35.
65. Sidney Goldberg (1908-1970), father of the author.
66. J.C., 4/15/35, p. 2.

67.   Glaser, "The German-American Bund," p. 36.
68.   N.N., 3/25/35, p. 19. Also scheduled for the event were Professors Albert Abarbanel and Sol Flink (both of Dana College), to speak against the bill and Harold Lett of the Urban League to speak for it.
69.   Ibid., 4/9/35, p. 20.
70.   The ACLU did not believe in the New Jersey Legislature's *bone fides*. Within six months of the Senate vote, the ACLU retreated from a principled stand because of fear of a "Red-hunt" by the legislature.
      Previously an anti-Nazi professor of German was dismissed from Rutgers University on the recommendation of his department head who was openly pro-Nazi. In May 1935, three members of the ACLU's New York Committee on Academic Freedom held a meeting with the dismissed professor, Lienhard Bergel. On the basis of the interview and other information, the ACLU said they would press for Bergel's reinstatement and pursue a charge that the German Department had engaged in Nazi propaganda. Three members of the New Jersey ACLU then visited the president of Rutgers, Robert C. Clothier, to discuss the case with him and to go over the ground rules for an investigatory panel that Clothier had committed to.
      Bergel's dismissal was upheld in August by the Rutgers panel after lengthy hearings. The ACLU issued a report disagreeing with the decision and threatening to go to the New Jersey Legislature if Bergel was not reinstated. However, within a few days it changed its position after Bergel's Rutgers faculty supporters convinced the ACLU that "a Nazi-hunt [by the legislature] could easily turn into a Red-hunt with themselves as victims." Bergel was left hanging in the wind. David M. Oshinsky, Richard P. McCormick, Daniel Horn, *The Case of the Nazi Professor*, New Brunswick, NJ, 1989, pp. 52-77.
71.   N.N, 4/11/35, p. 6.
72.   Papers of Arthur Garfield Hayes, Box 3, Folder 6, Resolution to Governor Harold G. Hoffman from Herman Von Busch, Secretary, Captain Hexamer Unit 73 of the Steuben Society of America, 5/7/35.
73.   Ibid., Box 6, Folder 1, "Memorandum of Law and Policy" prepared by the ACLU, 4/1/39. The document claims that, other than one person, the only ones persecuted under the Rafferty Law were members of Jehovah's Witnesses who were accused of circulating anti-Roman Catholic tracts.
74.   Glaser, "The German-American Bund," p. 45.
75.   NYT, 10/21/34, p. 27.
76.   N.N., 10/15/34, p. 9.
77.   Ibid., 6/7/35, p. 28.
78.   Ibid., 6/13/35, p. 15.
79.   Interview Walter Rayelt, 6/4/96.
80.   Union City, with its large German population, served as the headquarters for Bund activities in Hudson County. It was the largest Bund in New Jersey (Newark was second largest).
81.   N.N, 6/25/34, p. 24.
82.   Ibid.
83.   NYT, 6/26/34, p.10.
84.   Glaser, "The German-American Bund," pp. 35, 36.
85.   N.N., 6/18/35, p. 6.
86.   Ibid., 8/27/34, p. 28; 8/30/34, p. 13; 9/2/34, p. 6.
87.   The Friends were so incensed at Mayor McManus that they scheduled a demonstration in front of the Linden City Hall. The Minutemen and others threatened to counter the demonstration and the Friends backed down. See N.N. 5/28/35, p.12.
88.   N.N., 5/13/35, p. 7.
89.   Ibid., 10/3/33, p. 5; 11/3/33, p. 14.
90.   Ibid., 1/9/34, p. 5; 4/3/34, p. 11.
91.   Ibid., 9/11/34, p. 5; 10/2/34, p. 21.
92.   Ibid., 4/19/34, p. 11.

93.   Papers of Dr. S. William Kalb, DAWA Trade Guide for New Jersey; DAWA Trade
       Guide for Newark and Vicinity. Retail stores and services (barber and beauty shops,
       travel agencies, funeral directors, etc.) provide the majority of the listings. Under
       dentists and physicians a note reads, "Our Physicians (Dentists) prefer not to be listed.
       When in need of medical aid, call the DAWA office: Tel.: ESsex 2-1195."
94.   N.N., 7/3/34, p. 26; 9/8/34, p. 17; 12/4/34, p. 19.
95.   Ibid., 10/18/33, p.1;11/2/33, p. 22.
96.   Obermuller was observed at a German-American Bund meeting on October 17,
       1937, heiling with the audience, and in his capacity as a former National Commander
       of the German-American War Veterans, suggesting to the audience that all German-
       Americans in the United States be loyal to Hitler. However, when war began with the
       Nazi invasion of Poland, Obermuller publicly disapproved of Hitler's action. See,
       JBC, Box 4, *Jewish Veteran*, October-November, 1937, "German Veterans Groups in
       America," p. 11; N.N., 9/1/39, p. 21.
97.   N.N., 11/12/33, p. 22; 11/24/33, p. 11; 11/25/33, p. 23; 12/9/33, p. 7.
98.   Ibid., 12/13/33, p. 12.
99.   Ibid., 12/15/33, p. 22.
100.   Ibid., 3/29/34, p. 20.
101.   Ibid., 1/14/35, p. 6.
102.   Ibid., 5/22/35, p.13; 5/25/35, p. 4.
103.   Dr. Just's increasing role in pro-Nazi activities prompted the Newark NSANL to
       investigate him during the Saengerfest incident. The report claims that Dr. Just,
       although a Nazi sympathizer, was not a member of the Friends of the New Germany.
       Kalb Papers, Reports 16, 16A, "Re: Dr. Just."
104.   N.N., 5/21/35, p.19.
105.   Ibid., 5/22/35, p. 13.
106.   Ibid.
107.   S.C., 5/26/35, p. 14.
108.   N.N., 5/28/35, p. 6.
109.   Ibid., 5/31/35, p. 16.
110.   Lewy, Guenter, *The Cause that Failed: Communism in American Political Life*, New
       York, 1990, pp. 30-32.
111.   N.N., 5/31/35, p. 16.
112.   S.E., 5/31/35, p. 2.
113.   N.N., 5/31/35, p. 20.
114.   Ibid., p. 10.
115.   Ibid., 6/1/35, p.1.
116.   S.C., 6/2/35, pp. 1, 2.
117.   N.N., 6/3/35, p. 8.
118.   Ibid., 6/18/35, p. 14.
119.   Otto Stiefel (1876-1943) was a controversial figure who through two world wars
       consistently backed German nationalism. Active in German-American and in Newark
       civic groups, he espoused isolationist and Anglophobic positions. Stiefel denounced
       President Woodrow Wilson as a "Benedict Arnold" in 1916 and 1917 over the president's
       neutrality policies. After World War I, he criticized those who fought the Germans.
       Prior to World War II, he likened Hitler to George Washington and attacked President
       Roosevelt as a war-monger. See, N.N. Morgue, "Otto Stiefel."
120.   N.N., 8/5/35, p. 10.
121.   Ibid., 8/6/35, p. 14.
122.   Ibid., 8/21/35, p. 2.
123.   Ibid., 10/7/35, p. 34.
124.   Ibid., 11/5/35, p. 28.
125.   See Diamond, *The Nazi Movement in the United States*, p. 169, 172-174. Before
       Spanknoebel left the country, he named Dr. Ignatz Griebl his successor as bundesleiter.
       However, Fritz Gissibl, a NSDAP member and an early and ardent Nazi, had not
       given up his ambition for the post. Using his many contacts within the Friends and
       help from Berlin, Gissibl soon supplanted Griebl. For the next two years, Gissibl was

first the titular head of the Friends and then the behind-the-scenes leader when he named Dr. Hubert Schnuch, an American citizen, as bundesleiter at the Friends' second national convention in July 1934. With Gissibl's blessing, Schnuch was successful in establishing good relations with the myriad of German-American groups in New York. Because many of these groups lacked funds and were no longer supported by UGS, which had been factionalized by the Spanknoebel affair of 1933, he was able to get over twenty of them to affiliate with the Friends in 1934-1935. This increased the Friends' New York membership and consequently the national membership, to its peak of 10,000. Yet this success was converted to a failure as Gissibl's enemies, seeing a rejuvenated Nazi group, decided they wanted to take control of the Friends. Anton Haegele, a deputy Bundesleiter to Schnuch, and a group of dissidents including the former and deposed leader, Dr. Ignatz Griebl, attacked Schnuch and Gissibl as mismanaging the Friends' affairs. They also said it was time for the "old guard" to step aside and let new and creative people take over. The group was able to gain control of the party paper in New York City and gain the support of the president of the Steuben Society, Theodor Hoffmann. However, they were neither able to take control of the Friends' headquarters in Yorkville nor get the support of the O.D., the Nazis' fighting arm. These failures prevented members of the Friends in other cities from joining the revolt. The total number of dissidents never exceeded 200.

126. Frye, *Surrender on Demand*, pp. 62, 63; Diamond, *The Nazi Movement in the United States*, pp. 190-193.

127. Canedy, *America's Nazis*, p. 66.

4

Dr. S. William Kalb and the Anti-Nazi Boycott

The boycott against German goods and services was an effort by American Jewish organizations to relieve the terror wrought on German Jews by the Nazis. It was hoped that if the German economy could be damaged enough through depriving its industry of markets, enough pressure could be brought upon the Nazis by manufacturers to force the regime to ease up or cease its persecution of Jews. From 1933 through 1939 the boycott was pursued with varying degrees of effort and success.

An important aspect of the boycott is that there was never a unified effort among American groups, nor among its international proponents. The reasons for this failure were the egos of the leaders, differences in strategy and tactics, and the unwillingness of the groups to relinquish the necessary amount of autonomy to pursue a single effort.

Another hindrance to the boycott was the lack of any governmental support in either the United States or Europe. Government leaders saw German anti-Semitism as a Jewish problem and were concerned that a boycott would worsen political and economic relations with the Hitler regime. Cordell Hull, Secretary of State from 1933 through 1944, was a preeminent exponent of this thinking, and an early boycott opponent.[1] It is open to question whether, given the American government's disinclination to support a boycott, a unified effort among Jewish and labor groups would have been able to help the plight of German Jews. What is not open to question is the historical precedent of Americans using boycotts to redress grievances. The boycott was used successfully against Great Britain in the creation of the United States.[2] The most recent successful boycott by Americans helped end apartheid in South Africa.

The Non-Sectarian Anti-Nazi League (NSANL) and similar groups used the boycott to redress grievances in a peaceful way. Whether or not leaders of the boycott campaign in the 1930s knew they were acting in accord with principles drawn up by the country's founding fathers, domestic foes of the boycott could not reasonably oppose it on grounds that it was un-American. There were four large organizations running anti-Nazi boycott campaigns by February 1934: NSANL, the American Jewish Congress (AJC), the Joint Labor Committee (JLC), and the Jewish War Veterans (JWV). All were based in New York City. The NSANL was solely dedicated to the boycott, whereas the other groups had multiple agendas, with the boycott increasing in importance over time.

The NSANL became the successor to the American League for the Defense of Jewish Rights on December 23, 1933. The reorganization occurred because Samuel Untermyer, president of the league and its most influential leader, wanted non-Jewish support for the boycott. He therefore chose a name that would be more appealing to Christian groups and individuals. Untermyer became president of the new group, replacing Abraham Coralnik, the league's founder and first president.

Untermyer, a brilliant lawyer and skilled publicist, had a long and successful career behind him when he began his boycott work. He was often uncompromising in his dealings with other boycott groups, and unwilling to cede any significant amount of his group's autonomy. Under his leadership, the NSANL worked with other boycott groups, but on his terms. The NSANL's mission remained the same as its predecessor's—to pursue the boycott as the only effective weapon for the defense of fundamental human rights.

The AJC set up a boycott committee in the summer of 1933, and soon after established a research bureau to aid in identifying boycott violators as well as items to replace boycotted German goods. The AJC delayed any direct action by its members until 1934, in the hope it could avoid duplication of efforts with the already established American League for the Defense of Jewish Rights. Negotiations for a unified boycott effort between Rabbi Stephen Wise, president of the AJC, and Samuel Untermyer produced no results.

The AJC did have a major success in this period. It helped persuade the American Federation of Labor (AFL) to endorse the anti-Nazi boycott in the fall of 1933. AFL president William Green had denounced Nazism for its persecution of labor and Jews at an AJC rally earlier in the year, and since that time had worked with union officials to support the boycott.[3] Green, at a December meeting in

Washington with Rabbi Wise, agreed on joint boycott activities. In February, 1934, Rabbi Wise appointed Dr. Joseph L. Tenenbaum, a national vice president of the AJC, as its boycott chairman. Wise spoke out nationally and internationally for the boycott, while Tenenbaum did the administrative and coordinating work.

The boycott movement had its origin at a March 19, 1933 meeting of Jewish organizations sponsored by the AJC, the American Jewish Committee, and B'Nai Brith. J. George Fredman, commander of the Jewish War Veterans, proposed an anti-Nazi boycott, but no vote was taken because a majority of delegates would have voted negatively. Judge Joseph M. Proskauer, a leading member of the American Jewish Committee, denounced the proposed boycott and any demonstrations against the Nazi government. Rabbi Wise, to maintain unity, did not challenge Proskauer.[4] The JWV within a day passed its own boycott measure and soon began an active campaign to implement it.

The JWV was not as influential as B'Nai Brith, AJC, or the American Jewish Committee. When it announced a boycott there was scant general press notice, both because the JWV did not represent American Jewry at large and because it lacked any real relationship with important press personalities.[5] Cognizant that the group lacked the resources to carry the boycott on its own shoulders, it sought aid from other Jewish groups. Once such groups as the NSANL and AJC took up the boycott effort, the veterans continually called for a unification of efforts. As early as September 1933, Fredman requested American boycott organizations to unite under one banner and for a worldwide boycott effort.[6] Unfortunately, these goals were never attained, despite the efforts of the JWV and others. The veterans' group remained a stalwart force in the boycott movement until the war.

A fourth important boycott group was formed in February 1934 when the Jewish Labor Committee (JLC) was founded as a Jewish-American defense group. From its inception, the JLC had the support of the AFL and its president, William Green. An AFL affiliate, the committee represented nearly 400,000 Jewish workers from such organizations as the United Hebrew Trades, the International Ladies Garment Workers' Union, the Workmen's Circle, the *Forward*, and the Amalgamated Clothing Workers of America. The JLC constitution clearly states its aims:

> To give aid to Jewish and non-Jewish labor institutions overseas; to provide succor to victims of oppression and persecution and to combat anti-Semitism and racial and religious intolerance abroad and in the United States.[7]

In line with this credo, the anti-Nazi boycott was the JLC's first major activity. The campaign's initial success was keeping German machinery out of union shops.

Baruch Charney Vladeck, editor of the *Jewish Daily Forward*, was founder and leader of the JLC. A leading Socialist, journalist, orator, and civic reformer (particularly in the field of housing), Vladeck was one of the most charismatic and well-known people in the Yiddish- speaking labor movement. He and Joseph Tenenbaum founded the Joint Boycott Council (JBC) in February 1936.[8]

Newark had representatives from all the national groups. The American League for the Defense of Jewish Rights had set up a committee in the city in the fall of 1933. However, existing mainly on paper, it had no plan of action, no office or staff, and very little money. When the league closed its national office in New York in December 1933, the group's files were shipped to Untermyer's law suite, which became NSANL headquarters. It took many months before the NSANL established an operating organization in Newark.

The AJC, like the NSANL, had neither office nor staff in Newark. Meetings were held on an *ad hoc* basis, and there would not be a separate Newark-area division of the group until May 28, 1935, when delegates from more than sixty fraternal and religious groups formed an Essex County branch. The Newark AJC branch was formed to investigate Nazi propaganda in America, to develop public opinion concerning Jewish interests and problems, and continue the anti-Nazi boycott. Judge Joseph Siegler was elected president and State Assemblyman Sidney Goldberg chairman of the executive board.[9] The Essex branch of the AJC periodically engaged in boycott activities.

The JLC had no office in Newark, but many of its constituent groups, particularly the Workman's Circle, had branches in the city. The Circle's five branches, locals of the Amalgamated Clothing Workers of America, and the International Garment Workers Union were active boycott supporters.

The group that led the boycott in Newark was Post 34 of the JWV, which had been formed in December 1931 with an initial membership of thirty-five. Its first commander was Michael Breitkopf. Other aspiring leaders also became officers of the new group, including Dr. S. William Kalb and Joseph Heimberg.[10] After the National JWV passed its boycott resolution, it determined that each post would conduct its own campaign, with support and advice from New York headquarters. With the encouragement of the JWV national commander, J. George Fredman, who lived in Bayonne near Newark, Post 34 became a boycott leader.

One of the first activities undertaken in New York by the JWV, and subsequently taken up by many local posts, was a campaign to persuade department stores and other large retailers not to sell German goods. If retailers continued to sell such merchandise they would be picketed. Fliers circulated by the picketers were intended to impress the boycott message on shoppers. One of the JWV fliers read:

> Don't Buy German Goods
> Don't Sell German Goods
> Don't Ship American Merchandise in German Ships
> Don't Patronize German Moving Pictures
> Do It Yourself. Tell Your Family and Friends To Do It,
> But by All Means, Boycott, Boycott, Boycott![11]

* * *

S. William Kalb, organizer of Newark Post 34 JWV in 1931, was one of its most active members. His offer to be the post's boycott chairman in 1933 was readily accepted by the membership. Kalb possessed organizational abilities, good public speaking skills, and persistence.[12] He was a thirty-six-year-old physician who, although not affluent, was earning enough to provide for his family. What made him decide to take valuable time away from his practice over the next seven years to lead the anti-Nazi boycott effort in Newark?

Samuel William Kalb was born in Newark on November 12, 1897, the son of immigrants from the Galician part of Austria. One of six children, he had four sisters. His father was a tailor who made small investments in real estate and gradually became financially secure but never wealthy. Little is known about Kalb's early life other than the fact that he became a Bar Mitzvah in Newark at a synagogue in the Third Ward. Soon after high school he enlisted in the Marines and served for more than a year in Europe during World War I. While he was in service, two sisters and his brother died in the influenza epidemic of 1918.[13] Kalb's military service made a deep impression on him; from that time on patriotism became a major force in his worldview.

After his discharge from the Marines, he enrolled at Indiana's Valparaiso University, earning a degree in pharmacy in 1922. The many extracurricular activities listed in his graduation yearbook suggest that he did not have to work his way through college.[14] Kalb's daughter Pat Einhorn remembers one oft-related incident from her father's college career that had a profound effect on him. As the cheerleader for the Valparaiso football team, he was caricatured in a school newspaper on the occasion of a Valparaiso-Notre Dame game. Kalb was shown kneeling in his cheerleader's uniform with a pawnbroker's symbol over his head, three footballs replacing the traditional three round balls. Kalb often said that although he had experienced anti-Semitism in the Marines, this public humiliation was the worst he suffered in his youth. He kept a copy of this paper until he died.[15]

After one year as a pharmacist, Kalb decided he would rather be a doctor and was accepted at the University of Cincinnati Medical School, from which he received his M.D. degree in 1925. Kalb met Amelia Segal while in medical school and they married in 1926. He practiced medicine in Cincinnati for five years before returning to Newark in 1931. He secured part-time positions with two Newark meat packing firms, examining their employees two mornings a week and on Saturdays. This work kept the family going while Kalb began building his practice.[16]

KUVs—burial and welfare societies organized by Jews from the same town of origin in Eastern Europe—proved fertile ground on which to establish a practice in Newark. There were too few Jewish doctors, particularly those who spoke Yiddish as Kalb did, to service Newark's working-class Jewish population. Upon his return to the city, Kalb made the rounds of all the KUVs,[17] offering cut-rate fees for members and their families in return for a monthly payment from the KUV based on the number of patients seen. In the 1930s, it was common for KUVs and other Jewish organizations to have such arrangements, particularly with physicians, dentists, and lawyers.[18] Kalb became the physician for a number of KUVs, including two of the largest, the Israel Verein and the Erste Bershader.[19]

Kalb also became active in veterans' groups in Newark, including the American Legion, Marine Corps League, Veterans of World War I, and most importantly as a founding member of Post 34 of the JWV. It was through this group that he first became known in the city. As the officer in charge of the anti-Nazi boycott, Kalb attracted publicity in the city's newspapers and the Jewish press. He was also the JWV physician under the same type of arrangement he had with the KUVs.

Kalb became politically active, working for the successful candidacy of Meyer Ellenstein in the 1933 Newark City Commission election. In January 1934, Kalb was elected a vice-president of the Joseph Heimberg Political Club, one of the largest and most potent in the city.[20] This group was predominantly Republican, but because it was active in non-partisan municipal elections it didn't use a party label. The Heimberg Club had a substantial overlap in membership with Post 34 of the JWV. However, since the JWV was supposedly non-political, it was the Heimberg Club that openly aided Ellenstein's election efforts.

As an inveterate meeting-goer, Kalb was out of his house almost every night. Within a short time, he gained recognition as a person who could be trusted with responsibility. His ebullient personality was an asset in gaining allies for all his endeavors, including building his medical practice. He undertook activities to make himself a popular and influential member of the community as well as to increase his income. Barbara Rachlin, Kalb's other daughter, believes her father was always torn between making money and being a humanitarian, but when "push came to shove he was a people person, not a money person."[21]

Patriotism was a major component of Kalb's persona, as was his loyalty to the Jewish people. He was a fierce foe of both Nazi Germany and domestic Nazis. By 1933, Kalb had established a practice that provided a comfortable income for his family. His children were in private schools and he lived in a large house in one of Newark's best neighborhoods. Yet for the next seven years, as leader of the anti-Nazi boycott through his role in the JWV and his later chairmanship of the New Jersey NSANL, he spent as much time fighting Nazism as he did practicing medicine. Active in the KUVs, veterans' groups, the AJC, and in politics, Kalb obtained various degrees of support from all of them in his anti-Nazi work. He was often busy seventy hours a week and thrived on the recognition and sense of accomplishment from this work.

Nat Arno was the only other Newark resident who spent as much time fighting Nazism. With such a common interest it is not surprising that they became allies. What is surprising is that a friendship developed between the rough-and-tumble pugilist Arno and the well-educated physician. Both of Kalb's daughters recall the affection between the two men. Pat Einhorn vividly remembers Arno as a regular visitor at their house, especially on Sunday mornings. During these visits she would climb onto Arno's lap and listen to the two men talk.

There was frequent laughter during these conversations. Barbara, the younger of the Kalbs' daughters, remembers the visits less well but nevertheless recalls Arno as "short and brawny." She also remembers that whenever her father talked about his anti-Nazi activities he would always talk fondly of Arno. Both daughters smile when they recall the line Arno often repeated to their father, which became part of their family lore: "Doc, is there anyone I can kill for you?" Barbara hastened to add that Arno meant with his fists, not with a gun.[22]

The close tie between the two men augured well for the cause they espoused. Cooperation between the Minutemen and the NSANL in the anti-Nazi struggle made both groups stronger. The Minutemen used Kalb's editorial skills for many of its statements, which were published in the daily newspapers. Arno and some of his men were present at many of the NSANL rallies in case of attacks by Nazis. Kalb apparently was also good with his fists and not afraid to "mix it up." He sometimes accompanied Arno on raids to break up Nazi meetings. Whenever the doctor went with Arno on such missions, Mrs. Kalb worried that her husband would hurt his hands in the fighting, thus curtailing or ending his career as a physician. She would wait up all night until he returned from the skirmishes. Luckily, he was never injured.[23]

* * *

While the JWV was waging an active boycott campaign in Newark, the NSANL was yet to make its presence felt. Although Kalb and Michael Stavitsky were officers and had conversations on how to proceed, no funds were allocated to the Newark branch nor was there correspondence from New York. In fact, most anti-Nazis in Newark did not even know a local branch of NSANL existed. Irving Piltch, who had volunteered for anti-Nazi causes with the Young Men's Hebrew Club, sent a letter to Untermyer in March offering his services. He told the NSANL he was active in several groups that could be effective in the boycott movement. Another letter volunteering services to the NSANL came from N.P. Leiter in June. He had received a solicitation letter from NSANL and in replying offered both himself and his automobile for "any type of work which will aid you in the present struggle for religious freedom."[24] No replies were found to either man in the NSANL files.

The national office of NSANL did cooperate with Kalb in providing research and advice for his boycott efforts. He was its representative in New Jersey, but he carried out his campaign in the name of the JWV rather than the NSANL. Most of his correspondence was on JWV stationary, but when appropriate he used NSANL letterheads with the New York address and list of officers. He listed himself as "Chairman New Jersey Division."

Since Newark was the major New Jersey city and the home of a large and influential Jewish population, Samuel Untermyer wanted to establish an NSANL branch there. As late as October 1935, George Harriman, the executive secretary of the NSANL, asked Rabbi Julius Silberfeld of Temple B'Nai Abraham to organize a Newark branch.[25] But it took until mid-1936 for the NSANL to become a force in Newark.

* * *

The first correspondence regarding Kalb's involvement in a Newark boycott case is an early-1934 letter to him from Schraffts Restaurant Corporation in New York, replying to allegations that the company's Newark eatery was "unwilling to cater to parties held by people of the Jewish faith." Schraffts denounced the "malicious rumor" as "untrue and absolutely without foundation." Kalb was invited to submit the names of any Jews interested in a catered party to them so it "may explain our service to them." It is not known if the anti-Semitic allegations against Schraffts were true, but Kalb's intervention in the matter ensured that if there had been anti-Jewish discrimination at the chain it would cease, at least in Newark.

Although Kalb's boycott efforts were mainly with the JWV, in March he reactivated a small leadership group from the Central Committee for the Protection of Human Rights. This was founded in October 1933 as an umbrella group for the three major boycott groups and other Newark Jewish fraternal and welfare organizations. It had not held a meeting since then, but some of its leaders remained active in boycott work. With Michael A. Stavitsky of the Newark Conference of Jewish Charities and Nathan Franzblau of the Order of Brith Sholem, Kalb met with executives of the city's department stores to persuade them not to buy or sell German goods.[26] The men thought they had a major success in early April when Abraham Schindel, vice president of Kresge's Department Store in Newark, announced "this store has not made any purchases from Germany since the Hitler regime." He added that the small amount of German merchandise in the store was all bought before Hitler.[27] However, despite Schindel's promise and verbal commitments by other stores, German goods were periodically advertised and sold at Kresge and other Newark department stores through 1939.

Kalb constantly spoke before Jewish organizations, urging them to participate in the boycott movement. By the end of the year, women from the auxiliaries of the AJC, JWV, and KUVs were visiting retail stores to dissuade them from buying German goods. The Israel KUV urged its membership to advise the boycott leader, "our own brother Kalb," if they found German goods in any store.[28] Some of the boycotters supplied stores with lists of American-made products to substitute for German products.[29]

In their zeal to fight Nazism in the most practical way available to them, the KUVs and other Jewish benevolent and fraternal societies began their own boycott operations. The Israel and Erste Bershader KUVs set up boycott committees, which gave progress reports at biweekly meetings. These multiple campaigns brought about duplication of effort and even bickering. The need for a unified boycott organization in the Newark area was obvious. Kalb called a meeting of the Newark division of the Committee for the Protection of Human Rights for mid-April 1934. Among the committee's officers were some of the most influential Jews in Newark, including Stavitsky, Aaron Lasser, and Samuel Kessler. Stavitsky chaired the meeting. Seventy Jewish groups were invited and most sent delegates. Stavitsky told them that so many Jewish organizations were attempting to set up their own boycott operations that they were counterproductive. He pointed out that the committee had succeeded in obtaining the cooperation of some of the leading department stores in Essex County, and that several had agreed to stop selling German merchandise. Uniting the boycott groups under the committee's leadership would intensify the boycott.

Kalb then addressed the group on the spread of Nazism in Essex County by the Friends of the New Germany and the efforts of anti-Nazis to combat the Hitlerites. The only resolution passed by the meeting endorsed U.S. Rep. Emmanuel Celler's bill to make an exception to the stringent 1924 immigration law and permit German-Jewish refugees to settle in the United States. The attendees agreed to another meeting to which all Newark-area synagogues would be invited. No action was taken toward unifying boycott efforts.[30]

The first boycott campaign in Newark involved L. Bamberger, Newark's and New Jersey's largest department store. The campaign had its origin in New York, where the American League for the Protection of Human Rights and its successor the NSANL, following the lead of the JWV, determined to rid New York's department stores of German-made goods. By the end of 1934 New York stores including Macy's, Gimbel's, Saks, and Hearn's had agreed to the boycott. Even John Wanamaker, one of the few non-Jewish-owned department stores in the city, went on record as supporting the ban on sales of German goods.[31]

Macy's, the owner of L. Bamberger since 1929, was the leading retailer in New York. It had a buying office in Berlin and was a large importer of German goods. As early as the fall of 1933 the store took out ads in metropolitan New York newspapers, including the *NewYork Times* and the Jewish press, replying to complaints about its policies regarding German merchandise. The company claimed that the boycott would harm German Jews because some of the products bought by American stores were from Jewish sources and because it would create more ill will in Germany towards Jews.

Untermyer determined to force Macy's to change its pro-German policy. The AJC entered the campaign later and separately. After months of negotiations, threats, and publicity, Macy's issued a press release in March 1934 agreeing to close its buying office in Berlin and to no longer buy German-made goods. In their own releases both the NSANL and the AJC took credit for the capitulation of the world's largest department store. There was no agreement on the disposition of German goods still in the store. Knowing they were being monitored by at least two boycott groups, the management of Macy's attempted to find a way of disposing of these goods without either taking a loss or risking bad publicity.[32]

Soon after the agreement, there were rumors that Macy's was using L. Bamberger in Newark to sell its stock of German goods. L. Bamberger was one of the highest-volume retail establishments in the country. Louis Bamberger, along with his brother-in-law Felix Fuld, had sold the store to Macy's in 1929. However, Bamberger was still associated with the store under a contract with Macy's and was there every day watching over the operation.

Bamberger had never married and the store was the focus of his life, along with his philanthropic interests. Newark's premier philanthropist both for secular and Jewish causes, he was one of the most generous contributors to Newark's Community Chest and the prime source of funds for the Newark Conference of Jewish Charities. Along with Fuld, Bamberger built and presented to the city the Newark Museum in 1924. In 1928 he was the largest contributor in the building of Newark's Beth Israel Hospital. Bamberger was the major donor for Newark's YM&YWHA on High Street. In 1930 he funded the Institute of Advanced Studies at Princeton University with his sister Carrie, Fuld's widow.[33]

Bamberger was modest and reserved and not inclined to public speaking or leadership roles in the various charities he supported. However, every Jewish organization in the area sought his advice and his donation. When he accepted leadership roles his usual title was Honorary President. Bamberger was by far Newark's most influential Jew. Any public accusations against the L. Bamberger store would inevitably involve Bamberger himself.

The impetus for a confrontation with the store over its sales of German goods came from J. George Fredman. He called Kalb, recently elected National Surgeon General of the JWV and the group's boycott chairman in Newark, and asked him to become involved. Kalb's investigation found that L. Bamberger was indeed selling German-produced goods. Kalb first discussed the problem with the Newark Post 34 commander Louis B. Freeman, a popular tavern owner and politician. Freeman said that any action against L. Bamberger would be unwise, and that JWV participation in such a cause would be self-destructive.

Kalb then turned for advice to Stavitsky. President-elect of the Conference of Jewish Charities, he was well connected with all groups representing the middle and upper classes of Newark's Jewish community. Kalb and Stavitsky met at Newark's Progress Club, a bastion of the city's German-Jewish aristocracy. It was Kalb's first visit to the club. Like Freeman, Stavitsky warned against any public protest against the store. He said that perhaps Louis Bamberger could be approached to speak to the Straus Brothers, owners of Macy's, to rid their Newark store of German goods. Kalb asked Stavitsky to set up a meeting between him and Bamberger for that purpose. Stavitsky said that Kalb was not the right person for such a conference and that he would think about who should meet with Bamberger. It is doubtful that any meeting occurred because L. Bamberger continued to sell German-made merchandise.

Kalb was determined not to let Macy's off the hook. But the organized Jewish community could not act against the store for fear of offending Louis Bamberger. There was one person Kalb knew who would not be afraid to address the situation—Nat Arno. The two men met and the Minuteman immediately agreed to cooperate. Arno called a meeting of several men in his group that evening, with Kalb in attendance. They decided on direct action.

The next day four Minutemen appeared in front of L. Bamberger on Market Street in downtown Newark. Two carried picket signs reading, "L. Bamberger buys and sells goods made in Nazi Germany." The two picketed in an orderly manner for about twenty minutes undisturbed by the traffic policemen on the street. Then a patrol wagon appeared and police arrested the picketers, Joseph Kaplan and Jacob Stacher, on charges of disorderly conduct. When a newspaper photographer tried to take a picture, a third Minuteman attempted to wrest the camera away from him. In the struggle, the anti-Nazi threw a cigar in the photographer's face. Hyman Trugman was arrested for assault after the victim identified him as the assailant. The fourth Minuteman, unidentified, was also placed in the police van. The police said the arrests took place because of a complaint from L. Bamberger. When questioned by newsmen about selling German-made merchandise, the director of publicity for the store said that only the company president could discuss the issue.[34]

Soon after the incident, L. Bamberger issued an official statement claiming that German goods had not been purchased for many months, but that the company was still selling items purchased earlier. Police adjourned the hearing of the three arrested men after the photographer said he had mistakenly identified Trugman. He now said that the fourth Minuteman was his assailant. According to police, this unnamed anti-Nazi somehow disappeared before the wagon got to headquarters.[35] Within a few days all charges were dropped. Given the circumstantial evidence— the cigar in the face and the "escape" from the wagon—it can be assumed that the unidentified Minuteman was Arno, who was known to use his ever-present cigar as a weapon. Although appreciative of all the publicity, Arno was still on parole for the May 21, 1934 Irvington riot, and another arrest could have sent him back to jail. Presumably, Longie Zwillman used his influence with the Newark police to protect the commander.

These events were not reported in the two Newark dailies, probably because L. Bamberger was the largest advertiser in both papers. This was similar to events in New York when Untermyer's criticism of Macy's went unreported in the New York dailies. The JWV and Kalb were lauded a week before the L. Bamberger incident by the *Jewish Chronicle,* Newark's English language Jewish weekly, as leaders in defending "the Jewish name in a practical way."[36]

The only mention of the picketing, but not the arrests, was in an end-of-the-year insert in the *Jewish Chronicle* paid for by the JWV. Kalb was quoted in an article in the supplement as giving full credit to the Minutemen for forcing L. Bamberger to say it hadn't purchased German goods in many months. This statement put the store on record, and Kalb hoped it would discourage the store from such purchases in the future. Even without unpaid publicity crediting the organization, the Newark JWV saw the effectiveness of the picketing and passed a resolution to employ it as a means to further the boycott.[37]

* * *

Immediately after the L. Bamberger incident, Kalb wrote a report to the Newark JWV on his boycott activities. After a brief description of the events at L. Bamberger, he told of visits made to the three other major Newark department stores, Hahne & Co., Ohrbach's, and Kresge. They had all recently advertised fall sales of German gloves, and Kalb sent a woman to each store to purchase a pair of gloves. Germany had been the major source of imported gloves in America for many years, and this was an opportunity for Kalb to strike a quick blow to a major German export and to educate the department stores on the need for the boycott. According to his report, Kalb then contacted executives of each of the stores, eliciting promises to stop purchasing German goods.[38] Prior attempts to convince the Newark department stores to subscribe to the boycott had been unsuccessful.

An important recommendation in Kalb's report was that each JWV member who was in business send him the names of all suppliers of manufactured goods. Kalb would check to see if the supplier was handling German products. Kalb clipped out the foreign ship arrivals every day from the *Journal of Commerce.* Listed was the name of the ship, its country of registry, the name and address of all cargo recipients, and a description of the type of cargo for each destination in the United States.[39] If a supplier was handling German goods, a JWV member could try to persuade it to switch to other merchandise, preferably American. The research for replacement goods was usually done by the NSANL in New York. Another suggestion in the Kalb report was that the JWV make a strong effort to gain synagogue support for the boycott.[40]

Such attempts were made by the JWV prior to the Jewish High Holy Days. There was one success at a major congregation. Rabbi Julius Silberfeld of Temple B'Nai Abraham endorsed the boycott in a Rosh Hashonah sermon. In justifying his stand Silberfeld said that Hitler was planning "the complete extermination of 600,000 human beings on no ground whatsoever except that they belong to a particular race and religion."[41] However, most Rabbis spoke on the Jewish tragedy in Germany without reference to the boycott. Rather, they posited Palestine or a return to religious values as solutions to the tragedy.[42] An exception was Rabbi Marius Ransom of Temple Sharey Tefilo in East Orange, a Newark suburb, who urged his congregation to give "greater consideration to world problems" than to the "isolated phenomena of anti-Semitism in Europe." Ransom optimistically added "the world is getting better."[43] Facing harsh criticism for his remarks by members of his synagogue and Jewish leaders, Ranson soon reversed his position. He announced his support for the anti-Nazi boycott, even if "the German people should suffer for the sins of the Hitler administration."[44]

Kalb continued his appearances in Newark promoting the boycott. Over a two-month period, he spoke before more than fifteen groups in his capacity as Surgeon General of the National JWV and boycott chairman of the Newark JWV.[45]

Women's groups were extremely important in the boycott movement. Women shoppers became enthusiastic detectives in search of German-made goods. An example is a September 6, 1934 letter from Gertrude Levine:

> This is to certify that I have personally examined the contents of the following counters in Hahne & Co., and have found them as listed below: The China and Glassware Dept. where all the merchandise is from China, Japan and Czechoslovakia. The Linen Dept. where the merchandise is imported from Holland, Belgium and Czechoslovakia. The Glove Dept. where I asked to see the new fall line and all the gloves shown me were from Nuremberg, Whittenberg [sic] and Saxony. When I told the salesgirl that I understood that they had discontinued the sale of German gloves she very emphatically informed me that they sold any number of German gloves.[46]

Ms. Levine's report came less than one month after Kalb had received assurances from Hahne & Co. that it would stop selling German merchandise. Usually after a store was reported selling German merchandise, Kalb or an associate would make an appointment to see an executive and explain the importance of the boycott. If the retailer persisted in selling German merchandise, the store's name would be circulated among participating boycott organizations, whose memberships would boycott the store.   Kalb wanted to print lists of boycott violators under the aegis of the JWV since this was a far more intimidating device than word-of-mouth. He printed 10,000 circulars, sending one to Fredman for approval before distribution. Fredman, fearing legal repercussions, asked Untermyer for advice. The lawyer cautioned against circulating names of any violators until he could research possible anti-trust implications. Kalb then requested a ruling by the JWV national commander or judge advocate.[47]

Impatient to start his boycott violators list campaign, Kalb again turned to his ally Nat Arno. The doctor knew the Minuteman leader would not be deterred by anti-trust considerations. By the end of the summer, the first boycott list was printed and distributed by Newark's Minutemen. Twelve companies were listed, among them four large retailers, three with branches in Newark: Sears Roebuck & Co., S. H. Kress, and Woolworth & Co.; four drug companies, including Hoffman LaRoche Inc., of Nutley, New Jersey; and two food companies, Atlantic and Pacific Tea Co., with many branches in New Jersey, and the Kraft Food Company.[48]

Kalb soon received permission from national JWV to begin publishing a state-wide boycott violators list. Untermyer had determined that there were no legal ramifications as long as there was proof that the violating companies imported German goods. The first circular contained thirty-four companies, mainly from New York City. Only one, Hoffman-LaRoche, was headquartered in New Jersey. The original 10,000 JWV circulars were destroyed because they contained companies that were negotiating with either the JWV or the NSANL to cease buying German goods or services. The new list contained only concerns that had been identified by the NSANL as violators.[49]

During 1934, Kalb succeeded in establishing a network of Jewish groups that were active participants in the boycott campaign. At the same time, a small group of dedicated men were contacting the larger enterprises in Newark to persuade them not to buy or sell German goods. An end-of-the-year tribute to Kalb by Louis Freeman, Commander of Newark Post 34 of the JWV, read: "Had it not been for Dr. Kalb's wholehearted interest in this anti-Nazi boycott movement, I venture to say little would have been accomplished in this community."[50]

Kalb's attitude toward anything but direct action against the Nazis was made manifest in a letter he sent to Herman Weckstein, a JWV boycott activist. Not pleased with the JWV role in Minutemen

operations, Weckstein urged Kalb to work "on a program of dignified propaganda." Kalb in response said that the Minutemen activities were carried out "with the consent, approval, and under the advice of the JWV." Regarding "dignified propaganda," Kalb said,

> I don't know what you mean by dignified propaganda. If you mean to send speakers
> out to Jewish groups such as the AJC, American Jewish Committee, Anti-Nazi League,
> etc., then I say forget it![51]

The end of the year also saw the first and only support of the
boycott by the Newark Conference on Jewish Charities. It allocated
$100 for the national NSANL toward its 1935 budget. It is possible
that this gift was made because Stavitsky was the conference's chairman as well as an officer of NSANL. This small amount, even by
1934 standards, can be compared to the other allocations to other
Jewish defense groups: Anti-Defamation League of B'Nai Brith,
$3,000; American Jewish Committee, $500; AJC, $500.[52]

The pressure of the boycott work on Kalb's family and medical
practice was enormous. His income had not increased even though
his family's expenses mounted as his children grew. He announced
in January 1935 that he was withdrawing from all boycott work for
the JWV to devote full time to his medical practice.[53] This news,
which appeared in the *Jewish Chronicle,* shocked those in the Jewish community participating in the boycott movement. He was im-
plored by Stavitsky, Fredman, and other Jewish leaders to change his
mind, which he did within a week. What caused his about-face is not
known. There is no evidence that he received any additional help in
carrying on as the self-appointed anti-Nazi leader. And yet, during
the next year, Kalb's activities increased on behalf of the boycott.

In early 1935, Kalb began pressing the local AJC to become active in the boycott campaign. Under the presidency of Judge Joseph
Siegler, the Newark AJC had been mainly concerned about the plight
of Germany's Jews.[54] The AJC's Essex Women's Division was ahead
of the men and set up its own boycott committee in April 1935.[55]
Tenenbaum organized the first national AJC boycott conference in
the fall, which included three Newark residents.[56] Kalb urged
Tenenbaum to begin an active program in New Jersey. Describing
himself as the boycott leader in New Jersey for the past two years,
Kalb told Tenenbaum that the results of AJC research should be made
available to all states where it was needed.[57] Kalb remained in touch
with the national AJC office and became its *de facto* boycott leader
in Newark and northern New Jersey.

Kalb requested the Essex County AJC to send out a letter to all member groups in August to appoint delegates for a boycott committee.[58] When no action was taken, Kalb sent Judge Siegler the following letter:

> On August 14, I sent you a copy of a letter which I sent to Bruno Berk with reference to some real active Boycott work. Up to this time nothing was done. I want to know if the Congress in Newark is going to be a speech-making organization or will we actually avail the organizations the privilege of doing something worthwhile. The necessity for constructive boycotting in and around Newark is as acute. As president of the local Congress YOU should insist on the secretary carrying out his duties or else get a paid secretary, even if its only a girl.[59]

This prompted action, and by the middle of November over thirty organizations had submitted names for an AJC sponsored Executive Boycott Council. Most were KUVs; others were labor groups such as the Federation of Kosher Butchers, Hatter's Benefit Association, and Jewish Worker's Club. Also included was the Young Men's Hebrew Club, an early boycott supporter.[60] It was Kalb's intention to have the first meeting by the end of the year.[61] One was announced for November, but never took place.[62]

Kalb's efforts with the AJC continued in 1936. He used his position in the Essex County AJC to urge it into boycott action. At a June meeting, Kalb told of the need for strict enforcement of the boycott and asked for volunteer investigators. Kalb was one of those chosen to attend a Washington D.C. convention to elect American delegates to the World Jewish Congress in Geneva. [63] Before the trip, Kalb again pressed support for the boycott at the annual meeting of the Essex AJC in December. In response to his request, the group reaffirmed its adherence to the boycott. Kalb was elected treasurer for the next year.[64] The Essex County AJC gave public support for the boycott, but through 1936 never directly participated. Rather, it allowed Kalb, an officer of the group, to carry the fight forward.[65]

As New Jersey JWV Boycott Chairman, Kalb activated boycott committees at all posts in the state. He issued specific orders to each post's boycott chairmen. His main instructions concerned the violators' lists, which he wanted each post to issue monthly. Proof of violation for any company had to be documented and submitted to Kalb before publication. Each post was told to place no more than eight names on its monthly violators' lists. Names were eliminated only if affidavits of compliance were submitted to the post's boycott committee. Temporary removal was possible if the violating company was currently in negotiation with the committee.[66]

* * *

An example of Kalb's boycott work was the case of Food Sales Company, Inc., a major distributor for Kraft Foods. Kalb and the national office of NSANL identified Kraft in 1934 as a significant importer of German dairy products, all shipped on German vessels. Kalb contacted Kraft, told executives the objectives of the boycott, and asked for cooperation. He said that records indicated that Kraft had imported 660 tons of German products in the previous year. In reply, Lester Claster, president of Food Sales, claimed that this figure had been reduced to 100 tons in the first nine months of 1935 and that he would cooperate with the boycott effort. [67] Research by Kalb and NSANL indicated that the correct figure for 1935 was 362 tons.[68]

The two men met. Kalb told Claster of his tonnage findings and stressed that he wanted a reduction of German imports to forty tons for the coming year (1936). An excerpt from a follow-up letter is indicative of the tactics Kalb used:

> Since you were here I have had requests from some more of your competitors for circulars and letters with reference to disseminating propaganda against Kraft Phenix products. This I have refused to do. I am looking forward to a letter from you which will settle the question so far as your organization is concerned. Be sure to make it specific because I have 125 cities to whom I must send copies of your letter. These letters will not be published but will be for the information of the chairmen only.[69]

Kraft was Food Sales' largest client, and a boycott of its products would be disastrous for Food Sales.

Kraft Phenix was well aware of the potential boycott of its products, having already been contacted by NSANL's national office about its shipping Swiss cheese on German vessels. It was not surprising that Food Sales agreed to import all the Swiss cheese for Kraft on the Holland American Line rather than on North German Lloyd. The company asserted that this change in shippers had been planned "some time ago" but was delayed by price considerations, which had since been worked out.[70] In his final meeting with Claster, Kalb elicited a promise that as of January 1, 1936, no cheese would be imported from Germany, except a few cases of Gruyere, which were needed by a limited number of German merchants.

The successful resolution of the Kraft case was recognized not only by the JWV but also by the NSANL. In a year-end report of its research division, the NSANL listed this case as successfully resolved "largely due to the efforts of Dr. S. William Kalb."[71]

Kalb rewarded Claster with a letter of thanks for his cooperation and a promise of assistance if there were any further complaints against his company. Kalb made good on this promise when the JWV North Hudson County Post included Kraft Phenix in its February 1936 boycott violators list. After Claster informed Kalb, the latter immediately contacted the post's boycott chairman, Sam Spiegel, to chastise him for circulating a name without clearing it with him. Kalb asked Spiegel what proof he had that the company was a violator and suggested that Kraft Phenix's name had been copied from a previously issued list.[72]

After the incident with Kraft, Spiegel conscientiously sent his monthly boycott list to Kalb for clearance.[73] Kalb continued to aid Spiegel in his boycott campaign. When the North Hudson chairman was having trouble with a Union City concern he asked Kalb for help. A Western Union telegram by Kalb to the potential boycott violator settled the issue:

> Understand you contemplate making large order on German merchandise. We are now making up circular containing names of violators of anti-Nazi boycott in Hudson County. Do you think it advisable to include your name? Please advise.[74]

*   *   *

Newark's department stores remained under surveillance by the boycott forces during 1935, L. Bamberger again being the main concern. The national offices of both the JWV and NSANL contacted Kalb whenever they heard that the store was selling German goods. In March 1935, at the behest of the NSANL, Kalb sent ten women into L. Bamberger to go through the entire store in search of German merchandise. According to the report of Mrs. Bessie Ross, there were no German goods in the store.[75] Later in the year J. George Fredman chided Kalb that "Newark has fallen asleep" and that Macy's was again shipping German merchandise to L. Bamberger.[76]

Kalb investigated complaints against Woolworth, Hahne & Co., Sears Roebuck, and Kresge. On a national basis, Woolworth, with its 1,941 stores, had promised to comply with the boycott in March 1934, citing sales resistance to German goods as its rationale. Conversely, Sears Roebuck never agreed to the boycott, despite having a Jewish chairman, Lessing J. Rosenwald.[77] In the Newark cases,

Kalb found that either the charges were without merit or that the stores stopped selling German goods.[78]

Despite its earlier adherence to the boycott, Woolworth continued to buy merchandise in Germany and sell it at branch stores. In Newark, L.Bamberger and Hahne & Co. periodically violated the boycott. Kalb and his allies continued to monitor Newark's department stores throughout the decade. Even if there were some violations, the amount of goods imported from Germany decreased each year of the boycott.

Newark's boycott efforts were the exception to the national and international trend of the boycott movement. Kalb and the many Jewish organizations influenced by his leadership had prevented German-made goods from being sold in most of the city. However, by 1935, there was a decrease in boycott activities in both Europe and the United States. Nazi Germany was making an economic comeback because of its rearmament and an easing of trade rivalries with major European nations. Germany negotiated a barter system with these countries, which obviated the need to deal with companies and individuals. Direct trading between nations made it extremely difficult for European Jews to prosecute the boycott, lest they be accused of being unpatriotic.[79] In the United States, the rivalry between the AJC and the NSANL hurt the boycott effort, as did the knowledge by boycott activists that despite their two years of struggle the Nazis were stronger than ever.

Despite all this, Kalb escalated his boycott activities during 1936 and was the point man for all boycott matters in New Jersey. His correspondence with the JWV, AJC, and NSANL abounds with requests for information on companies that might be violating the boycott. In the course of the year, Kalb traveled to Bergen, Passaic, Hudson, Union, and Middlesex Counties to either investigate or mediate violation complaints. At the same time he was frequently involved in Newark and Essex County boycott matters. Some of the companies Kalb was asked to investigate were huge, such as the Botany Worsted Mills and the Forstmann Woollen Co., both in Passaic.[80] Others were small, such as Nock's Cut-Rate store in Jersey City. Nothing escaped Kalb's attention, even pencils. The major utility in New Jersey, Public Service Electric and Gas Company, wrote in response to a letter from Kalb that the wood pencils it purchased "are all manufactured in the southern part of the United States."[81]

While Kalb was close to a one-man operation, he did receive some help. When he became state chairman of the JWV boycott committee, Kalb appointed Herman Weckstein, a Newark attorney, chairman of the JWV Newark boycott effort. During 1935 and part of 1936, Kalb directed Weckstein in investigations of such German goods as harmonicas, cutlery, flower pots, and baked goods sold at the bakery of Meyer Tulbowitz.[82]

Since 1933, Kalb had unsuccessfully argued for unification of the city's boycott efforts. By 1935, anti-Nazis recognized him throughout New Jersey as the "Boycott Chairman." With his well-earned reputation, Kalb was ready to make another attempt at merging the effort in Newark. The NSANL, which wanted a strong Newark presence, had been unsuccessful in finding a leader with the time, energy, and skills to establish an active Newark group.

Michael Stavitsky, the most prominent Jewish leader in Newark, originally agreed to lead the NSANL. However, time constraints made him give up the job. Others, including Joseph Kraemer and Rabbi Julius Silberfeld, were approached. Why the feisty Kalb was not asked to head a Newark division is not known. Perhaps he did not quite fit the image sought by the NSANL's aristocratic leader, Samuel Untermyer. Despite Untermyer's reservations by 1936 it was obvious to the NSANL that Kalb was the best choice to raise funds, organize, and operate a boycott.

The impetus for Kalb and the NSANL to begin negotiations came from Abraham Harkavy, a young lawyer who headed Temple B'Nai Abraham's boycott committee. Harkavy contacted G. E. Harriman, executive secretary of the NSANL, to offer his group's support. Harriman asked Harkavy to bring his committee to New York for a meeting. [83] Harriman then told Kalb about the proposed gathering and asked him to participate. According to the secretary, the committee could aid Kalb's boycott efforts in Newark.[84] In December they met in New York and began negotiations for a formal tie between Harkavy's committee and the NSANL, which would include an advisory role for Kalb.

The talks lasted several months and brought about an unexpected agreement. Kalb would become president of the Newark Division of NSANL. Harkavy and his committee would work with Kalb as members of NSANL. Kalb would establish a Newark office with full-time secretarial help. The local group would pay for these expenses and in return keep all fund-raising proceeds. Fifty percent of all membership dues collected by the Newark division would be remitted to the national office. To Kalb, the key element in the agreement was the authorization to collect money in the name of the NSANL. With the imprimatur of the NSANL, a nationally respected organization, he hoped to raise sufficient funds to manage a strengthened boycott campaign in the city. A well-financed effort would enable him to unify the Newark boycott forces under the umbrella of the NSANL.

Harriman's major concern was the lack of cooperation between the NSANL national offices and the AJC. Would the situation repeat itself in Newark? Harriman said that in cities outside the New York area local branches of the two groups did cooperate,[85] but Newark was only nine miles from New York.[86] Kalb assured him that he had worked with the Essex AJC in boycott matters and it would welcome participating under an umbrella group.

Enthusiastic about the new arrangement, Kalb quickly gained support for the unification drive and establishment of a Newark division of NSANL. The JWV, the KUVs, and the AJC readily agreed to combine their boycott efforts under Kalb's leadership and the NSANL banner. To mark the event, The JWV honored Kalb at a testimonial dinner at Krueger Hall on April 26, 1936. Over 350 attendees heard speeches from Michael Stavitsky, Congressman Samuel Dickstein, G. E. Harriman, Louis Freeman, and Judge Joseph Siegler.[87]

The day after his dinner, Kalb was back at work on the boycott. For several months he had been pressuring Newark's many beer breweries to cease importing malt, hops, and barrels from Germany. Kalb visited at least two of these establishments—Oldberger and Krueger, receiving promises from both to either stop or limit their German imports.[88] This was the last investigation Kalb made under the aegis of the JWV. For the next four years his boycott activities centered on the NSANL.

Kalb built and maintained a successful boycott movement in the Newark area. Through perseverance and hard work, he enlisted the JWV, AJC, KUVs, and other Jewish organizations to participate in the NSANL boycott. Kalb's success in Newark as a leader, organizer, propagandist, and researcher was unmatched in any other American city.[89]

Notes

1.   Gottlieb, Moshe R., *American Anti-Nazi Resistance, 1933-1941*, New York, 1982, p. 298.

2.   The economic policy of Great Britain toward the colonies was to extract as much income as possible from them. In March 1765 Parliament passed the Stamp Act which

was intended to bring revenue into England by forcing the use in the colonies of stamped forms for all public papers including deeds, leases, and warrants. All business documents would be illegal and void unless written on the stamped paper. The cost of the stamped forms was expensive and had to be paid in cash. This was the first direct tax placed upon the colonists by Great Britain. Up to that time only the legislatures of each colony had taxed their citizens. To fight this measure, colonial businessmen agreed not to buy any British goods until the act was repealed. England's colonial trade fell so precipitously that Manchester manufacturers petitioned Parliament to repeal the law. This was done in February 1766. Thus the first important boycott in American history was successful.

England, to show the colonies who was in charge, passed the next year, duties on glass, paper, tea, and painters' colors. A boycott was called again, and in 1769 the three major ports of entry: Boston, New York, and Philadelphia agreed to joint action in regard to the non-importation of English goods. In 1774 the First Continental Congress met and declared a boycott on all British goods. The opening lines assert:

> To obtain the redress of our grievances... we are of the opinion that a non-importation, non-consumption, and non-exportation agreement, faithfully adhered to, will prove the most speedy, effectual and peacable measures...

See *Americans.Journals of the Continental Congress*, Vol. 1, pp. 75,76 as quoted in *Yad Vashem Studies, III,* 1959, Joseph Tenenbaum, "The Anti-Nazi Boycott Movement in the United States," p. 143.

The boycott stayed in effect until the Revolutionary War was won by the United States.

3.   Green appeared as guest of honor at a NSANL dinner on February 14, 1934 and attacked the Hitler regime for its anti-Semitic and anti-union ideology. He also called for a boycott on German goods. Louis Bamberger, Mrs. Felix Fuld, Joseph Kraemer, Joseph Siegler, and Rabbi Solomon Foster were on the dinner committee. See N.N., 2/15/34, p. 8.

4.   Gottlieb, *American Anti-Nazi Resistance*, p. 30.

5.   Ibid., p. 56.

6.   Ibid., p. 97.

7.   Ibid., p.177.

8.   Ibid., p. 178.

9.   N.N., 5/29/36, p. 4. Within five months, another national organization formed a county division, the Essex Post of the Catholic War Veterans. As with the Essex AJC, their aim was defensive. According to Bishop Thomas J. Walsh founder of the group, the Essex Post would fight communism and other influences seeking to destroy religion, country, and home.

10.   Ibid., 1/8/32, p. 20.

11.   As quoted in Gottlieb, *American Anti-Nazi Resistance*, p. 46.

12.   Dr. Kalb's last Curriculum Vitae, prepared in 1980 when he was eighty-three, contains seven pages. In it are listed sixty awards and honors, including the Vatican Humanitarian Award from Pope Pius XII in 1952, the Rehabilitation Award from the American ORT Federation in 1963, and the Humanitarian Award from the American Medical Association for Service in Vietnam in 1966. Listed as one of twelve items under "other activities" is "President, Non-Sectarian Anti-Nazi League." See, Papers of Dr. S. William Kalb, Curriculum Vitae of S. William Kalb, M.D., 1980.

13.   Interview, Patricia Kalb Einhorn, 1/12/1997.
      The influenza epidemic of 1918 killed 1,747 Newarkers. In contrast during all of World War I, 255 Newarkers were killed in action. See, John T. Cunningham, *Newark*, Newark, 1988, p. 261.

14.   *The Record*, Valparaiso University, 1921, p. 75.

15.   Interview, Patricia Kalb Einhorn, 1/12/97.

16.   Interview, Barbara Kalb Rachlin, 2/3/98.

17.   Ibid.

18.   The author remembers that his father served as the attorney for Newark's Admiral Sampson Lodge, and that his first doctor and dentist also served the lodge.

19. Papers of The Israel Kranken Untersteutzung Verein (KUV), RG 4700, Box 2, Minutebook, 4/18/29-1/9/41, pp. 179, 182, 186, 188, 197, 201, 207, 211. In a nine month period, in 1933 and 1934, Kalb received $350 for his medical services from Israel Verein.

20. N.N., 1/12/34, p. 8.

21. Interview, Rachlin.

22. Interviews, Einhorn and Rachlin.

23. Interview, Rachlin.

24. NSANL, Geographical Files, Box 11, Folder 1, Letter from Irving Piltch to NSANL, 3/16/34; Letter from N.P. Leiter to NSANL, 6/15/34.

25. Ibid., Letter from G.E. Harriman to Rabbi Julius Silberfeld, 10/11/35.

26. The group of officers were the same as those who had been elected in October 1933 for the American League for the Defense of Jewish Rights. However, since the league had been dissolved in December, and Untermyer had not yet reconstituted the Newark branch of the League into the NSANL, the men decided to use the name "Central Committee for the Protection of Human Rights" which had originally been suggested by Kalb.

27. N.N., 4/6/34, p. 4.

28. Israel Verein, *The Israel Verein Messenger*, October 1935, p.1.

29. J.C., 8/13/34, p. 2

30. Ibid., 4/13/34, p. 3

31. Gottlieb, *American Anti-Nazi Resistance*, pp. 135, 136

32. Ibid., pp. 131-134 See also pp. 111-118, 129 for an account of the Macy's incident.

33. JHS, Biographical File, Louis Bamberger.

34. NYT, 8/13/34, p. 3.

35. Ibid., 8/14/34, p. 7.

36. J.C., 8/10/34, p. 6.

37. Ibid., 12/7/34, p. 1.

38. Papers of Dr. S. William Kalb, Report on Boycott Activities in Essex County, 8/8/34, p. 1.

39. Ibid. Copies of daily arrival listings were annotated in Kalb's handwriting for boycott purposes and periodically placed in envelopes throughout the archive. Thus he knew what companies in New Jersey and New York were shipping on German ships, and/or receiving German goods and what the contents of the shipments contained.

40. Ibid., p. 2.

41. N.N., 9/10/34, p. 14.

42. Ibid.

43. Ibid., 9/11/34, p. 18.

44. S.E., 10/7/34, p. 4.

45. N.N., 10/26/34, p. 28; JC, 11/9/34, p. 2. Among the organizations he addressed were the German-Jewish Club, Israel KUV, Erste Bershader KUV, Young Men's Tarnopol Society, Liberty Young Men, United Hebrew Krakower, Chechanovitzer Ladies, Kurlander Camp, Lunizer Ladies, Bershader Ladies, Bialystoker Ladies, Liberty Ladies, Knights of the Round Table, Louis D. Brandeis Lodge, and the Odessa Ladies.

46. Kalb Papers, Letter of Gertrude Levine to Kalb, 9/6/34.

47. Ibid., Letter from Kalb to J. George Fredman, 8/2/34; Report on Boycott Activities in Essex County, 8/8/34.

48. Ibid., Circular from Newark Post No. 1 Minutemen of America, "Buy American Boycott German Made Goods," undated but probably late August, early September, 1934.

49. Ibid., Circular from New Jersey JWV, "Why Do These Firms Continue to Handle Nazi Merchandise or Use Nazi Services?" undated but prior to November 1934.

50. J.C., *JWV Supplement*, 12/7/34, p. 5.

51. Kalb Papers, Letter from Kalb to Weckstein, 2/26/35.

52. Minutes of the Executive Committee, Newark Conference of Jewish Charities, 12/26/34, p. 1.

53. J.C., 1/11/35, p. 7.

54. Ibid., 1/26/35, p. 1; S.C., 2/11/35, p. 8.
55. J.C., 4/20/35, p. 7.
56. JBC, Box I, Folder "Boycott Committee," Letter from Tenenbaum announcing national boycott conference, 9/25/35. The three Newark attendees were Dr. Kalb (representing the JWV), Mrs. Samuel Schulsinger (Hadassah), and Joseph Bohrer (Independent Order Brith Abraham).
57. Kalb Papers, Letter from Kalb to Dr. Joseph Tenenbaum, 9/26/35.
58. Ibid., Letter from Kalb to Bruno Berk, 8/14/35.
59. Ibid., Letter from Kalb to Judge Joseph Siegler, 9/9/35.
60. Ibid., Undated list of delegates, probably 11/35.
61. Ibid., Letter from Kalb to Bruno Berk, 10/6/35.
62. J.C., 11/1/35, p. 4. In an early March 1936 letter to I. Posnansky, secretary of the National AJC Boycott Committee, Kalb said, "It has been very difficult to arrange an open mass meeting with the various organizations to propagate the Boycott." See, Kalb Papers, Letter from Kalb to I. Posnansky, 3/4/36.
63. J.C., 5/22/36, p. 1; N.N., 5/26/36, p. 38.
64. N.N., 12/7/36, p. 7.
65. JBC, Box 5, Folder "S-1937-1938," Letter from Joseph Siegler to Tenenbaum, 11/13/36.
     In response to a letter from Tenenbaum asking about Essex AJC work on the boycott, Siegler tells Tenenbaum that he is referring the letter to Kalb, who "is chairman of the boycott committee of the local Congress section [and] also in charge of boycott work for the NSANL." Siegler adds, "There is very good work being done under Dr. Kalb's leadership, and he will be very glad to report to you about it...For anything further on the subject, I suggest that you communicate with Dr. Kalb."
     Kalb replied to Tenenbaum with a four-page letter outlining boycott activities for twenty-five industries within Essex County. He then remonstrates with Tenenbaum: "at no time during the year has the JBC interested itself sufficiently to send me a letter asking for information about any violators or advising us of any national firms that are dealing in Nazi merchandise, and who may be selling in our area of New Jersey." See, JBC, Box 19, Folder "Newark," Letter from Kalb to Tenenbaum, 11/14/36.
66. Kalb Papers, Letter from Kalb to Sam Spiegel, 3/30/35.
67. Ibid., Letter from Lester Claster to Kalb, 11/2/35.
68. Ibid., Letter from Kalb to Lester Claster, 11/18/35.
69. Ibid.
70. Ibid., Letter from M.L. Bauer to J.R. Moulder, Kraft Phenix Cheese, 11/22/35.
71. Ibid., Report of Research Department to Women's Division, 12/2/35.
72. Ibid., Letter from Kalb to Sam Spiegel, 3/24/36; Letter from Kalb to Dr. David Coyne, 3/24/36.
73. Ibid., Letter from Sam Spiegel to Kalb, 3/23/36.
74. Ibid., Telegram from Kalb to Louis Goldstein, 11/8/35.
75. Ibid. Letter from Samuel Feller to Kalb, 3/5/35; Letter from Kalb to Feller, 3/18/35. According to the investigation, Bambergers' most inexpensive goods came from China and Japan, while the better imported goods were from Italy, England, Czechoslovakia, and Bulgaria.
76. NSANL Papers, Box 11, Folder 1, Letter from J. George Fredman to Kalb, 5/27/35.
77. Gottlieb, *American Anti-Nazi Resistance*, pp. 226-228.
78. Kalb Papers, Letter from Kalb to Woolworth, 11/26/35; Letter from George Harriman to Kalb, 4/21/36; Letter from Kresge to Kalb, 4/11/36; Letter from Kalb to Every Friday Publishing Co., 11/26/35.
79. Ibid., pp. 167,168. Joseph Tenenbaum presents evidence that a year earlier, in mid-1934, that the anti-Nazi boycott made Hitler "uneasy," and that the German foreign minister, Constantin von Neurath, complained that the boycott had contributed to a decrease in German gold reserves. See, *Yad Vashem Studies*, op. cit., p. 151.
80. Kalb Papers, Letter from G.E. Harriman to Kalb, 6/9/36.
81. Ibid., Letter from J.T.Foster to Kalb, 4/27/36.

82. Ibid., Letters from Kalb to Herman B. J. Weckstein, 3/10/36, 3/13/36, 4/2/36, 5/4/36.
     In the Tulbowitz case, Weckstein was proud to report that he had employed Yiddish in
     determining that the baker was selling German goods. Kalb also used other allies in
     Newark for investigative purposes, such as the dentist, Leonard S. Morvay, to check
     whether certain dental supply houses were selling German manufactured equipment.
83. NSANL, Geographic Files, Box 2, Folder 2, Letter from Abraham Harkavy to G.E.
     Harriman, 11/27/35; Letter from E.G. Harriman to Abraham Harkavy, 12/13/35.
84. Kalb Papers, Letter from G.E. Harriman to Kalb, 12/14/35.
85. Samuel Untermyer Papers, Box 1/2, Letter from G.E. Harriman to Samuel Untermyer,
     6/29/35 The St. Louis Council of the AJC sent a $500 contribution to the national
     NSANL with a note of appreciation "of the fine work you have been doing."
86. An example of the hostility in the New York area between the NSANL and AJC is
     exemplified in a letter from the national NSANL office to Kalb. It contains a remark
     about the Research Director of the Boycott Committee of the AJC as follows:
         Posnansky called us a little while ago and tried to chisel some information. The
         conniving methods by which he attempts to secure important data is hardly ex-
         pected of one doing boycott work for any organization.
     Kalb Papers, Letter from F. Berkowitz to Kalb, 3/2/36.
87. J.C., 5/1/36, p. 1.
88. Kalb Papers, Letter from Kalb to NSANL, 3/11/36; Letter from Matthew F. Dornes to
     Kalb, 4/14/36; Letter from G.E. Harriman to Kalb, 4/27/36.
89. NSANL, Boxes 4, 5, 7, 10, 17, 18, 19. Other than in New York, major cities with
     active boycott movements were Chicago, Detroit, Boston, Philadelphia, Cleveland,
     and Pittsburgh. These groups worked with paid executives or with a committee of
     volunteers. Only Cleveland and Detroit had boycott movements as effective as
     Newark's, and this is at least partly because these were the only two cities where the
     Jewish Federation participated.
         Chicago, Boston, and Philadelphia set up boycott groups in 1933 which lasted
     several years and then became inactive. Chicago set up an NSANL division in 1938
     which operated through 1939. Boston organized a NSANL division in April 1939
     which lasted until January 1940. Philadelphia's NSANL division was organized in June
     1938 and closed its office in September 1939. Pittsburgh organized a NSANL affiliate,
     the Anti-Nazi Boycott Council in 1935, with help from the Pittsburgh American Jewish
     Congress. The council received significant help from labor unions such as the United
     Mine Workers and the Central Labor Union, both of which sent out anti-Nazi boycott
     fliers to their members. The council does not seem to have operated after 1936.
         Detroit organized the League for Defense of Jewish Rights in 1933 which was
     renamed the League for Human Rights and remained active until June 1940. The
     Board of Governors of the Jewish Welfare Federation of Detroit was behind this
     group for its duration. The league issued bulletins, sometimes including boycott
     violators. Cleveland, the home of Rabbi Abba Hillel Silver and friend and supporter
     of Untermyer and the NSANL, set up the League for Defense of Human Rights in
     January 1934 renamed it the League for Human Rights and operated it through most
     of 1940. Rabbi Silver was its first chairman and with his involvement in the Jewish
     Welfare Federation of Cleveland it received Federation support until 1940. In the
     scope of its work it closely resembled the Newark NSANL. Detroit's boycott group
     was unique in that more than 60 percent of its board members were Christian. The
     New York NSANL office ran the entire country and in the city concentrated on
     department stores and other large businesses. There were several branches, notably in
     the Bronx, which existed for only a short period of time.

5

The Failure of Liberalism

On April 29, 1932, Newark's Contemporary Club met at the YWCA on Washington Street. The featured speaker was thirty-two year-old Luke Hamilton Garner, minister of the city's Universalist Church of the Redeemer.[1] His topic was "the New Patriotism," which he defined as ultra-nationalist and militaristic. In his three years in Newark, Garner had earned the reputation as a leader in the fight for economic and racial justice. Because of this, Amelia Berndt Moorfield had invited him to share his views with the Contemporary, Newark's premiere women's organization.

Moorfield, fifty-three, was the head of both Newark's and New Jersey's peace movements. On that afternoon, there was only one man at the meeting other than Garner, Dr. Frank Kingdon, minister of Calvary Methodist Church of East Orange. Kingdon, thirty-five, had come to New Jersey about the same time as Garner, and like him, had gained a reputation as an outspoken liberal. Kingdon's presence at the meeting reflected the informal coalition formed by Kingdon, Garner, and Moorfield. Pacifism and support for society's persecuted bound the three together. An anomaly of the coalition was that the two clergymen were socialists, whereas Moorfield was a Republican Party activist.

Garner, after his presentation, moved to the rear of the room to converse with Kingdon and Moorfield. The trio caused many heads to turn. The two clerics were both handsome and over six feet tall. Garner was described at the time as "tall, lean, with fiery red curly hair."[2] Kingdon, thin and handsome with straight brown hair, had a patrician mien. Both towered over the five-foot-three Moorfield who looked matronly in her black dress and white lace collar.

Garner, Moorfield, and Kingdon personified Newark's liberalism. Each enjoyed a platform from which to espouse his or her ideology, and each received coverage from Newark's two daily newspapers. Garner, pastor of one of Newark's influential churches, was founder of the Community Forum, which in presenting well- known and controversial speakers attracted Newark liberals. Moorfield was the legendary leader of the city's women's suffrage movement. Kingdon sponsored weekly open meetings to discuss social and political problems at his East Orange church. After his 1934 appointment as president of Dana College, one of Newark's two small liberal arts colleges, Kingdon became a leader of the city's liberals.

Hitler's ascension to the German chancellorship in January 1933 resulted in Nazi outrages against German Jews and Nazi-sponsored anti-Semitic incidents in large American cities including Newark. Garner, Moorfield, and Kingdon became Newark's most outspoken Christian anti-Nazis. Yet this highly visible liberal trio was unsuccessful in influencing their audiences to adopt anti-Nazi policies.

The reasons for this failure on the part of Christian Newark include: traditional Christian anti-Semitism; accusations of pro-Communist sympathy; the position of Newark's Catholic Church, which was always anti-Communist but, until America's entry into World War II, seldom anti-Nazi; and the fear of offending the city's large German-American population which might interpret anti-Nazism as pro-Jewish and anti-German rather than as humanitarian.

What makes the lack of Christian support for anti-Nazism even more troubling is that although Newark was not a liberal city, there were liberal individuals and organizations within the city. Liberalism in the 1930s supported the underdog, and Jews in Germany certainly fit that description. Likewise, the Jews of Newark, who were mostly poor and working class, were underdogs in the battle against the anti-Semitism of American Nazi groups.

To understand the failure of Newark's liberals to fight Nazism in the 1930s, it is necessary to assess liberalism's influence as well as its strengths and weaknesses. It will also be helpful to explore the careers of Kingdon, Garner, and Moorfield, leaders of the Christian liberals.

Amelia Moorfield, Newark's pre-eminent liberal woman was involved in anti-Nazi activities, including the NSANL boycott. She spoke out against Nazism to the Newark branch of WILPF and to the American League Against War and Fascism (ALAWF), with its mainly Jewish membership.[3] However, she was unable to transmit her anti-Nazism to the predominantly Christian women's groups that contained the bulk of the city's liberals.[4]

Luke Garner and Frank Kingdon preached anti-Nazism to a Christian community that was conservative and, save a few examples, unsympathetic to Jews. Garner and Kingdon's main admirers in Newark were the few liberal Jews who saw the pair as the "only Gentiles in the city speaking out for them."[5] The two men were far and away the most active of the Christian clergymen participating in the paltry number (approximately six) of interfaith events in Newark between the 1933 outrages against the Jews in Nazi Germany and the November 1938 Kristallnacht pogrom.[6]

The Protestant elite of the city was well educated and fully informed on Nazism's domestic and foreign advances. Many of them were descendants of Newark's Puritan founders, and they retained a major influence on the city's economic and social fabric. Although many were now living in Newark's suburbs, and although they had lost control of the municipal government, these Puritan descendants still controlled the city's Republican party, as well as the banks, insurance companies, and larger industrial concerns. From the Newark Board of Trade, the Essex Club, and their media voice, the *Newark Evening News,*[7] they set the city's economic, social, and cultural agenda.

Was Newark's Protestant elite anti-Semitic? Not overtly, since they maintained correct behavior in business and personal contacts. However, they harbored traditional Christian attitudes towards Jews, and discrimination occurred, particularly in the social sphere. The Essex Club, the major bastion of Newark's Protestant business class, had no Jewish members in the 1930s.[8] The *Newark Evening News* was indifferent at best to Jewish interests except during particularly horrifying events in Germany such as the 1933 anti-Jewish riots and Kristallnacht. In February 1935, Rabbi Julius Silberfeld publicly chided the *News* for its editorial, "Hitler's Second Year," which praised the Führer for unifying Germany.[9]

It is not surprising that Newark's three major liberals of the 1930s, Moorfield, Garner, and Kingdon, all were born and spent their formative years far from the city. A fourth well-known liberal, Dr. Wells P. Eagleton, one of the city's most prominent physicians and civic leaders, was also born and raised outside of Newark.[10]

* * *

The Great Depression threw millions of people out of work and posed a significant threat to American democracy. While responses ranged from fascist schemes on the right to communism on the left, an overwhelming majority of Americans eschewed these extremes and struggled to find a way to deal with the Depression within existing democratic institutions.

When Franklin Delano Roosevelt established the New Deal, the Depression was attacked with liberal solutions. The New Dealers were liberals who wanted to save democracy by helping the country's increasingly impoverished and unemployed citizens. Roosevelt's policies soon transformed both Garner and Kingdon from socialists into New Deal Democrats. Moorfield supported many New Deal measures but remained a loyal Republican.

FDR's New Deal liberalism ignored certain liberal tenets. Political reform, including the fight against governmental corruption, was not on FDR's agenda, since he needed the continued political support of big city bosses like Frank Hague of New Jersey. Roosevelt also avoided contentious social issues such as racial equality, since his New Deal coalition included Southern Democrats. When FDR took office in 1933, it was economic institutions that most Americans wanted reformed. Liberalism as defined by FDR was "plain English for a changed concept of the duty and responsibility of government toward economic life."[11]

Economic reform does not fully capture the resonance of liberalism in the 1930s. The growth of fascism throughout the Western world, with its attendant wars of conquest, palpable social ills manifested in the continuing lynchings in the South, and the industrial exploitation of women and children gave rise to an unprecedented range of responses. Students, teachers, clergymen, political activists, and ordinary citizens participated in efforts to help those threatened by violence, intolerance, and poverty. Many efforts were devoted to a single issue—unemployment, pacifism, African-American rights, worker's rights, or women's issues. On the other hand, since the problems were often overlapping, some organizations, especially women's groups, became involved in a wide range of political, social, and economic issues.

Newark's ethnic groups first embraced Roosevelt and then his New Deal. Presidential election results bear this out. New York Governor Alfred E. Smith received 10,000 more votes in Newark than the Republican Herbert Hoover in the 1928 presidential election (68,586 to 58,901). In 1932, after three years of the Depression, FDR beat President Hoover in Newark by 32,000 votes (76,796 to

44,883). After almost four years of the New Deal, Roosevelt beat the Republican Alf Landon in 1936 by 52,000 votes (99,277 to 37,495).[12]

It was FDR's definition of liberalism that captured the hearts and minds of Newark's white ethnics. Beaten down by the Depression, they welcomed New Deal economic measures that provided welfare, governmental work, pensions, and hope for a better future. On the other hand, they neglected tenets of liberalism such as equality for African-Americans and for women, political reform, and pacifism; the first two because of racist and patriarchal attitudes, and the second two because of disinterest.

The white ethnic groups that arrived in Newark during the nineteenth and early twentieth centuries were conservative. Germans quickly assimilated into the city's economic and political life and by the end of the nineteenth century had already elected their first mayor and gained control of the city's board of aldermen. By the 1930s, except for social, athletic, and singing societies, German Americans were indistinguishable from the city's other Protestants. The Depression affected them less than the city's other groups because they were employed primarily as civil servants, skilled workers, and as business owners.

Irish Catholics did not achieve the economic success of the Germans. However, by the second decade of the twentieth century they were challenging them for political control of the city and its patronage. Hard hit by the Depression, the city's Irish Catholics, already Democratic voters because of the 1928 candidacy of Al Smith, flocked to Roosevelt and the New Deal. Despite their support of the New Deal and their role in Newark's labor unions, the Irish remained conservative, largely because of the influence of the Roman Catholic Church whose fear of communism made it oppose social activism.

The bulk of Italians arrived in the early twentieth century. Because they were not native English speakers, they were slower to integrate into Newark's political life. The Depression harmed Newark's Italian Americans more than any other white ethnic group because of their preponderance as unskilled laborers. Mussolini's fascism had already attracted some Newark Italians in the 1920s, but more joined various fascist groups in the 1930s looking for a way out of the Depression. Over a score of Italian political clubs were founded in the 1930s, most under the banner of individuals. These clubs were parochial in nature and centered on political patronage and social activities. Newark's Italian Americans, including most of the fascists, were enthusiastic backers of Roosevelt and the New Deal. Like the Irish, the Italians were basically conservative eschewing social liberalism.

The Jews who immigrated to Newark in the second half of the nineteenth and first quarter of the twentieth centuries did not espouse liberalism either. German Jews, who arrived in America in the mid-1800s, quickly gained economic success and adopted the dominant conservatism and Republicanism. Many Eastern European Jews, arriving in great numbers between the 1880s and World War I, were accustomed to the political process from their experiences in Eastern Europe. Until the Depression, many followed the lead of German Jews and voted Republican. However, from then on, most became Roosevelt and New Deal supporters. Newark Jews who were politically active either adopted the self-interest of the two major political parties or brought to the city the socialism of Russia and Poland. A minority became communists or sympathizers.

The Depression hurt African Americans more than any other ethnic group in Newark. By 1932, African Americans, although comprising 8.8 percent of Newark's population, made up over one-third of the welfare cases (2,080 out of 6,186). This situation continued throughout the 1930s—by the end of the decade African-American families constituted 37.5 percent of the relief cases. Private relief agencies such as the Salvation Army and the Goodwill Home and Rescue Mission housed indigent whites but not African Americans. The Family Department of the American Red Cross and the Newark Female Charitable Society also discriminated against African Americans. Only the Urban League tended to the African-American community in the city. The Director of the New Jersey Urban League in Newark, Thomas J. Puryear, stated that on one day in December 1931, he had 112 African-American Newarkers in his office that had not eaten in from one to five days.[13]

Newark's African-American working class supported Roosevelt despite his failure to attack racial discrimination in America. The small middle class retained its Republican affiliation that African Americans had adopted after the Civil War. The great majority of African Americans was so beaten down economically and socially that they could not afford the luxury of liberalism. Harold Lett, Puryear's successor as director of Newark's Urban League, was an exception. He became the city's most influential African-American liberal voice.

* * *

Of the four political parties that ran candidates for office—Republicans, Democrats, communists, socialists—only the latter could be termed liberal. Republicans and Democrats were interested in government contracts and patronage rather than ideology. Communists often supported liberal positions but did so to advance party interests, mainly to gain the membership and/or sympathy of unionists, pacifists, African Americans, and others dissatisfied with American social, economic, or political policies. Newark's Socialist Party adopted the entire range of liberal positions, but was largely ineffective because students, who made up the core of its activists, followed the lead of Norman Thomas, Socialist Party chairman, whose agenda was national and international in scope and included civil liberties, the rights of migrant workers, and pacifism. This agenda cut the party off from Newark's trade union socialists who were older and whose leaders focused on bread and butter issues.

Most union members in Newark were involved with economic issues rather than with ideology or politics. The Essex Trades Council, composed of skilled workers, was the strongest labor force in the city and the most political. It was moderate rather than liberal despite the presence of secret communists—who didn't acknowledge their party membership—operating in some of the locals. Many trade union socialists worked in the needle trades, had Bundist and/or Workmen's Circle ties, and spoke Yiddish. Among the communist union activists were members of the International Worker's Order, a communist faction that left the Workmen's Circle in 1930.

The arrival of the Congress of Industrial Organizations (CIO) in Newark in 1936 added to the conflict between the Socialist and Communist parties, with each endeavoring to gain a strong foothold in the nascent industrial labor movement. The year before, John L. Lewis and Sidney Hillman had founded Labor's Non-Partisan League to engage in political activity favorable to industrial unionists.[14] A Newark unit of that group did not form until 1938, when Jack Lerner became its president. Thereafter, the group, under communist influence, cooperated with liberal and leftist causes in the Newark area but failed to attract a mass base.

Newark's educational system, with few exceptions, was not liberal, since it was staffed largely by conservative Protestant (including German) and Irish Catholic teachers and administrators.[15] Politically active high school students gravitated toward either the Young People's Socialist League (YPSL) or the Young Communist League

(YCL). This was especially true of South Side, a predominantly Jewish high school, where each group had about 100 members. The five small colleges in the city were minimally active until Frank Kingdon became president of Dana College, a small liberal arts college, in 1934 and then in 1936 led the merger of the five schools into Newark University. He encouraged political diversity, including liberal, socialist, and even communist activity, among the student body and faculty. Eventually there were several hundred activists at the university.

The American Civil Liberties Union (ACLU) was the most influential liberal organization in Newark during the prewar period. The ACLU's academics and lawyers saw free speech as the most pressing issue facing America in these years. Nazism was to be deplored and even condemned, but the Nazis' civil liberties were to be defended. When Nazi propaganda calling for the destruction of Jews was prohibited by local and state laws, the ACLU attacked these laws in the courts. The belief that free speech is an absolute right was shared by many Newark liberals of the pre-World War II era who failed to recognize the threat of Nazism.

The ACLU had an unofficial presence in Newark as early as 1934, when Kingdon and two associates served as an *ad hoc* executive board of the New Jersey Committee of the ACLU. The first correspondence between Newark and the national office related to the breakup of a Nazi meeting in Elizabeth.[16] In less than two years, the New Jersey ACLU had a Newark office and about 100 dues-paying members. Serving on the state board were Luke Garner, Dr. Milton Konvitz, and Helen Stevenson, all well known Newark liberals.[17] Another board member was Abraham Isserman, a Newark lawyer, who served as general counsel to the group. Also on the ACLU national board, Isserman was a secret member of the American Communist Party.[18]

A smaller and less influential liberal group was the German-American League for Culture, founded in 1935 to combat Nazism in America and to foster and preserve German culture. Its early leaders were liberals and socialists affiliated with pro-labor German-American organizations. The Anti-Defamation League (ADL) of B'Nai Brith was a financial and organizational supporter, and Jews were active in the organization. There were fifteen branches operating in the United States by the late 1930s. Almost from its inception, German communists attempted to wrest control of the league. According to the FBI, communists gained control of the national office in 1938.[19]

The Newark branch of the League had about forty members and several affiliated "sick benefit" groups. Adolph Friederich, an outspoken non-Communist anti-Nazi, led the Newark branch from its inception in 1935 through 1939.[20] He fought Nazi influence among German Americans in the Newark area, and at the same time, supported Jewish causes in the face of the growing Nazi menace. However, the group's focus and membership were too narrow to attract substantial backing in Newark, and it served primarily as an irritant to the Nazis.

* * *

Women's organizations were the major component of Newark's liberalism. Most of these groups were created in the first two decades of the twentieth century in the wake of the women's suffrage movement. With the February, 1920 ratification of the Nineteenth Amendment, it was hoped that a women's voting bloc would solve society's ills.[21] However, no such bloc arose, and society's ills were addressed by fewer American citizens than before World War I.

The "Roaring Twenties" provided escapism from the tensions the war and its aftermath. Women, like men, were more interested in self-gratification than social and political activism. Contrary to the suffragists' expectations, few women exercised their right to vote during the 1920s, and when they did, they voted like their husbands. The suffrage movement splintered into many groups with often competing interests. As a result of the conservative political climate, women's groups saw their memberships decrease.[22]

The Depression reversed the decline of interest in social and political issues. In the 1930s, women's groups became both creators and transmitters of the liberal agenda. In Newark, women became leaders in the union, peace, and radical movements. As mothers, they backed child labor laws; as wives they backed wage, hour, and pension legislation; and as wives and mothers they backed efforts to prevent war. Since women knew the sting of discrimination, many of them also sought fairer treatment of African Americans. Jews were obviously under attack in both Germany and in America. Thus women's groups should have included anti-Nazism in their liberal agenda.

Women became knowledgeable in international affairs as part of their opposition to war. Certainly they knew of Hitler's persecution of German Jews, which was well publicized from his first days in office. Likewise, they took note of Newark's Nazis and their opponents in the front-page headlines of both Newark dailies. The women were familiar with other anti-Semites such as Father Charles E. Coughlin, the radio preacher who castigated both President Roosevelt and the Jews on his nation-wide broadcasts each Sunday.

Four of Newark women's organizations stand out as liberal institutions during the 1930s—the Women's International League for Peace and Freedom (WILPF), the Contemporary Club, the Business and Professional Women's Club (BPWC), and the National Council of Jewish Women. WILPF began as a peace group; the next two as social and charitable groups; and the National Council of Jewish Women as an "immigration aid" organization. All four were well informed on current events, active in their community, and progressive. It was no coincidence that Amelia Moorfield was active in the three secular groups and cooperated with the National Council of Jewish Women, especially on peace issues.

* * *

Amelia Berndt was born in Newport, Kentucky in 1876, the only child of Caroline and Gustave Berndt. As a youngster, she developed sympathy for the area's illiterate African Americans, and remembered reading letters to them. She also recalled collecting shoes from the more comfortable residents of her town to give to the poor (African American and white). She aspired to a career in social work or teaching.

The Berndt family moved to Newark when Amelia was a young adult. She married Frank Moorfield, a wealthy inventor and manufacturer of watch components. She gave birth to her only child, Hannah, in 1909. She enjoyed homemaking and also held a part-time job in her husband's factory.

Moorfield began her volunteer work in 1914 with the Newark Branch of the Women's Political Union (WPU).[23] The WPU, a national women's suffrage group, had organized a Newark chapter in 1908. It hoped to achieve women's voting rights through an amendment to the United States Constitution. A rival suffrage group, the New Jersey Women's Suffrage Association, was successful in getting a women's suffrage amendment to the New Jersey Constitution on the ballot in 1915. The WPU decided to back this amendment and Moorfield, already financial secretary of the state organization, became chief fundraiser for the effort. She also became an authority

on the amendment so she could be a source of information to suffragists in debates with opponents.

Despite the efforts of Moorfield and her cohorts, the state amendment failed. She then turned her attention to a United States constitutional amendment.[24] From 1915 to 1920, Moorfield worked with
the WPU to raise funds and educate the public on the necessity of
women's suffrage. After ratification of the Nineteenth Amendment
in 1920, the WPU merged with the newly formed League of Women
Voters (LWV). The Newark branch of the WPU, largest in the state,
gave its property to the league, and Florence Peshine Eagleton, president of the branch, became the first president of Newark's LWV.[25]
Moorfield helped found both the New Jersey LWV and its Newark
branch (as late as the mid-1930s she was president of the Newark
LWV and a board member of the state LWV).[26]

Frank Moorfield died in 1923, leaving Amelia with a substantial
inheritance. Financially independent and able to devote her life to
organizational work, she was experienced in organizing, fund raising, and propagandizing. She decided that the peace movement would
be her major cause. Moorfield joined WILPF, and in 1925 was one
of the founders of its New Jersey branch. She worked with the organization until her death in 1950. WILPF was founded in 1919 by
Jane Addams as a successor to the Women's Peace Party, which
Addams had established in 1915 to keep America out of World War
I. Disarmament for peace was WILPF's first priority.

Moorfield was elected state vice-chair of WILPF and her daughter, Hannah, secretary in 1926.[27] The next year she was made chairman, a post she would hold for over a decade. Moorfield proceeded
to organize WILPF by congressional districts, instructing the leader
in each district to direct letter-writing campaigns to its U.S. Representative. This tactic, along with free air time offered by radio stations, allowed WILPF to become the most powerful force in New
Jersey's peace movement.

When the Japanese invaded China in 1932—in violation of the
1928 Kellogg-Briand Pact—Moorfield urged the United States to
work with the League of Nations to localize the conflict. In April
1934, she told her members: "With militarism again gaining the ascendancy in Europe and the Far East, it behooves America to take
the lead in reestablishing world peace."[28] Her slogan "Do not give
way to pessimism" became a rallying cry for peace advocates
throughout the country.[29]

Cooperation between WILPF and other groups was the hallmark of Moorfield's strategy. This was facilitated by her active role in many Newark women's social and advocacy groups. These organizations included: the LWV, which worked for political reforms, particularly expansion of the state civil service system, and for the improvement of women's and children's working conditions; the New Jersey Consumer's League, which had as its sole agenda improvement of working conditions for women and children (its state office was in Newark); the Contemporary; the Newark Interracial Council; the Newark Urban League; the Newark Branch of the BPWC; and the New Jersey League of Women Shoppers.[30]

By the mid-1930s, Moorfield's influence was at its peak. She was profiled in a book on twenty-seven successful New Jersey citizens. Of the subjects, only three were women, all were Protestants, and about half were from Newark. In her interview for the profile, Moorfield took exception to being described as a "welfare worker." She said her role was to provide women with information and education in order to manage the crisis of the Depression. [31]

Moorfield carefully followed the national WILPF line on all issues. In domestic affairs, she supported interracial cooperation and legislation for the protection of women and children in the workplace, both of which had long-standing support from both the WILPF and suffragists. Since WILPF existed to promote peace, it opposed aggressors throughout the world, including the Nationalists in Spain, the Japanese in China, the Italians in Ethiopia, and Nazism everywhere. However, with the outbreak of World War II in September 1939, WILPF muted its opposition to the aggressors and instead concentrated on preventing the United States from entering the conflict.

Moorfield reported to the WILPF board in 1935 that the Newark BPWC was cooperating with it on a number of legislative and other issues.[32] This club, founded in 1921 with ninety-six charter members, was an outgrowth of a group of women who worked in Newark during World War I in influential positions. By 1928 the club had affiliated with both state and national federations of business and professional women.[33] The club's constitution provided for a non-sectarian and non-partisan membership devoted to promoting the interests of and networking among business and professional women. Its charter members were mainly Protestants who continued to run the club until after World War II. The club's first Jewish member, Esther Untermann, was admitted in 1933.

The group's roster remained at just over 100 for most of the 1930s. Despite this relatively small number (compared to almost 400 at the Consumer's League and over 1,000 at the Contemporary) most of its members worked in high-level influential positions.[34]

The club's original activities included sending girls to summer camp, scholarships for young women for professional schools and colleges, student loans, milk money for poor high school girls, and Christmas baskets for "old ladies."[35] The Depression changed the club's mission from predominantly charitable and social to political and social action. Amelia Moorfield was a leader in this change.

An active member of the Inter-Racial Council of Newark, Moorfield invited BPWC members to the city's annual Race-Relations Sunday. She asked them to attend Frank Kingdon's Roundtable discussions at Dana College, which featured controversial political topics. Moorfield worked on many women's issues that were under the domain of the New Jersey Legislature. Using her suffrage background, Moorfield convinced the BPWC to engage in letter-writing campaigns to legislators to achieve its aims. Some of the issues on which the BPWC used this approach were the regulation of night work for women; increase in the percentage of state jobs currently under civil service; elimination of the "veteran's preference" on civil-service tests; opposition to limiting women to a forty hour week; and prevention of anti-birth-control legislation.[36]

Moorfield encouraged her fellow BPWC members to become active in the peace movement. She invited representatives of the Institute on the Cause and Cure of War to meet with BPWC members, some of whom she later invited to the Institute's annual convention. She urged members to attend a Contemporary meeting to hear Norman Thomas speak on disarmament and peace, and to lobby Congress to deny relief funds for the building of armories.[37]

If Moorfield spoke to the club against Nazism or tried to get them to support the anti-Nazi boycott, she was unsuccessful; there is no record that the Business and Professional Women's Club of Newark ever officially discussed or took a stand on domestic or foreign Nazism.

Amelia Moorfield was also active in Newark's Contemporary Club, which unlike the WILPF and the BPWC began as a social group for upper-middle-class women. The Contemporary was founded in 1909 by thirty-three women from Newark's most prominent families. The group reached its pinnacle in the 1920s when Newark, like most of America, enjoyed a booming economy. Because of the Depression, the Contemporary's 1931 membership showed a decrease of several hundred to just over 1,000, including eight Italian-Americans and twelve Jews. There was also one Jew on the nine-person executive board, Mrs. Abram Unger.[38]

With the onset of the Depression, the group's activities turned to political, social, and economic problems. The legislative committee studied pending measures, endorsing some bills and protesting others. Its main interests were child welfare, unemployment relief, and retirement pensions. A prime example of the international affairs committee's work was a campaign for the entry of the United States into the World Court.[39] Early in the Nazi regime, the Contemporary heard a former German Army officer, Colonel Roddle, speak. He told them how Hitler had saved Germany from the communists but, with the threat of prison and the firing squad, had robbed his people of free thought, free speech, and free action.[40] Despite sponsoring this anti-Nazi event, the Contemporary, like the BPWC, never put itself on record to protest either domestic or foreign Nazism.

The failure of the two women's groups to speak out against Nazism indicates that their liberalism did not extend to sympathy for Jews. Additionally, World War I had not made the world safe for democracy, ingraining in them a pacifism that was stronger than any distaste of Hitlerism.

The National Council of Jewish Women is older than the other three groups, having been founded in New York in 1896. The Newark section was organized in 1912 by women from the German-Jewish elite, including Sadie Levy Foster, wife of Temple B'Nai Jeshurun's Rabbi, Solomon Foster.[41] The council's purpose is to help refugees. Like other women's groups in the 1930s, it also raised money for needy children; worked with the deaf and blind; backed legislation strengthening women's rights, including birth control; and worked with peace groups. In this latter regard the council came into contact with Amelia Moorfield.

When German-Jewish refugees started to arrive in the United States in 1933, it was natural for the Conference of Jewish Charities to turn to Newark's National Council of Jewish Women chapter for resettlement aid. The two groups were intertwined, with many of the conference's board members married to women who were active in the council. The council organized a service bureau with a full-time staff to work with the refugees, in 1937 it handled 1,774 cases alone.[42] The volume of cases became so great that the conference established a coordinating committee to help with the work, which included representatives of the council, conference, and the Jewish Social Service.[43] Within a year the coordinating committee had allocated funds to the council to hire more social workers.[44]

Unlike the Contemporary and the BPWC, the council took a stand on Nazism. It established an educational program called "Contemporary Jewish Affairs" to educate Jewish women on how to best combat Nazi and other anti-Semitic propaganda. Among its speakers were Luke Garner and Frank Kingdon. The council was also a dues-paying organizational member of the Non-Sectarian Anti-Nazi League (NSANL).[45] Undeniably, the council was a liberal organization that was also anti-Nazi.

Other than the German-American League for Culture and the National Council of Jewish Women, there were no liberal institutions or organizations in Newark that espoused anti-Nazism. However, neither of these groups had the influence to spread anti-Nazism. Rather it was left to Garner, Kingdon, and Moorfield, all of whom had city-wide platforms and were sympathetic to the Jewish predicament, to try to influence Newark's citizens to adopt an anti-Nazi stance.

* * *

When Kingdon and Garner arrived in Newark in the late 1920s, Amelia Moorfield befriended the two men, both of whom were young enough to be her sons. Kingdon and Garner were dynamic speakers who preached a gospel of brotherhood, peace, and social awareness. Moorfield gave the clerics exposure to her women's groups through speaking engagements. Garner and Kingdon's liberalism was anathema to much of the male Protestant community, but within the confines of Newark's women's groups, the clerics' views were more than merely acceptable, they were stirring.

Garner and Kingdon were both from poor families in which religion played an important role. Brilliant students, they both overcame obstacles to obtain an education and were elected to Phi Beta Kappa in college. During their careers they were educators and volunteer social workers. Both were excellent preachers and liked to be center stage.

By 1933, Garner and Kingdon had close ties to the Jewish community in Newark and had made their anti-Nazi views known. A difference between the two was that Garner was satisfied in the city and did not seek a wider audience, whereas Kingdon, an excellent writer and perceptive political commentator, eventually left Newark for the national stage.

Garner's sons remember that there was a mutual attraction between Jews and their parents. David Garner remembers telling his classmates at Ridge Street School in Newark that he was Jewish. When he told his mother, she laughed and subsequently told the story to all her Jewish friends. David said the Jewish population of Newark had a substantial influence on the Garners, and if it hadn't been for the Jews, his parents would have been "intellectually dead." David pointed out that he had married two Jewish women.[46] Another son, Peter, does not remember seeing Italians or Irish in his parents' house, only Jews and a few African Americans.[47]

Kingdon spoke and dressed like an aristocrat and was much less approachable than Garner.[48] Most of his Newark friends were upper-middle-class Protestants. However, by the late 1930s when he moved from Newark, he had become friends with several wealthy Jewish New Yorkers. One of these was Peter Strauss, owner of the radio station WMCA. After his divorce from his first wife, in 1940 Kingdon married a Jewish actress, Marcella Markham. He then moved permanently to New York City, where most of his friends and business associates were Jews.

Garner and Kingdon were outspoken advocates for liberal causes in a city still run by a conservative male Protestant elite. They were spokesmen for racial justice, toleration of leftist ideologies, and support for Jewish causes. As their voices resounded beyond their institutions and their stature grew among Newarkers with liberal inclinations, they became commensurately disliked by the city's establishment.

Members of the establishment who consistently supported liberal causes could be counted on the fingers of one hand. Thus, the two clerics had few influential defenders. Kingdon left the clergy voluntarily in 1934 to become president of Dana College and its successor, Newark University. In 1941, his liberalism cost him this job. Garner was fired by the trustees of his congregation in 1937 over charges of "radicalism," and became the executive director of Newark's Labor Relations Board.

* * *

Lucius Hamilton Garner was born in 1899 in Waverly, Alabama.[49] The name Lucius was soon abandoned in favor of Luke. His parents were third-generation Americans of Scotch-Irish descent. His father was a pecan farmer who also served as a lay Congregationalist preacher. His parents entrusted Luke's primary education to an itinerant minister of the same denomination who was reputed to possess a brilliant mind. Luke enrolled in a local high school and after only one year sat for the state teaching exam. At sixteen, he was awarded the highest honors for the test. At seventeen, he was appointed principal of his hometown grade school, which had 150 students and three teachers.

Garner successfully completed the school year as principal. However, the position's low pay, World War I's demands for manpower, and Garner's technical aptitude all contributed to his becoming an electrician for the United States Steel Corporation in Birmingham, Alabama. He stayed there until 1921, saving enough money to enroll at a theological college. Although the work was infinitely harder at the mill, he earned much more money than he would have as a principal.

In 1921 Garner entered St. Lawrence University in Canton, New York, from which he graduated Phi Beta Kappa in 1925. Two years later, he received a B.D. from St. Lawrence's Theological School, delivering the commencement address. Garner's first pulpit was in Potsdam, New York at the Universalist Church, where he remained until 1928. He then became Associate Minister at the Universalist Church of the Redeemer in Newark, a provisional position to judge whether Garner would succeed Dr. Henry R. Rose, the long-time minister who was to retire in a year.

For a year, Garner served the congregants of his church diligently. He also began to make a name for himself in Newark from his work with volunteer social-service groups. One of his early interests was marriage counseling, an activity that presaged his later career as a labor mediator.[50] Dr. Rose and the congregation were duly impressed by the mature twenty-nine-year old and in April 1929 elected him their new minister. He was installed as minister of the Church of the Redeemer on May 1, 1929.

At the Church of the Redeemer, Garner became a force in Newark's social, political, and intellectual life. He believed the church should be an educational medium for all, especially the underprivileged. To this end, in November 1929, barely six months into his tenure, Garner created the Community Forum, a Sunday night program at which people of all races and religions were invited to hear speakers voice their opinions on critical issues of the day.

The Community Forum at the Redeemer Church lasted almost eight years. The Forum was a success from its inception, attracting crowds of up to 1,000 that filled the church and its social hall to standing room only. The average crowd numbered about 800, and there were always at least 500 in attendence.[51] The Forum's first board of trustees consisted of twenty-two members, including members of the Redeemer congregation, as well as seven Jews, two African Americans, and seven women.

The Forum's opening program, on November 3, 1929, was a debate: "Is Liberalism a Menace?" Arthur Garfield Hays argued in the negative and V.F. Calverton (according to the promotional flyer, author of "Sex in Civilization") argued in the affirmative.[52] One of the most controversial issues the Forum debated was African-American rights, a cause Garner consistently supported. Within months of his installation, he delivered a Sunday sermon, "Black and White—Is the Color Line Crumbling?"

Interracial issues were at the heart of Garner's friendship with Amelia Moorfield, which started in the late 1920s. In May 1931, Moorfield invited Garner to speak on race relations at the annual meeting of the New Jersey Branch of the WILPF, paying him a $10 honorarium.[53] Along with Moorfield, several other ministers, and Rabbi Julius Silberfeld, Garner was one of the organizers of a 1932 discussion held at Temple B'Nai Abraham on "A Technique for Racial Understanding." [54] These activities presaged his later leadership in both the Urban League and the Newark Interracial Council.

Although he never joined the Socialist Party, socialism was another of Garner's interests. In a 1931 speech before Newark's Young People's Socialist League, he said that the social implications of Christianity were similar to the principles underlying the philosophy of socialism. He lauded the pacifism of socialism as consonant with the teachings of Christ. However, Garner was careful to add that there was a difference between socialist principles and a political platform. It was not by accident that he described Judaism as the "un-renounced religion of Jesus," which has its roots "springing directly out of the socially minded teaching of that magnificent succession of Hebrew prophets."[55] The audience undoubtedly contained many young Jews, who comprised the majority of Newark's "young socialists."

His congregation, other ministers, and Newark's elite did not always judge kindly Garner's support for African-Americans, Jews, socialists, and freethinkers. By 1932, he had been called "heretical, radical, 'red,' and worse." Barred from certain ministerial organizations, Garner's activities were branded "blasphemy in the pulpit." A sympathetic newspaper feature marking his fourth anniversary in Newark, said his career "has been more of an uphill fight than that of any other local pastor." However, the article claimed that the trustees of the Redeemer unanimously endorsed their minister's policies.[56] This public endorsement hoped to give the appearance of church solidarity. The reality was that some of the trustees were extremely hostile to Garner's views and also to the minister himself.

Other religious groups in Newark had ambivalent feelings about Garner. The Catholic Diocese of Newark was more conservative than the Protestants, and many of the topics presented at the forum, such as birth control, were anathema to it. Liberal Jews supported Garner and the forum from its beginning. Temple B'Nai Abraham, the most progressive of the city's Jewish congregations, and its Rabbi, Julius Silberfeld, often collaborated on programs with Garner. Much of the area's Protestant clergy was conservative and had little or nothing to do with Garner and his forum. The most notable exception was Kingdon, then the Minister of East Orange's Calvary Methodist Episcopal Church. An early forum program about African-American rights, "Fighting Lynch Law in America," featured Kingdon.[57]

* * *

The story of Frank Kingdon, university president, author, national leader in World War II refugee rescue efforts, civil rights activist, radio personality, and *New York Post* columnist, is best summed up by President Franklin Delano Roosevelt, who told Kingdon in 1938 "Frank, you will always be a man of influence but never a man of power."[58]

Kingdon was an ardent New Dealer and supported FDR on his radio program, in his newspaper column, and in his speeches at election time. Roosevelt asked Kingdon to be the Democratic candidate for the United States Senate in 1940. Roosevelt told Kingdon the nomination was his if he could get the okay from Frank Hague, Jersey City mayor and New Jersey's most powerful Democrat. The two men met, but Kingdon refused to agree to follow Hague's advice on patronage. This marked the end of Kingdon's political aspirations with the Democratic Party.[59]

Frank Kingdon was born in the heart of London near King's Cross Station, in 1894, the son of John and Matilda Caunt Kingdon. He was the youngest of six surviving children—seven additional siblings died during infancy. His parents were ardent Methodists, and their lives centered on religion and family. Both were constant in their attention to those in their church in need. Frank remembered that as a boy he carried food baskets to the sick and poor. Kingdon absorbed the Methodist teachings and by the time he was seven or eight began preaching at his house before a dozen or so neighborhood children. After several years, he moved to a nearby park where he developed his craft further. Throughout his youth, Kingdon continued to speak on religious topics for his Methodist church.[60]

Kingdon went to a local grade school filled with working-class students. When he was eleven, he won a scholarship to the elite University College School. He studied Latin, Greek, French, and classical and English literature, all of which he absorbed and came to enjoy. At sixteen, Kingdon passed his matriculation examination and graduated. Unlike his classmates he had no family connections, and he took a job as a bookkeeper. Through church work Kingdon established a close relationship with a couple planning to emigrate to the United States. The husband, an ordained Methodist minister, had accepted a pulpit in Maine and urged Kingdon to follow him. Already fascinated by America, Kingdon sailed to the United States in 1912 at the age of seventeen with the hope of becoming a Methodist minister. With the help of Methodist activists he found living quarters in Maine and began to preach and study toward ordination. Years later, Kingdon told his children that he left England because he didn't want to live in a monarchy and chose America for its freedom and democracy.[61]

He was soon licensed by the Methodists to preach and was sent to rural areas. In 1914, Kingdon obtained his first pulpit in Harmony Village Maine, where he also found a wife, Gertrude Bailey.[62] In 1916, his bishop transferred him to a position in Hull, Massachusetts so he could attend Boston University. He worked for the Democratic Party and spoke in the Boston area in favor of United States entry into World War I.

In 1920, Kingdon received an A.B. degree from Boston University, where he was elected to Phi Beta Kappa, and won a fellowship to Harvard Graduate School to study philosophy and religion. He was at Harvard in 1921 and 1922 while continuing to serve as pastor in Massachusetts. By this time the Methodist hierarchy was well aware of Kingdon's capacities and he was recommended for a more important pulpit, the Central Methodist Church in Lansing, Michigan. After hearing Kingdon preach, the church hired him, despite some misgivings about his liberal reputation.

East Orange, New Jersey, then an affluent suburb of Newark, was Kingdon's last pulpit. In 1929, he was hired as the minister of Calvary Methodist Church, a wealthy conservative congregation. From Calvary Methodist's pulpit, Kingdon's liberal political and social views gained substantial publicity and catapulted him into prominence in Newark and beyond. He organized a Sunday evening young men's club, which soon outdrew the attendance at Sunday church services. The club's meetings dealt entirely with contemporary issues. Many church members resented Kingdon's views and success at attracting new people to Calvary. They said that the new people did not pay membership dues and often took pews that paying members were accustomed to sitting in. With complaints similar to those leveled against Luke Garner, congregants protested that Kingdon "brings people off the street into our services."[63]

When the stock market collapsed on October 29, 1929, many congregants lost their wealth and often their jobs. Kingdon's wife, Gertrude, set up a makeshift soup kitchen in the back yard of their house in East Orange to help feed less fortunate parishioners.[64] With the help of Calvary's treasurer—himself now unemployed—Kingdon set up a "make-work" program for the unemployed, who were paid with scrip redeemable at a few stores. However, as conditions worsened the program was no longer affordable.[65]

In 1932, the Republicans nominated President Herbert Hoover and the Democrats Franklin Roosevelt. Kingdon could back neither. Hoover had already failed to end the Depression, and FDR's positions were too vague to inspire confidence in him. Norman Thomas, the Socialist Party candidate, was the man Kingdon felt could best deal with the Depression.[66] The minister joined the Socialist party, endorsed Thomas, and led his New Jersey campaign. Speaking before 200 at a newly organized Socialist party of the Oranges, Kingdon said he knew of no community that needed socialism more than the Oranges. While extolling Thomas, he deplored the rift between socialists and communists, calling the latter "socialists with swords in their teeth."[67] At another event in the Oranges he claimed that capitalism had failed because 30 million Americans were starving.[68]

Calvary's parishioners, overwhelmingly for Hoover in 1928 and already unhappy with Kingdon's liberalism, were relatively calm in 1932 when their minister became an active socialist. However, Kingdon was ready for a new challenge. "Newark loomed bigger and bigger as East Orange grew staler and staler," Kingdon said, describing his feelings in 1932.[69]

After Roosevelt's election, Kingdon continued speaking against lynchings, Nazism, and fascism. His pastorate in East Orange was no longer an important enough platform, as he sought wider recognition. His friendship with Beatrice Winser, director of the Newark Public Library, led to his next position. Miss Winser was one of the few women in Newark who constantly interacted on an equal footing with the male leadership. Professionally accomplished, energetic, and dedicated to Newark's welfare, she served on many boards that influenced the city's intellectual and cultural life. A trustee of Dana College, she recommended Kingdon for the vacant presidency and persuaded the other trustees to back him, despite their misgivings over the cleric's socialistic and liberal tendencies.

Kingdon started his presidency at Dana College in the fall of 1934. His first test came quickly. The school's Liberal Club called for an anti-fascist and antiwar conference and rally over the Christmas holiday. It would be the first such conference in New Jersey. The club learned that the National Student League was calling for a nationwide high school and college student strike on November 9. Representatives of the league and the club met and decided on a joint action for a conference on November 8, and a strike and demonstration in Military Park the following day. Kingdon agreed to be the featured speaker at the conference and to support the student strike and demonstration. The students were impressed with Kingdon's decision and he was praised in the school newspaper:

> Though Dr. Kingdon has been long known to be a Socialist and a liberal thinker, there has been some doubt as to how he would line up with the students on certain issues of the day. One readily sees that there is complete accord between him and the student body.[70]

The Thursday conference was held in the Dana College library, and Kingdon urged all those attending to join in the strike. The following morning 300 students marched from the college to the war monument in Military Park. They carried placards denouncing fascism, war preparations, and the Reserve Officer Training Corps

(ROTC), and in support of academic freedom. Contingents from Essex County Junior College and two elite Newark high schools, Arts High and Newark Institute of Arts and Science, also participated. Arts High students were required to get parental permission before being excused from class. The affair was entirely peaceful, with no heckling or counter-demonstrators.[71] In his public statement in support of the students, Kingdon said, "It is inevitable that those who oppose war shall also oppose fascism for in the latter all the seeds of the former germinate."[72]

* * *

Kingdon, Garner, and Moorfield shared a tendency of many 1930s liberals throughout America. In the absence of liberal organizations they sometimes accepted communists in their own projects or joined communist front groups working for issues they supported. From 1934 through 1936 the trio was active in the ALAWF, nationally a communist front, but in Newark controlled by liberals.

The ALAWF was an outgrowth of the International Bureau for the Fight Against Imperialist War and Fascism created at a convention in Amsterdam in 1932, under the initiative of the Communist International (Comintern). Many representatives of labor peace and groups attended, including Dorothy Detzer, National Secretary of WILPF, who believed the new organization could aid in the struggle for peace. She returned to the United States and along with Roger Baldwin, director of the American Civil Liberties Union, Earl Browder, secretary of the American Communist Party, and J.B. Mathews, a socialist leader, sponsored a 1933 call to form ALAWF.

By 1934, Detzer was successful in persuading reluctant national board members of the WILPF to sponsor ALAWF. She justified her cooperation with communists by citing the need to counter the emergence of fascist Italy and Nazi Germany. Detzer said, since "Soviet philosophy now dominated a sixth of the earth's surface, and was the creed of political minorities in every country, it was essential to me for all groups working against war and fascism to find a way to work with the communists."[73]

The WILPF instructed its United States branches to cooperate with local leagues against war and fascism. Moorfield was successful in recruiting Kingdon, newly named president of Dana College, to lead the ALAWF's Newark branch. Moorfield's other collaborator, Garner, became active in the league and permitted it to hold meetings in his church. Soon the league was holding weekly meetings with 100 people in attendance. Newark's communist leaders were livid about the situation. Rebecca Grecht, the Party's Newark district organizer, complained to national party chairman Earl Browder in January 1934:

> although an unrepresentative group calls itself the Newark branch of ALAWF they do not represent ideas of league. We cannot build a league in Newark by capitulating to petit-bourgeoisie intellectuals. We should make a new call in 4 or 5 weeks to establish a new Newark branch of the ALAWF and [the] existing league shall not participate in the call. It will be made by Communist Party.[74]

With the leadership of the Newark Branch clearly in the hands of Moorfield, Kingdon, and Garner, the communists were unable to implement their plan. Grecht complained: "We can't find a capable Party member to work in the ALAWF."[75] In October, the communists were still incensed. Harry Sazer, Grecht's successor, said,

> We find a terrible situation in the ALAWF. A number of liberals, petit-bourgeois elements have joined the league as individuals. A number of these liberals were elected to the Executive Committee and at the last meeting of the Committee not a single delegate from the mass organizations attended. This is impermissable.[76]

Soon afterward communists were participating in the Newark ALAWF. By the spring of 1935, Moorfield was under considerable pressure by WILPF members to justify their coalition with the communists in ALAWF. She reported to WILPF, "that of the thirty-odd organizations in the league, the Communist Party has one vote as have all the others."[77] However, Moorfield didn't know that many of those "thirty odd" groups were either Communist Party fronts or paper organizations the party controlled.[78] The communists were about to demonstrate that even without control, they could impose their will on the Newark ALAWF.

* * *

Events in Italy proved to Moorfield that peace was not possible when aggressors violated international treaties and ignored world opinion. Until then she had tried to work for peace through the League of Nations and diplomatic initiatives. Italy's invasion of Ethiopia roused WILPF and Moorfield to take a firm stand against fascism. At the age of sixty, she led an anti-fascist demonstration in the streets of Newark that was co-sponsored by WILPF and the Newark Branch of the ALAWF.

The invasion of Ethiopia released nationalistic feelings in Italian Americans. In Newark, fascist groups collected food, clothing, and money to send to Italy. Italian agents in America recruited men to fight in the war. Taking its lead from New York, the Newark Communist Party determined to use this issue for maximum propaganda, particularly among Italians and African Americans. On October 4, 1934, the Newark Communist Party proposed to organize a committee of Italians and African Americans to oppose the invasion. Furthermore, they planned to use the ALAWF to protest the recruitment of Italian workers in America, and to demonstrate in front of the Italian Consulate in Newark.[79]

Unaware of the Communist plan to use the ALAWF, Moorefield accepted suggestions to stage an anti-fascist demonstration. She organized fifty supporters of the WILPF and the ALAWF, joined by members of the Newark ACLU and Communist Party.

On October 20, 1935, protestors marched to the downtown Newark office of the Italian vice consul, Dr. Carlos Franchis. A request by protest representatives to see him was refused. After picketing in front of the building and passing out anti-fascist handbills, the protestors dispersed. Moorfield was satisfied with the event and stated in a report to Detzer that among the protestors were anti-Mussolini Italians and a small group of African Americans. She summarized, "It was a quiet friendly affair, we got the publicity we sought."[80] In another letter to a WILPF official, she said the demonstration was a success because while Mussolini was recruiting among Italian Americans some from that same group were picketing Mussolini's aggressive policies.[81]

Moorfield spoke publicly against Nazism in May 1935, at a rally against foreign and domestic Nazism sponsored by the Newark ALAWF held at the YMHA. Orchestrated by the Newark Communist Party,[82] the event was held to protest arrests and the breaking up of a demonstration of the American Youth Congress (AYC) by Newark police. Garner presided at the event.[83] Several months later, at a state board meeting of the WILPF, Moorfield asked for ratification of a resolution against the persecution of Jews in Germany.[84]

In the spring of 1935, another anti-war student event was planned for the country's high schools and colleges. As with the previous fall's protest, Kingdon approved Dana College participation and again said he would address the student assembly.[85] Four of the seven high schools in Newark (Central, Weequahic, Barringer, and South

Side) agreed to participate. There was consternation among veterans' groups and Catholic clergy who equated student activism with communist influence. The Young Communist League, with 110 members in the Newark area,[86] and the AYC, a communist-financed adjunct,[87] were the most active communist youth groups in the city. Their frequent demonstrations received newspaper coverage. It was fair to assume that the anti-war rally would have communist participation. This was made manifest when Newark's Young Communist League and the ALAWF became the rally's most vocal proponents. This gave fuel to the charges that the entire rally was a communist undertaking. Veterans' groups led the opposition to the event.

Dr. S. William Kalb, Newark's anti-Nazi boycott leader and veterans'-affairs activist, was particularly vehement in his denunciations of "communist influence" among the students. The Veterans' Alliance of Essex County, an umbrella group, appointed Kalb chairman of a counter-demonstration to be held at the same time as the students' march. Kalb said the counter-demonstration was needed to "prevent a communist-inspired student strike." He accused some Weequahic High School students of not taking the Pledge of Allegiance. Monsignor Francis J. Monaghan, president of Seton Hall College, agreed. "Communism is a menace in institutions of learning," he said.[88]

But the opposition had over-reacted. Student organizers of the anti-war event denied communist affiliation. Principal Max J. Hertzberg of Weequahic denied the accusation that some of his students refused to recite the Pledge. Arthur W. Belcher, the principal of South Side, said that the city's most influential rabbi, Solomon Foster of Temple B'nai Jeshurun, was to be one of the speakers at that school's peace activities. Raymond B. Gurley, principal of Barringer, informed Kalb that the school could run its own affairs. Kingdon's two allies, Moorfield (for WILPF) and Garner (for Redeemer Church), issued statements criticizing the veterans' group's proposed action.[89]

The Veterans' Alliance of Essex County retreated from its position, canceling the counter-demonstration. Kalb explained "the radicals have been using our name as ammunition for the students." He said that the students were told that the veterans' group was for war. On the contrary, Kalb continued, "We are not for war; we know what war is." Representatives of some veterans' groups argued that they should no longer oppose the student event. The veterans decided to "watch the situation."

The anti-war assembly was held at Dana College with Kingdon the main speaker. He told the students that they were the soldiers of tomorrow and that only they could prevent war by making it clear to the leaders of nations that they will not "pay in blood the price of bungling diplomacy." Kingdon also decried dragging out "the bogey of Communism to discredit the idealism of youth."[90] The following day, Luke Garner spoke to the students and faculty after a peaceful march to Military Park. For the next two years, the students held their parades without opposition. At an April 1937 rally, students from Princeton, Rutgers, and New Jersey State Teacher's College joined Newark University and heard Kingdon say, "No price is too high to pay for peace!"[91]

* * *

By the time of the 1935 spring rally, Kingdon had been president of Dana College six months. He had already led two anti-war, anti-fascist rallies at the college and was active in many other liberal causes. Whether it was a conscious decision on his part to become more mainstream or whether he was becoming more conservative as he approached middle age, Kingdon began to change direction in 1935. One week after the anti-war rally, he resigned from the Socialist Party, citing its "haziness" over its own objectives and the consequential divisions within the organization. He said that party labels, including Democratic and Republican, had become meaningless.[92] In the fall of 1935, he was named the 1936 campaign chair of the Newark Community Chest.[93] The Chest raised funds for the Newark Welfare Federation, the umbrella organization for the city's major charities. The welfare federation was a Protestant bastion whose directors included many of Newark's leading business and social leaders. His effectiveness as campaign leader soon became apparent. The chair of the campaign's men's division told the press that Kingdon had instilled more unity among the volunteers than in previous years.[94] Kingdon's success with the Community Chest Campaign prompted his elevation to a two-year term as president of the NewarkWelfare Federation in December 1937.[95]

Another accomplishment that added to his repute was the successful consolidation of Newark's five colleges into Newark University, a task that took almost two years.[96] Despite many obstacles, Kingdon's negotiating skills helped create the university. By its second semester, the institution had its own building, enrolled nearly 2,000 students, and established a unified curriculum.[97] As the president of a university in one of America's major cities, Kingdon was firmly established as an intellectual and political spokesman for liberalism throughout New Jersey and the northeast.

Kingdon's leadership at the University of Newark and the Newark Welfare Federation made it much easier for him to continue to pursue his liberal agenda. Previously his activities made him suspect to a broad segment of Newark's leaders. His new positions, combined with his withdrawal from the Socialist Party, made it more difficult for conservatives to attack him. Yet Kingdon remained distrusted by many in the Newark establishment, who waited for an opportunity to destroy him.

Kingdon's entry into mainstream Newark activities did not prevent him from continuing his support for Jewish causes. In November 1936 he became a New Jersey sponsor of the American Christian Conference on Palestine, which sought to speed emigration of Central European Jews and to maintain an open-door policy in Palestine for Jewish refugees. The other two sponsors in the state were Governor Harold Hoffman and the president of Rutgers University, Robert Clothier.[98] A few months later, he was the featured speaker for the annual meeting of the Federation of Jewish Philanthropies of New York City at Temple Emanuel in Manhattan.[99] Soon after, Kingdon gave the closing remarks at a celebration of the thirty-fifth anniversary of Rabbi Julius Silberfeld at Temple B'Nai Abraham.[100] An organizer of Essex County's Brotherhood Day, he was the spokesman for Protestant Churches, warning of a wave of nationalism sweeping the world, particularly Nazism.[101]

From 1934 on, Kingdon became increasingly active in the National Conference of Christians and Jews, later serving twelve years on its executive committee. He credited the conference with introducing him to the American Jewish community and the struggle against anti-Semitism.[102] Roger W. Strauss, a co-founder of the conference, was so impressed by Kingdon that he contributed $5,000 for the administration of a series of community seminars on intergroup relations at the University of Newark.[103]

* * *

While Kingdon's actions were increasingly mainstream, Garner was headed toward disaster with his congregation because of his liberal policies. In early 1935, urged on by disaffected board members, the church's former pastor, Dr. Henry Rose, accused Garner of causing congregants to leave the church because of the secularism he fostered, especially through the Community Forum. [104] Kingdon rallied to his ally's defense and spoke at Redeemer on "Why I Support the Newark Universalist Church." He praised the church's mission and its accomplishments under Garner.[105] The controversy subsided over the course of the year, but a determined band of anti-Garner members waited for an opportunity to eliminate both Garner and the forum.

The occasion used by the trustees to precipitate a showdown was a November 15, 1935 forum talk by Tony Sender, "Fugitives from Fascism." An elected member of the German Reichstag from 1920 to 1933, Sender left the country to avoid being arrested by the Nazis. A self-described moderate Social Democrat, Sender had spoken in Newark two years earlier without incident. However, this time some church trustees branded her a "radical."[106] The Board of Trustees of Redeemer met on November 4 and passed a resolution to bar the speech. They also decided that the board would have to clear all future forum speakers and their topics. They called Garner, told him of their decisions, and ordered that he substitute another speaker for Sender.

As the trustees anticipated, Garner refused to cancel Sender's talk on the grounds that their decision constituted violation of free speech—the major principle motivating the forum. Garner's act of defiance and his subsequent actions forced a showdown, which a majority of the trustees eagerly sought.[107]

Garner called Kingdon to discuss the crisis. Kingdon suggested a meeting with Beatrice Winser and Mrs. Parker O. Griffith, a liberal patron of the arts. The four met and agreed to remove the forum from church sponsorship and place it under the aegis of a non-profit group of prominent Newarkers. The new forum was incorporated as "The Community Forum and Institute."[108]

Garner then obtained a site for the forum and Sender's talk. He called his colleague Rabbi Julius Silberfeld of Temple B'Nai Abraham and asked if the congregation's auditorium could be used for the event. Garner had spoken at the Temple several times and had participated with the rabbi at various interfaith and community events,[109] and B'Nai Abraham often sponsored controversial speakers. Silberfeld readily gave his assent to the request and the date was set for Sunday, November 15, the same night it was originally scheduled. Frank Kingdon agreed to act as chairman.

On Sunday night, a capacity crowd of over 700 assembled in Temple B'Nai Abraham's auditorium. After Kingdon's introduction, Garner addressed the audience. He thanked Rabbi Silberfeld for his generosity in allowing the forum to be held at the temple. He asked the community to withhold judgement as to the "real liberalism" of the Redeemer Universalist Church, since the congregation had "fearlessly upheld" the forum principle each and every time it had been attacked over the past seven years. He announced he would call a special meeting of his church to consider its future policies. He would resign his pastorate if the congregation did not endorse the forum.

In throwing down the gauntlet to the trustees, Garner was taking an enormous risk, especially a financial one. Garner had a wife and three young sons to support. Not independently wealthy, Garner had made the last $5.00 payment for his student loan from theological school only one year earlier.[110] To uproot his family for another parish was not what he desired; he had close friends in the Newark area and wanted to remain there. If he lost his job, there was no guarantee that he could find a position in the Newark area that would pay the $5,000 he earned at Redeemer. But he wouldn't and couldn't back down. Both Newark dailies and the *New York Times* reported on the upcoming speech—all stressing Garner's threat to resign.[111]

The special session of the congregation was held in the auditorium of the Redeemer Church on December 14 at 8 PM. The minister, worried about the open rift, addressed his congregation briefly, telling them not to ignore the international scene and to remember that the church had a humanitarian mission in the world. Before the end of the meeting two-thirds of the congregation aired their views. At midnight the vote was taken and Garner and his policies were endorsed by a vote of 62 to 39. Garner told those assembled he would "carry on the program I have been following the past seven years," including opening the Redeemer to all races, creeds, and opinions.[112]

The anti-Garner trustees concentrated their efforts on the January 12, 1937 annual meeting. They packed this event with former Redeemer members who had left the church because of Garner. That evening, the board of trustees presented their report. Its main thrust was Garner's insubordination—he had violated an agreement with the board that they approve for all forum speakers. Two objectionable speakers had appeared at the forum, causing "an injury to the church." After insistent requests from Garner supporters to identify the speakers, a church official reported that they were Roger Baldwin, director of the American Civil Liberties Union, and Scott Nearing (a communist, according to the official).

Anti-Garner forces pointed out that the *American Mercury*, a reactionary periodical of the time, termed the ACLU "radical." A passage attacking the ACLU as "Communistic," purportedly extracted from a hearing of the House Committee on Un-American Activities, was read. Dr. Henry Davidson, a close friend of Garner, rebutted the article by pointing out that the portion quoted was from testimony of a witness and not the committee's conclusion. Another speaker linked the ACLU with ALAWF calling them "radical Communist" groups. At 1:30AM, after five hours of acrimonious debate, the question was called. By a vote of 88 to 56 the trustees passed a resolution to replace their minister. Garner was given three months severance and instructed to leave the church within a month.[113]

For days afterward, the newspapers ran articles protesting Garner's dismissal from various groups and individuals. Among those speaking out were Dr. Wells P. Eagleton, director of the Newark Eye and Ear Infirmary,[114] and Milton R. Konvitz, a lawyer, future legal scholar, and presidential advisor.[115] The *Newark Ledger* (formerly the *Star Eagle*) supported Garner editorially. It said that the trustees of Redeemer think it is heresy even to listen to any opinion that differs from their own. According to the paper, the trustees allowed Garner to speak on anything he pleased as long as he expressed their views.[116]

Public support could not pay Garner's bills, and his last pay from the church was in mid-April. His wife Genevieve immediately took a job as a saleswoman.[117] Kingdon, as president the newly incorporated Newark Community Forum, named Garner its executive director.[118] It was hoped that the weekly forum could generate enough income to pay Garner a living wage. The new forum became operational about the same time Garner left Redeemer in February. The *Newark Ledger* urged the public to patronize the forum and "help light the way toward the understanding and solution of many of the vital problems of the day."[119] To gain financial support, Kingdon sponsored a dinner at Newark's Essex House.[120]

Fortunately, some of Garner's Jewish friends were able to come to his aid. Michael Stavitsky, a supporter of the NSANL, suggested to Samuel Untermyer, the group's founder and president, that Garner would be an ideal candidate to rally liberal Christian clergymen (mainly in New York) in support of the boycott. An agreement was reached and Garner joined the league's paid staff. Garner began a campaign to enlist Protestant and Catholic clergymen in support of the league and the anti-Nazi boycott. However, after several months of disappointing results, Garner parted ways with the NSANL.[121]

It was a politician who finally provided Garner with a job that suited him well and provided a lifelong profession. Garner and Newark's mayor, Meyer Ellenstein, were well acquainted. The mayor's populism was complementary to the clergyman's liberalism. While serving as a pastor, Garner eschewed partisan politics in favor of his universalistic social gospel. However, once he was dismissed from Redeemer, he became actively involved in the 1937 Newark municipal election. He worked for Ellenstein's candidacy, making speeches and using his influence in liberal circles. Ellenstein was reelected with the highest vote total of the five elected commissioners, and following precedent, the other four commissioners chose him mayor for a second term.[122] Several months later, Garner was appointed to serve as executive director of the Newark Labor Relations Board, at a yearly salary of $5,000.[123]

Less than two months after he began his new job, Garner was forced to resign as director of the Community Forum. Several members of the Labor Relations Board publicly complained that Garner's continued activity with the forum—given its "radical" reputation—might hinder public confidence in the board.[124] This was a step Garner was loath to take, but after his recent bout with unemployment, his obligation to his family overcame the disappointment of abandoning his beloved forum. Although he curtailed some of his liberal activities, Garner continued to work with Moorfield and Kingdon.

When Garner served his brief stint with the NSANL, he enlisted Moorfield as a volunteer in the boycott. She worked with Kalb, the league's chairman, to persuade companies selling German-made goods to desist. Her efforts were rewarded by her election as one of five vice presidents of the New Jersey NSANL at its annual convention in April 1938.[125] She was one of two women—and the only non-Jew—ever elected to the organization's board.

* * *

Newark was a bastion of the New Deal during the 1930s. However, a great majority of the city's population did not support other aspects of the decade's liberalism, particularly its social agenda. Anti-Nazism never made the liberal agenda. The battle against Nazism in Newark was undertaken by Jews and precious few others until the late 1930s. It is all the more remarkable that Newark's three great liberal leaders, Moorfield, Garner, and Kingdon, remained steadfast in their anti-Nazism despite an absence of support from other Christians.

Notes

1. New Jersey Division, Newark Public Library, The Contemporary of Newark New Jersey, Yearbook 1931-1932, pp. 6,33
2. Garner Papers, unidentified newspaper, circa 9/29.
3. WPA New Jersey's Writer's Project, Subgroup New Jersey Enthological Survey, Box 2, Folder 25, ten-page undated survey (probably 1939) of fifty-four Jewish organizations, p. 2.
4. Other than in her pacifist and anti-Nazi activities, Moorfield had minimal contact with Jews. In the scores of interviews for this work, no Jewish person could recall her name. Her extensive social and recreational activities, which received ample press coverage, evinced no evidence of Jewish participation.
5. Interview, Joe Lerner, 5/16/97.
6. N.N., 1/26/34, p. 23; 2/22/35, pp. 6, 9; S.C., 1/5/36, p. 4; N.N. Morgue, undated, 1937; N.N., 3/23/38, p. 14. During these five years, there were six interfaith events in the city, and five of these were sponsored by the Essex County Conference of Christians and Jews at which Kingdon and Garner spoke twice each. Only one interfaith event was held in a church, at Garner's Universalist Church, while twice the men spoke at synagogues.
7. The *Star Eagle*, the other Newark daily, was geared toward the city's working class, and was generally favorable to both Mayor Ellenstein and the Democratic Party.
8. Lowenstein, Alan V., *Alan V. Lowenstein: New Jersey Lawyer and Community Leader*, New Brunswick, 2001, p. 8.
9. N.N., 2/9/35, p. 4.
10. Dr. Wells P. Eagleton (1865-1946) came to Newark in 1888 to serve his internship at Newark City Hospital and eventually became its chief brain and eye surgeon. An author of a medical text on brain surgery, he was the founder and then medical director of the Newark Eye and Ear Infirmary for over 25 years. In 1934, he was elected president of the American Academy of Opthamology. His many civic roles included the presidency of the Newark Council of Social Agencies (predecessor to the Newark Welfare Federation). Eagleton, in both public speeches and in the press, supported health legislation to aid the needy and opposed political interference in medical matters. He fought for mandatory health insurance, dismissing those who criticized him for promoting "socialized medicine." He posited that the quality of medical service was more important than economic consideration. See, N.N. Morgue, "Dr. Wells P. Eagleton."
11. Brinkley, Alan, *The End of Reform, New Deal Liberalism in Recession and War*, New York, 1995, p. 8.
12. New Jersey Legislative Manuals, 1929, 1933, 1937, Trenton.
13. Grover, Warren, "Relief in Newark, 1929-1933," M.A. Dissertation, 1962, pp. 52-55. For an unsuccessful attempt to send African Americans back to their former homes in the South, see pp. 98-102.
14. Klehr, Harvey, *The Heyday of American Communism, The Depression Decade*, New York, 1984, p. 187.
15. It was not until the second term of Mayor Meyer Ellenstein (1937-1941) that Jews and Italians were hired as teachers in the Newark other than as tokens. Interview, Ben Epstein, 6/19/98. Even before this, there was a small group of educators led by South Side High School's Helen G. Stevenson who were often associated with liberal causes.

The committee for a testimonial dinner for Stevenson, in June 1935, was a "who's who" of Newark liberalism and included Garner, Kingdon, Moorfield, Bernice Winser, Edward Fuhlbruegge, and Mrs. Parker O. Griffith.

16. ACLU Papers, Reel 113, Vol. 749, Letter from L.B. Milner to Kingdon, Edward P. Fuhlbruegge, Stephen Haff, Jr., 10/26/34.
17. ACLU Papers, Reel 153, Vol. 1051, Letter from Miss Nancy Cox to Lucille B. Milner, 10/8/37.
18. Walker, Samuel, *In Defense of American Liberties: A History of the ACLU*, New York, 1990, p. 121.
19. German-American League for Culture, FBI file 100-HQ-131905, file 100-1362 RCF.
20. No details could be found on Adolph Frederich's life. He is not mentioned in FBI files on the League nor in the Morgue of the *Newark Evening News*.
21. Gordon, Felice D., *After Winning, The Legacy of the New Jersey Suffragists*, 1920-1947, New Brunswick, NJ, 1986, p. 1.
22. Ibid., pp. 1, 2.
23. The Women's Project of New Jersey, Inc., *Past and Promise-Lives of New Jersey Women*, Sylvia Strauss, "Amelia Berndt Moorfield," Metuchen, NJ, 1990, p. 360.
24. Ibid.
25. Gordon, *After Winning*, p. 34.
26. Allan, Douglas, *Building Careers*, Newark, 1934, pp. 17, 18.
27. WILPF, Essex County Group, New Jersey Branch Papers, in author's possession, Minutes State Board Meeting, 6/16/26.
28. As quoted in Gordon, *After Winning*, p. 156.
29. As quoted in The Women's Project, *Past and Promise*, p. 361.
30. Gordon, *After Winning*, 143, 151, 156.
31. Allan, *Building Careers*, pp. 17,18, 20, 21.
32. WILPF, Essex County Group, Minutes Annual Meeting New Jersey, 5/17/35.
33. Newark Business and Professional Women's Club, Box II, Alice M. Garthwait, *History of the Business and Professional Women's Club of Newark*, 1961. The last set of minutes for the organization is from 1/20/65.
34. Ibid., Box I, Minutes of Business Meetings, 1933-1937 All the members of the club were not influential. In a democratic spirit, there was at least one housekeeper on the roster (a notation on an application indicated that Miss Price was not accepted for membership because "the housekeeper's quota was filled").
35. Ibid.
36. Ibid.
37. Ibid.
38. The Contemporary, op. cit., pp. 2, 43-67.
39. Ibid., pp. 8, 42-44.
40. N.N., 11/7/34, p. 10.
41. Papers of the Essex County Section, National Council of Jewish Women, Essex County Bulletin, 1/73, p. 12.
42. Conference of Jewish Charities, Minutes of Board of Directors Annual Meeting, 5/10/34, p. 3.
43. Conference of Jewish Charities, Executive Board Minutes, 4/27/37, p. 2.
44. Ibid., Minutes, 3/28/38, "Report on the Coordinating Committee of Essex County."
45. NSANL, Box 11, Folder 5, Organizational Members of the NSANL of N.J., p. "o."
46. Interview, David Garner, 6/27/98.
47. Interview, Dr. Peter Garner, 6/28/98.
48. Interviews, Alan Lowenstein, 6/9/98, Vivian Mintz Barnert, 1/21/2000.
49. Andover-Harvard Theological Library, Archives Office, biographical file on Rev. Lucius Hamilton Garner; Interviews, Fradleigh Garner, 7/16/98, David Garner, 6/27/98 These three sources are used for the early career of Garner.
50. Interview, Fradleigh Garner, 7/16/98.
51. Papers of Hamilton Garner, unidentified newspaper article on the 100th Anniversary of the Redeemer Universalist Church, 1935.

52.   Op. cit., "The Newark Universalist," 11/29.
53.   Papers of Essex County WILPF, in author's possession, "Checkbook 5/31-5/33."
54.   S.C., 2/7/32, p. 22.
55.   N.N., 6/6/31, p. 11.
56.   NPL, NJD., Folder, "Newark Clergy," S.C., 2/28/32.
57.   Garner Papers, Notebook, "Forum," undated entry, circa 1930.
58.   Kingdon Papers, *Inside The Golden Door, A Personal Report on American Institutions and Men Observed Through Fifty Years After Immigration,* Unpublished manuscript, circa 1962, p. 16.
59.   Kingdon Papers, Unpublished manuscript in possession of John Kingdon, p. 67.
60.   Kingdon, Frank, *Jacob's Ladder,* New York, 1943, pp. 186, 187.
61.   Interview, John Kingdon, 5/31/98.
62.   Kingdon, *Jacob's Ladder,* pp. 295-297.
63.   Interview, John Kingdon, 5/31/98.
64.   Interview, Getrude Kingdon Behrle, 5/8/98.
65.   Kingdon Papers, Unpublished manuscript in possession of John Kingdon, p. 57.
66.   Ibid., p. 58.
67.   N.N., 9/9/32, p. 10.
68.   Ibid., 10/22/32, p. 4.
69.   Kingdon Papers, p. 59.
70.   Rutgers Special Collections, *Dana College Chronicle,* 10/11/34, 10/18/34, 10/25/34.
71.   Ibid., 11/15/34.
72.   N.N., 10/18/34, p. 4.
73.   Detzer, Dorothy, *Appointment on the Hill,* New York, 1948, pp. 188-192.
74.   CPUSA, Reel 281, Delo 3619, Letter from Rebecca Grecht to Earl Browder, 1/23/34, p. 2.
75.   Ibid., Letter from Rebecca Grecht to ORG Commission, 3/26/34.
76.   CPUSA, Reel 280, Delo 3615, Report of H. Sazer to district plenum, 10/13/34, p. 5.
77.   WILPF, DG 43, Box 2, Folder 4, Annual Report, New Jersey WILPF, 1935.
78.   It was estimated that at the League's 1934 national convention over 70 percent of the 3,332 delegates were members of the Communist Party or its auxiliaries. See, Guenter Lewy, *The Cause that Failed,* New York, 1990, p. 172.
79.   CPUSA, Reel 297, Delo 3877, Minutes of the Newark Communist Party, 10/4/35, p. 2.
80.   WILPF, Reel 130.59, Letter from Moorfield to Dorothy Detzer, 10/23/35.
81.   The Women's Project of New Jersey, *Past and Promise,* p. 361.
82.   CPUSA, Reel 281, Delo 3619, Rebecca Grecht, "Report on the Situation in the New Jersey District," 5/15/34, p. 13.
83.   N.N., 5/31/35, p. 10.
84.   WILPF, Essex County, Minutes of State Board Meeting, 10/18/35.
85.   N.N., 4/3/35, p. 21.
86.   CPUSA, Reel 255, Delo 3300, Minutes Newark Communist Party, 11/9/33.
87.   CPUSA, Reel 297, Delo 3875, Harry Sazer's Report to the Newark District Plenum, 6/9/35, p. 4.
88.   N.N., 3/21/35, p. 5.
89.   Ibid., 4/11/35, p. 5.
90.   Ibid.
91.   Kingdon Papers, Volume "6," S.E., 4/23/37.
92.   N.N., 4/17/35, p. 15.
93.   Ibid., 9/19/35, p. 7.
94.   Ibid., 10/12/35, p. 3.
95.   Kingdon Papers, Volume "4" 1933-1937, N.N., 12/17/37.
96.   Kingdon Papers, Volume "2" 1925-1936, Annual Report of the President of the University of Newark, 5/13/36. The spring 1936 enrollment prior to the fall consolidation was 1886 consisting of

Mercer Beasley Law School	152
New Jersey Law School	426
Institute of Arts and Science	635
Dana College	393
Seth Boyden	280

97.   Ibid., Volume "3" 1936, NYT, 9/30/36, 9/27/36.
98.   Kingdon Papers, Vol. "4" 11/12/35.
99.   Ibid., Volume "5" 1937, 2/7/37.
100. Ibid., 2/22/37.
101. N.N., 2/22/35, p. 9.
102. Kingdon Papers, "Inside the Golden Door," pp. 118-120.
103. Ibid., Volume "5" 1937, S.E., 2/4/37. Strauss was a New York philanthropist who was vice president of American Smelting and Refining.
104. S.C., 2/24/35, p1; N.N. 2/25/35, p. 2.
105. Garner Papers, *The Newark Universalist*, 4/18/35, p. 1.
106. N.N., 11/11/36, p1; S.E., 11/12/36, p. 3.
107. Garner Papers, "Statement on the Program and the Policies of the Church" delivered by Rev. L. Hamilton Garner before the congregation of the Universalist Redeemer Church, 11/22/36.
108. Ibid., Certificate of Incorporation, State of New Jersey, for "Community Forum and Institute," 11/27/36.
109. N.N., 2/22/35, p. 6.
110. Garner Papers, Letter to Garner from Comptroller, St. Lawrence University, 3/29/35.
111. Ibid., N.N., 11/22/36; N.L., 11/23/36; NYT, 11/23/36.
112. N.N., 12/15/36, p. 1.
113. Garner Papers, N.N., 1/12/37; S.E., 1/12/37; *Christian Leader*, 2/19/37
114. Ibid., S. C., 1/31/37.
115. Ibid., S.C., 2/14/37.
116. Ibid., N.L., 2/9/37.
117. Interview, Ida Weiner, 7/16/98.
118. Garner Papers, Letterhead of Community Forum, 3/29/37. Of the thirty-eight trustees of the new Forum, twelve were Jews, including Rabbi Julius Silberfeld, Drs. Max Danzis and Eugene V. Parsonnet, Dr. Milton Konvitz, and Aaron Lasser; two were African-Americans, Dr. Walter G. Alexander and Thomas L. Puryear; eleven were educators, mainly connected to Newark University; ten were Protestant civic leaders in Newark, including Beatrice Winser, Dr. Wells P. Eagleton, Mrs. Parker O. Griffith, and Franklin Conklin, Jr.; one was Garner; two could not be identified.
119. Ibid., N.L., 2/9/37.
120. Kingdon Papers, Volume "5" 1937, "Community Forum and Institute Invitation", 2/8/37 Two weeks after this invitation, Kingdon presided and gave the closing remarks on the second day of Rabbi Silberfeld's thirty-fifth anniversary at Temple B'Nai Abraham. See, 2/22/37.
121. Garner Papers, Draft Letter from Garner to Samuel Untermyer, undated.
      The document indicates that Garner was successful in meeting with about a dozen New York Protestant clergymen, including Dr. Henry Emerson Fosdick, Rev. William B.Spofford, and Dr. Everett R. Clinchy. According to Garner, they were all sympathetic to the aims of the NSANL but were unable to give him institutional aid because of the resistance of their board and executive committee members. As to reactions from the Catholic clergy, Garner characterized them as "encouraging but evasive."
122. Stellhorn, Paul, "Champion of the City; Reflections on the Political Career of Meyer C. Ellenstein," unpublished manuscript based upon paper given to the Jewish Historical Society of Metro West, 6/9/97.
123. N.N., 9/27/37, p. 7.
124. Garner Papers, S.C., 11/14/37.
125. J.C., 4/29/38, p. 1; N.N., 4/25/38, p. 25.

Louis Slott's membership card
in the Minutemen

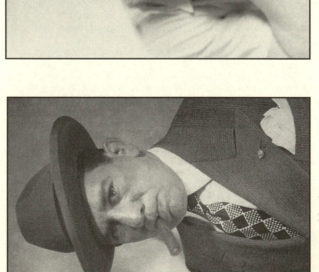

Louis Slott
First Commander of the Minutemen

Nat Arno
Commander of the Minutemen, 1934-1940

Minuteman Alex Portnoff, 1942

Minuteman Max "Puddy" Hinkes

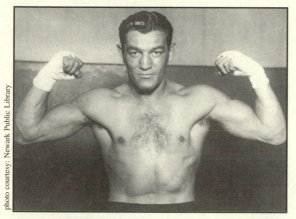

Minuteman Abie Bain

Minuteman Lou Halper

Minuteman Moe Fischer

Abner "Longie" Zwillman,
late 1920's

Meyer Ellenstein
Newark Mayor, 1933-1941

Abner "Longie" Zwillman, 1938

Minuteman Benny Levine (*right*) and Benny Leonard, 1931

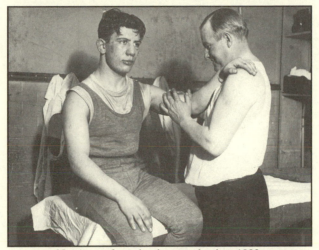

Nat Arno after a boxing match, circa 1932

Nat Arno and Benny Leonard in Newark gym, circa 1927

Nat Arno (*center*) and Dr. Kalb (*second from right*) at
Chris Chop House on Clinton Avenue in Newark, 1940.

Nat Arno (*with cigar*) and Minutemen including Julius "Skinny"
Markowitz (*with hand on Arno's shoulder*) at Krueger Auditorium, 1936.

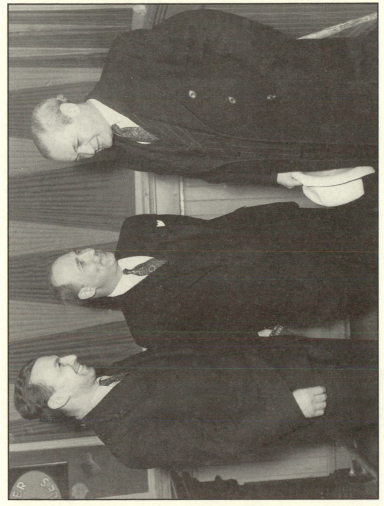

Dr. S. William Kalb (*center*) and Congressman Samuel Dickstein (*right*) at an anti-Nazi meeting at Krueger Auditorium, March 1937.

Advertisement for Schwabenhalle, 1933

Schwabenhalle, 2002

Newark Bund leader
Matthias Kohler, 1940

Walter Kauf, Friends of the New
Germany, arrest photo 1933.

Rabbi Joachim Prinz
Temple B'Nai Abraham

Michael Stavitsky
President of the Newark Conference
of Jewish Charities, circa 1935.

Rabbi Julius Silberfeld
Temple B'Nai Abraham

Rabbi Solomon Foster
Temple B'Nai Jeshurun

Reverend Luke Garner, 1935

Luke Garner and Eleanor Roosevelt in Newark, circa 1944.

Frank Kingdon

Frank Kingdon and Erica Mann, 1941

Amelia Moorfield, 1935

Nancy Cox, press photo from 1937

Jack Malamuth, circa 1935

Arthur Bell, N.J. Grand Dragon, speaking at joint meeting of the German-American Bund and Ku Klux Klan at Camp Nordland, Andover N.J., August 1940.

Fritz Kuhn, leader of the German-American Bund, reviews goose-stepping Nazis at a May Day celebration before 4,000 Nazi sympathizers at Camp Nordland in 1940.

August Klapprott, New Jersey Bund leader, delivering opening
speech before 8,000 people at Camp Nordland, July 1937.

Norman Thomas laughing at photo of him being
egged in Newark's Military Park, June 1938.

Minuteman contingent picketing Bund rally at Schwabenhalle, September 26, 1938.
(Jack Rothseid, Nat Arno, and Irving Edisis in front row)

"Left" and "Right" unite to picket September 26, 1938 Bund meeting.

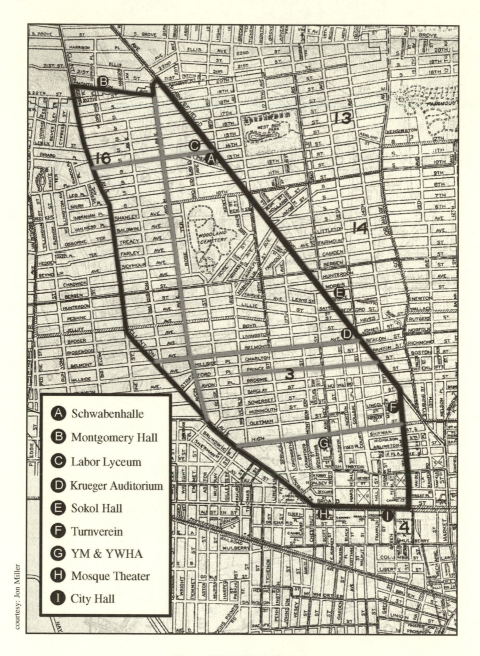

courtesy: Jon Miller

A Schwabenhalle

B Montgomery Hall

C Labor Lyceum

D Krueger Auditorium

E Sokol Hall

F Turnverein

G YM & YWHA

H Mosque Theater

I City Hall

Map of Third Ward, Newark

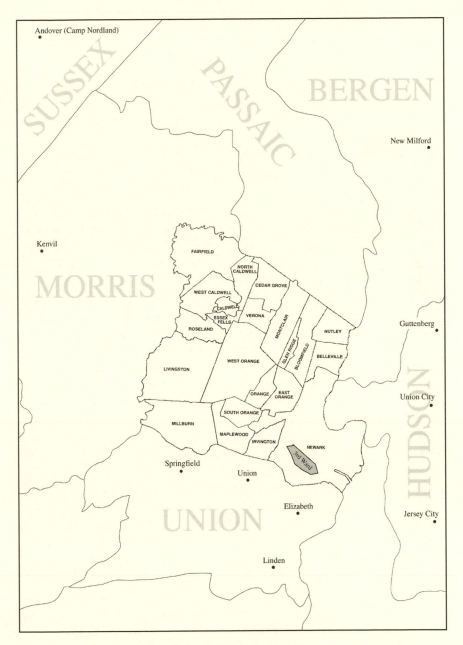

Essex County and surrounding areas

6

The Rise of the German-American Bund, 1936-1937

Anti-Nazism was well established in Newark by 1936 when the German-American Bund replaced the Friends of the New Germany as the major Nazi organization in the United States. Newark's major anti-Nazi groups, the Minutemen and the Non-Sectarian Anti-Nazi League (NSANL), worked together through their respective leaders, Nat Arno and Dr. S. William, Kalb to battle Nazism through education, propaganda, and physical force and intimidation. These tools were even more necessary as the German-American Bund built a formidable organization during the next two years.

Liberals and communists were also part of the anti-Nazi response. The Reverends Luke Garner and Frank Kingdon, as well as Amelia Moorfield, lacked a substantial base of support for their liberal anti-Nazism. Sometimes unknowingly, they worked with Newark's well-organized and skillful Communist Party in pacifist and anti-Nazi causes. Even the socially and politically conservative NSANL was not immune to communist infiltration.

Berlin's order to all German nationals to withdraw from the Friends of the New Germany by December 31, 1935 was a serious threat. Refusal would mean loss of German passports and possibly German citizenship. German officials hoped the withdrawal of German nationals from the fractious and undisciplined Friends would result in the collapse of an organization that had embarrassed Nazi leaders in Berlin too many times. Berlin hoped to create a unified movement made up of U. S. citizens of German descent to which it could feed propaganda about German patriotism, racial doctrine, and Nazi aspirations. To complement this effort, Berlin unleashed a ceaseless stream of propaganda directed at non-German extremist groups in

America with pro-Nazi, anti-Semitic, or anti-communist agendas. The Nazis became the chief supplier of anti-Semitic and Anglophobic literature to such groups as William Dudley Pelley's Jew-baiting Silver Shirts and C. F. Fulliam's White Shirts.[1] Berlin hoped that nativist movements would grow along with the Friends' successor into a revolutionary movement, creating a Nazi-type regime in America.

But Berlin underestimated the Friends' success in putting down strong roots in parts of the German-American community. In Newark, for example, the Friends had gained control of the important German-American League of Essex County. With the ascent of Fritz Kuhn to the Friends' national leadership in November 1935, Nazis in America had a charismatic and intelligent leader. Rather than a collapse of the Friends and the creation of a new independent Nazi movement in America, Berlin watched as Kuhn retained the structure and principles of the old group, and simply renamed it the German-American Bund. Under Kuhn's leadership, the Bund became a visible and cohesive force that Americans correctly perceived as an increased threat. For Nazi diplomacy in America, the Bund was to become a more serious problem than the Friends.

The Bund grew from 1936 to 1938. This was due to Kuhn's abilities; the acceptance of Nazi propaganda by increasing numbers of German Americans; the propaganda success of the Berlin Olympics; and the growth of non-German extremist groups, some of which cooperated with the Bund. The Bund gained an increasingly prominent spotlight in the United States. Despite this notoriety, or more likely because of it, the Bund was never successful in making itself an American organization. Berlin's threats to confiscate passports and cancel citizenship were never carried out. The group's leadership remained largely in the hands of German immigrants who had recently become U.S. citizens or were becoming citizens specifically so they could work for Nazi Germany.

* * *

Fritz Kuhn was born in Munich in 1886 and died there in 1951 soon after his release from a jail term imposed by the Bavarian de-Nazification court. At the outbreak of World War I, Kuhn joined a Bavarian infantry unit and served as a machine gunner in France. After Germany's collapse in 1918, he joined the right-wing Frei Korps, which fought the socialists and communists in Bavaria. He then enrolled in the nascent National Socialist German Worker's Party (NSDAP) while attending university in Bavaria. Kuhn graduated in 1922 with the equivalent of a master's degree in chemical engineering but, unable to find satisfactory work, immigrated to Mexico, where he worked as a chemist and teacher until he entered the United States in 1928. After a brief stay in New York, Kuhn moved to Detroit and, like many other immigrants, sought work in the burgeoning automobile industry. Kuhn worked at Ford Motors until 1935.[2]

Kuhn joined the Friends of the New Germany in the summer of 1933 and steadily rose through the ranks over the next two years. He became leader of the Detroit chapter by displaying strong organizing abilities. This talent, a university education, prior membership in the NSDAP, and service in the Frei Korps made Kuhn a standout in the Friends. After two years, he was appointed Midwest leader by Fritz Gissbl. After the December 1935 Berlin edict for all German nationals to leave the Friends by the end of the year, Gissibl and Sepp Schuster, commander of the Ordnungs-Dienst (the O.D., a paramilitary group modeled after Hitler's Storm Troopers), returned to Germany. Before leaving the U.S., Gissibl named Kuhn the Friends' provisional Bundesleiter.[3]

The first tasks for the new leader were to attain unity of the different Friends' factions and ensure the personal loyalty of its members. Kuhn was successful in both efforts. After the internal conflicts, the blows of the Dickstein Committee, and Berlin's order, members were eager for the strong leadership Kuhn promised. He required that each member of the O.D. take an oath of fidelity to him, and increased the size of the group to ten percent of the Friends' total membership. He gathered a group of close collaborators who would be loyal to him and to whom he could delegate responsibility. Among this group was Gerhard William Kunze, who would become Kuhn's successor in 1939.

After Kuhn made substantial progress toward his objectives, he called a convention for March 1936 in Buffalo New York. The Friends and numerous splinter groups attended for what amounted to Kuhn's coronation. As soon as he was elected Bundesleiter he declared the Friends of the New Germany defunct and asked delegates to adopt a new name: Amerikadeutscher Volksbund (German-American Bund). The new name reflected Kuhn's desire to Americanize the group to promote friendship between Germany and America.[4] The result was that all Nazi factions—with a few minor exceptions—became united for the first time since the 1920s. The first official announcement of the German-American Bund stated its purpose:

> to combat the Moscow-directed madness of the Red world menace and its Jewish bacillus-carriers.[5]

Kuhn built the Bund into the largest and best-financed Nazi group operating in America during Hitler's reign. In 1937 and 1938—the Bund salad days—membership grew to 25,000.[6] There is no evidence that Germany financed the group.[7] Kuhn's public relations efforts and business acumen, along with Hitler's continued successes in Europe, kept American Nazi money pouring into its coffers.

Kuhn retained his O.D. as the main instrument of control over the Bund. It served as Kuhn's bodyguard and as security for Bund events. Membership in the O.D. was open to all male Bund members eighteen or older. Instruction was given in marching, riflery, and calisthenics. The American press referred to the O.D. as Kuhn's storm troopers. Newsreels and print media of the time showed them marching in columns in a parade wearing their armbands, Sam Browne belts, and jackboots, and giving Nazi salutes to their leaders and the swastika flags.[8]

Family togetherness was one of Kuhn's tactics for building the Nazi movement in America. He set up youth groups in many large Bund chapters, including Newark. He intensified efforts to set up Bund camps, attracting families with German food and beer, entertainment, and Nazi propaganda. These camps featured overnight facilities for children, who received uniforms, were instructed in drill, learned German, and were subjected to Nazi propaganda in an attempt to set up a parallel group to Germany's Hitler Youth movement.

Kuhn sought to keep the existence of local cells and names of cell members a secret. The swastika symbol was de-emphasized in favor of the American flag, and English rather than German was favored at meetings. Commanders of the various Bund units concluded every meeting by leading members in the Nazi salute and reciting the motto,

> To a free, Gentile-ruled United States and to our fighting movement of awakened Aryan Americans, a three-fold, rousing "Free America! Free America! Free America!"[9]

Kuhn, with the aid of his propagandists, established a cult of personality. His activities were publicized far beyond those of his mostly colorless predecessors. Kuhn imitated Hitler in every pos-

sible way. He was usually dressed in uniform with black leather jackboots, and stood with his legs apart and his thumbs fixed in his Sam
Browne belt. He often announced loudly that he was the American
Führer.[10] Unlike Hitler, Kuhn was over six feet tall and had an imposing countenance. Some laughed at him, as many had laughed at
Hitler, but his followers believed in him and saw Kuhn as the per-
sonification of their Nazi hopes.

Kuhn's creation of a unified Nazi movement in America was front-
page news in the *New York Times*, the *Newark News*, and the *Jewish
Chronicle*. In assessing Kuhn's change of the Nazi organization's
name, the *Chronicle* stressed that its purpose was to Nazify the more
conservative German-American element. According to the editorial
"Nazifying America," Kuhn's objective was to lead America in the
same direction as Germany.[11] Kuhn's penchant for public relations
allowed Newark's anti-Nazis to be well informed of the danger a
resurgent Bund presented. They soon proved themselves equal to
the challenge.

* * *

Kuhn tried to emulate Hitler, and in turn, the American Führer
had his own emulator in Newark in the guise of Hermann Von Busch.
However, Von Busch, a supervisor for Public Service Electric and
Gas Company, New Jersey's dominant utility, was no Fritz Kuhn. A
1930 photo of Public Service employees shows Newark's Führer-
to-be average-height, squat, bald, and jug-eared.[12] In addition, Von
Busch was an uninspiring speaker who lacked Kuhn's charisma and
intelligence.

Von Busch was born in Germany in 1889 and emigrated to the
United States in 1909. He became an American citizen in 1919 while
living in Jersey City (seat of Hudson County). His career was spent
at Public Service, where he started in 1911 and with a few interrup-
tions remained through the 1950's. In an FBI interview in 1942, Von
Busch's former wife, Sophie, claimed that Hermann worked long
hours at his twelve-dollar-a-week job. He spent all his spare time
with her and their three children and was not active in German affairs until 1925, when he left his family and moved to Newark with
another woman.[13] Another source told the FBI Von Busch was very
active in German-American organizations in Hudson County, including the Captain William Hexamer Unit of the Steuben Society.

After moving to Newark, Von Busch remained in the organization, eventually becoming its secretary.

Von Busch joined the Friends of the New Germany when the Newark Branch was organized in 1933. He was accepted into the O.D. and often dressed in Nazi uniform. At Public Service, where he worked the night shift, he was sometimes seen with his Nazi uniform under his work clothes. He became a recruiter for the Friends, especially among recent German immigrants.[14] Although popular within the organization, he was not part of the core group, which consisted of newer immigrants to America, many with Nazi ties.

When Fritz Kuhn dissolved the Friends and created the Bund in 1936, Von Busch saw his opening. Newark's Nazi old guard, mainly German nationals, withdrew from center stage and sought American leadership. From 1936 through 1939, Von Busch, serving as "political leader," was the Newark Bund's most visible and vocal personality,

Von Busch lived on South 17th Street, a predominantly German-American neighborhood, in a former single-family home he converted to a boardinghouse. At any given moment, there could be three or four German immigrants renting rooms from him. These men would stay with Von Busch until they got jobs and became established. A number of boarders told the FBI their landlord had recruited them to join the Bund. Several joined, most did not. Busch also got these men jobs at Public Service, some in his department. One of the boarders alleged that Von Busch demanded a kickback from each man Public Service hired. Another FBI informant claimed that Von Busch was running a Nazi cell from his house and that the roomers were Nazis sent by Germany as agents.[15]

***

Matthias Kohler, a member of the Newark Friends of the New Germany, served as the unit's O.D. leader in 1934. With the 1935 dissolution of the Friends, he, along with Von Busch, became a leader of the Newark Bund. Kohler initially kept more to the background, perhaps because he had only received his American citizenship in mid-1935. There is strong evidence that Kohler was a member of the NSDAP (German Nazi Party). Kohler was elected Bundesleiter of the Newark unit at its first meeting, a position he held until the fall of 1939.

A World War I veteran of the German army, Kohler immigrated to the United States in 1927. He worked as a watchmaker for Wiss &

Co., a large Newark jeweler, from 1928 to 1938 when he started his own watch-making business at his home in Irvington. Kohler was known as an extremist who believed that the Bund should be more militant. He was active in the local, state, and Eastern regional branches of the O.D. At Camp Nordland, established by the Newark Bund in July 1937, he served as a rifle instructor. [16] Kohler was Von Busch's superior, but he allowed his colleague to be the mouthpiece for the Newark Bund.

* * *

Beginning in 1936, Nat Arno to help support himself and several Minutemen friends, began visiting local Jewish businesses requesting money. Alone or with an associate, Arno would describe the work of his organization, and ask the businessman to contribute from one to ten dollars. In return, Arno would give the donor a Minuteman membership card. Periodically thereafter he would revisit the "member" for dues. Most businessmen knew of Arno's reputation as a boxer, enforcer, and commander of the Minutemen. Few refused to join.[17]

The Newark Bund's first public event was an April 1936 birthday celebration for Hitler, slated for Montgomery Hall in Irvington. The Friends had quietly celebrated this event for the last two years. The Minutemen had broken up a publicly advertised Hindenburg birthday party in 1933. In keeping with Kuhn's policy of maximum publicity, the Newark chapter heralded the Hitler celebration.

Arno and his ally, Dr. S. William Kalb, requested a meeting with Irvington Magistrate Thomas J. Holleran to protest the celebration as a violation of the 1934 agreement between the anti-Nazis and the Irvington police. Arno, accompanied by two lieutenants, Lazer Schwartz and Max Goldberg, and by an attorney, Abraham Harkavy, an official of the NSANL, met with Holleran and other police and public officials. Arno objected to the birthday celebration on the grounds that the Bund was un-American and anti-Semitic. He warned of violence if the event included Nazi propaganda or a display of the swastika. Holleran said Irvington officials would not tolerate any un-American display, but any Minutemen violence would be dealt with harshly. Arno replied that his group was not violent except when incited by anti-Semitism. He threatened that if the Irvington police did not respond to anti-Semitic provocations at the event, the Minutemen would. Schwartz added that although the Minutemen prefer "peaceful methods," they would not necessarily listen peacefully to Nazi propaganda.[18]

The Hitler birthday celebration was held at Montgomery Hall without incident. The Minutemen did not appear, since Holleran's position was unambiguous, and the anti-Nazis were not ready to face certain arrest if they attacked the Bundists. However, the meeting with Holleran was a partial success, Irvington officials told the Bund that no further Nazi rallies would be permitted, explaining that it was not only the threat of violence that concerned them but the negative publicity the town received following each public Nazi event. For the rest of the year, the Bund held no public rallies in the city. The Bund did, however, indirectly sponsor one public event. It concerned the 1936 Summer Olympics held in Berlin.

* * *

American participation in the 1936 Olympics was predicated on Nazi promises to allow Jewish athletes to compete for Germany. Fearing that the United States would withdraw from the games in 1934, Germany announced that twenty-one Jewish athletes had been nominated for Olympic training camps. The American Olympic Committee sent Avery Brundage to Germany to investigate whether Germany was complying with its promises. Mindful of the importance of Brundage's visit, the Nazis successfully overwhelmed him with propaganda. Brundage returned to America with optimistic news about Nazi Olympic preparations and fair treatment of Jewish athletes. The American Olympic Committee voted to participate in Berlin.[19] The only body that could reverse this decision was the executive committee of the Amateur Athletic Union (AAU), which had jurisdiction over all American amateur teams and individuals.

Anti-Nazi forces in America protested the 1936 Summer Olympics because of the obvious propaganda boon it would provide the Nazis. Indeed, most Jewish groups opposed United States participation in Berlin. There was also significant Christian opposition. A resolution against holding the Olympics in Berlin was passed by the National Council of the Methodist Church. The liberal Catholic magazine *Commonweal* said Nazi youth organizations were "pagan" and that to support the Olympics would be to approve the "radically anti-Christian Nazi doctrine of youth." The American Federation of

Labor declared itself against American participation in the Olympics because the Nazis were anti-labor and because there was nothing noble in the persecution of 600,000 Jews by 60 million Germans.[20]

From June through September 1935, over 100 organizations in Newark put themselves on record against America's participation in the Olympics.[21] Rabbis Julius Silberfeld of Temple B'Nai Abraham and Solomon Foster of Temple B'Nai Jeshurun endorsed a boycott.[22] As part of a national effort to influence the AAU to vote against American participation, a November "Olympic Boycott Rally" was held in Newark sponsored by Dr. Frank Kingdon, Dana College president. At the event, well attended by representatives of Jewish, labor, and education groups, a resolution was passed urging the AAU to reverse the decision of the American Olympics Committee.[23] Despite petitions from organizations representing 1.5 million members and the signatures of 500,000 people opposing American participation, the executive board of the AAU at a December 1935 meeting voted to take part in the Olympics. Avery Brundage's report was the deciding factor.

The Bund wanted to celebrate the Nazi victory, but it had promised Holleran it would not sponsor any public rallies. Dr. Francis Just filled the breach. In May 1936, using the Bund-controlled Essex County German-American League as the sponsor, Just announced a concert and athletic contest to benefit American sports clubs sending members to the Summer Olympics. Just planned to use the benefit as a showcase for Bund propaganda.

The Essex County branch of the German-American League for Culture protested to the president of Olympic Park in Irvington, where the festivities were to take place. The branch claimed the purpose of the event was to raise funds to provide visitors to Berlin with Nazi propaganda. Adolph Friederich, the group's chairman, said Just and his organization were a propaganda agency for Nazism and had merged their activities with the Bund.[24] Just denied Nazi ties to his group and claimed his organization was a coordinating body for German-American groups to provide mutual assistance. Henry Guenther, Olympic Park president, replied that Just had promised there would be no Nazi propaganda at the event. The last word was Friederich's, as he quoted the official invitation to the benefit that openly called for funds to enable the conversion "of many visitors to the Olympic Games at Berlin to Nazism."[25]

Other groups protested against the benefit. Kalb wanted to raise money for the NSANL to print circulars condemning the rally.[26] The Newark and the New Jersey Committees of the American League Against War and Fascism (ALAWF) added a feminist motivation for opposing both the games and the benefit.[27] Mrs. Frances Dodge, secretary of the committee, quoted a Nazi sports leader: "We National Socialists reject sports for women," and she asked rhetorically whether the American Olympic women swimmers would appreciate the Nazi sentiment.[28] Fearing continued protests might force a cancellation, Just promised the Irvington public safety director, Edward D. Balentine, there would be no swastikas, armbands, or uniforms.[29] Irvington police guarded the gates and grounds of Olympic Park to ensure that no trouble broke out.

Over 3,000 visitors attended the event. The afternoon's athletic events were undisturbed. During an evening concert of band music and chorale societies, fire broke out near the crowded dance hall auditorium. The lights went out and smoke filled the room, causing the crowd to panic and flee. There were only a few minor injuries and property damage was minimal. Unwilling to admit that Irvington police had botched their assignment, the city's investigators attributed the flames to paint and turpentine stored in the basement. Just more accurately blamed the fire on the Minutemen.[30]

Controversy also broke out in Newark over the Berlin Olympics. The City Commission voted $200 to Jenny Caputo, a sixteen-year-old Newark gymnast, to help pay expenses for her trip to Berlin. The grant was made because Caputo's sponsor, the Newark Turn Verein (sports club), said it could only provide $300 of the $500 needed. Commissioner Anthony Minisi sponsored the resolution, which was passed by the commission with no discussion. Immediately, the NSANL and Newark Post 34 of the JWV, protested the grant on the grounds that the Olympics were to be used to disseminate Nazi propaganda.[31]

Minisi defended the grant, saying the Turn Verein "is noted for developing the youth of our city" and is non-political. Judge Joseph Siegler, a prominent Newark Jewish leader, countered by praising Caputo as a great athlete and a credit to Newark whose skills should not be displayed in "despotic" Germany.[32] Adding their voices to the protest were the Essex Trades Council and the Delicatessen and Cafeteria Workers' Union.[33] As a result of the opposition, the City Commission rescinded the grant. The City Clerk told Kalb the action was taken because the commissioners lacked both authority and funds to approve the resolution.[34] By this time Jenny Caputo was already half way across the Atlantic on her way to the Olympics.[35]

* * *

The Rome-Berlin Axis agreement was signed on October 25, 1936. It is doubtful that the pact played a part in the barring of the German and Austrian War Veterans from participating in the Newark Armistice Day Parade two days later. The anti-Nazi record of the group's commander, Richard Krueger, and the fact that the group had a few Jewish members meant little. Although the group had been allowed to parade for the two years prior to 1933, 1936 marked the fourth straight year it was banned. The persuading argument against the group's participation was the event honored America's war dead. The parade marshal, Louis Freeman, Commander of Newark Post 34 of the Jewish War Veterans, argued "they're not Americans." Kalb also spoke against participation by the German-Austrian group.[36]

During this period, one of Kalb's concerns was the lack of unity in the national anti-Nazi movement.[37] A major problem was that the NSANL president, Samuel Untermyer, wanted to control any unified group. He criticized the American Jewish Congress (AJC) for not separating the boycott from its other work, which Untermyer claimed hurt the national effort.[38] While neither the AJC nor the Joint Labor Committee (JLC) components of the Joint Boycott Council (JBC) would cede control of their boycott efforts to the NSANL, they would have welcomed the NSANL as an equal member of the JBC.

The situation would have been ludicrous had it not been tragic. The NSANL and the JBC had separate offices and research divisions in New York. Each issued press releases and other publicity on boycott matters. Each had a newsletter listing boycott violators and other related information. The NSANL published "Anti-Nazi Economic Bulletin" and the JBC mailed out "Boycott." The latter publication was first produced in early 1937 and was obviously a take-off on the NSANL periodical, which had been circulating for over three years.[39]

The rivalry between the JBC and the NSANL hampered the boycott effort. A letter from Kalb to the JBC chairman, Joseph Tenenbaum, illustrates this point. Kalb complained that the research chair of the JBC, Israel Posnansky, refused to grant him information on a boycott case because Tenenbaum said, "I was affiliated with the NSANL." Kalb was not only the ranking New Jersey boycott official for the JWV and the NSANL, but also for the AJC, a partner in the JBC. "If you, Dr. Tenenbaum, really left such instructions you are to be severely criticized," Kalb continued. In the same letter, Kalb complained that at no time in the nine months of the JBC's existence had it contacted him for boycott information or advised him of any violators dealing in Nazi goods "selling to stores in this section of New Jersey."[40]

By June of 1937, the governing council of the AJC told the JBC that it would cooperate with the NSANL but would no longer seek a merger with that group. In fact, during the previous year there had been suggestions that the JBC and NSANL cooperate on a case-by-case basis. A recommendation that the JWV be included in talks was accepted. On behalf of the national office of the NSANL, Kalb sent a letter to the JBC that the NSANL had agreed to participate in a "council on decisions."[41] In November, the national boycott committee of the JWV unanimously voted to appoint two board members to serve with two each from the JBC and the NSANL to establish such a council.[42] The next month, the organizations agreed to set up a joint action committee (usually referred to as the Committee on Joint Cases). Its purpose was to investigate and recommend action on boycott cases brought to its attention by any of the three participants.[43] Kalb was the NSANL signatory on the agreement.[44]

Kalb frequently traveled to New York to participate in NSANL board matters and to represent it on the Committee on Joint Cases.[45] In October 1936, he was named national research director for the NSANL. Once the Committee on Joint Cases began to function, Kalb helped coordinate NSANL and JBC research on possible boycott violators.[46] Inquiries from New Jersey on boycott matters were routinely forwarded to Kalb not only from the NSANL, but also from the JBC, despite the earlier difficulty.[47]

Kalb found the financial demands of running a boycott organization formidable. In order to maintain a small NSANL office, pay one full-time employee, rent halls for public meetings, and print bulletins and other materials, he had to spend considerable time fundraising. Through speaking engagements and frequent fund appeals, Kalb and his leadership cadre assured the Newark NSANL a constant flow of small contributions from KUVs and other Eastern European immigrant welfare societies.

One of Kalb's most effective fund-raisers and speakers for the NSANL was Jacob Malamuth, whom Kalb had met in the early 1930s through KUV activities. Malamuth was a tall, powerfully built activist who often accompanied Kalb as a bodyguard and companion to NSANL events. Malamuth's sister, Charlotte, remembers Kalb as a frequent visitor to their house.[48] In addition to his NSANL activities, Malamuth was involved in Yiddish and leftist causes. Unknown to the staunch anti-communist Kalb was that Malamuth was chairman of the Newark Communist Party's Jewish bureau, a position he had held since 1933.[49] An organizer for Newark's three Jewish sections of the International Worker's Order (IWO), Communist Party leaders valued Malamuth's work, and promoted him to Newark District Organizer for the Language Bureau (the body set up to supervise the foreign language speakers' sections of the party) in September, 1935.[50]

Malamuth was also active along with Kalb in the AJC. Kalb needed financial help from the Essex unit of the AJC, a broad-based middle-class Jewish organization that was committed to the boycott. As treasurer of the Essex AJC and its boycott chairman, Kalb worked closely with Judge Joseph Siegler, chairman of both the Essex and New Jersey AJC. Kalb, it would seem, was in an excellent position to merge the efforts of that group and those of Newark's NSANL.[51]

Kalb made several attempts to coordinate the anti-German boycott efforts of the Jewish community in early 1937. Newark's NSANL sent letters to 340 Jewish organizations asking for their cooperation in the boycott. Forty-five responded that they were willing to set up a permanent organization of English- and Yiddish-speaking groups to unite in boycott efforts.[52] Nothing further was heard about this effort, and it can be assumed that it never came to fruition. Kalb made another effort to unify Newark-area groups when he called a special meeting of the NSANL, at which delegates from over 100 Jewish organizations, including the AJC and the JWV, gathered at the Y. Speaking for the AJC, Judge Siegler urged all groups to cooperate in supporting the boycott. [53]

Cooperation, of course, did not mean unification, nor did it mean mutual financial support. Two months prior, in November 1936, Kalb presided at the annual conference of the New Jersey Division of the NSANL, held at the Y. The convention's major objective was the launch of a $10,000 fund-raising effort for anti-Nazi activities, particularly the boycott of German goods. This was New Jersey's quota for a NSANL national campaign to raise $250,000.[54] Kalb said substantial contributions were needed immediately, since the Germans were going through tough economic times and the "time to press the boycott is now."[55]

Within two weeks, the Essex County AJC met and Kalb asked Siegler to support the NSANL fund-raising effort. Siegler urged the 200 in attendance to fight anti-Semitic propaganda that was being imported into the United States. He also had his organization reaffirm its adherence to the boycott. However, he made no request for a financial contribution to the NSANL effort.[56] An Essex AJC contribution to the Newark NSANL might incur the wrath of national AJC leaders, and Siegler was determined not to take that risk. Without AJC support, Kalb's mission to raise $10,000 was in jeopardy. The AJC was the only mainstream Jewish organization supporting the boycott that had both the financial resources and influence among middle-class Newark Jews to guarantee the NSANL's campaign goal. Responses to the NSANL appeal for funds were reported in both the *Newark News* and the *Jewish Chronicle*. By the end of the year the *Chronicle* listed thirty-three contributions, all from Eastern European working-class sources: KUV's (eighteen), other men's and women's welfare associations (ten), and Orthodox synagogues (five), with the two largest gifts coming from the Erste Bershader KUV ($115), and the Israel KUV ($75).[57] By February 1937, the appeal was quietly dropped, with a total of $1,000 collected.[58]

Despite lack of financial support, Kalb kept the boycott campaign alive with speeches and his local boycott-violators list.[59] He organized a week long NSANL exhibition at the Y illustrating how millions of dollars were being spent by Nazi Germany for anti-American and anti-Semitic propaganda and on the activities of Nazi groups in America.[60] The AJC praised the exhibit, which drew thousands of visitors.[61] During the High Holy Days in 1936, Kalb once again called on rabbis to include support for the boycott in their sermons.[62]

In his end-of-the-year report to the NSANL, Kalb listed twenty-five industries included in the boycott. A major focus continued to be Newark department stores. He asserted that L. Bamberger and the Kresge Department Store "have called or written me frequently requesting information on jobbers and importers relative to their position on the anti-Nazi boycott. They have cooperated completely. Hahne & Company, Goerke's, and Sears Roebuck are still handling German goods in spite of the fact that they are constantly receiving complaints. These stores have been circularized and I am sure they are feeling the effect of the boycott." Another important Newark industry was beer. Kalb reported: "Krueger and Hoffman are not handling German goods. United and Feigenspan are using German malt and other products." [63]

Women remained important in the boycott movement as investigators and enforcers. Kalb often stressed the importance of the Newark NSANL Women's Division, which attempted to enlighten women about Nazi Germany's degradation of women.[64] However, the men were not always eager to allow women to act on their own. When Bertha Koretz of New York, national chairman of the JWV's "Ladies Auxilliary National Boycott Committee," was about to issue her organization's first bulletin, she met with resistance from the JWV national commander, Edgar H. Burman. A friend, Betty Lazarus, a member of the Newark NSANL's Women's Division, sent a good-luck letter telling her not to let Burman stop her. " Tell him you are the LADIES National Boycott Chairman," urged Lazarus.[65]

In mid-1937, Kalb remarked on the success of the boycott at the national level. Citing a NSANL report that showed German trade with the United States amounted to only 3.2 percent of America's total foreign trade, as opposed to 5.6 percent before the boycott began in 1933. Kalb pointed out that the figure would be lower but many German manufacturers had made their "Made in Germany" markings easy to remove. By the time the goods were sold in the United States the markings had been replaced with those of another country. A subsequent NSANL report showed that for the first four months of 1937, German trade had fallen to 2.7 percent of total American foreign trade.[66]

Despite these optimistic figures, German rearmament and political successes made it evident that the Nazi regime would continue with or without the boycott. By the time the New York office of the NSANL issued these reports, the Nazis had already retaken the Saarland, resumed conscription in violation of the Versailles Treaty, marched into the Rhineland, and formed the Rome Berlin Axis. All this had been done without intervention by the democratic powers. As early as October1936, Rudolf Höss, subsequently commandant of the Auschwitz death camp, bragged that the boycott had been defeated.[67] If the boycott forces heard Höss's remarks, it did not stop them.

* * *

Bund strength increased in key areas of the United States beginning in 1936. By the fall of 1937, the U. S. Department of Justice estimated Bund membership exceeded 8,000, spread over fifty local chapters; over 5,000 members were in twenty-six chapters in New York, New Jersey, Connecticut, and Pennsylvania. New Jersey had five chapters, in Essex (Newark), Hudson, Passaic, Bergen, and Mercer counties, with the Newark chapter the second largest.[68] As with the Friends of the New Germany, the Bund also operated in smaller New Jersey towns where it was under less scrutiny. From 1937 through 1940, Bund activities were reported in Englewood, West Orange, Newfoundland, New Milford, Carlstadt, Glendale, Paramus, Hanover, and Bloomingdale.[69]

The Bund's growing membership was not the only anti-Nazi concern. Fritz Kuhn's provocative pronouncements and penchant for publicity guaranteed constant press and radio coverage. The *New York Times* ran a feature story on the Nazi group in March 1937 that asserted that the movement had failed to make headway in an "American democratic setting." The article reported that the average Bund meeting in Yorkville attracted an audience of 1,500 with seventy-five O.D. troopers. Apparently this number was insufficient for the *Times* to be alarmed; it cited internal dissension and an undemocratic message as the chief reasons for the Bund's inability to make more headway among Manhattan's estimated 200,000 Germans.[70]

However, New York's Mayor Fiorello La Guardia expressed outrage at the Bund's increased activities and visibility. At a meeting of the AJC women's division, La Guardia said he would like to have "a figure of that brown-shirted fanatic (Hitler) who is now menacing the peace of the world" in a chamber of horrors at the New York World's Fair. The Nazi government criticized La Guardia's remarks, causing Secretary of State Cordell Hull to send a letter of regret to the German government. Hull's action was bitterly denounced by Samuel Untermyer of the NSANL.[71]

Two weeks after La Guardia's anti-Hitler remarks, over 20,000 jammed into Madison Square Garden for an anti-Nazi rally. JBC organized the event, which featured John L. Lewis, President of the Congress of Industrial Organizations (CIO), who told the crowd that industrial democracy was the best guarantee against fascism in the United States. Rabbi Stephen Wise announced that one of the greatest living Americans was in attendance. The spotlight lit on Mayor La Guardia. The loudest ovation of the evening broke out as the crowd cried, "We want the Mayor!" Rabbi Wise called La Guardia to the speaker's podium, where he gave an impromptu speech again denouncing Hitler.[72]

As in Yorkville, Kuhn's policy of Americanization attracted members and supporters to the Newark Bund. Some had sympathized with the Friends, but because of that group's obvious alien character had not openly participated in its activities. Friends' meetings had drawn fifty to sixty people each week. Now Bund gatherings in Irvington grew to over 200 and were sometimes held twice a week; in early 1937, the *New York Times* estimated the Newark Bund's membership at between 100 and 285.[73]

The Nazis met in the evening in the backroom of the Apollo Restaurant on Springfield Avenue, a location known to Irvington police, the Minutemen, and the NSANL. The city's sizable Jewish population lived on the same streets as the German Americans. They could not help but see Nazi activities, particularly since the O.D. had established a branch and often wore their uniforms to meetings. The frequency of and growing attendance at Bund meetings caused apprehension among both Jews and Irvington officials.

Fritz Kuhn made his first recorded trip to Irvington in February 1937 to meet with the Newark Bund. Non-uniformed O.D. members accompanied him. The American Führer addressed the Nazis on the need to become more public in their activities and to fly the swastika at every opportunity in order to gain recruits and forge alliances with other extremist groups.

It may have been at this event that Kuhn first discussed setting up Camp Nordland, in Andover with Von Busch. (Andover is a community in rural Sussex County, an hour and a half from Newark.) Von Busch had a small summer cabin in Andover, and later claimed it was his idea to build the camp there. Nazi camps, because of the privacy they afforded and the revenue they raised, were a prime item on Kuhn's agenda. A score were already operating or on the drawing board.

Arno and Kalb soon heard about Kuhn's appearance in Irvington. Arno wanted to send the Minutemen to battle the Bundists. Kalb prevailed upon his friend to give diplomacy a chance. Since Arno and his group were *persona non grata* in Irvington, it was the NSANL that sent a letter to Irvington officials protesting Nazi activities. Kalb sent a copy of the letter to the *Irvington Herald* rather than to the two Newark dailies or to the *Jewish Chronicle*. German Americans were the largest ethnic group in Irvington, and up to this point, the *Herald* had studiously avoided the topic of Nazism in Irvington. Kalb hoped to force the newspaper and city officials to get off the fence on the issue of Nazism. While the Bund kept a low profile, it operated in Irvington with impunity because the police protected it from the Minutemen. When the Nazis began open agitation in 1937, the attendant publicity was not good for the city.

Longie Zwillman controlled most of Irvington's illegal gambling, including the slot machines installed in vacant stores throughout town. He paid protection money to both the police and politicians for their cooperation. However, once the Bund threatened the Jews, he did not hesitate to unleash the always willing Arno and his Minutemen, even if it meant disrupting his "business." It was in the interest of Irvington officials and police to restrain the Bund and keep the Minutemen out of their town.

To increase pressure on Irvington officials, Kalb called a March meeting of the NSANL at which Representative Samuel Dickstein would speak. Dickstein was a household name for most Newark Jews and the press gave substantial space to the upcoming event. Dickstein, whose Congressional investigation into the Friends had been a major factor in the group's demise, had continued his attacks on its successor, the German-American Bund. At an Atlantic City convention of B'Nai Brith, he charged that almost every German ship entering an American harbor carried, in addition to its regular crew, a large number of "seamen" whose mission was to help Nazi groups in America. He also claimed that his investigators had discovered German aliens holding trials for countrymen who refused to join the Hitler movement.[74]

Over 2,000 people packed Newark's Krueger Hall to hear Dickstein. He did not disappoint the audience as he delivered a thirty-minute exposé of Nazi activities in America. The Congressman claimed that there were 100 Nazi spies in America and that twenty-five of them were in New Jersey. He also said that the Bund had 50,000 followers in the state, and that Irvington was a key Nazi stronghold. Although Dickstein inflated some of his figures—as he was prone to do—his speech served as a call to action. After Dickstein spoke of the vital need to continue the anti-Nazi boycott, Kalb made a plea for funds.[75]

As pressure increased in Irvington, city officials met with *Herald* executives. It was decided that the weekly would serve as a spokesman for the municipal authorities. One week after Dickstein's charges a *Herald* headline announced, "Police Authorities to Receive Formal Notice of Alleged Activities." Without naming the NSANL, the article said a letter sent to the Irvington police alleged that regular Bund and O.D. meetings, complete with swastikas, were being held in the town. Two meetings had taken place in the past week at the Apollo Restaurant, both with over 200 attendees. Kuhn's February appearance in Irvington was also mentioned. The *Herald* said that the letter emphasized that Irvington officials had barred un-American meetings after the 1934 riot.[76] The article put the Bund on notice that it was embarrassing Irvington. As planned, Balentine answered Kalb's letter with a phone call. He asked Kalb whether he would be willing to have a confidential meeting with Irvington Bund leaders to work out a truce, and if he could speak for Arno. After checking with Arno, Kalb called Balentine and agreed to the meeting.

Balentine, Kalb, Abraham Harkavy, attorney for the NSANL, and Von Busch met in late March at the same time newspapers were reporting that Representative Dickstein had launched a new attack on the Bund. In a speech on the House floor, he had challenged the Bund to deny that its oath required members to swear allegiance to Adolph Hitler and to grant the Führer and his surrogates absolute obedience.[77] Whether this was brought up at the Irvington meeting is unknown. The meeting resulted in an agreement that neither uniforms nor the swastika would be displayed in public and that no anti-Semitic propaganda would be distributed in Irvington. In return, Kalb promised that there would be no attacks on private Bund meetings. Balentine promised Von Busch that the Bund could continue to hold private meetings as before, with no interference. The agreement also provided for a statement to the upcoming *Herald* article in which Von Busch could stress the Bund's Americanism, as long as the statement had no anti-Semitic content.

The headline of the April 2, 1937 *Herald* proclaimed "Opponents Reach Agreement on Nazi Charges." The paper took credit for bringing about a peaceful settlement of the dispute. It claimed that representatives of the factions reached an agreement that would eliminate the threat of violence in Irvington. The paper concluded its article with Von Busch's statement, which claimed that German Americans were not traitors and that Bund meetings were not Nazi or un-American but rather peaceful gatherings of Christian American citizens who "realize the terrible menace to America through the preaching of atheism, Communism, Godless Bolshevism, and bloody red terrorism."[78]

In its lead editorial, "Trouble Forestalled," the *Herald* congratulated the NSANL, the Bund, and itself for preventing potential violence. It also said "racial animosities have no place in Irvington."[79] The *Herald* was overly optimistic and naive. The newspaper's voice was the voice of its advertisers and the Irvington political establishment both of whom hoped to buy time before the next crisis. They could not know that 1938 would see an increasing number of Bund activities that could not be peacefully accommodated.

As a dubious peace was being announced in Irvington, Representative Dickstein introduced a resolution to investigate "un-American activities," which was quickly reported out of the Rules Committee and awaited a full House vote. Dickstein's ally, McCormack, requested an appropriation of $30,000 to fund a thorough examination of anti-American groups. During the House debate, the resolution was assailed as a possible attack on freedom of speech and as a tool for Dickstein's self-aggrandizment. Others opposed the bill because such a committee could stir up racial bias, an argument that had been brought up against creation of the original McCormack-Dickstein Committee. Despite the two Congressmen's efforts, the resolution was tabled in early April by a vote of 184 to 38.[80]

Dickstein himself was one of the reasons the resolution did not pass. House members were jealous that he had a national reputation because of his anti-Nazi work. His well-publicized speeches, radio addresses, and general flamboyance irritated many Congressional colleagues. Dickstein's prominence was anathema to some House members because he was Jewish. Finally, there were those lawmakers who objected to his attacks on Nazism, and felt that only Communism was anti-American. It would be more than a year before an un-American Activities Committee was created by the House, and it would be a far different body than the one McCormack and Dickstein ran four years earlier.

* * *

During the summer of 1937 a not-so-new Nazi phenomenon appeared—the summer camp. The Friends of the New Germany had run camps for Nazi youth indoctrination in 1934 and 1935, but these were not successful and were soon out of business. When the Bund took over the American Nazi movement, Fritz Kuhn organized an extensive camp network. He believed the camps should educate not just children but entire families and serve as family entertainment centers during the summer. As part of Kuhn's strategy for Nazifying German Americans, there were over twenty Bund camps operating in the United States by the summer of 1937. Bund officials provided propaganda, drilled youths and O.D. forces, and conducted all business away from prying eyes. Perhaps one reason Von Busch made the agreement with Balentine and Kalb was that he knew Camp Nordland would be ready in a few months, and he could use it for events originally planned for Irvington.

Members of the Newark Bund used the camp more frequently than any other New Jersey Bund division.[81] Camp Nordland was incorporated in March 1937 with August Klapprott, New Jersey Bundesleiter, as the registered agent. Among the eight trustees were Fritz Kuhn and Hermann Von Busch. Klapprott, a former mason, had joined the Friends of the New Germany in 1933 but had never been a leader. His rise to prominence in the Bund was attributed to his friendship with and loyalty to Kuhn.[82]

Camp Nordland included ninety-seven wooded acres and a lake.[83] In Nordland's first summer, close to 400 boys and girls enrolled in the youth program.[84] All conversations among the campers were required to be in German. Adjacent to the camp were lots for rent at $15 per year, where families could build cottages. Von Busch stressed that the camp was an outdoor gathering place for "all" German-American families.[85] After hasty renovations it opened on July 18. Over 8,000 German Americans from New Jersey and New York attended. They had come by car or by a special train from Hoboken for the festivities, which included swastika waving, marching, speechmaking and beer drinking.

The day began with a parade of O.D. troopers, Italian-American black shirted Fascists, and uniformed youths. Klapprott presided and introduced Sussex County State Senator William Dolan, who welcomed the Nazis and Fascists to Sussex County. Kuhn was the featured speaker. However, neither Klapprott nor Kuhn attacked Jews by name, instead referring to "a certain minority" threatening America. The leader of the Blackshirts, Dr. Salvatore Caridi of Union City, praised Germany and Italy as the "two best nations in the world" and contended that each was a "model of order and discipline."[86]

Camp Nordland's opening received wide press coverage, and protests were immediate and intense. Two of the first attacks came from
Newark Post 34 of the Jewish War Veterans and from Kalb, who
demanded that the camp be closed because it was a military training
ground for a foreign power. Another early protester was Robert
Parker, secretary of the Newark branch of the International Labor
Defense Group, a communist-sponsored organization. The New Jersey regional director of the CIO, William J. Carney, sent a telegram
to Dickstein calling for a Congressional probe. State veterans groups,
including branches of the VFW and American Legion, called for
either an investigation or the camp's closing.[87]

Newark Post 34 of the JWV convened a meeting within a week
after Nordland's opening to discuss possible actions against the camp.
The veterans were emotional. Kalb asserted that America was now
facing an enemy more dangerous than that in World War I. Louis
Freeman, State Commander of the JWV, castigated the Bund for
teaching children to salute the swastika rather than the American
flag "for which we fought for overseas." William Becker, Judge
Advocate of the Post, argued that the only way to halt the Bund's
subversive activities was with fists. He said, "Let's not pussyfoot
about the matter. Let's go out there like men, fight it out and break it
up."[88] After resounding cheers for Becker's speech had subsided,
Herman Weckstein, the Post Commander, argued that the JWV objectives would be better served without violence. He recommended
lobbying for a Congressional investigation. His view carried the day.
The post unanimously passed a resolution assailing Nordland as
"completely un-American and contrary to principles of patriotism
and democracy," and it appointed three delegates to present the communication to Dickstein.[89]

The Nazis and their sympathizers also lobbied Congress. A form
letter designed by supporters of the camp was mailed to congressmen to oppose the creation of an "un-American" committee. Charles
Kraft, proprietor of Kraft's Hardware in Irvington, sent this letter to
Representative J.J. O'Connor and others. It complained about the simultaneous persecution of the Bund and tolerance of communists openly
agitating for the overthrow of the government. The letter added that
although the writer was not a Bund member, he had attended the first
meeting at Nordland and neither saw nor heard anything that "any
good American would find fault with." The note added that communists were attacking Bund meetings with "bricks and bats."[90]

In response to veteran's groups and others, Dickstein said he would again urge an investigation of un-American activities. Dickstein sensed, however, that if he introduced the bill personal animosity and jealousy would again reduce its chances for success. He had heard on the floor of the House Representative Shannon of Missouri remark that "An investigation of this kind should not be headed by a foreign-born citizen."[91] Facing reality as he had three years earlier, when he declined the chairmanship of the initial committee to investigate the Friends, Dickstein became the chief advocate of an un-American activities investigation bill introduced by Representative Martin Dies of Texas.

Martin Dies and Samuel Dickstein were both Democrats, but their differences were more pronounced than their similarities. Dies grew up in rural Texas, whereas Dickstein was raised on New York's Lower East Side. Dies' father was a successful businessman who served in Congress from 1909 to 1919. Dickstein's father was a tailor. Dickstein championed the immigrant throughout his Congressional career whereas on his first day in Congress, in 1931, Martin Dies sponsored a bill to suspend immigration to the United States for five years.[92] Whereas Dickstein was the Nazi's fiercest congressional foe, Dies became the *bête noire* of communists. Dickstein was an outsider in the "old boy" network of the House. Dies, on the other hand, was a consummate insider. The New Yorker had to earn his chairmanship of the House Committee on Immigration through seniority while Dies, after only a few years in Congress, obtained a seat on the powerful House Rules Committee because of the patronage of Vice President John Nance Garner. Dies was tall and an indifferent dresser; Dickstein was short and impeccably attired. The qualities they shared, however, were powerful; a fondness for the spotlight and a hatred of those they perceived as a threat to the United States.

Dies yearly sponsored bills aimed at deporting alien communists, none of which were enacted. In 1935, he added fascists to his agenda and introduced a bill to deport alien communists and fascists. The measure was reported out of committee but died.[93] By 1937, Dies had a reputation as a flamboyant and ambitious legislator. Sensing an opportunity to get the headlines Dickstein garnered, and having witnessed the defeat of Dickstein's bill, Dies decided to capitalize on the twin threats of communism and Nazism. Backed by Vice President Garner, House Speaker William B. Bankhead, and House Majority Leader Sam Rayburn,[94] Dies introduced Resolution 282, calling for the formation of a committee to investigate un-American activities. The measure was submitted to the Rules Committee in June 1937, one month before Camp Nordland's opening.

Dickstein's support of the resolution included publishing lists of Nazi sympathizers, speaking to the House on the Nazi menace (three times in September), and publishing a list of the printed matter in German or English to stir up German Americans in the *Congressional Record*. Predictably, Representative Harold Knutson of Minnesota denounced Dickstein in the House by for being obsessed with Nazism and by Representative Maury Maverick of Texas for being a witch hunter.[95]

Dickstein addressed the House specifically about Camp Nordland and suggested that State Senator William Dolan, who had welcomed the Bund to the camp be impeached. He also accused New Jersey politicians, including Dolan, of being involved in the sale to the Bund of the 100-acre property in Sussex County. Dolan claimed that his law office had only done title work for the Bund. Several days later, Representative J. Parnell Thomas of Sussex County interrupted Dickstein in the middle of a speech supporting the Dies resolution. Thomas, a Republican, reminded House colleagues that Dolan was a Democrat, as were the other county officials who invited the Bund to Sussex County. He claimed that the Democrat-controlled Andover County Township Board had granted a liquor license to the camp. He said he supported an investigation of the camp but insisted that Democrats were responsible for it.[96] The next day Thomas made his own speech in support of the Dies resolution and attacked Camp Nordland. He coupled this denunciation with a demand that the Communist Party also be investigated. His remarked, "Even in one small section in New York City there are more Reds than there are Nazis in the entire United States."[97]

New Jersey veterans' groups continued to press for an investigation of the Bund and Camp Nordland. They would have to wait over a year before such a probe began. In the meantime, a meeting of thirty New Jersey post commanders of the American Legion, Veterans of Foreign Wars, Jewish War Veterans, Irish Veterans, and Order of the Purple Heart was held in Newark at which a resolution passed condemning the Bund for preaching Nazism and race hatred, and requesting both state and Congressional investigations of the organization. Louis Freeman, JWV state commander, requested that the resolution be sent to Governor Harold Hoffman, who had not yet expressed an opinion on Camp Nordland or the Bund. On the other hand, Hoffman had recently expressed his opposition to the C.I.O., which was organizing labor unions in New Jersey. Kalb asked for an investigation of Bund finances, noting that Camp Nordland had cost $16,000. Arthur Coakley of the Irish War Veterans urged a widespread school program to combat "the goose-step, Hitler salute, and disregard for our flag." Several speakers condemned beer drinking at Nordland, calling it a demoralizing influence on the camp's youths. Most speakers said they represented themselves and not their posts.[98] Nordland's second weekend saw the number of attendees decline to 2,000 people. Martial music, heiling, and marching were temporarily suspended in favor of beer and waltzing. Klapprott spoke in the camp's beer hall to a small audience, including newspapermen. He said he would welcome a federal investigation of the camp since the Bund was doing nothing wrong. When asked about the protests of veteran's groups, Klapprott said they had no right to call for an investigation since the Bund was a private group just like a synagogue, and that his group "never investigates Jewish synagogues."[99] Prior to Nordland's third weekend, Dickstein published the names of seventeen Nazi propagandists in the *Congressional Record* to add to the forty-six he had previously publicized. He included Klapprott, who the Congressman stated had been arrested on a morals charge.[100] When the Bund met in the camp that weekend, Klapprott said he would refute the "lies" against him and the camp. He claimed he had many witnesses who would defend him on the morals charge, but was not more specific. Von Busch told those assembled that German Americans were a menace only to the lawless elements of the country. He said the Bund was not afraid of any investigation because "we have the support of all real American people."[101]

With no Congressional investigation in the offing, Dickstein indirectly answered Klapprott and Von Busch from the floor of the House. He demanded that subpoena powers be granted the House Immigration Committee to enable it to expose the "well-organized and well-financed" Nazi movement in the United States.[102] The House leadership had no intention of granting this power to his committee, so Dickstein was again stymied. Many months would pass before the Dies committee saw the light of day. Attacks on Bund camps, if they were to occur in 1937, would not be made by the government.

* * *

Arno and Kalb faced several problems with regard to Nordland. First, the camp was almost two hours from Newark, and a cavalcade of cars containing armed men might be stopped on the road, resulting in arrests for carrying weapons. Second, the anti-Nazis had every reason to believe that Sussex authorities would forcibly repel an attack on the camp. Rather than do nothing, the decision was made to attack the camp without weapons. The Minutemen passed the word to their fighters to assemble on Prince Street and Springfield Avenue at 9 AM Sunday August 8 for the trip to Nordland. Word of the impending attack got to the Nazis and Von Busch put the press and Sussex authorities on notice. He issued a statement that the camp would provide for its own protection and that the Sussex Sheriff Sidney Webster was aware of the situation.[103]

On Sunday morning, eight cars containing approximately forty unarmed men left Newark for Camp Nordland. They arrived around noon and saw hundreds of men, women, and children entering the facility and thousands more already inside. The press estimated the crowd at 5,000. There were over 100 local police on the scene, armed in combat gear. The Minutemen saw no Nazis in uniform. The atmosphere was one of a carnival as the Nazis had proclaimed that Sunday "Youth Sports Day." Arno and his men spent an hour driving and walking around the camp perimeter before returning to Newark.[104]

Although Arno and Kalb's efforts against Nordland had not succeeded, other groups joined them in attacking the camp. The State Council of the Knights of Columbus, an influential Catholic lay group, condemned Nazi activities at Camp Nordland and warned against "a harvest of religious intolerance in America." Newark Post 10 of the American Legion, explaining that some of its own members were of German origin, passed resolutions against the Bund and Camp Nordland, including a demand that both the state and national conventions of the legion take action against the Bund. Post 10 went further than most veterans' groups in its condemnation of the Bund, claiming Nordland to be "an unwanted, unparalleled bit of brazen effrontery on the part of the subjects of a nation which so recently as nineteen years ago was fighting against the citizens of this country."[105]

The calls by local posts of veterans' groups to act against the Bund soon were countered by other local posts and by the American Legion's state committee, which refused to approve a resolution to investigate Nordland because it "specified no overt act." At the same time, twelve members of different posts of the Essex County American Legion, VFW, and DAV, after a visit to Nordland, gave it a "clean bill of health." A spokesman for the group said, "I have seen nothing un-American here. It's a fine thing." A month later at its state convention in Atlantic City, The American Legion reversed the decision of its executive committee. The delegates approved, without debate, a resolution opposing establishment of camps, societies, or organizations that promote allegiance to foreign governments.[106]

Dickstein pressed his attack on the camp. In a speech before Congress he said, "New Jersey contains the worst hotbed of Nazis and Fascists that you and I could ever dream of." The Congressman again asked the House to approve the Dies resolution to investigate alien activities. He claimed that the Justice Department didn't have sufficient authority to make a thorough probe. United States Attorney General Homer Cummings said the investigation of complaints against German-American "military training camps" was in the preliminary stages.[107]

Kalb continued to hammer away at the Bund and its camps. At a press conference at the New Jersey NSANL headquarters, he claimed that hundreds of German youths between the ages of twelve and sixteen were being sent to America as exchange students but were really here to spread propaganda among young German Americans. Their destination was German-American communities and camps such as Nordland. He noted that at Camp Nordland these youths spoke exclusively in German to American campers. Kalb charged that these German youths were abusing diplomatic privilege and their American visas. He urged that the exchange program with Germany be halted, New Jersey Attorney General David Wilentz to investigate Nazi activities in the state, and for Congress to approve the Dies resolution.[108]

Acting on complaints from Congress, the public, and the press, Attorney General Homer Cummings authorized J. Edgar Hoover and the FBI to investigate Nazi military training camps throughout the country to determine if any federal laws were being violated. Cummings said some of the complaints charged Nazi sympathizers with placing firearms in interstate commerce while transporting them from one camp to another. The Bund immediately denied this charge. Klapprott said the only arms at the camp were Boy Scout knives. He said that military discipline and drilling kept the boy campers in order. He blamed Dickstein for the complaint and said that Congressman William Criton of Connecticut, who had made the charge on the House floor, was Dickstein's mouthpiece.[109]

The New Jersey division of the AJC weighed in against Nordland and the Bund at its organizational meeting in the fall. Nordland and other Bund camps were attacked for "alienating children from American ideals of social justice and fair play." Over $3,000 was raised statewide to fight "subversive Nazi camp activities," and to aid other AJC activities. The guest of honor was Rabbi Stephen Wise, who said Americans should strengthen the hands of governmental leaders such as President Roosevelt to keep democratic principles alive. Among the resolutions approved by AJC were continued support for the anti-Nazi boycott and an end to discrimination against Jews in the professions, trade, and industry. Two NSANL stalwarts were made officers of the new division, Michael (Mickey) Breitkopf and Jacob Malamuth.[110]

Interest in Nordland waned in the press and with the public by the end of the summer. Other than the AJC protest, only Kalb continued attacking Nordland and the Bund. He did this at both NSANL meetings and before Jewish organizations such as the Israel KUV.[111] Kalb consistently maintained that the best weapon against the Nazis was the boycott.[112] At an Essex County branch meeting of the NSANL, in late December, more than 250 delegates met in Krueger's Auditorium in Newark. Kalb reported that an early supporter of the boycott, the Young Men's Hebrew Club, would conduct a boycott rally at the club's headquarters in early January. [113]

At the end of 1937 an observation about the Nazis struck a pessimistic but prescient note. Delivering a guest sermon during a December Friday-night service at Temple B'Nai Abraham, Rabbi Joachim Prinz spoke on "Why Hitler Is Not Overthrown" before an overflow audience of 1,200.[114] Prinz, former rabbi of the largest synagogue in Berlin, had been exiled by the Nazis for his vigorous defense of Jewish rights. Prinz assessed the situation in Germany and posited that the Nazis would stay in power. He said, "There is no future for the Jews of Germany. They are condemned to extinction. The last chapter in the history of German Jewry is now being written, and it is necessary to recognize this fact and to make no attempt to preserve any illusions about the matter."[115]

By the end of 1937, Nazi Germany had signed a military and political pact with Japan and was well on its way to complete rearmament. Britain and France were both divided on how to deal with Hitler, and Russia was in the midst of a debilitating purge of its military hierarchy. Nazi strength was reflected in the corresponding growth in numbers and confidence of the German-American Bund; it was reported the Bund had enlisted almost 5,000 new members during the year.[116] At the same time, there was no consensus on how to deal with the Bund. Congress had still not brought up for vote the Dies resolution, which had languished in the House Rules Committee since June. The FBI, which began an investigation of the Bund camps in August, had not yet made a report of its findings. Twenty Bund camps were operating unhindered in the United States. Despite the efforts of anti-Nazis and other concerned groups and individuals in New Jersey, Camp Nordland seemed a permanent fixture in Andover.

In New York City, the Nazis flaunted their strength in Yorkville. At the end of October, the Bund held a parade in that neighborhood with 800 uniformed marchers. There would have been 3,000 if New Jersey and Pennsylvania contingents had not pulled out at the last moment. Over 5,000 spectators were at the start of the parade route at 86th St. and East End Avenue. The vanguard of the marchers carried American flags along with six swastika banners. The "Stars and Stripes," however, predominated among the 12,000 to 15,000 spectators. Over 1,300 police were stationed along the parade route and on rooftops to prevent disturbances.[117]

The Bund's growing confidence was also obvious in New Jersey. Over 400 Bundists met in an atmosphere of militaristic uniforms, clicking heels, and Nazi salutes at a rally in Hackensack to denounce New Jersey Justice Joseph Leyden, who said he would deny American citizenship to any member of the Bund. Klapprott was master of ceremonies and one of the speakers. Fritz Kuhn was the featured speaker. As he approached the podium, a column of 100 O.D. troops marched down the aisle two by two, snapped to attention, and gave their leader the Nazi salute accompanied by shouts of "heil." Kuhn said Leyden was unfit to be a judge and should go with "the Jews and the communists." He excoriated President Roosevelt for sending Joseph Stalin a telegram of congratulations on the twentieth anniversary of the Bolshevik revolution and for not sending one to Hitler "for the marvelous work he has done over there." After his address—delivered in German—Kuhn translated his words into English "for the benefit of the press." Other speakers claimed that Jews ran the country and that the Bund had done the United States a great favor by fighting the Jews and the communists. Newspapers that were unsympathetic to Hitler were referred to as "the Kosher press." Gerhard Kunze, a ranking Bund officer who would be Kuhn's successor, began his speech with the Nazi salute and a shout, "Heil, Der Fuhrer and white Gentile Americans." Treasury Secretary Henry Morganthau, Rabbi Stephen Wise, Samuel Untermyer, and Representative Samuel Dickstein were called menaces to America.[118]

1937 Nazi Germany possessed both national unity and military preparedness. It had already reversed important results of the Versailles Treaty. The Bund seemed in a position to attract further German-American and nativist support. In 1938, Hitler's troops would occupy much of Central Europe and commit atrocities against German Jews with little resistance. But those successes in Europe would not be reflected in the Bund. Rather, as European events unfolded in 1938, the Bund came under increasing attack by federal, state, and local governments. By the end of 1938, although Hitler was the dominant power in Europe, the Bund was in decline.

Notes

1. Diamond, Sander A., *The Nazi Movement in the United States, 1921-1941*, Ithaca, NY, 1974, p.193.
2. Ibid., pp. 211, 212.
3. Ibid., 213; Canedy, Susan, *America's Nazis*, Menlo Park CA, 1990, pp. 77-81.
4. Bell, Leland V., *In Hitler's Shadow — The Anatomy of American Nazism*, Port Washington, NY, 1973, p. 17.
5. NYT, 4/1/36, p. 22.
6. Other figures for Bund membership are lower, from 6,600 to 20,000. See Canedy, *America's Nazis*, p. 86. However, no true figure can be ascertained because the Bund burned most of their membership lists when Congressional investigations began.
7. Ibid., p. 31.
8. Ibid., pp. 91-94.
9. Frye, Alton, *Nazi Germany and the American Hemisphere 1933-1941*, New Haven, CT 1967, p.15.
10. Diamond, *The Nazi Movement in the United States*, p. 205.
11. J.C., 4/10/36, pp. 2, 4.
12. PSE&G Archives, *Public Service News*, 4/15/30, supplied to author by Public Service Electric and Gas, 6/25/98. The author's request for access to the archive for information on Herman Von Busch was denied on the basis that personnel records were not available to the public.
13. FBI File # 100-25344, Hermann Von Busch, Reports, 11/12/42, 2/6/43.
14. FBI Von Busch, op. cit., Reports, 2/6/43, 2/13/43.
15. Ibid., Report, 2/13/43.
16. FBI File # 100-9464, Section 1, Matthias Kohler, Report 8/5/42, pp. 1, 5, 8, 11, 14.
17. FBI file # 60-15, 67C, OS, Nat Arno, 6/30/39, p. 9. Arno was not loath to intimidate those who were reluctant to join his organization, or were giving less of a contribution than Arno expected. In the latter group was Hoxie Rabinowitz, a men's clothing merchant, who had a store on Branford Place in Newark. One day, Arno appeared and asked for Hoxie's "membership dues." Hoxie reached into the breast pocket of his suit, took out his wallet, and extracted a $1 bill which he gave to Arno. The next thing the diminutive Hoxie knew was that he had been lifted a foot off the ground by one hand of Arno while his wallet was being pulled out by the commander's other hand. Hoxie was then set down and given back his wallet $5 lighter. Interview, Hoxie Rabinowitz, 1/7/97.

18. N.N., 4/10/36, p. 16.
19. Mandell, Richard D., *The Nazi Olympics*, New York, 1971, pp. 71-73.
20. Ibid., pp. 77, 78.
21. J.C., 6/28/35, 8/16/35; N.N. 8/14/35.
22. Silberfeld's leadership in the Olympic boycott was praised by the NSANL. See NSANL, Box 11, Folder 1, Letter from G. E. Harriman to Rabbi Julius Silberfield, 10/11/35.
23. Rabbi Solomon Foster, reversing his previous stand, refused to attend the rally saying it was now up to the Olympic Committee and Christian leaders to settle the dispute. When he was attacked by Kingdon for his flip-flop, the Rabbi sent a letter to influential Newark Jewish leaders saying that because of the American Olympic Committee vote, "it would be futile and undignified for the Jewish people to protest further." See, Kalb Papers, Letter to "Friend" from Solomon Foster, 11/20/35.
24. N.N., 5/4/36, p. 5.
25. Ibid., 5/6/36, p. 4.
26. Kalb Papers, Letter to "Joe" from Kalb, 5/9/36.
27. N.N., 5/7/36, p. 26.
28. Ibid., 5/12/36, p. 16.
29. Ibid.
30. Siegel, Alan A., *Smile, A Picture History of Olympic Park, 1887-1965*, New Brunswick, NJ, 1995.
31. N.N., 7/3/36, p. 8; Kalb Papers, Telegram to Newark City Commission from Kalb, 7/2/36 Another response against the grant came from Attorney Samuel M. Hollander, who wrote the five commissioners decrying the support of anything with the "slightest tinge of the Nazi regime." He said the $200 would better be spent to help "the starving and unfortunate citizens of the City of Newark." See, Kalb Papers, Letter to Newark City Commissioners from Samuel M. Hollander, 7/2/36.
32. N.N., 7/7/36, p. 1; J.C., 7/10/36, p. 1.
33. N.N., 7/9/36, p. 19.
34. Kalb Papers, Letter from City Clerk to Kalb, 7/9/36.
35. N.N., 7/17/36, p. 1. For more on Jenny Caputo, see Warren Grover, "In Search of Jenny Caputo," *New Jersey Italian Tribune*, 5/18/00, p. 3; "In Search of Jenny Caputo-Part II," 8/17/00, p. 6.
36. N.N., 10/27/36, p. 18.
37. While Kalb was leading the boycott in Newark, another physician, Dr. Abraham Grossman, led a brief-lived movement in the Bronx which incorporated both the AJCongress and the NSANL. Grossman, an activist with the Bronx AJCongress, was able to set up a unified group, "United Non-Sectarian Boycott Council of the Bronx," in July, 1937. Representatives from the area's NSANL and JWV joined in the effort. As in Newark, support for the boycott effort came from KUVs and Workmen's Circle lodges. In the preface for the minutes of the first meeting of the new organization, Dr. Grossman said: "At last my dream of a united boycott activity in the Bronx became an accomplished fact." The NSANL, as a condition for its participation, forbade their name to be used on the letterhead of the group and stipulated that the no funds be raised by the United Boycott Council.

Grossman used the research departments of the NSANL and the JBC, and initiated his own investigations when possible. Also, like Kalb, Grossman worked to enforce the boycott by authorizing picket lines against boycott violators. The meetings of the United Boycott Council were much smaller than those of Newark's NSANL, averaging less than ten per session. Grossman was probably not as politically conservative as Kalb, since he applauded efforts of the League Against War and Fascism and Progressive Women's Council in picketing a Bronx Nazi meeting hall (Hunts Point Palace). Grossman's activities paralleled Kalb's, but in covering the Bronx, he had much more territory and population to deal with than his Newark counterpart. Also, Jewish institutions were relatively centralized in Newark while in the Bronx they were mainly branches of Manhattan organizations. See, Papers of Dr. Abraham Grossman, Box 1, Folder 1B, Grossman memos, 7/24/37, 7/27/37; also Folder 1A, Grossman memo, 11/9/37; Minutes of meetings, 5/19/38, 11/11/38.

38. Gottlieb, Moshe R., *American Anti-Nazi Resistance, 1933-1941*, New York, 1982, pp. 193,194. Untermyer's arguments that the "League be retained as the sole instrumentality for the boycott" were that the NSANL was (1) the first group to take up the boycott; (2) dedicated exclusively to the boycott; (3) non-sectarian and therefore in a better position to get funds from Christians; and (4) recognized throughout the country as *the* boycott organization.

39. Fredman Papers, "Boycott," 2/37.

40. JBC, op. cit., Box 19, Folder "Newark, N.J.," Letter from Kalb to Tenenbaum, 11/14/36.

41. JBC, op. cit., Box 4, Folder "J," Letter from Kalb to Israel Posnansky, 11/15/37.

42. Ibid., Letter from Edgar H. Burman to JBC, 11/22/37.

43. Gottlieb, *American Anti-Nazi Resistance*, pp. 195,196.

44. JBC, op. cit., Box 3, Folder "NSANL," Undated agreement to set up "Actions Committee on Boycott Cases."

45. Ibid., Box 4, "J" Folder, Letter from Dr. Robert Marcus to Kalb, 2/13/39.

46. Ibid., Box 3, Folder "NSANL," Letter from Kalb to Poznanski, 11/10/37; Letter from NSANL to Poznansky, 11/17/37.

47. Ibid., Box 5, Folder "S-1937-1938," Letter from Joseph Siegler to Joseph Tenenbaum, 11/13/36; Letter from Joseph Tenenbaum to Miss Bertha Yuker, 12/6/37.

48. Interview, Charlotte Gelb, 4/19/98.

49. CPUSA, Reel 255, Delo 3300, Minutes District 14 (Essex, Hudson, Passaic Counties), 11/9/33 The Party had Language Bureaus in most districts which supervised the activities of the foreign language branches of communist members and sympathizers. Each language group had their own weekly paper published in New York. In Newark, other than a Yiddish group (the largest), there were Italian (second largest) Polish, German, Slovak, Ukrainian, and Czech organizations.

50. Ibid., Reel 297, Delo 3878, Directive from the "National Org Department" to "The National Language Buro," 9/14/35. Malamuth used his Party connections to secure Dr. Benjamin Epstein a teaching job in the Newark school system. He knew Epstein from the AJC. Before Malamuth's help, Epstein couldn't "get to first base" despite finishing first in Newark's teaching exam. Interview, Dr. Benjamin Epstein, 6/19/98.

51. JBC, Box 5, Folder "S," Letter from Joseph Siegler to Joseph Tenenbaum, 11/13/36.

52. AJArchive, RG 307, Nazism Manuscript Collection, Box 1, Folder 1, Report of Inter-State Conference of NSANL, 3/7/37, p. 4.

53. J.C., 1/15/37, pp. 1, 6.

54. Ibid., 12/4/36, p 1.

55. Ibid., 12/11/36, p. 1.

56. N.N., 12/7/36, p. 7.

57. J.C., 12/18/36, p. 1; 12/25/36, p 1; N.N., 12/28/37, p. 29.

58. J.C., 1/15/37, p. 1.

59. Ibid., 11/13/36, p. 1.

60. Ibid., 11/20/36, p 2.

61. JBC, Box 5, Folder "S-1937-1938," Letter from Joseph Siegler to Joseph Tenenbaum, 11/13/36.

62. NSANL, Geographic Files, Box 11, Folder 2, Letter from Isidore Dworkin to NSANL, 9/23/36.

63. JBC, Box 19, Folder "Newark N.J.," Letter from Kalb to Tenenbaum, 11/14/36. Two futile boycott efforts undertaken by Kalb in 1936 concerned the German boxer, Max Schmeling, who was a favorite of Hitler. Schmeling's claim to fame was a knockout victory over Joe Louis in 1936, before "The Brown Bomber" became the World Heavyweight Champion. At the December 1936 Annual Meeting of the New Jersey NSANL, the convention voted to urge a ban on the Max Schmeling-James Braddock heavyweight boxing match set for Madison Square Garden in New York. This followed the initiative of Samuel Untermyer, national leader of the NSANL, who threatened a boycott of the match if it was held. Schmeling took a pro-Nazi stance, and his share of the fight gate would generate significant taxes for the Nazi regime. The boycott attempt turned into a futile exercise because a contract dispute sent Schmeling back to Germany without a match with Braddock.

Kalb's second effort was incorporated in a letter of warning to Loew's Theaters upon hearing that they were about to sign a contract with the boxer to appear throughout the country at their locations. The doctor threatened a one-year boycott against Loew's Theater in Newark if it hosted Schmeling. However, the contract was never signed.

64. N.N. 11/30/36, p. 6.
65. AJArchive, R.G.307, Nazism Manuscript Collection, Box 1, Folder 1, Letter to Mrs. Bertha Coretz from Mrs. Betty Lazarus, 11/1/37.
66. J.C., 5/21/37, p.1; 7/30/37, p. 6.
67. Gottlieb, *American Anti-Nazi Resistance*, p. 212.
68. NYT, 4/4/39, p. 1.
69. Glaser, Martha, "The German-American Bund in New Jersey," New Jersey History, Vol. XCII, No. 1, Spring 1974, pp. 40-42; N.N., 3/11/38, p. 11; 2/26/39, p. 1; 5/11/40, p. 6.
70. NYT, 3/21/37, Section IV, p. 11.
71. Ibid., 3/8/37, p. 13.
72. Ibid., 3/16/37, pp. 1, 2.
73. N.N., 4/4/39, p. 17.
74. NYT., 5/4/36, p. 11.
75. N.N., 3/12/37, p. 7.
76. I.H., 3/19/37, p. 1.
77. N.N., 3/24/37, p. 14.
78. I.H., 4/2/37, p. 1.
79. Ibid., 4/2/37, p. 4.
80. Ogden, August Raymond, *The Dies Committee—A Study of the Special House Committee for the Investigation of un-American Activities 1938-1944,* Washington, DC, 1945, pp. 41,42.
81. N.N., 9/10/40, p. 30. A survey of license plates by the New Jersey State Police disclosed that over 40 percent of the regular attendants of Camp Nordland were from Essex County.
82. Diamond, *The Nazi Movement in the United States*, pp. 312, 314, 338. According to an archival report, Klapprott was a Nazi Party member in Germany who participated in the murder of another Nazi in 1923. He was convicted for the crime in 1927 and sentenced to death. Klapprott was pardoned under a political amnesty ruling and soon emigrated to the United States. See, Fredman Collection, Box 4, File "Nazism," 4-page report.
83. Samuel Dickstein Papers, Series A, Box 2, Folder 4, Copy of Incorporation Papers, German-American Bund Auxilliary, 3/25/37.
84. Canedy, *America's Nazis*, p. 97.
85. Ibid.
86. N.N., 7/19/37, p. 1; J.C., 7/23/37, p. 1. Italian-American Fascist activity in New Jersey had existed since the 1920s. With the Nazi rise to power, and the subsequent alliance between Hitler and Mussolini in October 1936, both the Bund and Italian-American Fascist groups gave support to each other as in the case of the Camp Nordland opening. However, the ultra-nationalist agendas of each group prevented any strategic cooperation. Morristown, New Jersey was the site of one of the largest Italian-American Fascists rallies ever held on American soil. In August 1936, over 10,000 Italian-American Fascists rallied on the grounds of the Maestre Pie Filippini nuns, who managed many Italian schools in the United States. The men wore the Fascist black shirts and most women and girls were in uniform. A large group of Catholic Italian clergy attended and a Mass was celebrated. It was claimed that Newark Bishop Thomas Walsh sent a representative to the event, Monsignor F. Di Persia. After the Mass speeches were made lauding Mussolini and the correlation between Christianity and Fascism. No mention could be found of any Nazi presence. However, as the departing motorcade passed through German-American neighborhoods, people in the streets and from their windows answered the Fascist salute by "giving the Hitlerian salute of the German comrades." See, Gaetano Salvemini, Italian Fascist Activities in the United States, New York, 1977, pp. 209-214.

87. N.N., 7/21/37, pp. 3, 19; J.C., 7/23/37, p. 2.
88. N.N., 7/22/37, p. 2.
89. Ibid.
90. Dickstein Papers, Series A, Box 3, Folder 4, Letter to Hon. J.J. O'Conner from Charles P. Kraft, 7/22/37.
91. Goodman, Walter, *The Committee—The Extraordinary Career of the House Committee on Un-American Activities*, New York, 1968, p. 20.
92. Ibid.
93. Ogden, *The Dies Committee*, p. 39.
94. Goodman, *The Committee*, p. 16.
95. Ogden, *The Dies Committee*, pp. 42, 43.
96. N.N., 7/28/37, p. 11.
97. Ibid., 7/29/37, p. 9. Rep. Thomas was referring to Manhattan's Lower East Side.
98. Ibid., 7/27/37, p. 18.
99. Ibid., 7/26/37, p. 1.
100. Ibid., 7/30/37, p. 11.
101. Ibid., 8/2/37, p. 4; NYT, 8/2/37, p. 4.
102. NYT, 8/4/37, p. 2.
103. N.N., 8/2/37, p. 4.
104. Ibid., 8/9/37, p. 1.
105. Ibid., 8/5/37, p. 13.
106. Ibid., 8/8/37, p. 1; 8/9/37, p. 1; 9/10/37, p. 32.
107. Ibid., 8/12/37, p. 5.
108. Ibid., 8/4/37, p. 15.
109. Ibid., 8/18/37, p. 1; 8/19/37, p. 24.
110. Ibid., 10/4/37, p. 16; J.C., 10/8/37.
111. JHS, Israel Kranken Untersteutzung Verein, R.G. 4700, Box 2, Minutes 4/18/29-1/9/41, p. 365, 9/16/37.
112. J.C., 9/3/37, p. 2; 9/17/37, p. 11; 10/8/37, p. 1; 10/15/37, p. 1; 11/26/37, p. 1; 12/31/37, p. 1. N.N., 9/7/37, p. 11; 9/11/37, p. 7.
113. J.C., 12/31/37, p. 1. Other support for the NSANL came from the Plain Talk Club, a women's group, which organized a shoppers committee to visit and to dissuade merchants who were still distributing Nazi merchandise. Also, David Kent, president of Erste Bershader KUV, announced that every member of his group had volunteered one dollar each to support the League.
114. N.N., 12/8/37, p. 32. Ironically, two years later Silberfeld was replaced by Prinz as Rabbi of B'Nai Abraham.
115. J.C., 12/17/37, p. 2.
116. Diamond, *The Nazi Movement in the United States*, p. 315.
117. NYT, 10/31/37, p. 7.
118. N.N. 12/3/37, p. 19.

7

1938 and Kristallnacht

For Jews, 1938 was the cruelest of the interwar years. That year, Germany demonstrated to the world that it would move with impunity in Europe and violate Jews' most basic rights: Jewish community organizations lost their official status and recognition (March); the registration of all Jewish property became compulsory (April); over 1,500 German Jews were arrested and imprisoned in concentration camps (June); Jewish physicians could no longer treat Christians (June); Nazis ordered the destruction of the Great Synagogue in Munich (July); All Jewish men were required to add "Israel" to their name and all Jewish women "Sarah" (August); Jews were barred from practicing law (September); German Jewish passports were marked with the letter "J" for *Jude* (October); and finally Kristallnacht (November). Neither Europe nor the United States opposed any of the 1938 measures other than with diplomatic protests, encouraging Hitler to unleash World War II and the Holocaust.

The list of countries in which Jews were endangered grew significantly. Germany occupied Austria in April and the Sudetenland (a portion of Czechoslovakia) in September. Anti-Semitic laws were announced in Italy in October. In Poland, Romania, and Hungary, Nazi ideology fueled traditional anti-Semitism, causing a worsening of conditions for those countries' Jews. Seeking to appease the Arabs, England continued its retreat from the Balfour Declaration and further closed Palestine's doors to Jewish refugees.

Between the 1935 Nuremberg Laws—which deprived Jews of German citizenship; excluded them from public places, including theaters, shops, and hotels; and barred marriage and non-marital sexual contact between Christians and Jews—and 1938, few significant anti-Jewish measures were enacted in Germany. The 1936 Nazi Olympics, which Germany used for maximum propaganda effect, and

Hitler's ambition to achieve complete rearmament contributed to the cessation of anti-Semitic decrees. Hitler's abstinence from aggressive actions against his neighbors, with the exception of the March 1936 seizure of the Rhineland, earned him a degree of respectability in international affairs. Although many still mistrusted him, others thought he was becoming more politically moderate and would be useful as a strong counter to communism. Some optimists even predicted that the Jewish situation in Germany would normalize. Few in the West could have predicted the terrible events about to unfold.

* * *

Fritz Kuhn's German-American Bund basked in the reflected light of Nazi Germany's economic growth and increased respectability. Under his leadership the Bund grew in numbers and financial strength. Its 1937 nationwide summer camp program had been an unqualified success, and the Bund's Youth Division recruited a host of campers. Despite opposition from anti-Nazi forces, no camps had been forced to close. The Bund began publishing a youth magazine, *Junges Volk*, which praised the role played by Germans in the development of America, vaunted German heroes and the Aryan race, and dehumanized Jews.[1]

The Bund's strength was reflected in an increase in Nazi rallies and parades, which in turn drew additional visibility and publicity. Newspapers, magazines, and newsreels featured Bund events, especially those with goose-stepping and Nazi-saluting uniformed troops. Coupled with similar pictures of uniformed youths at Bund summer camps, many Americans who had previously ignored the American Nazis felt uncomfortable with an alien militaristic group in their midst.

Bund militancy in America's large cities brought about a corresponding response by anti-Nazis. In the first three months of 1938, Bund meetings were broken up in Buffalo, Chicago, and Philadelphia. In a separate Philadelphia incident, anti-Nazis bombed a meeting hall. Bund activities were investigated in Ohio. In New Jersey Bund meetings were attacked up in Englewood and New Milford.[2]

Anti-Nazis were disappointed in January 1938 when Attorney General Homer Cummings and FBI Director J. Edgar Hoover—after much delay—announced that the long investigation into the Bund's internal affairs did not uncover any violations of federal statutes.[3]

Thus the Bund could continue its activities without fear of federal interference. The problem for the Bund was clearly political, not legal. Influential German officials, particularly Hans Dieckhoff, the new ambassador to the United States, were well aware of the Bund's damaging effect on German-American relations. Like the Friends of the New Germany, it increased American sentiment against the Nazi regime. Dieckhoff counseled his government to disavow the Bund.

The German government agreed with Dieckhoff that the group was a liability. To appease American public opinion, German leaders issued a statement through the Ambassador in February immediately ordering all German citizens out of the Bund and its associated organizations. The majority of Bund members and supporters were still not citizens, despite the German government's ultimatum in December 1935 that had led to the dissolution of the Bund's predecessor, the Friends of the New Germany. As early as March 1936, Kuhn had purposely ignored the edict and established organizations of German citizens to serve as fronts for Bund activities.

Herman Von Busch said the new order from Berlin would not affect his organization, since most Newark branch members were American citizens. He also predicted that Nazi officials would not attempt to interfere with the American organization. Von Busch was correct. German citizens remained active in the Newark branch, particularly Matthias Kohler. When asked how many members the Bund had in Newark, Von Busch refused to answer. An anonymous source estimated the number at 500.[4]

There had been no public Nazi events in Newark since May 1934, when a Minuteman-inspired anti-Nazi riot in Irvington spread to Newark. During that riot, Newark Police Chief James A. McRell promised the Minutemen that no Nazi demonstrations would be allowed in the city. He kept his word. However, early in 1938 New Jersey Bund leader August Klapprott announced a Washington's Birthday celebration for Sunday, February 20 at Newark's Turn Verein. In likening Adolph Hitler to George Washington, he declared "Hitler has done as much for the new Germany as Washington did for the United States." Klapprott said Fritz Kuhn would be the main speaker and that the Ordnungs-Dienst (uniformed service) troops would act as policemen.[5]

The announcement of the Washington's Birthday celebration drew no comment from either Newark's press or its mainstream liberal and Jewish groups. The event also demonstrated the growing acceptance of the Bund. The Turn Verein was an old-time German venue where Nazis had not been welcome before. Unlike Schwabenhalle, located several miles away from downtown Newark, the Turn Verein was on William Street, only a few blocks from the city's heart. The upcoming event broke a tacit agreement between the Newark police and the Minutemen that no Nazi activities would be allowed in the city. Despite the negative publicity generated by the Bund over the previous six months, there was no response to Klapprott's provocative statement that uniformed O.D. troops would be at the celebration to act as "policemen."

Leaders of the Minutemen, the Non-Sectarian Anti-Nazi League (NSANL), and the Jewish War Veterans (JWV) met to plan a strategy to prevent the Bund event. They agreed to press the Newark police. Louis Freeman, Commander of Newark Post 34 of the JWV, gave Police Inspector John Brady two reasons for barring it— the prior agreement between the police and the Minutemen, and the probability that anti-American activities would occur. Brady responded that he had not been party to the agreement and did not feel bound by it. As for anti-Americanism, he wondered how a birthday party for George Washington could have that potential. Brady promised Freeman that neither Bund leader Kuhn nor the Nazi insignia would be in attendance.

With the Bund event two days away, Kalb called a meeting of Newark's NSANL. The Minutemen and Post 34 of the JWV were also represented. The group voted to send a delegation of fifty men to petition Brady to ban the celebration. If this failed, Kalb urged the men to buy tickets to the event and monitor it for anti-American and anti-Semitic propaganda. Kalb told them to act if necessary, but he hoped there would be no violence.[6] The Essex County American Legion sent a letter of protest to Brady as well.

The next day the delegation appeared at Brady's office hoping, but not expecting, that the inspector would reverse himself. He refused to cancel the celebration, predicting that no anti-Americanism would occur. Kalb and Arno called the Minutemen[7] and other anti-Nazis and told them to organize a demonstration and to expect trouble. If the monitors inside the Turn Verein signaled, they were to storm the hall.

The Newark police and Mayor Ellenstein quickly learned of the plans to picket the Bund celebration. The mayor told Brady that if the event became anti-Semitic and a riot ensued, he would blame the police department. Despite assurances by Von Busch that the affair would be a pro-American rally, he was called in again to police headquarters, where Brady told him that Kuhn was prohibited from appearing and no further Bund activities would be allowed in Newark if any anti-Semitism was expressed.

On Sunday evening over 500 Bundists and supporters filled the hall. Seventy-five police were stationed inside and outside the building to prevent any disturbance. Another 300 were on alert at nearby police stations. Over 200 Minutemen and other anti-Nazis demonstrated in front of the Turn Verein. The police kept them one block from the hall. Following Kalb's directive, a number of anti-Nazis paid the twenty-five-cent admission and sat in the auditorium.

The Bund leadership was aware of the consequences if the Washington's Birthday celebration was not "American." Prior to the rally, Klapprott, Von Busch, and Mathias Kohler agreed that their strategy would be to praise America and democracy and to attack communists without mentioning Jews. They assumed that after years of conditioning, a Bund audience would know that attacks on "Reds" was a proxy for attacks on Jews.

The program began as uniformed men, boys, and girls marched into the hall led by a fife and drum band. They gave the Nazi salute and heiled the Newark Bund leader, Mathias Kohler, who was standing on the speaker's platform. The only picture in the hall was of George Washington. However, contrary to Brady's assurances, swastika banners were intermingled with American flags around the speaker's stand. A large American flag hung from the ceiling. After the audience sang the "Star Spangled Banner," Kohler, speaking in English, welcomed the audience and told them that he anticipated trouble from the protesters but his troops were ready for any contingency. He claimed that Bund members were not German Nazis but American National Socialists whose main objective was to fight communism.

The next speaker was O. K. Wegener, a Bund official. He addressed the audience as "fellow Americans of German extraction," and gave a brief presentation on Washington's career as a soldier and leader. Then, like Klapprott, he compared Hitler to George Washington, pointing out that both led revolutions in their countries. Wegener boasted that Hitler had lifted Germany from slavery and other nations were jealous of his accomplishments. He urged all German Americans to join the Bund because "we are surrounded by enemies that we must smash to bring victory."

In his address, Von Busch stressed the Bund's Americanism, and, in answer to American Legion protests, said that the Newark Bund would aid the Legion in the fight against communism. The two groups would ensure "that the reins of government in the United States [will] never fall into the hands of godless atheists and racketeers." The final speaker was August Klapprott, who spoke in German. He castigated the communists and called on the Bund to adhere to the American principles of democracy. [8]

To conclude the event, uniformed boys and girls gave a demonstration of flag maneuvers. As the audience filed out, Von Busch answered questions from the press. He agreed that the uniforms worn by both children and adults resembled Nazi outfits, but he denied that the Bund had any connection with the German government. He further claimed that the uniforms and the salutes were part of German-American custom rather than an attempt to ape the Nazis. He admitted that the Bund principles resembled those of the Nazi party in Germany, but he insisted that his group's aims were "absolutely and fervently for the American system of government." Finally, he claimed that the "heil" accompanied by the Nazi salute was a "typical" German greeting.

There was no mention of Jews, and Kuhn did not appear. The only provocation was the presence of the swastika, but it had not been enough to unleash an attack. Additionally, a heavy police presence deterred the demonstrators. The police were escorted the Bundists home while the protestors left the area on their own.[9] Despite the non-violent outcome, the anti-Nazis were deeply resentful of both the lack of public support for their position and the heavy police protection afforded the Nazis. A new precedent had been set. Bund meetings were now allowed in Newark.

* * *

Encouraged by the Washington's Birthday celebration success, the Bund escalated its efforts, announcing another event at the Turn Verein for April 16 at which the featured speaker was to be the nationally known Bund leader Wilhelm Kunze, Kuhn's unofficial deputy and public relations director. The Young Men's Hebrew Club, an ally of the Minutemen, wrote a letter to the owner of the Turn Verein warning him not to rent the hall to the Nazis. The proprietor took the letter to the Newark police, who promised him protection. The Minutemen and other anti-Nazis were in a quandary over how to react to the Bund's escalation. After much discussion, it was decided not to fight with the police and the Bundists, but to concentrate their efforts on Wilhelm Kunze. Arno picked about a dozen of his toughest men for this effort.

The April 16 event drew 300 Nazis to the Turn Verein. Brady commanded the significant police presence. Arno's forces did not picket the hall. Instead he and seven other men, including ex-boxers Puddy Hinkes and Abie Bain, paid admission to the meeting and sat in the back of the auditorium. They told police they were there to monitor the evening's speeches for any anti-Semitic remarks.

Twenty-five uniformed O.D. "ushers" were at the meeting to keep order. Standing at attention around the perimeter of the audience were twenty boys between the ages of eight and sixteen dressed in scout-like outfits. Unlike the Washington's Birthday celebration, the American Flag at this event shared the spotlight with a swastika banner of the same size. As the Bundists entered the hall, they gave the Nazi salute, and they heiled and saluted Kunze before and after he spoke. The speakers prior to Kunze spoke German, assailing the press and the communists. Kunze, who spoke in English, railed against the "anti-German" media. No one mentioned Jews. The Minutemen sat quietly and left as the event ended.

It soon became apparent why there were no Minutemen demonstrators, and why Arno was inside the hall. Prior to the meeting, Kunze had parked his car in a garage near the Turn Verein. While Kunze was speaking, several Minutemen slipped into the garage, threatened the attendant (they gave him a bribe and promised to come get him if he revealed anything), and tinkered with the carburetor wiring of Kunze's car. They wanted the car to start and leave the premises but then to stop dead. One block away, just outside the area of police patrol, a parked car faced east. Inside were four Minutemen armed with rubber-covered iron bars.

The police and the press surrounded Arno as he left the Turn Verein with his men. A reporter asked Arno why the Minutemen made no protest. He answered that no one said anything anti-Semitic. Arno, his aide Lazer Schwartz at his side, continued bantering with the group. The other Minutemen slipped out of the crowd and rendezvoused with the Minuteman car, where they received weapons.

The Bundists left quickly. Soon only the police, a few newsmen, and Arno and Schwartz were in front of the hall. Brady told his men to return to headquarters.

Kunze waited for the crowd to disperse and then departed with his bodyguards out the back door. As they entered the garage, the attendant immediately told them what had happened. Having had similar experiences in the past, one of the bodyguards, a cracker-jack auto mechanic, repaired the wiring on Kunze's car. Forewarned about Arno's plan, the Nazis left the garage and turned west rather than east on Williams Street.

Unprepared, the Minutemen lost time making a u-turn to chase Kunze. The men, hiding in an alley east of the hall, now had to run a full block to get to their target. Just as the Minutemen were about to catch up, a woman jumped in front of their car. It came to a screeching halt as the woman fell into the street, blocking their way. She screamed, "No, you stay here!" They tried to move her, but she continued to scream and flail her arms and legs. By the time she was carried to the sidewalk, Kunze's car was out of sight.[10] The Nazi leader escaped and the identity of the Bundist heroine was never determined.

At about the same time, a Bund meeting in Yorkville was the scene of a serious altercation. Over 3,500 Bundists attended a Hitler Birthday Party rally at the Yorkville Casino on East 86th Street. About 100 anti-Nazi members of the American Legion, many of them Jewish, were among the crowd. When one of them objected to remarks made by a Nazi speaker, he was attacked by uniformed O.D. members. The other legionnaires, sitting nearby, came to their comrade's aid and a free-for-all broke out. The O.D. forces used blackjacks and belt buckles from their uniforms to subdue the legionnaires, resulting in the latter's retreat to the exits. Seven legionnaires were hospitalized and three Bundists and one legionnaire were arrested.[11]

* * *

German military forces occupied Austria on March 13, 1938. The "Anschluss" received worldwide headlines and alarmed American Jews, who feared for their 180,000 Austrian brethren. Throughout America, Jewish community organizations protested the takeover. In Newark, Michael A. Stavitsky, president of the Conference of Jewish Charities, called a meeting to raise $100,000 for the United Jewish Appeal, in part to help Austrian Jews. He asserted that

Germany's takeover of Austria had "tragic implications for Jews there."[12]

The executive committee of the Conference, visualizing a fresh flow of refugee families to Newark, made an arrangement with the Hebrew Free Loan Society to grant conference-guaranteed loans of up to $250 to immigrant families.[13] At its quarterly meeting, the Conference heard the author and lecturer Pierre Van Paassen assert that Palestine was "the only haven of refuge for stricken Jewry in Europe." After the speech, Stavitsky urged generous gifts to the UJA campaign to aid resettlement of European Jews to Palestine.[14]

Kalb called a special meeting of the New Jersey NSANL at Krueger Auditorium to consolidate efforts "against the Nazi menace which has caused the rape of Austria." He warned that a similar fate awaited America if the Nazis continued to import their ideas unhindered.[15] The next day, Kalb wired President Roosevelt that the NSANL had worked for five years warning Americans to combat Nazism and predicted that events like Austria were what Americans could expect if "we don't eliminate from our environment those who want to bring such conditions over here."[16] Kalb also spoke on the Austrian situation before the Israel KUV, a Jewish fraternal and benevolent organization. Michael Alenick, the KUV's president, urged the membership to continue to support the NSANL's activities and to "pour your treasure into this fight!"[17]

Two notable Newark clergymen were among nearly 100 signatories of a statement sponsored by the National Council of Christians and Jews. They were Rev.William Hiram Foulkes, moderator of the United States Presbyterian Church and pastor of "Old First" Church, and Rabbi Joseph Konvitz, president of the Union of Orthodox Rabbis of the United States and spiritual leader of Anshe Russia, Newark's largest Orthodox synagogue. The statement warned that the same arbitrary measures of coercion and oppression prevailing in Germany would now be "relentlessly" applied in Austria. It called on Catholics, Protestants, and Jews, despite their historical differences, to stand together in defending human rights and liberties.[18] The statement was released three days before German Field Marshal Hermann Goering, in a speech in Vienna before a cheering crowd of 50,000, warned all Austrian Jews to leave the country.[19]

Not all religious groups in Newark were concerned about events in Austria. One day after Goering's speech, the Catholic War Veterans held its state convention in Newark. The major topic was communism. This was in keeping with Pope Pius XI's 1937 encyclical, *Divini Redemptoris*, warning that communism was the greatest menace in the world and calling for a Catholic crusade against it.[20] There was no mention of Hitler's aggression in Austria. Instead, Dr. James F. Kelley, President of Seton Hall College, attacked the Loyalist side in the Spanish Civil War, stating that it was a foe of the Catholic Church, and specifically accused the *New York Times* of favoring the Loyalists with inaccurate and misleading reports. The only mention of Nazism during the day's speeches came from Father Matthew Toohey, chaplain of the veteran's group and pastor of Newark's St. James Church. Toohey, like Kelley, denounced the Loyalists and their American supporters, particularly those at Newark University. He declared that the faculty and administration of the college was "honeycombed with radicals of the most extreme type." He also complained that Catholics were continuously asked to protest against the Nazi regime and to boycott German goods, yet among those making these requests were communist sympathizers. Father Toohey noted, "Where are they when we need their help? On the other side of the fence—our enemies."[21]

* * *

Disappointed but not discouraged by the Kunze fiasco and the legionnaire's defeat in Yorkville, Kalb and Arno were determined to intensify their anti-Nazi campaign. Kalb announced the fourth annual convention of the New Jersey NSANL. The arrangements committee included representatives of three of Newark's largest KUVs —Israel, Erste Bershader, and Rzezower; Newark Carpenters and Cloak and Shirt Makers unions; and two Jewish women's groups— Hadassah and First Ladies Felix Fuld Lodge. Kalb invited Newark's Archbishop, Thomas Walsh, to be the principal speaker.[22] Walsh was Father Matthew Toohey's superior. Perhaps the latter's attack on the boycott movement several weeks earlier was the reason for this invitation. In any event, Walsh did not reply to the invitation.

The convention met on Sunday April 24. The first order of business was Bund activities. Kalb suggested, and the delegates agreed, that the NSANL would attempt to prevent Nazi meetings wherever they occurred, and if unsuccessful would organize peaceful counter activities. The meeting also enacted a resolution calling for state and municipal laws to bar Nazi organizations. It pointed to the establishment of Nazi camps, Nazi influence in public schools, an increase in meetings preaching hatred, and support given Nazis by "reactionaries and indifferent politicians."[23] The next order of business was the anti-Nazi boycott. Kalb stressed that an increase in this effort was needed to prevent the spread of Nazi slaughter and persecution. To this end, he announced the creation of a youth division and the launch of a major educational campaign. The convention voted to raise $10,000 to aid educational and youth activities in New Jersey. Michael Alenick, a Newark lawyer and Kalb's brother-in-law, was elected president of the group, replacing Kalb, whose national duties for NSANL required him to relinquish local day-to-day operations. Kalb was named "honorary chairman" of the New Jersey NSANL, and Amelia Moorfield and Jack Malamuth were elected vice-presidents.[24] Alenick had served as president of the Israel Verein, a KUV that had been very active in the boycott campaign. He was to prove an energetic and effective leader of the NSANL during the next year.

Unfortunately, the new president found himself in the same position Kalb had been in, having to constantly raise money to continue operations. Under the agreement with the National NSANL, all branches were to be self-sufficient, and indeed were supposed to contribute to headquarters. Just prior to the launch of the $10,000 campaign, Kalb made formal application to the United Jewish Appeal of Essex County (UJA), the fund-raising arm of the Newark Conference of Jewish Charities, for $8,500 to cover the New Jersey NSANL's 1938-1939 budget.[25] Two attachments to the application are of interest. One was a letter from the Cleveland branch of the NSANL attesting that it received its entire budget from the Jewish Welfare Federation of Cleveland. The second was a financial statement of the New Jersey NSANL showing receipts of $4,000, including $3,300 from individual and organizational memberships and fundraisers, and $700 in loans for the year ending February 1938.[26] In 1934, Kalb's organization had received $100 from the UJA, but had received nothing since. The UJA refused the request, giving no explanation.[27] However, its allocations committee probably disapproved of direct action groups such as the NSANL. It is also possible that Kalb's alliance with Arno, which was no secret, was viewed negatively.

Kalb never discussed the UJA refusal for the record. However, at a meeting of the speaker's bureau to help raise the $10,000, Alenick said,

In the face of the praiseworthy activities conducted by the League, it is almost incomprehensible why the League was not included in the UJA Campaign.[28]

Alenick stated that the NSANL was the only agency in the state actively engaged in compiling reliable lists of merchants distributing Nazi-made merchandise. In addition, the League was the sole body in New Jersey actively combating Nazi race and religious hatred.[29] The new president, in a speech to the Israel Verein, again decried the UJA decision.[30]

A month later, Alenick announced gifts from twelve organizations and a score of individuals. The total, however, was under $500.[31] Previously Alenick had learned that the NSANL's New York headquarters was engaged in its own fund raising effort and was soliciting New Jersey donors. He sent two letters to New York, one asking the national organization to stop soliciting in New Jersey, and the other offering 20 percent of all money collected in the New Jersey campaign to national headquarters.[32] Like Kalb's effort in 1936, the fundraising effort was only minimally successful, and there was no further mention of the $10,000 campaign after June.

With summer approaching Alenick began a petition to urge the New Jersey legislature to investigate Camp Nordland in Andover. Kuhn had announced that he would be the main speaker at Nordland's first-anniversary celebration on June 5, and he predicted a crowd of 10,000 for the event.[33] Alenick claimed the facility was under direct Nazi control and that activities there violated the state's 1935 anti-Nazi Law. The petition urged that Americas should drive Nazis out of the country just as Nazis were driving Jews out of Germany.[34]

Nationally, Congress seemed ready to act, despite the FBI report that the Bund had broken no federal law. In May, the House Rules Committee submitted its response to Martin Dies' Resolution 282 to investigate un-American activities. A seven-man committee was proposed to investigate the extent, character and objectives of un-American propaganda in the United States; the diffusion of such propaganda from foreign countries or of domestic origin; and all other issues that would aid Congress in formulating legislation. Nazism, fascism, and communism were not mentioned in the resolution.

A heated two-week debate took place. Among those arguing against the investigation was Maury Maverick, who claimed that the resolution was really Dickstein's and not Dies', that it would engender race hatred, and that its only result would be publicity for members of the committee. New Jersey Representative J. Parnell Thomas spoke in favor, citing the activities at Camp Nordland and arguing that communism should not be neglected in the probe. When the bill was up for final consideration, Dickstein's request to speak for three minutes was refused.[35]

The resolution passed in early June, and House Speaker William B. Bankhead appointed Dies chair of the new committee. Thomas was appointed to the committee but Dickstein was not. The opposition to the New Yorker came from midwestern Congressmen who felt he was too partisan and anti-German.[36] Dickstein was apparently embarrassed, since he had expected to be "drafted" onto the committee. When questioned as to the reason for his omission, he was unable to come up with one.[37] As another concession to the committee's opponents, the $100,000 budget requested for the investigation had been reduced to $25,000.[38]

The Dies Committee, the Special House Committee for the Investigation of Un-American Activities, informally known as HUAC, began operations in June 1938 and held its first hearings in August.[39] Many including Alenick and the New Jersey NSANL believed Dies' major focus would be Nazi activities in the United States. In fact, Alenick telegrammed Speaker Bankhead to request a substantial increase to the $25,000 appropriated for the new committee.[40] But without Dickstein, the Committee's summer sessions were almost totally dedicated to communist subversion.[41] Comments by Thomas, in whose district Camp Nordland was located and who previously suggested calling out the state militia to close down the camp, were illustrative of the tenor of the Dies Committee. After his appointment to the committee, he mentioned the Nazi camps but then said,

> But behind the scenes, perhaps, lies an even more startling discovery. I am certain we will be able to present to Congress an amazing amount of evidence that, in my opinion, will show many high officials of the New Deal are aiding the Communist cause.[42]

By the end of August, Dickstein, who had been instrumental in creating the Committee, denounced it for "red-baiting" and neglecting to investigate Nazis.[43] In September a front-page editorial in Newark's *Jewish Chronicle* criticized the Committee for "comic" testimony and asked it to probe the Bund.[44] The politically artful Dies continued his communist-centered probe, but allowed the Committee's expert on Bund affairs, John C. Metcalf, to question witnesses in several cities in order to gain Nazi-related headlines.[45] The results of a nation-wide Gallup poll, taken at the end of 1938, indicated that 74 percent of those polled favored a continuation of the Dies investigation.[46]

Kalb expanded his activities in the national NSANL day-to-day operations and relied on Alenick to run the New Jersey branch. As a NSANL representative on the Joint Action Committee of Boycott Cases, Kalb was busy in New York hearing cases.[47] He also became involved in the NSANL's internal politics, especially after the ailing eighty year-old Samuel Untermyer resigned the presidency.[48] At a full board meeting to discuss Untermyer's resignation, Kalb lobbied for the presidency but could not get the required votes. At the one-day national NSANL convention in May, Kalb presided over the afternoon session and Dr. Benjamin Dubovsky presided over the morning one.[49] The thrust of the convention was the fight against domestic Nazism rather than the boycott. Kalb had always given more weight to combating local Nazis than had the national NSANL, and with Dubovsky's concurrence, he began to press this policy. (In a report sent the next year to the New Jersey league on the national office's achievements, Kalb wrote that the most important new development was the establishment of a bureau of un-American activities to combat anti-Semitism and fascism. Material in its possession and collected in the future would be at the disposal of all members and branch offices.)[50]

Despite the change in the NSANL's focus, the boycott continued to have a substantial effect on Germany throughout 1938. A November memorandum from the German Foreign Ministry to Hitler showed that between 1932 and 1937 the value of exports to the United States was down 25 percent and the value of imports from the United States had declined over 50 percent. The decline was attributed to the depreciation of the dollar and "the anti-German trade boycott." German exports to the United States continued to decline in 1938.[51]

***

Despite his busy schedule in New York, Kalb continued his Sunday morning meetings with Nat Arno. The two met at Kalb's house to discuss the coming week's actions. Their determination to intensify anti-Bund activity came to fruition in May when the Minutemen instituted their full-scale attacks on Bund gatherings in Irvington. With an excellent intelligence network built up over five years, Arno often knew the time and location of un-publicized Nazi meetings.

Usually such events were held in back rooms or over taverns in Irvington and had from ten to thirty participants.

Arno's methods were direct and effective. Only three or four Minutemen were involved in each confrontation. A larger group would have attracted too much attention. At small meetings the Minutemen would rush in and attack the Bundists with baseball bats or rubber-encased truncheons. At larger Bund meetings, they would use a ruse to lure several attendees out into the street, where they would attack them. As other Nazis came out in response to the noise, they too would be set upon. The Bundists were usually no match for the former boxers. The cast of Minutemen changed, but among the regulars were Arno, Lazer Schwartz, Max "Puddy" Hinkes, and Abie Baim. Minutemen attacks on Bund meetings did not make the newspapers because they were often not reported to the police, neither the Bundists nor their foes wanting to be identified. Irvington officials were not keen on the publicity associated with such skirmishes either, and the police were probably instructed not to respond unless a complaint was made. The Bund did not curtail its meeting schedule because of the Minutemen attacks, but provided better protection or chose new locations.

In the beginning of 1938, Schwabenhalle was being used covertly as a propaganda center. Campers at Nordland provided the Newark Bund with the nucleus of a youth group. To expand its base, the group showed Nazi propaganda films at Schwabenhalle, and parents brought their children to these unpublicized screenings. Arno found out about them several weeks after they began. Obviously, the Minutemen could not attack children. A different tack was needed.

On Sunday evening, May 26, there was a well-attended screening of Nazi films, including one titled "Jugendschaft" (Youth Movement of the German-American Bund). When the show was over, August Hambach, a New York Bund member who had brought the films to Schwabenhalle and was the projectionist, departed for the Newark Post Office to ship the films to the San Francisco Bund. As he followed a car with two Newark Bundists, brothers Walter and Charles Burkhardt, down Springfield Avenue toward the post office, a car containing Louis Lieberman and his two passengers, Al Fisher and Philip Small, was right behind him. About one mile down Springfield Avenue, Lieberman's car sideswiped Hambach's, forcing it to the curb at Mercer Street. Another car containing Seymour Byock and David Jacob forced the Burkhardt car to the curb. Lieberman,

Fisher, and Small attacked the Bundists when they left their cars, and Byock and Jacob took the films and disappeared. Police soon arrived and broke up the fight. The three Nazis were taken to City Hospital for stitches and X-rays. The police arrested Small and Fisher on assault charges, while the other three Minutemen escaped. After a night in jail, Hymie Kugel bailed Small and Fisher out using funds provided by Longie Zwillman.[52] Small, Fisher, and Lieberman (who had surrendered after being identified) were eventually convicted of assault and battery and received suspended sentences.[53]

The Minutemen did not enjoy their success for long. In an ill-advised adventure precipitated by Mayor Frank Hague of Jersey City and orchestrated by Longie Zwillman, Arno was arrested and convicted of disorderly conduct for taking part in the attempt to prevent Norman Thomas, the Socialist party leader, from speaking at a rally in Newark's Military Park, a well-documented incident that garnered more Newark press coverage than all foreign and domestic Nazi activities from 1933 to June 1938 combined. Thomas was to speak on behalf of the Congress of Industrial Organization (CIO), which had been engaged in a major organizing effort in New Jersey since 1936. The state was generally anti-labor, and its only organized unions were in the building trades, printing, and transportation, all affiliated with the State Federation of Labor. Partly to meet the CIO challenge, the State Legislature enacted a law in 1936 that gave police wide powers to arrest and disperse strikers.

The center of CIO action was Jersey City, where Mayor Frank "I Am the Law" Hague had seen to it that not a single strike prevailed from 1931 to 1937. Hague suspended civil liberties and Jersey City police prohibited pro-CIO meetings, speakers, and writings.[54] His anti-union stance wooed hundreds of sweatshops from New York to his "oasis of unorganized labor." Hague called the CIO communistic and enjoyed the support of business, the Catholic Church, and the State Federation of Labor. The CIO accepted Hague's challenge, and for the next several years its leaders and organizers were beaten, arrested, and run out of town. The CIO was allied with the ACLU, which handled the legal work, and the Communist and Socialist parties, which handled the organizational and propaganda work. Norman Thomas was the head of the Socialist Party of America and a civil libertarian. From the earliest years of the CIO, there were significant numbers of socialists in its ranks. It was inevitable that Thomas would enter the Jersey City struggle against "Hagueism." Socialist Party members from Newark were already in Jersey City trying to organize workers. The Communist Party had also sent representatives from Newark to Jersey City.

On April 30, 1938, Thomas attempted to speak in Jersey City but was seized by police and forced onto a ferry to New York. Not one to give up easily, Thomas announced that he would speak in Newark's Military Park on "The Role of Hagueism in New Jersey," and had received a speaker's permit from the city. Hague called Longie Zwillman. They had a good relationship from Zwillman's earliest bootlegging days. It is alleged that Hague received a weekly cash payment from Longie as protection for gambling operations in a section of Hudson County.[55] Zwillman agreed to help Hague and lobbied several politicians including Mayor Meyer Ellenstein to prevent Thomas from speaking in the city. Ellenstein would regret his decision to allow Hague and Zwillman to dictate events about to unfold in Newark. In addition to Hague and the Catholic hierarchy, those against Thomas and the CIO included the State Federation of Labor and some veterans groups hostile to labor and socialism. Ellenstein's personal feelings about the upcoming Thomas speech are unknown, but he was responsive to Zwillman and the veterans groups. Nat Arno was called to participate in the action with his Minutemen, many of whom Zwillman sometimes employed as strikebreakers.

On Saturday evening, June 4, Thomas entered Military Park, where an audience of 200 awaited him. Clara Handelman, Newark's Socialist Party secretary, introduced him. When Thomas rose to speak, he was interrupted by a hooting crowd of seventy-five men led by a twenty-five-piece band that had appeared out of nowhere and was marching toward the speaker's stand. Many wore the blue caps of the American Legion and carried anti-Communist placards. Among the hooters were Nat Arno and a group of Minutemen. Thomas was pelted with a fusillade of eggs and tomatoes. The police refused to interfere, despite pleas from the audience. Thomas tried to continue but fights broke out between Thomas' supporters and opponents. Finally the police charged into the melee, overturning the speaker's platform in the process. A Newark police official stood on a bench and ordered the meeting to disband. Eventually, police escorted Thomas back to Socialist party headquarters.

Reports of the event were telegraphed throughout America and abroad. Photographs showed Thomas being hit by eggs and tomatoes in the heart of Newark. Newark officials, particularly the police, were excoriated for allowing the riot. Clergy, politicians, academics, and scores of organizations denounced them in the Newark press over the coming weeks. Newark opened an official inquiry into the riot and an Essex County Grand Jury was empanelled to examine the police role in the disturbance. Nat Arno was the first person detained as a result of the police inquiry. He was held for questioning because Clara Handleman said he had "insulted" her. He was eventually arraigned on charges of "interfering and shouting in the park." Found guilty of disorderly conduct, Arno was fined twenty-five dollars.[56]

* * *

The Newark press did not report the June 15 Nazi roundup of 1,500 "previously convicted" German Jews with past crimes such as traffic tickets and other minor offences, and their subsequent placement in a Nazi concentration camp. Nor did it mention the June 25 Nazi edict that German Jewish physicians were henceforth only to treat Jewish patients. However, a federal indictment of eighteen individuals engaged in an espionage network directed at American defense secrets did make headlines. Many were German residents, including two Reich war ministry officers. Among the others was Dr. Fritz Griebl, who had recently become an American citizen but had fled to Germany when the investigation began.[57]

Camp Nordland began its second season in June with Klapprott's announcements that over 300 boys and girls would be enrolled,[58] and the Bund had bought an additional 100 acres adjacent to the camp. Still in a buying mood, Klapprott acquired ten twenty-two caliber Remington rifles for camp use.[59] Michael Alenick charged that Nordland was now one of the largest breeding grounds for Nazism in America. The NSANL head also quoted a leading Bundist, George Froboesse, who said to a crowd of 4,000 at Nordland that Germans "have placed their feet in America soil in an honest way, and that Bund camps have been created to convince German Americans that they are standing on safe ground." Alenick wondered why Americans should allow such remarks from paid Hitler agents who would like to see America "turned into a place of madness—like Germany is today."[60] In protesting Nordland, Alenick was perhaps thinking about the arrest of six leaders from Camp Yaphank, a Bund camp on Long Island. The Bundists were charged with violating New York State civil rights law by not filing membership lists, as was required of an oath-bound organization, and—in a highly publicized case—found guilty by a Long Island jury. The Judge sentenced Ernest Mueller, Yaphank's president, to one year in jail and fined the others $500 each. Fritz Kuhn was promising to appeal the convictions.[61]

The NSANL was not the only Newark group publicly opposing Nordland. Adolph Friederich, president of the Newark German-American League for Culture, called for German-American workers from Irvington and Maplewood to join him at a rally against Nordland. This was the first such New Jersey event sponsored by German-American citizens. The League followed up the event with a call for New Jersey boards of education to hold special classes on "Americanism" for children of German descent who had attended the summer camp at Nordland.[62] Irvington members of the League also petitioned the Irvington Board of Education to teach "Americanism" in its schools.[63]

Camp Nordland operated without interference during the summer of 1938. The FBI report stating that the Bund had broken no federal laws, the unwillingness of New Jersey authorities to take action, and the Dies Committee's decision to investigate communists rather than Nazis, combined to create a climate in which anti-Nazi groups could do nothing more than protest. When Fritz Kuhn spoke at the camp to celebrate New Jersey German-American Day, there was no response. In announcing the event, Klapprott said it would stress "a strong, free, and independent German element in America [to act against] hatred, lies, communism, and the Jewish boycott of German goods."[64] Kuhn spoke again at Nordland at the end of the summer, soon after his reelection as national Bund leader. Over 2,000 heard him announce a nine-point program that featured a demand for "a socially just, white, gentile-ruled United States and gentile-controlled American labor unions free of Jewish-Moscow-directed domination." He added that Jews should also be purged from the government, defense forces, educational institutions, and the film industry.[65]

* * *

The summer was not yet over when Mussolini announced anti-Jewish legislation. A decree of September 2 ordered all Jewish students and teachers to leave their schools except university students who were permitted to finish their degrees. All Jews who had settled in Italy since January 1, 1919 were ordered to leave the country within six months. Rabbi Solomon Foster denounced the laws as Italy gone "mad." Michael Stavitsky said the decree indicated that Italy was being forced to accept German leadership in the extermination of both Jews and non-Jews alike. Michael Alenick said the Nazi virus had taken over the Italian body politic, and that the country "could no longer boast that it is an exemplar of liberty and tolerance."[66]

Within several months additional decrees were enacted that denied the Jews the right to be a member of the Fascist Party, serve in the government or army, or marry a gentile. These measures disturbed many of Newark's Italian Americans who enjoyed good relations with the city's Jews. For their part, Jews had made a distinction between Hitler's anti-Semitic Nazism and Mussolini's non-racial fascism. Brothers, Joe and Al Pisano were members of Arno's Minutemen (as well as associates of Longie Zwillman). Newark's Italians were proud of their homeland's accomplishments over the past decade under Mussolini. How could they speak out against Mussolini's racial laws without renouncing Italy? For a month Newark's Italian-American community remained silent.

New York City's Italian Americans, an older, more secure, and wealthier community, provided guidance. *Il Progresso*, the largest circulation Italian paper in the country, continued to support Mussolini, while condemning the racial laws. Italian-American leaders, including Mayor Fiorello LaGuardia and Congressman Vito Marcantonio, were quick to find fault with the decrees. New York State Supreme Court Judge Salvatore Cotillo sent a cable to Mussolini asking for the repeal of the laws because there was serious talk of boycotting Italian goods in New York "where we live in close interdependent relationship" with the Jews.[67]

The day before Columbus Day, the Giuseppe Verdi Society, Newark's most elite Italian-American organization, celebrated its 36th anniversary. Anthony R. Finelli, the society's president, sent a telegram to Justice Cotillo stating,

> Anti-Semitism is not congenial to Italo-Americans of Newark. We sympathize with [your] efforts to procure modification of objectionable policies. We are thriving in this city and with [the] cooperation of the Jewish race. We have always been connected with professional and businessmen of the Jewish race in this city. While we admire our race in Italy, we find it very embarrassing to cope with difficulties brought about by this order against Jews in Italy.[68]

Newark's 1938 Columbus Day was celebrated at a rally in Washington Park. A small procession of First Ward civic associations, led by St. Lucy's Church fife and drum corps, initiated the proceedings. Governor A. Harry Moore, the keynote speaker, compared the peacefulness of Washington Park to a park he had just visited in London, which had been dug up to provide ditches for shelter during air raids. He was followed by the Italian vice counsel for Newark, Count Renato Della Chiesa, who said the futures of Italy and the United States were assured, and that Italy was "travelling serenely onward." Master of ceremonies Commissioner Ralph A. Villani, seized the moment and rose to reply to Della Chiesa. After decrying Italy's anti-Jewish decrees, he said,

> There is a cloud existing between Italian-Americans and Jews. Italian-Americans, however, are not paying any attention to the decrees. We want the Jews as friends and they want us.[69]

Speaking before the Newark Chapter of the American Business Clubs, that same day, former Congressman Peter A. Cavicchia, a leader of Newark's Italian-American community, claimed that Americans bearing Italian names were disturbed at Mussolini's persecution of Jews. He said that Italians living in America believed in the principle of freedom of speech and religion, and that Columbus Day was an occasion when people of all races should join in a prayer of thanksgiving for the privilege of enjoying that principle.[70]

Jewish Chronicle publisher Anton Kaufman applauded Finelli, Villani, and Cavicchia. The journalist suggested that Italian groups should organize nationwide to protest Mussolini's imitation of Hitler and to impress upon the dictator that the boycott against German goods could just as easily be applied against Italy.[71] Michael Alenick, who was ambivalent about a boycott against Italian goods in New Jersey, was instructed by the national office of the NSANL that there would be no such action.[72] There was no need for an anti-Italian boycott in Newark. After briefly hesitating, Italian-American leaders made their rejection of anti-Semitism clear. The city's Jews and Italians wanted to retain the good economic, political, and social relations they had forged over the past decades. With the exception of a few groups and individuals, Newark's Italian Americans rejected anti-Semitism.

* * *

Italy was enacting its anti-Jewish laws at the very moment Hitler was threatening Czechoslovakia. An October rally in Newark with over 100 delegates representing Newark's 10,000 Czechs and Slovaks protested Hitler's demand that the Sudetenland, a former German area awarded to the new state of Czechoslovakia after World War I, hold a plebiscite on whether to secede from Czechoslovakia and join Germany. When news that the Czech government had refused Hitler's demand was announced at the rally, the delegates broke out in cheers. No counter German-American rally was held to back Hitler on this issue.[73] On September 29, however, the Munich Agreement was signed, ceding the Sudetenland to Nazi Germany. France and England agreed to the pact to appease the Nazis, and according to some observers, to give them both more time to prepare for war.

The American League for Peace and Democracy (ALPD), a communist-controlled organization, announced a Newark parade and mass rally to "Save Czechoslovakia." Nancy Cox,[74] the league's state secretary, asked all "peace-loving" Newark citizens to come to the event. "We Americans must make it known to the world that we support Czechoslovakia's resistance to Hitler." Senator Vojta Benes, brother of the Czech president, Edward Benes, was to be the rally's featured speaker. When the threat of a German invasion forced the Czechs to accept Hitler's occupation plan, Cox announced that the rally would still be held so Newarkers could show their solidarity with the Czechs. [75]

A parade of 2,500 assembled in Newark's Lincoln Park and marched to Sokol Hall, where they met another 2,500 people waiting to hear Vojta Benes. When he arrived, the former senator was cheered, and when he rose to speak the audience broke into the Czech and Slovak anthems. Speaking in Czech, Benes said his country had to capitulate to the Nazis because its population of 10,000,000 was threatened by 120,000,000 Germans, Poles, and Hungarians. The crowd booed when Benes named Hitler, Daladier, and Chamberlain, and when he told them England and France had let his country down. There were loud cheers when Benes praised Russia for its support. Czech organizations participated in the rally along with the ALPD. Other than Cox's group and a lone representative of the CIO, however, no outside groups were represented. [76]

* * *

The Munich Pact put the Jews of Czechoslovakia at risk. News from Britain made it unlikely that Palestine would be a refuge for either these or other threatened European Jews. The Balfour Declaration was in danger. A British commission was about to issue a report that stated that no Jewish state could be created which would be large enough to allow for new Jewish immigration.[77] Rabbi Julius Silberfeld interrupted Succot (the Feast of Tabernacles) services to ask his congregation to protest the proposal to Secretary of State Cordell Hull, as the United States "is party to fulfillment of the British mandate." The membership unanimously authorized the Rabbi to send Hull a telegram. New Jersey governor A. Harry Moore sent a telegram directly to President Roosevelt asking for his intervention with the British. Mayor Ellenstein issued a protest against the proposed British plan, and said it was an act of "extreme cruelty" to shut Palestine's door at "a tragic moment in the history of a suffering people."[78]

Joseph Kraemer, chairman of the newly organized "Palestine Emergency Committee," called a rally of Zionist and pro-Zionist fraternal and communal groups at Krueger Auditorium on Sunday October 23. Over 5,000 people attended, including an overflow crowd that listened to loudspeakers in the street. Kraemer read President Roosevelt's response to Governor Moore's telegram that America was legally powerless to prevent any changes the British made to the mandate. Despite this rebuff, the group adopted a resolution calling on President Roosevelt to urge Britain not to abandon its mandate. Mayor Ellenstein said the British were considering reneging on promises to Jews, on the basis of which the Jews had invested over $500 million in Palestine. Other speakers included Stavitsky, Rabbi Joseph Konvitz and Rep. Cavicchia.[79] Also protesting the proposed British action were Zionist women's groups, including Hadassah, the Emma Lazarus League, Mizrachi Women, and Pioneer Women, who sent a letter of protest to Hull.[80] The New Jersey delegation to the American Jewish Congress (AJC) annual convention in New York introduced a resolution urging Britain to stand by its Balfour Declaration commitment. Included in the delegation were Kalb, Jack Malamuth, Rabbi Silberfeld, and Benjamin Epstein.[81]

* * *

An informal coalition of the Minutemen, the NSANL, liberals, and communists and their front groups came together to challenge the growing strength of the Bund and other anti-Semitic groups, and to protest the Nazi threat to Europe. Communists were primarily concerned with the Nazi threat to the Soviet Union, whereas the other groups worried about the Jews and the European democracies. The coalition widened after Kristallnacht and lasted until the Nazi-Soviet Pact of August 1939.[82] September 1938 brought the first evidence of the coalition's strength, when Nancy Cox of the ALPD called for a demonstration against a meeting called by Matthias Kohler in Elizabeth to establish a branch of the Bund in that city. Adolph Friederich, chair of the Essex County German-American League for Culture, and Jack Malamuth of the NSANL said their groups would participate. Malamuth was the liaison between Cox, the Newark Communist Party, and the NSANL. In addition, civic and veteran's groups from Elizabeth and other parts of Union County also agreed to demonstrate. If these efforts failed to dissuade the assembled Nazis, Nat Arno and the Minutemen were prepared to break up the gathering.

Kohler ignored the warning of Elizabeth police chief, Frank Brennan, who several days earlier urged him to cancel the event. One hour before the scheduled meeting, the scene at Eintracht Hall was chaotic. Over 3,000 anti-Nazis filled the hall's seats and lined the rear wall. The street in front of the auditorium was packed; over 100 pickets circled with anti-Nazi signs. In addition to the Minutemen, there were scores of youths "eager for a fight." Kohler and other Bund officials were afraid to enter the auditorium, thus leaving the speaker's platform empty. Nancy Cox went to the lectern and told the crowd to clear the aisles. She said that when the Bundists appeared her group and others wanted to question the Nazis. The Bundists did not appear. After a half-hour Chief Brennan came to the lectern and said the Bund had cancelled the meeting. Cox again went to the lectern and to wild applause opened a meeting "for democracy." Brennan told the audience that the Bund had rented the hall and no other group could use it. He asked the crowd to leave, and after receiving guarantees that the Bund was not about to return, the anti-Nazis filed out. In the auditorium's anteroom, Kohler, who was surrounded by police, told a reporter that he had decided to hold the event despite the police warning because he was not going to allow a group of "communists and gangsters" to stop him. He said that the pressure to cancel the meeting had abrogated the Bund's constitutional rights. After about an hour, the crowd dispersed, and police escorted Kohler and some of his followers out of Elizabeth.[83]

The next New Jersey Bund meeting was announced for two weeks later. Fritz Kuhn said that after the closing ceremonies at Camp Nordland he would appear in Union City to speak at a German Day celebration. Arno called his Minutemen, arranged transportation, and selected a gathering place in Union City. Nancy Cox organized anti-Nazi and left wing groups into an ad hoc committee, the "Anti-Nazi Council." The Czechoslovakian Societies of Hudson County, and the International Labor Defense, a socialist group, also invited their adherents to the demonstration.

The afternoon of Kuhn's appearance, Czechoslovakian groups rented a hall in Guttenberg—a small town next to Union City—so that the protesting groups could assemble and write a press statement. Several resolutions were endorsed, including one condemning all "isms" in the country except Americanism. Cox introduced a resolution condemning Nazism and also France and England for "selling out" Czechoslovakia. When Charles W. Gilmour, the chair of the meeting, requested that she include communism in her resolution, Cox said communism was not under discussion. Gilmour refused to entertain her motion.[84]

Over forty Minutemen arrived that evening for the speech, along with hundreds of others from various anti-Nazi organizations. Scores carried anti-Nazi banners imprinted with the names of their groups. Hitler was burned in effigy. Soon the anti-Nazi crowd swelled to 2,000, discouraging many Bundists from attending the rally. Uniformed O.D. troops were among the 100 who braved the catcalls, curses, and rocks. Union City and Hudson County police had trouble containing the crowd, which threatened to storm the hall. Inside, the Nazis could hardly hear themselves talk above the din. The police warned Kuhn that he would be trapped inside the hall unless he left immediately. Kuhn called the meeting off and as he began to leave the building, surrounded by his uniformed bodyguard, the enraged crowd screamed "Kill him, kill him!" A brawl broke out that took several hours to contain. Kuhn was not injured, and after a brief press conference left the site while the melee continued.[85]

The Minutemen were instrumental in breaking up a third attempted Bund meeting in northern New Jersey in the fall of 1938. Gerhard William Kunze was set to speak in a large house in New Milford, about twenty miles from Newark. Arno, twenty Minutemen, and about thirty local anti-Nazis congregated outside the house. Since the meeting was on private property and there was no request from the owner to intervene, about twenty-five policemen stood by and watched. The crowd started screaming and throwing rocks at the house. The noise of the shouting and the crash of windows forced Kunze to end the meeting. The Nazis asked for police protection, and Kunze and the other Bundists were escorted to safety.[86]

The Bundists knew they were under siege in northern New Jersey, and with winter approaching and Nordland soon to be snowed in, they decided to again challenge the Minutemen in Newark. A Bund rally was called for Schwabenhalle for October 27. The Turn Verein Hall was no longer available to the group because the owners were now wary of being associated with the Nazis. The ostensible purpose of the event was a "pep rally" to increase the Newark Bund's membership. Schwabenhalle had been the scene of the first major anti-Nazi riot in America five years earlier in October 1933. Then it was Longie Zwillman's Third Ward gang, forerunner to the Minutemen, who had fought the Bund's predecessor, the Friends of the New Germany. In choosing Schwabenhalle for its 1938 event, the Bund was tempting fate. This time the Nazis would face the Minutemen, the NSANL, and Communist front and other left-wing organizations.

Events in Irvington in the two weeks leading up to the Bund rally had intensified the emotions of Jews and anti-Nazi groups. A nine-year-old boy, Bernard Cohen, had been walking in Irvington Park when he was attacked by two teenage boys. They dragged him behind some bushes and scratched a swastika on his arm with a penknife. The two boys were arrested when Bernard and his father Samuel serendipitously encountered one of the assailants. Police got the youngster to identify his companion.[87] Both boys appeared before the Irvington Recorder (magistrate) Thomas J. Holleran, who gave them a lecture on "Americanism" and elicited a promise that they would not repeat their action. Holleran also told the parents of the two boys to use "a big stick" on their sons. Two days later a wooden swastika was burned in front of the Cohen's home. A police investigation was inconclusive. Some Jews accused Holleran "of seeking by every possible means within their power to prevent any publicity in the case." [88] The fact that neither boy in the assault was identified publicly or charged with a crime, particularly when one was no longer a juvenile, and that no suspect was apprehended in the swastika burning, upset Irvington's Jews.

Twenty-five people attended a meeting to oppose the Bund rally called by Nancy Cox and Jack Lerner, president of Newark's branch of the Labor's Non-Partisan League, at the Irvington Elk's Hall. Several participants voiced disappointment that representatives of veterans and religious groups did not attend. The probable reason was the leftist agendas of the sponsors. Samuel Ribner, an official of Temple B'Nai Israel of Irvington, came to Elk's Hall expressly to protest that the name of his synagogue had been used without authorization in letters calling the meeting.[89]

Adolph Friederich, leader of the German-American League for Culture, asserted that the Bund was a nest of Nazi spies, and that Irvington was a center for Bund propaganda printing. He added that most of the campers at Nordland were from Essex and Union Counties. The groups agreed to carry picket signs and to meet in front of Newark's Labor Lyceum from which they would march the one block to Schwabenhalle. They also pledged to distribute 7,000 fliers in Newark and Irvington to enlist additional protestors. Jack Malamuth, representing the NSANL, said his group would help with distribution. Fliers were prepared and on the streets of Newark and Irvington within hours. Alenick and Malamuth supervised volunteers from the NSANL and the ALPD. Inspector John Brady of the Newark Police warned Friederich and Lerner that 200 police would be at Schwabenhalle to prevent members of their groups from picketing the Bund event. The two men received Brady's warning without comment.[90] Nancy Cox was adamant about the picketing; it was her constitutional right.

Early Wednesday night 200 Newark police, some on motorcycles and horses, arrived at Schwabenhalle. Nancy Cox was the first demonstrator to appear. She came in her roadster, piled with ALPD picket signs, which she unloaded and distributed.[91] Nat Arno arrived soon afterwards with a dozen Minutemen. Members of the Jewish War Veterans and the NSANL were among other early arrivals. Picketing began at 7PM when the Bundists began to trickle into the hall. Hundreds of spectators filled the sidewalks, kept back by the police.

As the Bundists arrived, the police cleared paths for them. By the time the rally began at 8PM, there were 200 Bundists in the hall to hear Hermann Von Busch and Matthias Kohler. Outside the crowd had swelled to over 2,000. Two hundred carried picket signs proclaiming, "We Prefer the Shag to the Goose Step," "Freedom, Not Concentration Camps," and " Nazism Means War, Democracy Peace." Adolph Friederich and members of his organization carried picket signs in German that read "For German Culture Against Barbarism."

Pickets from Labor's Non-Partisan League, the American Youth Congress, the International Workers Order, the Sign Painters, and the AFL's Auxiliary Baker's Unions were on hand. Minutemen ranks swelled to fifty, and Arno had his men join the picketing, forming a phalanx. Brady objected, ordering the men to march two abreast. They obeyed.

Most pickets left before the Bund rally ended at 10PM. Newsmen asked for a statement and Cox said,

> This demonstrates the fact that peaceful picketing can be conducted by persons of this community who resent the spreading of Nazi propaganda in this section. We are determined to continue our efforts to expose the actions of the Nazis here.[92]

Cox went home pleased at the successful action.[93] The crowd remained along with the Minutemen.

The meeting was over at 11PM, and about half the audience descended the one flight of stairs to the street. Police lined up into the street on both sides of the steps. As soon as the Bundists appeared the Minutemen surged forward, urged on by the crowd. The police line broke and the Nazis were attacked with fists and weapons. Surprised at the assailants' fury, Brady ordered police to attack the rioters. Mounted police charged into the mass, liberally employing their nightsticks. It took twenty minutes to restore some semblance of order.

More police arrived to escort the Nazis home or to their cars. This procession wound through Newark streets for over a mile. However, there were not enough police, and every group of Bundists was followed by increasing numbers of anti-Nazis the further they got from Schwabenhalle.[94] Some Nazis were attacked even while accompanied by police. Fearing the worst, Brady gave the order for the police and their charges to retreat to Schwabenhalle. Over 100 Bundists were brought back. The police tried to spirit them out through a back door and some windows, but most Nazis preferred to remain inside. It was several hours before the arrival of additional police made it possible to escort the Nazis out. It was not until 2AM that the last of the Bundists and Minutemen left the area.[95]

An estimated fifteen Bundists were injured. Five arrests were made, all Minutemen: Alexander Goldberg, David Kampf, Murray Jayson, Charles Zweigbaum, and Louis Anker. Three of the cases were settled in police court the night of the riot. Zweigbaum was found innocent of "creating a disturbance," while Goldberg and Kampf were found guilty and fined twenty-five dollars each for "interfering with an officer." The charges against Jayson and Anker were held over. Mickey Breitkopf, a close collaborator of Kalb in the NSANL, was the lawyer for all the defendants. Anker was later found guilty and fined for "creating a disturbance." Jayson, faced the most serious charge, "atrocious assault and battery," for knocking out Gottlieb Woehrle's front teeth. He had his trial postponed three times because no Bundist would testify. Jayson was helped by the testimony of Detective Nathan Harris, who when called as a witness by Breitkopf, testified that at the time of the assault one of the alleged witnesses could not recall Jayson.[96]

This was the last anti-Nazi riot to occur in Essex County. By 1939 events in America and Europe would force the Bund into decline. On October 27, 1938, however, the Bund was still a threat to Jews. That evening, an ideologically disparate coalition including veterans, unionists, youths, liberals, German Americans, communists, Minutemen, and the NSANL, protested Nazism in Newark. A newspaper photo shows Nancy Cox, Nat Arno, Jack Malamuth, and Irving Edisis (a young protege of Kalb) marching together in the front rank of the pickets.[97]

Far from appreciating the significance of this event, The *Newark Sunday Call* printed an editorial the next day called "Provocative Pickets," which castigated the groups that organized the picketing and left before the violence began. "They must have known that their parade would draw a large crowd and give the hoodlums the excuse to make trouble," it stated. The *Call* claimed that the picketing "served no useful purpose," and that it was better to let subversive groups operate in the open. The paper praised Brady for protecting the Nazis right of free assembly. Left unmentioned was Brady's publicized attempt to deny the anti-Nazis the same right.[98]

* * *

Newark's Catholic Church made its first declaration against anti-Semitism two days before the Kristallnacht pogrom. At a Knights of Columbus meeting the President of Seton Hall College, Dr. James F. Kelley, denounced the race theory Hitler espoused as "a leap backward over thousands of years" and decried the barrage of "anti-Semitic vilifications" sent through the mail by "unknown" sources. Specifically mentioning discrimination against Negroes, Japanese, and Jews, Kelley declared that America also suffered from racism. He linked Mussolini's anti-Jewish decrees to Italy's racist policies in

Ethiopia. He concluded by asserting that Germany was committing "slow suicide by cutting off many of its finest members."[99] Anton Kaufman, publisher of the *Jewish Chronicle*, applauded Kelley's words, particularly because the cleric had previously failed to condemn Nazism. Kaufman said Kelley "now regards Fascism and Nazism as at least equally great dangers [as communism] to mankind."[100]

The danger of Nazism was made clearer during Kristallnacht. The Kristallnacht pogrom began on the evening of November 9 and lasted through the next day. Using as a pretext the assassination of a minor Nazi official at the German Embassy in Paris by Herschel Grynzpan, a Jewish student, Hitler had Joseph Goebbels, Reich Propaganda Minister, order a pogrom. Almost 200 synagogues in Germany were set on fire and seventy-six more were completely demolished; 100 Jews were killed or seriously injured; over 20,000 Jews were put into concentration camps; and thousands of Jewish stores, apartments, and facilities were looted, set on fire or otherwise destroyed. The windows of Jewish shops were smashed, which gave the pogrom its name, Kristallnacht, the "night of glass." The Nazis carried out a similar pogrom in Austria on November 10. Forty-two synagogues were destroyed and 7,800 Jews arrested in Vienna alone. In all, twenty-seven Jews were killed and 680 committed suicide.[101]

American public opinion and press were unanimous in denouncing Kristallnacht. A poll taken in the days after Kristallnacht indicated that 94 percent of Americans disapproved of Germany's treatment of Jews.[102] It was even said that the "United States has not been so aroused since the Lusitania." President Roosevelt, who was usually cautious, at first, referred all comment on Kristallnacht to the State Department. However, five days later, when the depth of American revulsion at the Nazis was fully evident, Roosevelt issued an unambiguous statement expressing the shock of the American people over Kristallnacht. The President then added his own feelings:

"I myself could scarcely believe that such things could occur in a twentieth century civilization."[103]

The first public response to Kristallnacht in Newark came from the NSANL that called for a mass meeting in the city. Speaking as chairman of the league's national board of directors, Kalb said that the time for protests was over and that members of all organizations and religious groups should unite in a strong anti-Nazi boycott movement.[104] Soon thereafter, Charles Handler, president of the Essex

Council of the AJC, gave the press a joint statement from AJC, the American Jewish Committee, and the Jewish Labor Committee, which called Kristallnacht an attack against civilization rather than the "torture of a particular minority."[105]

Nat Arno's reaction to the pogrom was characteristic. Upon hearing that Fritz Kuhn was to appear at an unpublicized Newark Bund meeting at Schwabenhalle on November 16, he brought fifty demonstrators to the site. The Bund, however, was tipped off beforehand and moved the meeting to Bergen County. When the Nazis failed to appear at the hall, three Minutemen traveled several blocks to Herman Von Busch's house on South 17th Street and threw rocks, breaking windows and the glass in his door.[106] The *Newark Sunday Call* denied that the smashing of Von Busch's windows was a small retaliation for Kristallnacht and instead denounced Arno. Citing his arrest at the Thomas riot and his leadership in the previous month's Schwabenhalle riot, the paper accused him of being the stone thrower at Von Busch's house. "America wants no stone throwing or mob violence. Lawful meetings must proceed unmolested, whether they are Communist, Socialist, Fascist, or Nazi," it stated. In calling for police action to stop Arno's activities, the *Call* said, "the country is full of Nat Arno's, of men easily moved to violence. We have seen in Germany the terrible effect of mob action. It must not be permitted to stand here."[107]

A more conventional method of protest against Kristallnacht occured when eighteen Essex County rabbis designated Sunday, November 20 as a day of mourning and called for prayers on behalf of German Jews. Sunday saw packed synagogues, including over 1,000 at Temple B'Nai Jeshurun. Several rabbis praised non-Jews for condemning Nazism. Indeed, prayers for German Jews were offered in nearly all Newark's Protestant churches and at some Catholic ones. However, at the city's St. Patrick's Cathedral, Jews were not mentioned. Instead parishioners were asked at each mass to "pray for oppressed peoples throughout the world."[108]

Father James Kelley again spoke out against the Nazis. Addressing a meeting of the Seton Hall branch of the National Federation of Catholic College Students, he said Nazism was "no flash in the pan" but stemmed from the "might makes right" tribal philosophy preached by Germans in the nineteenth century. The students endorsed a federation-sponsored resolution, condemning anti-Semitism and expressing "deep anxiety" over the rising tide of anti-Jewish feeling in the world.[109]

* * *

Neither individuals nor organizations in Newark's African-American community issued public statements on Kristallnacht.[110] Beset by poverty and discrimination, international affairs were far from their minds in 1938. A report of the New Jersey Legislature on the condition of African Americans in New Jersey cities demonstrated the levels of hardship and discrimination faced by them. Among the findings, for the years 1934-1938, were that infant mortality in the city was 9 percent for African Americans and 4 percent for whites; that in a school population of 10,947 African Americans only eleven teachers were of their race; that of 6,037 Newark municipal workers only 116 were African American despite the fact that they represented almost 10 percent of Newark's population. [111]

Another reason that Newark's African Americans were less sympathetic than other groups to the Jewish tragedy of Kristallnacht was the poor relations between the two groups in the Third Ward. African Americans became the majority in the Third Ward during the 1930s. Their neighborhood was in an area off Springfield Avenue on Broome and Spruce Streets. These blocks had many retail businesses that were mostly owned by Jews who had been there since the time the area was predominantly Jewish. Most of these stores did not employ African Americans, and if they did it was as porters and janitors.

Located in the Third Ward since its inception in 1932, the Newark Communist Party had worked long and hard to radicalize the African Americans of the area. The results were meager, and by 1935 the Newark Party could boast only three African-American members.[112] In 1938 some younger African Americans joined the Newark branch of the Communist-controlled National Negro Congress and participated in the Congress' "Don't Buy Where You Don't Work" campaign. This effort spurred the growth of the group to forty-five members and several hundred sympathizers, according to an FBI informant. The Congress had fourteen sponsoring agencies, including five African-American churches and seven labor unions. Luke Garner was listed as representing Local 27, of the National Leather Workers Association.[113] The majority of the activists were not interested in the Communist Party, but rather supported the Congress's moderate aims, including better housing, fair employment practices, and an end to police brutality.[114]

On March 11, 1938, the Newark branch of the National Negro Congress picketed in front of the F.W. Grand Silver store on the corner of Springfield Avenue and Spruce Street. Albert Crome, a

Newark Communist Party leader and spokesman for the Congress, demanded that Grand dismiss some of its white salesgirls and hire African Americans. Grand refused. Four Jewish merchants sought an injunction against the picketing. They claimed the pickets were forcing their clients into the street and depriving them of business.

Congress counsel Roger M. Yancey, an African American, and Samuel L. Rothbard, counsel for the Newark Communist Party, defended the Congress. They argued that the Congress had a legal right to picket, the pickets were not harming the four plaintiffs, and the picketing was a "means of winning for Negroes their share of economic opportunities." Irving Mandelbaum, counsel for the plaintiffs, argued that charges of discrimination in Newark against African Americans were based upon "hearsay."[115] The judge in the case, Vice Chancellor John O. Bigelow, agreed with the defendants' counsel and ruled for the picketers, claiming that employment opportunities for African Americans were "pitifully small," and they could only find employment as common laborers, janitors, and domestics. Although condemning picketing, he said the objective of the pickets "must be applauded." Bigelow also pointed out that a recent survey of 361 Newark employers with 61,000 employees found only 2,180 African Americans, despite the fact that 10 percent of Newark's population was African American.

The picketing resumed, despite a Congress suggestion that F.W. Grand give an African-American salesgirl a trial. She would receive no salary during the trial, but Grand would give her full-time employment if she worked out. Morton Stone, personnel manager of the store, refused the offer saying Grand had a waiting list of thirty to forty girls. Stone also claimed that most of the store's customers were white.[116]

The events in Newark were repeated in other large cities in the North including New York, Chicago, Detroit, and Washington. On May 22, the *Newark Sunday Call* devoted its first page headline and its lead editorial to the "awakening Negro," claiming that a survey uncovered the "abandonment of slave psychology" and a swing toward radical beliefs. Citing the Grand event as the first incidence of racial picketing in Newark, the *Call* warned of the economic costs of discrimination:

> As long as he is overcharged for inferior housing and denied his proportionate share of jobs he is competent to fill, the Negro will be a menace to public health, welfare and safety. He will continue to be an enormous public expense. And the left wingers will continue to dazzle him with the promise of a new society which would have a place for him.[117]

The *News* reported that the Newark branch of the National Negro Congress was in the forefront of the drive against discrimination in the city. In interviews with Harold Lett, executive secretary of the Newark Urban League and Arthur W. Hardy, executive secretary of the Negro YMCA, both leaders praised the Congress's campaign. According to the *News*, these Negro leaders and others claimed that the Congress was encouraged by the communists but not controlled by them.[118]

The *Newark Herald News*, an African-American weekly, began publishing in Newark in May 1938 during the Grand incident. It endorsed the congress's campaign and claimed "never before have Negro citizens been so solidly behind a movement for racial betterment."[119] Unfortunately, circumstances dictated that this Newark movement featured a confrontation between African Americans and Jews. The *Herald* reported on a similar confrontation in Chicago that had stirred up anti-Semitism among Chicago African Americans, thereby pitting "one oppressed group against another."[120]

* * *

Kristallnacht increased the effectiveness of the anti-Nazi boycott, both in America and abroad.[121] The German military reported that many companies had lost between 20 and 30 percent of their export business. Hardest hit were the leather goods and toy manufacturing businesses.[122] In Newark, L. Bamberger was picketed by the NSANL during the 1938 Christmas season, partly over its sale of German toys.[123] After Kristallnacht, New Jersey NSANL fund-raising efforts were sufficient to pay the $450 it owed to the national office from 1937.[124] For the year ending March 31, 1939, the New Jersey NSANL reported income of $6,300 from individual and organizational memberships and from fundraisers.[125] This was a gain of almost 100 percent over the previous year.

Other Newark groups endorsed the anti-Nazi boycott. The recently formed Essex County Youth Division of the AJC began a campaign to sell boycott buttons on behalf of the Joint Boycott Council. It ran a highly successful contest to see who would be the top sales person. The contest was won by Ruth Mandel of Newark, who sold twenty-five dollars' worth of buttons.[126] At a symposium of Protestant, Catholic, and Jewish women's groups, Mrs. Charles Apps, president of the á Kempis Society, declared "united womanhood can bring

persecutor nations to their knees." She advocated an economic boycott against such countries. Representing Jewish groups, Mrs. Marius
Ranson, wife of Rabbi Marius Ranson of Temple Sharey Tefilo in
East Orange, said that persecution of one religion in Germany would
lead to persecution of all religions. Mrs. Frederick Knapp, a vice
president of the New Jersey Federation of Women's Clubs, spoke
for Protestant groups and condemned domestic Nazism, saying citizens must be vigilant against attacks on democracy in America.[127]
Dr. Frank Kingdon also warned that it was pointless to condemn
Hitler "if we ourselves toy with the idea that the Jew is not quite the
same as we are." He appealed to Essex County churches to make a
Thanksgiving Day request of their congregations to make contributions equal to their Thanksgiving expenditures for victims of oppression abroad.[128]

In December, 1938, anticipating a new surge of German-Jewish
emigrants to New Jersey, Michael Stavitsky called a state-wide meeting to discuss methods for dealing with the crisis. The Essex County
Jewish Coordinating Committee, established to coordinate the efforts of all groups dealing with Jewish refugees, reported that it was
working with 450 immigrants. A small camp was established for
mothers and children and a German-Jewish club for adults. The
Newark Board of Education held classes to teach refugees English
while the coordinating committee worked on citizenship papers. It
was estimated that there were between 1,000 and 1,500 Jewish refugees in Essex County.[129]

* * *

After Kristallnacht Christians took the initiative in an anti-Nazi
activity in Newark for the first time. A few days after the pogrom,
Reverend Clarence Bleakney called a meeting to organize a committee of Newark's business, religious, civic, and cultural institutions to protest the Nazi action. Bleakney, pastor of Newark's Roseville
Baptist Church, had been active in interfaith events, the prohibition-
ist movement, and social work. The horror of Kristallnacht had moved
this affable and well-liked cleric to take the lead in organizing a
citywide response to Hitler. At the meeting at the Hotel Douglas it
was decided to call the new group "The Committee of 100 for the
Defense of Human Rights." Bleakney was authorized to write prospective members inviting them to a meeting at Newark's City Hall.
The letter stated,

Owing to the fact of the unprecedented stand of our President over the persecution of Jews and Catholics in Germany, we are asking you to serve on a "committee of 100" to plan a program of action in their behalf.[130]

The City Hall meeting included religious, labor, political, and cultural leaders. Women's groups were well represented. The only Newark influentials not represented were industry and finance leaders. Institutions such as the Prudential Insurance Company (with over 10,000 employees in its Newark office), Mutual Benefit and Life, Fireman's Life, American Insurance Company, Public Service Electric and Gas, New Jersey Bell Telephone Company, Fidelity Union Trust, and National Newark and Essex Bank had little or no role in the Committee of 100. One reason was because the city's banks, insurance companies, and utilities employed an insignificant number of Jews in the 1930s.[131]

The Committee of 100's principal aims were to alleviate the condition of persecuted minorities in Germany, to prevent the infiltration of Nazi ideology into America, and combat Nazism. The committee adopted Peter Cavicchia's resolution urging immediate severance of diplomatic and commercial relations with Germany, and endorsed President Roosevelt's "action and attitude" in regards to Kristallnacht. A protest rally for early December at Krueger Auditorium was approved, and Bleakney was directed to appoint a twelve-member steering committee. Representing the Jewish community, Stavitsky suggested that steering committee duties should include preparing a slate of officers, formulating policies and procedures, suggesting fundraising methods, completing plans for the mass meeting, and arranging necessary details to make the organization permanent.[132] Bleakney's steering committee included Garner, Kingdon, Rev. William Hiram Foulkes, and a relative newcomer, Nancy Cox, who during her one year in Newark had proven her mettle as an activist. The steering committee organized two subcommittees, one to make the Committee of 100 countywide by selecting residents outside of Newark and one to confer with a similar group in New York planning joint strategy. The venue for the mass rally was changed from Krueger Auditorium to the Mosque Theater.[133]

Foulkes was named chairman of the Committee of 100. As pastor of Newark's most influential Protestant congregation, First Presbyterian ("Old First"), moderator of the General Assembly of the Presbyterian Church of America, and leader of the city's Protestant clergy, he was the logical choice for the position. Kingdon was named associate chairman, and Dr. Max Danzis, chief of staff of Newark's Beth Israel Hospital, was named vice chairman.[134] A meeting of the Committee of 100 ratified the steering committee decisions, and named Louis Bamberger honorary chairman, and Judge Daniel T. Brennan,[135] Newark commissioner, Vincent Murphy, Ralph Lum, prominent lawyer and former head of the Newark Welfare Federation,[136] and Mrs. C.H. Robbins, a well-known women's club activist, additional vice chairmen. New York Supreme Court Justice Ferdinand Pecora was selected as the main speaker.

Editorials in Newark's two dailies and the *Jewish Chronicle* praised the formation of the Committee of 100 and the upcoming rally. There were daily articles on preparations for the event. The *Newark Evening News* gave the event its imprimatur, and one of its officers, Robert R. Lane, was active on the committee. The *Chronicle* wrote, "Thank God that we here have Christians who take the lead in defending and protecting human rights."[137] Groups throughout the Newark area supported the Committee of 100 rally. The Essex County Branch of WILPF urged its members to attend the event.[138] The NSANL canceled its own anti-Nazi rally and urged its members to support the Committee of 100's assembly.[139]

A few days before the event, another anti-Nazi rally took place in Newark. In a hall festooned with anti-Nazi banners, the exiled German author Oscar Maria Graf urged the audience at the annual festival of the German-American Clubs of Newark to work against "manifestations of Nazism in the United States." The crowd sang the folk song "Lorelei," which was banned in Germany because Heinrich Heine, a Jew, had written it.[140]

On Monday evening December 12, a crowd of almost 4,000 filled every seat, corner, and doorway of the Mosque Theater to denounce recent events in Germany. Moved by the speeches of Judge Pecora and others, the audience adopted a resolution reaffirming faith in democracy. The declaration also endorsed Roosevelt's rebuke of the Nazis for their persecution of minorities and his call for "a conference of all democracies to adopt measures to safeguard the security of all liberty loving people."

Reverend Foulkes, the event's chairman, and Ralph Lum, its vice chairman, had received letters signed with the swastika telling them "to mind their own business." This phrase became a catchword; Foulkes, Pecora, and others repeated over and over again that the fate of an oppressed people is everyone's business. Foulkes said

that those assembled were not telling Germany what form of government to adopt but rather protesting her inhumane treatment of
fellow human beings. He also pointed out that America was not free
of prejudice towards minorities, particularly African-Americans. Pecora
noted that the United States was minding its business better than Germany, which was trying to spread Nazism in the Western Hemisphere.
Kingdon told the audience it was fighting against a spirit that, if allowed to spread, would "destroy everything precious in human experience." Dr. Walter G. Alexander, the sole African-American speaker, received great applause when he asserted that his race has a "sympathetic
understanding and feeling for those who are suffering abroad what we
have suffered for many generations."[141] The African-American *Herald
News* reported this applause, but claimed that Dr. Alexander "startled"
the audience when he said that African Americans in America were
being treated in the same manner as Jews in Germany.[142]

The *Newark Sunday Call* editorial "It Can't Happen Here" called
the event an "amazing" evening at which every group in the community was represented. Elements that were normally "uncoopera-
tive or actually unfriendly" stood together for a denunciation of the
savagery of the Nazis and for a reaffirmation of Newark's faith in
democracy. According to the *Call*, the rally should "reassure the
fears of those who worry about the fate of democracy in America."[143]

* * *

At 1938's end, some Newarkers who had previously been neutral
or silent *vis a vis* Hitler began to speak out. Nazi aggression in Europe, barbarities against the Jews during Kristallnacht, and newsreels and newspaper photos of ever-growing Bund rallies in America,
had alienated fair-minded Americans. The Bund was increasingly
seen as a fifth column and was the target of government inquiry and
regulation. Ironically the year ended not only with tragedy for European Jews but with an upsurge of anti-Semitism in the United States.[144]
Nativist anti-Semitic groups such as the Silver Shirts and Father
Charles E. Coughlin's Christian Front gained strength, while the
German-American Bund still posed a threat. 3.5 million Americans
listened each Sunday to Coughlin's anti-Semitic tirades on the radio
and another 15 million listened occasionally. A survey of Americans
showed a glaring ambivalence: while 88 percent disapproved of
Hitler's treatment of Jews, over 60 percent considered it partly or
fully the fault of the Jews themselves.[145]

Notes

1. Diamond, Sander A., *The Nazi Movement in the United States, 1924-1941,* Ithaca, NY, 1974, p. 242.
2. NYT, 2/14/38, p. 18; 2/21/38, p. 5; N.N., 2/15/38, p. 4; 2/24/38, p. 6; 3/11/38, p. 11;3/25/38, p. 8.
3. Diamond, *The Nazi Movement in the United States*, p. 295.
4. N.N., 3/1/38, p. 9.
5. NYT, 2/13/38, p. 28.
6. N.N. 2/18/38, p. 27.
7. By 1938, the majority of Minutemen no longer lived in the Third Ward, but rather on or adjoining Hawthorne Avenue, several miles South of the Third Ward. Jews left the Third Ward as it became more populated by African-Americans. The Hawthorne Avenue area replaced Prince Street both as the major residential area for the Jewish proletariat and as the center for Jewish gangs and illegal activities. Nevertheless, the gathering place for the Minutemen remained Prince Street in the Third Ward.
8. N.N., 2/21/38, p. 4.
9. Ibid.
10. S.C., 4/17/38, pp. 1, 12.
11. NYT, 4/21/39, pp. 1, 11.
12. N.N., 3/15/38, p. 17.
13. Newark Conference of Jewish Charities, Executive Committee Minutes, 3/28/38.
14. J.C., 4/29/38, p. 5.
15. Ibid., 3/25/38, p. 1.
16. NSANL, Box 2 , Folder 3, Telegram from Dr. Kalb to President Roosevelt, 3/25/38.
17. IKUV, IKUV Messenger, April 1938.
18. N.N., 3/23/38, p. 14.
19. S.C., 3/27/38, p. 1.
20. Bayor, Ronald H., *Neighbors in Conflict—The Irish, Germans, Jews, and Italians of New York City, 1929-1941*, Chicago, 1988, p. 87. The Pope in 1930 warned Americans to be wary of communism during their economic difficulties. In 1932, he further warned of the danger of militant atheism, which was using the press and political parties to achieve its ends.
21. S.C., 3/27/38, p. 1. Dr. Frank Kingdon, president of Newark University, was away on vacation and could not be reached for comment. The following day, Frank Harris, Dean of New Jersey Law School (part of Newark University) was summoned by Reverend Toohey to a meeting at St. James Church. At the meeting, Harris, a practicing Catholic, was asked if there were any communist students at the University. The educator responded that there were and that communists could be found at every college in the country. Toohey responded that as long as there was one he would fight it and that he had the backing of Archbishop Walsh. Toohey then asked if four recently dismissed professors were fired because they were "commies." Harris answered that they were fired for budgetary reasons. The Reverend said, "That is a lie and whoever said so is a liar." The dean responded that Toohey would have a tough time proving his allegation. The cleric then said that Harris was not a very good Catholic and there was no reason to continue the meeting. Toohey ended the interview by saying, "You can leave and don't send any Jews down to see me." Harris immediately executed a sworn affidavit of the meeting but never made it public. See, Newark College of Arts and Sciences, University of Newark Office Records 1934-1946 group I, RG N2/NO/I, Box 5, Sworn Affidavit of Dean Frank Harris, 3/28/38.
22. J.C., 4/22/38, p. 6.
23. Ibid., 4/29/39, p. 1; N.N., 4/25/38, p. 6.
24. N.N., Ibid.
25. JHS, RG 2, National Agencies File, "Questionnaire-the United Jewish Appeal of Essex County, 1938 Campaign," 3/28/38.
26. Newark Conference of Jewish Charities, Executive Director's Agencies Files, Box 18, Folder 5, Letter from the League for Human Rights to Kalb, 3/9/39; NSANL of New Jersey, Statement of Receipts and Disbursements, 3/23/38.

27. Ibid, Letter from Julius H. Cohn to Kalb, 4/21/38.
28. N.N., 5/6/38, p. 12.
29. Ibid.
30. IKUV, IKUV Messenger, November, 1938.
31. N.N., 5/27/38, p. 1.
32. NSANL, Box 11, Folder 5, Letters from Alenick to NSANL, 5/13/38, 5/16/38.
33. S.C., 6/5/38, p. 8.
34. Ibid., 5/29/38, p. 8; J.C., 6/3/38, p. 1.
35. Goodman, Walter, *The Committee—The Extraordinary Career of the House Committee on Un-American Activities*, New York, 1968, p. 22.
36. Bell, Leland, *In Hitler's Shadow: The Anatomy of American Nazism*, Port Washington, 1973, p. 68.
37. N.N., 6/8/38, p. 16.
38. Ogden, August Raymond, *The Dies Committee, A Study of the Special House Committee for the Investigation of Un-American Activities 1938-1944,* Washington, DC, 1945, pp. 43-46.
39. Ogden, *The Dies Committee*, pp. 46, 50.
40. Ibid, p. 45; S.C., 6/12/38, p. 10.
41. Bell, *In Hitler's Shadow*, p. 68.
42. Ibid., p. 64; N.N., 6/8/38, p. 16.
43. Bell, *In Hitler's Shadow*, p. 62.
44. J.C., 9/9/38, p. 1.
45. NYT, 10/7/38, p. 1; N.N., 11/5/38, p. 1.
46. Ogden, *The Dies Committee*, p. 101.
47. 1938 boycott decisions in which Kalb was involved included: Sears Roebuck & Company should not be taken off the boycott list because their claim of decreased imports from Germany was in dispute; Afga Film should not be taken off the boycott list because there was uncertainty as to the amount of money being sent back to Germany from film sales in the United States; the film *Carnival in Flanders* at the 68th Street Theater in Manhattan should be picketed because it was made by a German film company; and the boycott should be extended to Austrian made goods. See, JBC, Box 4, Folder "J," Letter from Kalb to Israel Poznansky, 2/7/38; Ibid., Minutes of the Joint Actions Committee, 2/11/38; Dr. Abraham Grossman Papers, RG 286, Box 5, Folder 8, Minutes of the Joint Actions Committee, 3/18/38.
48. Samuel Untermyer Papers, RG 251, Boxes 1 and 2, Letter from Untermyer to NSANL Board, 4/24/38; NYT, 4/28/38, p. 5.
49. IKUV, IKUV Messenger, June 1938.
50. NSANL, Box 11, Folder 4, report "To the members of the NJ Division of the NSANL," 4/12/39.
51. Yad Vashem Studies, III, 1959, Joseph Tenenbaum, "Anti-Nazi Boycott Movement," pp. 155, 157.
52. N.N., 5/26/38, p. 5; Interviews, Al Fisher, 4/7/98, Phil Small, 4/8/98.
53. N.N., 6/2/38, p. 30.
54. Vecoli, Rudolph J., *The People of New Jersey*, Princeton, NJ, 1965, p. 207.
55. Stuart, Mark A., *Gangster # 2, Longy Zwillman,* Secaucus, NJ, 1985, pp. 106,7. The same source claims that Hague was on the guest list for Zwillman's 1939 wedding (page 118).
56. N.N., 6/20/38, pp. 1,2; 7/28/38, p. 1; 8/18/38, p. 1.
57. Ibid., 6/20/38, p. 1.
58. S.C., 7/3/38, p. 12.
59. German-American Bund, RG 131, 304A, Box 2, Letter from Klapprott to Remington Arms, 6/11/38.
60. J.C., 7/1/38, p. 1.
61. N.N. 7/12/38, p. 1; The Appellate Division of New York overturned the civil rights conviction of the five in November on grounds of insufficient evidence. However, the one-year jail sentence meted out to Mueller was re-affirmed based upon his attitude of "contempt" toward the court. See N.N., 11/5/38, p. 7.

62.   Ibid., 7/22/38, p. 22; J.C., 7/29/38, p. 1; 8/26/38, p. 1.
63.   I.H., 10/28/38, p. 1.
64.   S.C., 7/31/38, p. 8.
65.   NYT, 9/5/38, p. 10.
66.   N.N., 9/1/38, p. 14.
67.   Bayor, *Neighbors in Conflict*, pp. 83, 84.
68.   N.N., 10/11/38, p. 22.
69.   Ibid., 10/13/38, p. 24.
70.   Ibid., 10/13/38, p. 9.
71.   J.C., 10/14/38, p. 4.
72.   NSANL, Box 11, Folder 2, Letter from Smertenko to Alenick, 10/6/38.
73.   NN., 9/14/38, p. 1.
74.   Nancy Cox (1913-2001), a direct descendant of the only female born aboard the Mayflower, moved with her family to Maplewood, New Jersey in 1922. Her father Philip Cox was an author and professor at New York University's School of Education. A well-known liberal, he served on the board of Newark's ACLU. Nancy inherited her father's ideology. By the time she graduated Antioch, a work-study college, she had been a teacher in a Jones and Loughlin Steel Company mill town where she witnessed the intimidation and terrible working conditions of the employees. After her junior year in 1935 she traveled to Europe, and following her parents' recommendation, she took a twelve-week course at a school in the Soviet Union. Nancy was impressed that women had a more advanced role in society than they had in the United States. She then traveled to Nazi Germany where she was repelled by the crude anti-Semitism and the militarism she saw there. She was no more impressed by Austria or Italy, which she visited next.

When she returned to the United States after a year in Europe, she finished her degree at NYU. Simultaneously, she volunteered with the League of Industrial Democracy (LID) and the Worker's Defense League both Norman Thomas projects. With the Defense League, she volunteered to be arrested for a test case to challenge the constitutionality of a newly enacted law in Edgewater, New Jersey prohibiting the distribution of handbills without submitting fingerprints, a photograph, and the text of the handbill to police for their approval. She was arrested on the steps of City Hall distributing copies of the Bill of Rights. Eventually the law was declared unconstitutional by the New Jersey Supreme Court.

Through her father's friendship with Roger Baldwin, in September 1937, she was offered the position as the executive secretary of the New Jersey ACLU, in Newark, at $10 per week. At twenty-three, the Mayflower descendant had a police record and a job with the ACLU. Her next paid job was as leader of the New Jersey branch of the ALPD. By the end of the year, until the Nazi Soviet Pact of August 1939, she was one of the leading activists in Newark. She married Robert Parker (Premo), a young communist in early 1938.

Before her death in 2001, she published a memoir, *My Story, 1934-1939* covering her days in Newark.
75.   J.C., 9/30/38, p. 1; S.C., 10/2/38, p. 6.
76.   N.N., 10/3/38, p. 16.
77.   Laqueur, Walter, *A History of Zionism*, New York, 1972, p. 522.
78.   N.N., 10/10/38, p. 9; 10/11/38, p. 34.
79.   Ibid., 10/24/38, p. 5.
80.   Ibid., 10/13/38, p. 4.
81.   Ibid., 10/30/38, p. 8.
82.   The existence of this informal coalition is confirmed by Milton Ritz, then a communist turned socialist, who said there was a steady flow of information between communists and anti-Nazis as to the timing and tactics of anti-Bund activities. Ritz claims that as early as 1933 there was informal contact between Longie Zwillman and the communists for purposes of actions against the Friends of the New Germany. The author could find no verification for this latter claim. Telephone interview, Milton Ritz, 4/5/98.

83. *Elizabeth Daily Journal*, 9/16/38, pp. 1,2.
84. N.N., 10/3/38, p. 7.
85. Ibid., 10/3/38, p. 1; S.E., 10/3/38, p. 1.
86. N.N., 10/11/38, p. 17.
87. Ibid., 10/14/38, p.5; 10/17/38, p. 12.
88. J.C., 10/21/38, p. 1.
89. N.N., 10/25/38, p. 12.
90. Ibid., 10/26/38, p. 13.
91. Interview, Nancy Cox, 4/17/98.
92. N.N., 10/27/38, p. 1.
93. Interview, Nancy Cox. The following morning, when Cox read about the riot in the newspaper, she was embarrassed that the caption underneath the front-page photo of the scene included her quote about "peaceful picketing."
94. NYT, 10/27/38, p. 4.
95. N.N., 10/27/38, p. 1; S. E., 10/27/38, p.1.
96. N.N., 11/17/38, p. 12.
97. Ibid., 10/27/38, p. 4.
98. S.C., 10/30/38, p. 16.
99. N.N., 11/8/38, p. 4.
100. J.C., 11/11/38, p. 4.
101. Hilberg, Raul, *The Destruction of the European Jews*, Vol. I, New York, 1985, pp. 38, 39; Heydrich, Reinhard, Preliminary Secret Report to Hermann Goering, November 1938 as quoted in *The Jew in the Modern World*, Edited by Paul Mendes-Flohr and Jehuda Reinharz, New York, 1995, pp. 651, 652.
102. Lookstein, Haskel, *Were We Our Brothers' Keepers? The Public Response of American Jews to the Holocaust 1938-1944,* New York, 1985, p. 42.
103. Lipstadt, Deborah E., *Beyond Belief: The American Press and the Coming of the Holocaust*, New York, 1986, pp. 104,105.
104. N.N., 11/11/38, p. 7.
105. Ibid., 11/14/38, p. 2.
106. Ibid., 11/17/38, p. 2.
107. S.C., 11/20/38, Part III, p. 12.
     When six months later, the front entrance to Mayor Meyer Ellenstein's house was defaced with large letters "GET OUT JEW," there was little newspaper response. N.N., 6/7/39, p. 1.
108. N.N., 11/16/38, p. 4; 11/21/38, p. 11; J.C., 11/18/38, p. 2.
109. S.E., 11/21/38, p. 7; N.N., 12/13/38, p. 17.
110. The only African-American voice speaking out against Kristallnacht in Newark was the weekly *Herald News*. In a strongly worded editorial, it condemned the pogrom and stated that despite lynching in the South and segregation in the North, African Americans in America did not suffer as much as the Jews in Germany. The *Herald* said despite battles, America's African-Americans have freedoms, including high governmental posts, elected officials, and beloved and wealthy celebrities. See, *New Jersey Herald News*, 11/19/38, p. 4.
111. New Jersey, State of, Report of the New Jersey State Temporary Commission on the Condition of the Urban Colored Population to the Legislature of the State of New Jersey, Trenton, New Jersey, 1939, pp. 56, 57, 61, 70. For the collaboration between vocational schools and labor unions that prevented African-Americans from gaining apprenticeships in craft unions in Newark, see Kenneth T. and Barbara B. Jackson, "The Black Experience in Newark: The Growth of the Ghetto, 1870-1970," as published in *New Jersey since 1860: New Findings and Interpretations*, edited by William C. Wright: New Jersey Historical Commission, Trenton, NJ, 1972, p. 49.
112. CPUSA, Reel 297, Delo 3877, Minutes Newark Communist Party, 12/27/35.
     Elwood Dean was the most active of the three Newark African-American communists in 1935 and throughout the 1950s.
113. National Negro Congress, FBI File 100-1467, Report of 2/1/43, pp. 3, 4.

114.   The National Negro Congress, a communist front, began operations in 1936, with a convention of 550 organizations, including Roy Wilkins of the NAACP, Lester Granger of the Urban League, as well as Republicans, Democrats, and Communists. A. Phillip Randolph, prominent Socialist and leader of the Brotherhood of Sleeping Car Porters, was elected the first president. Like others, he was prepared to work with communists because of the moderate aims of the Congress, which included much needed social and economic reforms, with no revolutionary program. See, Klehr, Harvey, *The Heyday of American Communism: the Depression Decade,* New York, 1984, pp. 346, 347.

115.   N.N., 3/30/38, p. 28; 3/31/38, p. 9; 4/19/38, p. 9.

116.   Ibid., 4/20/38, p. 1; 5/15/38, p. 1.

117.   S.C., 5/22/38, pp. 1, 5, Part III, p. 12.

118.   Ibid., 5/22/38, p. 1.

119.   *Newark Herald News*, 8/27/38, p. 7. In May 1938, the *Newark Herald News* changed its name to the *New Jersey Herald News*. The *News* was published by two brothers who manufactured hair products, Fred and Richard Martin. It was the guardian of African-American business interests. See, Price, Clement Alexander, *Freedom Not Far Distant: A Documentary History of Afro-Americans in New Jersey,* Newark, NJ, 1980, p. 234.

120.   Ibid., 7/2/38, p. 12.

121.   The horrors of Kristallnacht resulted in the creation of two Christian boycott organizations, the Volunteer Christian Committee to Boycott Nazi Germany (VCC) and the American Boycott Against Aggressor Nations (ABAAN). See, Gottlieb, Moshe, "Boycott, Rescue, and Ransom," YIVO Annual XV, 241-245.

122.   Hilberg, *Destruction of the European Jews*, p. 42.

123.   Interview, Irving Edisis, 4/15/98. Edisis claims he participated in an action with Dr. Kalb in front of L. Bamberger in protest against the store's sale of German-made guns. The two men shouted through a loudspeaker: "toys become guns-boycott is the moral equivalent of war!"

124.   NSANL, Box 11, Folder 5, Letters from Smertenko to Alenick, 11/17/38; from Jacobs to Alenick, 12/21/38.

125.   Newark Conference of Jewish Charities, Executive Director's Agencies Files, Box 18, Folder 5, New Jersey NSANL Statement of Income and Expenses for the Year Ended March 31, 1939.

126.   JBC, Box 3, Folder "Reorganization," Letter from Robert S. Marcus to Ruth Mandel, 11/28/38.

127.   S.E., 11/23/38, p. 2.

128.   N.N., 11/14/38, p. 19; 11/17/38, p. 6.

129.   Stavitsky Papers, Meeting to Organize Work with German-Jewish Refugees in New Jersey, 12/14/38, pp. 2, 3.

130.   N.N., 11/15/38, p. 28; 11/17/38, p. 6.

131.   Journal of Industry & Finance (New Jersey), Volumes 10-13, December 1935-May 1939. The names of the officers and directors of these companies are listed in various articles during this time period. None were Jews. Of all the names, only one, Ralph A. Lum, an attorney listed as a director of First Fidelity Bank served on the Committee of 100.

132.   N.N., 11/22/38, p. 3.

133.   S.E., 11/26/38, p. 4. Other steering committee members were: Jacob Baer of the Essex Trades Council (AFL), Herman Walker, Executive Secretary of the Newark Teachers Association, William Carney, state CIO organizer, Mrs. Patrick Henry Adams, President of the State Federation of Women's Clubs, Mrs. L. Crawford Russell, President of the Contemporary, Peter A. Smith, and Russell P. Walker, secretary of the Newark YMCA.

134.   Papers of Michael A. Stavitsky, Series 2, Box 6, Folder 2, Letter from Foulkes to Stavitsky, 12/1/38.

135.   Judge Daniel Brennan (1890-1958) was a prominent Catholic layman, who was probably on the Committee of 100 to represent the Catholic Church.

136. Ralph E. Lum was the only male on the Committee of 100 that represented Newark's old-line elite. He was a descendent of Abraham Pierson, one of the Puritan founders of Newark. An attorney, Lum was one of the city's most active civic leaders. His law firm represented successful financial, insurance, and business enterprises. He was a director of Fidelity Union Trust and L. Bamberger & Co. This latter position showed that he had the trust of Newark's most influential Jew.

137. J.C., 12/9/38, p. 1.

138. Essex County WILPF Papers, Minutes of meeting, 12/12/38.

139. N.N., 11/25/38, p. 7.

140. Ibid., 12/11/38, p. 2.

141. Ibid., 12/13/38, pp. 1,2.

142. *New Jersey Herald News*, 12/24/38, p. 2. Dr. Walter G. Alexander (1880-1953), was Newark's outstanding African-American from the 1920s through the 1940s. He was the first African American to serve in the New Jersey Legislature (1921-1922), and was appointed for two terms by two governors to serve on the New Jersey Board of Health. He was an organizer of the New Jersey Urban League and its former vice president. Throughout his career, he was an advocate of better health care for African Americans, particularly in regards to tuberculosis, which was a scourge of Newark's minority population. See, *Newark News* Morgue, Dr. Walter G. Alexander.

143. S.C., 12/18/38, Part III, p. 8.

144. N.N., 12/28/38, p. 4. An AJC report stated that discrimination against Jews had reached a new high since the advent of Nazism.

145. Lookstein, *Were We Our Brother's Keepers?*, pp. 78, 79.

8

The Nazi-Soviet Pact and World War II, 1939-1940

The Nazi-Soviet Pact, a ten-year non-aggression agreement between Germany and the Soviet Union, was signed on August 23, 1939. A secret clause in the pact provided for the division of Poland and the Baltic countries between the two dictatorships. One week later, Germany invaded Poland, and France and Great Britain declared war on Germany. Shortly thereafter, Soviet Russia occupied eastern Poland, Latvia, Lithuania, and Estonia, and invaded Finland. World War II had begun.

Prior to the outbreak of war, the brunt of anti-Nazi activities in the United States had been shouldered by predominantly Jewish groups engaged in boycott activities, demonstrations, and physical intimidation. With the exception of the Communist Party and its many front organizations, support from non-Jewish groups had been limited. With the advent of the Nazi-Soviet Pact, however, the Communist Party reversed its anti-Nazism and denounced both British and French imperialism and American support for the Allies.

Throughout 1939, but especially immediately following the signing of the Nazi-Soviet Pact, Nazi aggression in Europe increasingly turned American public opinion against Hitler. American anti-Nazi policies were based on the fear that Germany would upset the balance of European power and threaten American interests. In the same way, increased government action against the German-American Bund was grounded in the fear that an alien group would become a "fifth column" in the advent of war with Germany. Jewish interests were not a consideration in formulating America's foreign policy vis-à-vis Germany and the German-American Bund. The need for groups like the Minutemen and the NSANL receded as both Federal and local governments stepped up efforts against the Hitlerites.

As 1939 began, new voices in Newark's Christian community were raised against anti-Semitism. Conrad Hoffman, National Director for Jewish Evangelical Work, told over 150 pastors, elders, and women at a conference of the missionary societies of the Newark Presbytery that a tide of anti-Semitism was sweeping the world. He said that even American Jews were not immune to the threat because most Protestants here "are anti-Semitic in their outlook" and urged pastors and other church workers to educate people against anti-Semitism.[1] Seton Hall College established a "Student's Crusade for Americanism" and its first release denounced the Bund and similar organizations for infringing on American principles. Paul Brienza, president of the group, said that allowing the Bund to exercise its rights of assembly and free speech was injurious to the cause of Americanism.[2]

The Committee of 100 started the year with an announcement that it would become a permanent organization, a decision a *Jewish Chronicle* editorial opined was good for the Jewish community.[3] The group promised to defend minority rights and preserve democracy. The committee spawned an offshoot, the Non-Sectarian Committee in Defense of Human Rights of the Oranges and Maplewood. Organized by Judge Daniel Brennan and Luke Garner, the latter group passed a resolution at its first meeting asking President Roosevelt to permanently recall the American Ambassador to Berlin and to boycott German goods.[4]

The resolution did not go unchallenged. Benjamin Franklin Miessner, a Short Hills inventor, protested the use of the Orange High School Auditorium by a "Communistic and radical" group. He continued: "If these Communist Jews want to rail against the Germans or the German Americans let them hire a hall as others do." Judge Brennan replied that the committee was composed of members of all religions and worked in the interests of persecuted minorities everywhere. The judge also said the auditorium had been rented at the regular fee.[5]

* * *

Unlike the Committee of 100 and its offshoot, many groups operating in Newark in 1939 were communist organizations and fronts, part of what is known collectively as the Popular Front. The Popular Front strategy began in 1935 when Moscow, desperate to establish friendship with bourgeois nations in the fight against fascism, forged alliances with progressive political, peace, labor, and intellectual groups. Communist members adopted the programs of the groups they joined, while at the same time attempting to gain control of them.

The most successful front created by the Communist Party was the American League Against War and Fascism, renamed the American League For Peace and Democracy (ALPD) in 1937. The Newark league resisted communist domination until 1938. Prior to that, leadership of the league was vested in the community's three pre-eminent Protestant liberals, Amelia Moorfield, Frank Kingdon, and Luke Garner. Moorfield, the state secretary, consistently defended the league's non-communist character.[6] But, in truth, many members of the Newark branch were either communists or sympathizers.

In late 1937, Dorothy Detzer, national secretary of the Women's International League for Peace and Democracy (WILPF), withdrew her organization from the ALPD, claiming that the communists were distorting ALPD policies.[7] Subsequently, Amelia Moorfield resigned her ALPD position, and the New Jersey group languished until Nancy Cox became its executive secretary in the spring of 1938. Cox, who had resigned her position as the executive secretary of the Newark office of the American Civil Liberties Union (ACLU),[8] reinvigorated the ALPD and visited all of the state's twenty-three branches to co-ordinate activities. Much of her time was spent defending the Loyalist side of the Spanish Civil War, and on her trips to the branches she took a projector to show the anti-Franco film *The Fight for Peace* by Hendrik Willem Van Loon.[9]

The Spanish Civil War was perfect fodder for Popular Front activities. Liberal groups of all stripes backed the beleaguered Loyalists. One of the Spanish Republican government's last hopes was that the United States would reverse its embargo against both sides and allow shipments of arms to reach the Loyalists. Although the ALPD was active in this cause, the Communist Party organized another front to deal specifically with the embargo, the National Council to Lift the Embargo on the Spanish Republic. The council was active in Newark, and Garner, Moorfield, Dr. Wells P. Eagleton, and Dr. Eugene V. Parsonnet were among the signers of a January 1939 council appeal to President Roosevelt to lift the embargo. The leader of the council's Newark branch was Rev. William L. Tucker, assistant to William Hiram Foulkes at First Presbyterian Church and a leader in the Committee of 100.[10] The council dissolved after May 1939, when Franco formed his government in Spain.[11]

If Cox had any doubts about who controlled the New Jersey ALPD when she took the job, she learned soon enough. After about six months on the job, she was called to a meeting by Jim Nelson, the league's personnel director, and former leader in the Abraham Lincoln Brigade (a volunteer group dominated by communists that fought with the Loyalist forces during the Spanish Civil War). Nelson told her that some people in the organization wanted to replace her with a Spanish Civil War veteran. Nelson said he didn't want this to happen because the veteran had disobeyed orders in Madrid by not reporting to duty for a crucial battle. Nelson said he would instruct them not to replace Cox.

As predicted, Cox was called to a strange location to face a group of about twenty people she had never seen before. She did recognize the woman running the meeting—Lena Davis, Newark Communist Party chairman. The Spanish Civil War veteran, dressed in uniform, criticized Cox and explained why he would be a better executive secretary. Cox was asked to justify her performance. When she finished enumerating her accomplishments, she turned to Davis and asked if she could impart the knowledge she had gained from Nelson. In the absence of a response, Cox repeated what Nelson had told her about the veteran's war record. Silence ensued and she left the meeting. She went back to her job and never heard another word about the matter.[12]

Newark's branch of the ALPD was often called the "Mothers' Group" because its core consisted of 150 members who were female Jewish refugees from Russia's 1905 Revolution.[13] Nancy Cox, head of the New Jersey ALPD, had her office at the "Mothers' Group" headquarters in Clinton Hill (a Jewish neighborhood adjacent to downtown Newark) and remembers that whenever the league needed letter writers, demonstrators, audiences, or spokespeople the "Mothers' Group" was always there.[14]

Another communist labor front, The International Workers' Order (IWO), had a national membership of approximately 150,000 by 1939. Some of its members had joined because of the low-cost life insurance it offered them.[15] The insurance, in addition to other benefits, made it similar to a KUV or the Workman's Circle. Although most of its members did not belong to the Communist Party, the leaders did, and they used the IWO as a recruiting ground for the party. Rebecca Grecht, who served as Newark's Communist Party Secretary in the early and mid-1930s, was a district organizer for the

IWO.[16] The IWO had 1,800 members in Newark, including 500 members in four Jewish branches.[17] Long active in the anti-Nazi boycott, they held meetings to discuss the Bund and other fascist groups.[18]

The Workers' Alliance, a joint project of the Communist and Socialist parties, was a pressure group comprised of labor unions and the unemployed that tried to obtain more benefits for its constituents from the New Deal. By 1937, it was claimed that nineteen out of twenty-five members of the national executive board were communists. In 1936 and again in 1938 the alliance protested federal actions to reduce the number of WPA workers.[19] In January 1939, the Newark branch of the Workers' Alliance held a demonstration to protest recent WPA layoffs.[20]

Norman Thomas and the Socialist Party left the Workers' Alliance during early 1939 because of its communist domination. In Newark, seven out of the thirteen Essex County locals pulled out of the alliance charging that it was controlled "by Communists and Stalin stooges." As if to prove the charge, Newark Communist Party stalwarts denounced socialists and defectors at the alliance's first meeting after the pullout. The Communist Party used the opportunity to install its members as the leaders of the alliance.[21]

The New Jersey division of the Jewish Peoples' Committee, another front[22] and an affiliate of the IWO[23], held its organizational meeting at Krueger Auditorium in March 1939. According to its president, Dr. Samuel M. Goodman, the group's purpose was to fight Nazism and aid refugees.[24] In an obviously inflated claim, the committee claimed its membership consisted of seventy organizations representing 17,000 Newark Jews. Most of its members were unionists and belonged to KUVs.

The committee's communist pedigree must have been well known as a contemporaneous report underscored the "antagonism" toward the group displayed by the AJC and other organizations.[25] When New Jersey Governor A. Harry Moore was asked to send a statement supporting a Jewish Peoples' Committee anti-Nazi rally, Philip Foreman, a prominent state judge who was active in the Jewish community, advised the governor that the committee was communist and "not to dignify this meeting by a statement."[26]

The communists, as part of their Popular Front strategy, infiltrated a number of branches of Labor's Non-Partisan League, an affiliate of the Congress of Industrial Organizations (CIO).[27] In order to recruit new party members, the communists decided to organize neighborhood groups against Nazism in 1938, with the help of the Non-Partisan League. This policy was implemented in Newark in early 1939, particularly in Jewish neighborhoods. The West Side Neighborhood Committee[28] was one such group. It was established in February 1939 to fight anti-Semitism and Nazism in Newark. Harry Wendrich of the Non-Partisan League was elected chair and Jack Malamuth of the NSANL vice-chair. The West Side Committee petitioned Newark's Commission to ban Bund meetings in Newark and to adopt an ordinance against distribution of Nazi propaganda in the city.[29] Joseph Procida, secretary of the Non-Partisan League, sent a copy of the resolution to Governor Moore, who forwarded it to the Dies Committee.[30] The 9th-16th Ward Club was also organized under the banner of the Non-Partisan League. At the club's first meeting, Samuel Goodman urged Jews and Christians to unite in the fight against racial intolerance. He criticized Newark Jewry for not showing a united front.[31]

The Communist Party of Essex County sponsored a "Stop Hitler" rally in Newark in April 1939.[32] The meeting led to a "Stop Hitler" parade, led by an ad hoc front group, the Czechoslovakian Educational Federation of Newark, as well as by the German-American League for Culture. The purpose of the event was to protest the Nazi dismemberment of Czechoslovakia.[33] The parade drew 1,000 participants who marched from Lincoln Park to Washington Park. Speakers included such disparate individuals as Reverend William Hiram Foulkes, Chairman of the Committee of 100, and Samuel Goodman.[34]

Another ad hoc front group of foreign extraction, the Ukrainian Unity Society, called an anti-Nazi meeting at Newark's Ukrainian Hall. The co-sponsor of the event was the International Workers' Order. Over 200 persons heard a communist Ukrainian speaker, Michael Tkach, claim Nazi agents were responsible for nationalistic Ukrainian agitation in America. When a motion denouncing Nazi aggression was proposed, Bogdan Buchak, secretary of the Young Ukrainian Nationalists of Newark, demanded that the resolution also condemn Communist Russia, Poland, and Romania for their treatment of the Ukrainians. Buchak's remarks provoked a disturbance and a policeman stationed in back of the hall was summoned. He questioned Buchak and several others but made no arrests. Buchak's amendment was not discussed and the resolution passed without change. It included a recommendation that the United States, England, France, and the Soviet Union unite against Nazi Germany.[35]

The National Negro Congress was one popular front group in Newark without an anti-Nazi agenda. In March 1939, it organized Newark's first rent strike on Bedford Street in the Third Ward to protest the pitiable housing opportunities for African Americans in Newark. A survey conducted by the Newark Housing Authority found that sufficient housing was available for whites but negligible vacancies existed for African Americans. Over 60 percent of Newark's African-American population lived in the Third Ward and adjoining neighborhoods. The balance lived in a "factory strip" along the Pennsylvania Railroad tracks about four blocks into the city's Ironbound section. African Americans who were better off financially moved into East Orange, whereas those on relief or with minimal funds were forced to take whatever housing was available.[36]

The Congress, in its campaign against "disgraceful living quarters," organized a picket line in front of the "rat infested" Bedford Street tenement after five families were evicted for refusing to pay a rent increase. The tenants were represented by Samuel Rothbard, who had been successful in preventing an injunction against pickets in the May 1938 "Don't Buy Where You Don't Work" campaign (see chapter 7).[37]

During 1939 other groups took up the cause for African-American rights. The ALPD's Nancy Cox and the ACLU sponsored a conference to devise methods of eliminating discrimination.[38] Henry Jackson, the leader of a Third Ward African-American cult group, the House of Israel, had delivered street-corner orations urging African Americans to open their own stores since "the black race should not buy from Jews." Sued for "hate" speech by Alexander Abramson, a Jewish merchant, Jackson's supporters retained a legal team and the charge was dropped because of inconclusive evidence. Hundreds of spectators, in and out of the courtroom, cheered the verdict.[39]

* * *

The Dies Committee sent investigators to the Newark Police Department in October 1939 purportedly to seek material on the German-American Bund, the ALPD, and the Communist Party. When three months later the committee had still not taken action against the Bund, Louis Marciante, president of the State Federation of Labor, wrote a letter of protest to J. Parnell Thomas, New Jersey Congressman and committee member. Marciante applauded the committee's work against communists but chided it for ignoring New Jersey's "Nazi Bund."[40]

During 1939, the struggle against the Bund entered a decisive stage. Public opinion, alarmed by Hitler's successes and the Bund's increased visibility and activity, prodded national, state, and local governments into action. New York arrested Fritz Kuhn on May 26, 1939 and charged him with forgery and grand larceny. The indictment alleged that Kuhn had stolen Bund funds and used some of the money to pay a girlfriend's expenses.[41] While out on bail and awaiting trial, Kuhn was re-arrested in September by New York District Attorney Thomas Dewey's office and his bail increased from $5,000 to $50,000. Dewey claimed that Kuhn was planning to leave the country.[42] It took nine days for Bundists to raise the $50,000.

Matthias Kohler was one of many Bund leaders who testified that Kuhn was justified in using Bund funds for his personal use because of the Nazi "leadership principle." After a three-week trial in December, Kuhn was found guilty of stealing Bund funds and falsifying records to cover the thefts. The Bundesleiter was sentenced to two and a half to five years in prison. In imposing sentence, Judge James Garrett Wallace called Kuhn a "small timer" who was being punished for theft and not, as his attorney argued, for his beliefs.[43]

While the trial was taking place, Newark residents were receiving Nazi propaganda through the mail. The first piece was a circular accusing the British of supplying poison gas to Polish troops. The second was an eight-page brochure titled "Never Again," featuring a picture below of a woman holding an emaciated boy. The thrust of the latter piece was that although the 1919 British blockade of Germany caused starvation and sickness, Britain would not succeed similarly in 1939. It was never determined whether the cash-strapped Bund was responsible for the mailings.[44]

Publicity—perhaps a cash settlement—was on August Klapprott's mind when he filed a $1.95 million libel suit against the *Newark Star Ledger* for a series of articles that alleged, among other things, sexual improprieties at Camp Nordland. Bund lawyer, Wilbur V. Keegan, told the *Ledger* that his client originally only wanted more favorable coverage from the paper.[45] When it refused, the suit was filed. The attorney for the *Ledger* threatened to expose ties between the Bund and the NSDAP if the suit came to trial. When Klapprott and his attorneys failed to appear in the Newton courthouse on the day of the hearing, the judge dismissed the case.[46]

At the end of 1939, the United States Congress considered legislation that would affect the Bund and Nazi Germany. The Alien Registration Bill required aliens who were Bundists (and communists) to register as "foreign agents." The bill was opposed by both the German-American Club of Newark, a non-Nazi group that viewed the legislation as anti-German, and the Order of the Sons of Zion, which pronounced it unconstitutional. [47] The "Neutrality Bill," which became law in November 1939, amended arms-embargo legislation to allow belligerents to buy American arms on a "cash and carry" basis. Otto Stiefel, a Bund attorney and sympathizer, promptly denounced the bill for placing America "in a state of war with Germany," and correctly predicted that it would lead to Congressional action to give credits to the Allies for weapons.[48]

The New Jersey Legislature had enacted no anti-Nazi legislation since the 1935 "Anti-Nazi Law." The 1939 Foran bill provided for the registration, fingerprinting, and photographing of aliens; their mandatory possession of an alien registration card; and their arbitrary arrest and detention without warrant or charges for twenty-four hours. Passed by the Senate but not the Assembly, it was opposed on constitutional grounds by a Newark *ad hoc* "Committee of 15" composed of liberals including Luke Garner.[49] In June 1939 an amendment to the Anti-Nazi Law was enacted, making it illegal to appear in public in a military uniform similar to one of a foreign government. The new law may have been inspired by Mayor Fiorello LaGuardia's New York City order forbidding uniformed guards at meetings.[50] The amendment was specifically aimed at Camp Nordland, which was about to begin its summer session.

* * *

Bundists from New Jersey, New York, and Connecticut held a giant rally at Madison Square Garden in February 1939 under the pretext of celebrating George Washington's Birthday. The rally drew over 20,000, and raised $8,500 for the Bund through admission charges. The Newark unit sold over 500 tickets and hired buses to transport ticket holders to the Garden.[51] The event, which received national attention, focused on Jews. George Washington was all but forgotten except for a giant picture of him surrounded by the American flag and swastikas. Fritz Kuhn gave a speech almost entirely on the evils of the Jew. Other Bundist leaders denounced "international

Marxist Jews," "international Jewish financiers," and the Roosevelt administration. To the delight of the audience, Wilhelm Kunze, Kuhn's deputy, referred to Roosevelt as "Rosenfeld."[52]

Several days after the Madison Square Garden event the Newark Bund called a rally in a West Orange meeting hall. Kalb and Arno learned of the event and the NSANL and Minutemen distributed fliers appealing to citizens to come to West Orange to protest the rally. The owner of the meeting hall cancelled the event after receiving a letter from the NSANL. Arno and Kalb called off their protest, but Arno and several Minutemen arrived at the hall just in case there was a double cross. The police from West Orange and Orange were also worried that the rally would take place and stationed twenty-five police outside the hall while additional men armed with riot guns and tear gas bombs stood nearby.[53]

The Bund seemed to be increasing in strength. The Dies Committee, however, issued a report on its 1938 investigation of subversive activities that focused primarily on communist infiltration. Some of the targets were the Federal Writer's and Federal Theater projects, the CIO, and the U.S. Department of Labor. Communist-dominated organizations such as the ALPD were also targeted. The material on the Bund was taken entirely from the testimony of John C. Metcalfe, Dies Committee investigator, and probably written by him as well. A short account of native fascist movements concluded the report.

The committee's methods and procedures, as well as its final report, came under fire from friends and foes alike. Dies blamed a lack of funds for the committee's shortcomings. He said that if his committee received $150,000 for 1939 rather than the $25,000 appropriated in 1938, it could be more thorough. The Congressman noted that there was strong public support for the committee's work. After only an hour's debate, the House extended the committee through 1939 by a vote of 344 to 35 with 53 abstentions. The House Committee on Accounts reduced the $150,000 appropriation request to $100,000, and it passed.[54]

Samuel Dickstein reiterated his call for the committee to put more emphasis on investigating the Bund. The Madison Square Garden rally added import to this warning. Another Gallup Poll indicated that more people wanted Nazism investigated than communism. Mindful of these factors, Dies pressed United States Attorney General Frank Murphy to release the report of the 1937 FBI investigation of the Bund, which Murphy had held up for over a year.[55]

In Newark, the April, 1939 release of the FBI report made front-page headlines. The report identified Irvington as a "hotbed" of Nazi activities in Essex County, and provided information on Newark Bund leaders Matthias Kohler and Herman Von Busch. Of 285 members in the Newark group, 100 were from Irvington. According to the report, the Bund paid monthly rent of $25 for its headquarters on Nye Avenue. The FBI also claimed that the Bund often had problems finding meeting halls large enough to accommodate all its members and that it often had skirmishes with "local Communists."[56]

One consequence of the FBI report was that Herman Von Busch resigned from his Bund positions effective May 1, 1939. An executive of Public Service Electric and Gas pressured Von Busch into this decision because of negative publicity the utility had received. Von Busch, a gas works supervisor, told the executive that his job was more important than his "hobby positions." A Bund official accepted the resignation with regret, bemoaning the "persecution" of Von Busch, and told him "you had no choice in the matter." Public Service refused to fire him, stating that he was trustworthy and would not act "contrary to the interests of the United States."[57] Von Busch continued to attend Bund meetings until April 1940, despite his resignation.[58]

Other local responses to the two-year-old FBI report were instructive. The *Irvington Herald* minimized the report, contrasting the town's Americanism with the few named in the FBI report that "came to the United States about ten years ago."[59] The *Jewish Chronicle*, as if to answer the *Herald*, said it made no difference how many Bundists there were in Irvington since "they should be promptly weeded out and deported as aliens."[60]   Irvington mayor Herbert Kruttschnitt, caught by surprise, remarked, "If there is a Bund here, I don't know of it. At least I can't identify any of those said to be members and organizers." Arthur F. Huebner, president of the anti-Nazi German-American Political Club of Essex County, said that he was not surprised by the report but it underestimated the number of Bund members. The pro-Nazi Dr. Francis Just, president of the German-American Societies of Essex County, stated he hadn't read the report and "knew nothing about Nazi activities."[61]

The anti-Nazi German-American League for Culture held a two-day convention in Newark two weeks after the report appeared. Speakers urged Americans of German descent to "declare themselves" on the issue of Hitler, claiming that Nazi aggression in

Europe had produced a backlash against German Americans, including firings and refusal to hire those with German names. It was stressed that this provided fertile ground for the Bund to spread its message.

The convention adopted a resolution stating that the majority of German Americans opposed Nazi philosophy, its agents in the United States, and Hitler's expansionist policies. Nazi agents, it declared, were responsible for the distrust that many Americans harbored against citizens of German extraction. Lastly the resolution called upon Americans not to discriminate against German Americans, but rather to join them in the fight against the Bund.[62]

Attorney General Murphy announced that he would reopen the investigation of Camp Nordland, cited in the FBI report as the largest Bund camp in the country and a center for Nazi propaganda. Investigators found that the cover of the instruction book given to girl campers bore the message "By fighting the Jew I fight for the work of the Lord—Der Führer." They also said that anti-Semitism was the main theme of almost all the books used in the camp. Murphy said the new investigation would focus on espionage and passport, immigration, and firearms violations.[63]

Reacting to Murphy's statement, the Committee of 100 sent an open letter to August Klapprott, saying that if the reports of race hatred at the camp were true it was a menace to the people of the state. The committee asked Klapprott to answer thirty-three questions, most of which dealt with the camp's relationship with Nazi Germany, the source of its finances, and its educational goals. Rev. William Hiram Foulkes and Frank Kingdon signed the letter. [64] Klapprott declined to respond.

The Bund was under increasing pressure from state and local authorities as well as the FBI. On the defensive, Klapprott warned that no unofficial investigators would be allowed at the camp. Thumbing his nose at the Bund's enemies, he claimed that his organization was sponsoring over two-dozen German-language classes in the state, some in public schools. The New Jersey Bundesleiter denounced "worthless refugees... no good in their own countries," who were taking jobs from good Americans.[65] Nancy Cox answered Klapprott on behalf of the ALPD, countering his reference to "worthless refugees" by asserting the "the American people have spontaneously accepted the leaders in science, literature, and art driven out of Germany by persecution." Governor A. Harry Moore, speaking at an Elks convention in

Atlantic City, struck at the Bund, decrying that he was against the practice of "clothing American bodies in alien uniforms."[66]

Irvington was again off -limits for public Bund meetings until the "hotbed" epithet wore off. Instead, a meeting of the "Reich German Society" was advertised for the city's Montgomery Hall in May. The ostensible purpose of the event was to welcome the crew of the Hamburg-American liner *Hansa*. The program was mainly musical, with only one speech. However, to make sure that Irvington and Newark Bundists knew what the affair was about, the circular advertised in boldface letters that the door prize was a copy of Hitler's *Mein Kampf*.[67]

Dr. Francis Just also stepped in to provide a venue for the Bund. Under the aegis of the Essex County Federation of German-American Societies, Just announced a German Day celebration at Montgomery Hall in June. Adolph Friederich sent a letter protesting the event to Mayor Kruttschnitt, in which he advised him that the swastika would be displayed. He also pointed out that among those on the Federation's nine-man governing board were four Bund members listed in the FBI report.[68] Kruttschnitt asked the town attorney for a ruling on the legality of flying the swastika. It was rumored that the ACLU was ready to step in if the swastika was banned. The next day the mayor said the town attorney had ruled that it was not illegal to display the flag of a foreign country at the upcoming celebration.[69]

Irvington officials were again in an embarrassing position, and once more the *Irvington Herald* was involved. A front-page guest editorial placed above the paper's masthead delivered a not so subtle message. Richard Spitz, an activist German-American attorney, wrote the piece. He protested that the German Day event was an insult to the German Americans of Irvington. Irvington, he said had "suffered enough humiliation and embarrassment because of the Bund and the Nazis," and supporters of Hitler "should take the next boat and live under his regime."[70]

Just was called to Public Safety Director Edward Balentine's office where he was made to sign a statement that there would be no uniforms, pro-Nazi literature, or anti-American and anti-Semitic speeches at German Day. Only one German Flag (the swastika) would be displayed inside the hall. Balentine showed the statement to Friederich, who said "under the laws of a democratic state, they could do no better."[71]

German Day was celebrated without incident at Montgomery Park. Food, music, and Bavarian costumes were the main attractions. As promised, only one swastika was displayed inside the hall. No protest was made when Nazi literature was passed out in violation of Just's agreement with the police. Rev. Heinz Kugler, speaking in German, deplored the indignities being heaped on German Americans living in the United States. Speaking in English, Otto Stiefel pleaded for an American policy of isolationism. Adolph Friederich and his followers did not appear. He had told German Americans to celebrate German Day at the World's Fair in New York. But Nat Arno and twelve Minutemen did travel to Montgomery Park, where they were told by the police to either leave Irvington or be arrested. They left without comment.[72]

During 1939, Arno and his Minutemen continued their unpublicized efforts to break up Bund meetings in Irvington and elsewhere. With logistical and financial help from Kalb, Arno sent Minutemen as far as Maryland to break up Bund meetings.[73]

* * *

The Bund was a detriment to Nazi foreign policy, since it antagonized Americans and heightened enmity toward Germany. With war on the horizon, American non-intervention in Europe became the Reich's main priority. One of Germany's first steps toward influencing America into non-interventionism was the creation of the American Fellowship Forum (AFF) in March 1939. Dr. Friedrich Auhagen, a paid Nazi agent and former professor of German Literature at Columbia University, led the group. Auhagen came to America from Germany in 1923 and started to work for Nazi intelligence after Hitler came to power. His academic background gave him a good cover for his work. One of the AFF's first adherents was Philip Johnson, the world-famous architect, who also served as the "foreign correspondent" of Father Coughlin's publication *Social Justice*.[74] The purpose of the AFF was to spread appeasement propaganda, encourage isolationism, and promote opposition to the defense preparations being advocated by President Roosevelt. It hoped to appeal to businessmen and professionals, most of whom would have nothing to do with the Bund. Although anti-Semitism was evident in the AFF publication, *Today's Challenge,* Auhagen stressed that anti-Semitic rhetoric at meetings would be counterproductive. The AFF

earned sufficient early success in New York for Auhagen to establish branches in Philadelphia, Cleveland, Detroit, Milwaukee and
Newark [75]

Auhagen asked Otto Stiefel to be chairman of the Newark Branch
of the AFF. Stiefel, former president of the Steuben Society of
America, was an early member of the New York AFF, at whose meetings he talked of his love for Newark. He bemoaned the fact that
many of "his own" had gradually left Newark for the suburbs and
been replaced by a "new type" of people. The Newark AFF's initial
meeting was held in November 1939 at the Newark Athletic Club,
with a mainly German-American attendance. Auhagen, the featured
speaker, extolled the contributions made by Germans to America, complained about the abuse heaped on Germany by the British and French,
and urged the audience to speak out on behalf of Germany. [76]

The Newark AFF continued to hold meetings through the first
half of 1940, which provoked no response from Newark's anti-Nazis, since the organizers avoided publicity. Very little was accomplished: Influential Newarkers the AFF sought to recruit were wary
of joining the German-dominated group. Attendance, which was as
high as 100 for the early meetings in 1939, dropped considerably
throughout 1940. Only thirty participants appeared in February 1940
at the Newark Athletic Club, and they "bore all the earmarks of a
discouraged crowd." They were enthusiastic only when Stiefel endorsed American aviation hero Charles Lindbergh's[77] candidacy for
the upcoming presidential election.[78] Lindbergh, a prominent isolationist and idol of the right, was an admirer of the Nazi regime.

The Nazis abandoned the AFF after new isolationist groups led
by prominent Americans came on the scene. These included New
York Congressman Hamilton Fish's "National Committee to Keep
America Out of Foreign Wars" and Avery Brundage's "Keep America
Out of the War Committee." Both were forerunners of the America
First Committee (AFC). It was much safer for Nazi sympathizers to
support American-bred organizations than to remain with a group
whose connections to the Reich could be uncovered at any moment.
Indeed, by early 1940, the AFF was being investigated by the United
States Justice Department.[79]

In September 1940, the AFF closed its New York office and
Auhagen unsuccessfully tried to flee the country. He was arrested at
shipside, brought to trial, convicted, and sentenced to up to two years
in prison for failure to register as an agent of the German govern-

ment.[80] The Newark AFF held its last meeting in the summer of 1940. Stiefel said he had given up the struggle to keep America out of the war because neither the AFF nor any other organization was powerful enough "to thwart the plans of Great Britain and Roosevelt. It is plain now that despite the fine and great contributions to this country in the past, citizens of German blood are not wanted."[81]

* * *

The New Jersey NSANL began 1939 with the momentum gained from hostile reactions to Kristallnacht and Nazi aggression. Contributions and new members permitted it to employ a full time executive secretary and researcher, as well as a part-time investigator of boycott violators. There were about 200 NSANL dues-paying individuals in Newark, ninety-one in the rest of Essex County, and 228 in the other parts of New Jersey.[82] There were also 119 Newark organizations that belonged, four organizations from the rest of Essex County, and thirty-three organizations from other parts of New Jersey (mainly Elizabeth and Linden). The Newark organizations ranged from the mainline Temple B'nai Abraham, Hadassah, and National Council of Jewish Women to the proletarian Egg Inspectors' Union, Hebrew Sheet Metal Workers, and Newark Junk Peddlers Association.[83]

In announcing the NSANL's April 1939 convention, Michael Alenick said that Nazi aggression in Europe made the Newark Bund more dangerous.[84] The event drew 244 delegates, representing 186 organizations. Resolutions were passed calling for unification of all boycott groups, requesting Governor A. Harry Moore to begin an investigation of the Bund and other subversive groups in New Jersey, and supporting an embargo on all German goods.

In his valedictory address, Alenick urged boycott participation by Catholic organizations and groups such as the Kiwanis, Elks, and Lions. Abraham Harkavy, a young lawyer who served in the Meyer Ellenstein administration, succeeded Alenick as president. Among the other officers were Kalb, honorary president, Jack Malamuth, first vice-president, and Amelia Moorfield, Chair of the Women's Division.[85] Although the New Jersey NSANL appeared to be in good condition, it would not survive another year.

With Samuel Untermyer's departure, the NSANL national office was in chaos. Staff turnover, rivalries between board members, and questionable fund-raising activities all contributed to the decline. Kalb, Dubovsky, and Steele all attempted to succeed Untermyer.

Untermyer fretted about the inadequacies of his "child," and kept in contact with some board members, particularly Dubovsky. Conversely, Dubovsky and other executive committee members looked to Untermyer for advice and approval. Kalb sent a letter to Untermyer discussing the New Jersey league's accomplishments. The response, complaining that New Jersey was duplicating work done by the national office, went not to Kalb but to Dubovsky.[86]

During the period of uncertainty, the national office issued a circular entitled, "WANTED—Adolph Hitler for Kidnapping," which accused Fritz Kuhn of being Hitler's main spy in America. Kuhn threatened legal action against Kalb, whose name was on the circular as a director of the NSANL, unless the charge was retracted.[87] The controversy generated much publicity, but no retraction was made or legal action taken. Kuhn had more serious problems to contend with.

At the same time, despite a promising start to the year, the New Jersey NSANL was also experiencing serious difficulties. In June, its Union County branch disbanded.[88] In August, Newark released two of its three employees because the national office refused to subsidize the positions.[89] Press releases and Harkavy's speeches to KUVs, synagogues, and young people's groups were all that was left in New Jersey.[90] The lack of support for the NSANL was part of a growing realization that Nazi Germany had become too powerful, both economically and militarily, to be damaged by a boycott. It was soon to be obvious that only a military response could stop Germany.[91]

* * *

The Andover Township Commission held hearings on the re-issuance of Nordland's liquor license, which was to expire July 1. The deliberations had not yet concluded by the time of the camp's Independence Day celebration, but the commission revoked the license anyway, citing un-American activities. New Jersey alcoholic beverage commissioner D. Frederick Burnett stayed the order on the grounds that the camp was denied due process because the hearings had not been completed.[92] The stay allowed the camp to hold its July 4 rally with liquor. Over seventy-five uniformed O.D. troops took part in the festivities. Subsequently, Burnett revoked Nordland's liquor license, citing its violation of the "Uniform Law." The Andover Township Committee had also finished its hearings and denied the Bund a license renewal. At a German Day celebration with about 8,000 celebrants later in July, neither swastikas, nor formal uniforms were displayed, nor was beer sold. Kuhn said the Bund didn't need beer to draw a crowd.[93].

Over 1,000 Sussex County residents signed a petition asking the Andover Township Committee to close Nordland. The Committee chairman, Charles Barbay, stated that Andover was determined to rid itself of the Bund, and to this end increased Nordland's property assessment from $6,000 to $26,000.[94] It was hoped that the subsequent tax increase would serve the desired purpose.

The Dies Committee began its 1939 hearings at the end of May, concentrating on domestic anti-Semitic groups and individuals who were purportedly plotting to overthrow the government. However, the hearings turned into a showcase for anti-Semitic propaganda. Dies permitted witnesses to spin tales of "Jewish conspiracies" and Jewish control of the Communist Party. A member of the Committee, John J. Dempsey of New Mexico, objected to one witness's testimony, but was overruled. Dempsey later pointed out that there was not one word in the entire presentation about subversive activities.[95]

The investigation ended in June. No plots to overthrow the government were uncovered. Major news sources such as *Time* treated the committee's effort with sarcasm and disdain. Dies still had not exposed "un-American" activities. The next public committee session was set for August 16. Several days earlier, J. Parnell Thomas predicted that the committee had enough information to "kill off the Communist Party in this Country." Dies was shrewd enough to ignore Parnell's posturing and to now concentrate on the Bund.

Fritz Kuhn, who was out on bail, was the hearing's first witness. During two days of testimony he continually stressed the Americanism of the Bund and revealed nothing new.[96] The next witness was nineteen-year-old Helen Vooros, a former member of the Bund Youth Movement. Her detailed testimony contradicted Kuhn's statements that the Bund was a bona fide American group. A chart prepared by John Metcalfe buttressed this information by showing the connection between the Nazi government and the Bund.

The press preferred to report on sex rather than on Vooros's valuable testimony on Nazi indoctrination in Bund camps and on a Nazi youth trip to Germany. Front- page coverage was given to her testimony dealing with the reasons for her departure from the Bund Youth. She testified that at camp Nordland "the boys and girls did things they shouldn't do." When asked to be specific, Vooros asserted that after a youth leader made "advances" she complained to Theodore

Dinkelacher, adult leader of the Bund Youth, and was asked: "Can't you take it?" It was soon obvious why Dinkelacher was not the right person to complain to: He had previously been caught in bed with a seventeen-year-old Bundist under his supervision.[97]

After testimony on the Bund, Dies turned the Committee's attention to German consular officials who were alleged to have attempted to influence important Americans, and to the link between the anti-Semitic Silver Shirts and the German-American Bund. Further testimony linked the Silver Shirts to a host of other anti-Semitic groups. Dies said he was less interested in the anti-Semitic aspects of these movements than he was in their leaders' pro-Hitler and Mussolini public stances.[98]

* * *

By June 1940, Nazi conquests in Western Europe left Great Britain facing Hitler's armed might by itself. Pressure in the United States to aid Britain with armaments and other war materials grew more intense with the fall of France and the bombing of England and Scotland. A *Fortune* poll in July 1940 indicated that 67.5 percent of Americans favored aid to the Allies.[99] However, intervention was opposed by traditional pacifists (e.g., Socialists, isolationists, communists [after the Nazi-Soviet Pact and up to the Nazi invasion of the Soviet Union]), as well as by such anti-democratic and anti-Semitic groups as the German-American Bund, the Silver Shirts, and the Christian Front.

Hitler's threat to European Jewry convinced most American Jews to back aid to the Allies. Joachim Prinz, newly installed Rabbi of Newark's influential Temple B'Nai Abraham, was a major spokesman for intervention. He clearly stated his concerns in a Rosh Hashonah sermon, two weeks after the Nazi invasion of Poland. Prinz predicted, "This war will undoubtedly be long and cruel enough to destroy not only the European civilization and vast stretches of land, but it will wipe out millions of Jews."[100]

After Russia and Germany partitioned Poland at the end of September, the *Newark News* reported that 2,000 Polish Jews in Germany were arrested and taken to the Sachsenhausen concentration camp, where some had already died because of "mishaps."[101] In October, Newark residents learned that the first ghetto had been established in German-occupied Poland, and soon after they read that the Nazis had forced all Jews to wear the "Yellow Star." As the opportunity for European Jews to emigrate decreased, Jewish groups working on their behalf competed with each other for influence and funds. The American Jewish Congress (AJC), Zionist organizations, the Hebrew Immigrant Aid Society (HIAS), and the Federation of Polish Jews all ran publicized programs during the first two months of the war. The Newark Conference of Jewish Charities, which had consistently allocated funds for refugees, began a drive for increased relief for endangered European Jews. Youth Aliya, a Zionist group, ran a fund-raising ball at the Mosque Theater for the benefit of Jewish refugee children.[102] The Independent Order of Brith Shalom, a large and influential fraternal and benevolent organization, pledged its continued aid for refugees, citing a home for refugee children it sponsored in Pennsylvania.[103]

At a Newark Sons of Zion rally of 600 soon after the outbreak of the war, Joseph Kraemer stated pointedly that the Intergovernmental Committee on Refugees, which was then meeting in Washington, mentioned every location other than Palestine as a safe haven for European refugees.[104] He urged the committee to consider that most of the homeless in Europe were Jews, and that Palestine was their ancestral homeland.[105] The newly created New Jersey Conference of the United Palestine Appeal worked toward the same end. At its June 1940 organizational meeting in Newark, presided over by Michael Stavitsky, the conference unanimously passed a resolution that only in Palestine could millions of European Jews find refuge from Nazism. The United Palestine Appeal was made one of the three major beneficiaries of the Newark United Jewish Appeal. Rabbi Joachim Prinz urged the spread of Zionist ideology among Jews.[106]

The possibility of Palestine as a refuge became more remote as the war continued and Hitler's armies overran much of Europe. Even if the Nazis were willing to allow Jews under their control to immigrate to Palestine, the British would not let them enter. What could American Zionists accomplish? Thus, they were forced to shift their emphasis from immediate emigration of European Jews to Palestine to the protection and welfare of Jews already in Palestine.[107]

Polish Jewry was of immediate concern to the thousands in Newark who still had relatives in Nazi-occupied Poland. The American Federation of Polish Jews began operations soon after the outbreak of war. A Newark branch began activities in early 1941, when representatives from over seventy Jewish groups met at Krueger Auditorium to pledge funds for 2,500 food packages for Polish Jews.[108]

The few Gentile voices in Newark that spoke out for persecuted Jews and against Nazism prior to the war continued to do so. Rev. William Hiram Foulkes, chairman of the Committee of 100, sent a September 1939 Jewish New Year's greeting sympathizing with "the sufferings of Israel," and extolling the genuine liberty of religions and races in America.[109] Adolph Friedrich's New Year's message to the Jews of Newark contained the hope that "German people of all faiths and all other peoples in Nazi clutches will soon be liberated."[110]

National organizations to aid the allies and to prepare for the eventuality of war were organized during the spring of 1940. In the city, the most effective of these groups was the Newark Division of the Committee to Defend America by Aiding the Allies, known as the Committee to Defend America (CDA). The committee, established in May 1940 by William Allen White, the well-known journalist, and Clark M. Eichelberger of the League of Nations Association, was a propaganda organization that worked to persuade public opinion that America should provide the Allies with as much material and financial aid as possible in order to keep the United States out of the war.[111] Frank Kingdon and Rev. William Hiram Foulkes were original members of the National Committee, and Dr. and Mrs. Wells P. Eagleton soon followed.[112] By November 1940, the committee had 750 local chapters and about 10,000 members.[113]

The Newark CDA's first meeting was in July 1940 at City Hall. Protestant clergyman, Dr. Henry P. Van Dusen, and lawyer, David H. Yoneff spoke.[114] Diran Kurk, a Newark publicist and former field director for Near East Relief, volunteered to be chairman and to let the group use his office as headquarters. Frances Thomas, the national office's coordinator of local committees, asked Frank Kingdon, then splitting his time between Newark and New York, to recruit ten prominent Newarkers to join the committee and to assist Kurk.[115]

The CDA's first action was to lobby Congress to sell fifty World War I destroyers to Great Britain to replace ones that had been lost or damaged. Kurk used General John J. Pershing's words—"If there is anything we can do to save the British fleet...we shall be failing in our duty to America if we do not do it"—to convince committee members and supporters to send letters to Congress in favor of the sale of destroyers.[116]

The effort by the national committee and other pro-Ally forces was successful. President Roosevelt issued an executive order in September 1940 to trade the fifty destroyers to England in exchange for several naval bases. The results of a Gallup Poll in mid-August showed Americans favoring the sale by 62 percent to 38 percent. After FDR's order, Kurk asked Frances Thomas, "what will be our next pressure propaganda?" She told him that the next project was to get planes for England. In late October Congress authorized the sale of 12,000 airplanes to Great Britain, and Kurk sent another letter to Thomas requesting instructions.[117]

The Eagletons were among the first large contributors to the national committee[118] and continued to be among the committee's main financial supporters. Other important Newark participants included Judges Walter D. Van Riper and William Clark. Michael A. Stavitsky and five other Jews were part of the thirty- member Newark group. Efforts to attract prominent Irish and Italian Americans to the city effort were unsuccessful during 1940.[119]

* * *

The "Great Debate" over the American role in the war began with the Nazi invasion of Poland in September 1939 and ended in December 1941 with Pearl Harbor. The debate was between interventionists and isolationists (or non-interventionists, as they preferred to be called). It concerned aid to the Allies, the extent and form of such aid, and ultimately whether or not America should enter the war.[120] The Great Debate was epitomized by the struggle between the CDA and the America First Committee.

Among the isolationists were Irish Catholics who harbored traditional hatred of the British as well as an abiding abhorrence of communism. They saw no moral difference between the Nazis and the English, and were against aid to England in its life-and-death struggle with Hitler. In considering communism a worse threat to America than Nazism, they consequently believed that Nazi Germany was a bulwark against the "Godless" Soviet Union. Nationally, Father Charles E. Coughlin, the anti-Semitic radio priest, was a spokesman for the isolationist, anti-British, anti-communist point of view. His newspaper, *Social Justice,* quoted Hitler and Goebbels' venomous anti-Semitic diatribes almost line for line. Coughlin "branded Democracy a version of communism and communism an invention of the Jews."[121] *Social Justice* was sometimes sold at newsstands on three of Newark's "Four Corners" (the intersection of Broad and Market Streets—one of the busiest in the country).[122] Many in Newark's large Irish-Catholic population listened to Coughlin's Sunday broadcasts. Coughlin had asked Bishop Thomas J. Walsh, leader of the Newark Diocese, to send a representative to Royal Oaks Michigan ("all expenses will be paid by me") to discuss the theory of "social justice." Walsh's response cannot be found, but the conservative prelate never publicly denounced Coughlin.[123]

Because of Father Coughlin, the Bund was not the only concern of Newark's anti-Nazis in 1939. John A. Matthews was Newark's most prominent disciple of Coughlin as well as an important Catholic layman, Democratic politician, and jurist.[124] Matthews praised Hitler in a 1939 St. Patrick's Day speech to the Friends of St. Patrick in East Orange. An isolationist, he warned America to mind its own business and criticized President Roosevelt's condemnation of Germany's occupation of Czechoslovakia. He declared that Hitler had revitalized his prostrate nation and outwitted the "burglar nations at Versailles." He also excoriated America's "Anglophiles, Hitler haters, and Stalin stooges" for threatening the cause of American democracy.[125] Matthews questioned whether Americans were "the unwitting tutors of the European dictators in their un-Christian theory of racism."[126] According to the *Newark Star Ledger,* Matthews' remarks on Hitler drew both applause and catcalls. The *Newark News* did not comment on the audience reaction.[127] There were no public condemnations of Matthews' speech by either Christians or Jews.

By the summer of 1939 Matthews was making speeches on Coughlin's behalf in New York City.[128] When World War II began, Matthews' response to those who wanted to aid the Allies was quick and direct. In October he traveled to Royal Oaks to appear on Father Coughlin's regular Sunday radio hour. He argued against repeal of the Embargo Act, a law that forbade the United States from aiding the Allies. Matthews said the war was a struggle for power between Germany and England rather than a moral issue. He further claimed that communism and its "fellow travelers" were a "greater menace to Christian democracy than totalitarianism of any other form" and criticized Roosevelt's pro-repeal efforts, citing FDR's 1935 and 1936 speeches in favor of neutrality.[129] Matthews' appearance with Coughlin, like his remarks on Hitler, elicited no reaction from Newark Jewish groups, despite prior condemnations of Coughlin by the AJC, the NSANL, and other organizations. Newark Jews did not have the confidence to publicly rebuke one of the city's most prominent citizens.

The German-American Bund agreed wholeheartedly with Matthews' views. In Newark, Otto Stiefel blamed the British for the war and called on the United States to stay out of the conflict. According to Stiefel, "If England and America had allowed Europe to skin their own skunks there would have been no war." The only German-American leader in Newark to denounce Hitler was Adolph Friederich, who said: "after years of war of war, preparation and perpetual agitation, Hitler has finally succeeded in plunging the distressed German people and with them the humanity of the world, into a bloody war catastrophe."[130]

* * *

The Nazi-Soviet Pact of August 23, 1939 dealt the American Communist Party a blow from which it never recovered. Although there had been reports of an imminent rapprochement between the two arch enemies, the American Communist Party leader Earl Browder sneered at the rumors and stated that such an event was as likely to happen as his election as president of the American Chamber of Commerce. After the pact was signed, and Germany invaded Poland a week later, American communists were thrown into disarray. Moscow sent Browder a series of coded instructions for the American party's new course of action, which included praising the pact for promoting world peace.[131]

The orders from Moscow reversed three years of Popular Front strategy against fascism. The new line signaled the end of the campaign against Nazi Germany and the beginning of attacks on Britain and France. Denouncing the two nations as capitalist and imperialist warmongers, communists now posited that bourgeois democracy in France and England was an even greater enemy than fascism. This echoed the tragic position taken by German communists who equated social democracy with fascism that had aided Hitler's rise to power. American communists, under Soviet instruction, pulled out of all Popular Front organizations that refused to conform to the new line; ended cooperation with President Roosevelt, labeling New Deal measures capitalist palliatives; ended support for lifting the embargo and for interventionism; and attempted to forge alliances with American isolationists.

The American Communist Party had increased its membership and become a major force in many organizations because of its call for and involvement in the Popular Front against fascism. By reversing this stand and supporting the Soviet Union, the party lost membership (from 65,000 in January 1939 to 50,000 in January 1941),[132] alienated sympathizers, and made new enemies. Most importantly, the good will that it had engendered among liberals was lost. The Nazi-Soviet Pact ended the most successful era in the history of the American Communist Party. It was obvious that the Soviet Union's foreign policy dictated the American party's domestic policy. [133]

In its first statement after the pact, the Newark Communist Party tried to cling to its anti-Nazi credentials. While following the party line, it claimed that the agreement dealt German fascism a serious blow and helped to "block the duplicity and underhandedness" of the British "capitulationists." A month later, Lawrence Mahon, newly chosen leader of Newark's communists, didn't mention German Nazism when he defended the Soviet seizure of Eastern Poland because it saved the Poles from "capitalist oppression." Elizabeth Gurley Flynn, a member of the party's national committee, told a November 1939 Newark celebration of the twenty-second anniversary of the Bolshevik Revolution that Russia was pursuing a "peace policy" designed to "isolate and curtail the war." Flynn and other speakers stressed that the party's task was to keep the United States out of the war. Other than the party faithful, few attended the event. Krueger Hall, filled to capacity for the 1938 anniversary celebration, was half-empty in 1939.[134]

There were no resignations from the Newark party because of the pact, according to a communist active at the time.[135] This was surprising given that the American Communist Party lost almost 25 percent of its membership during the next year. How could Newark communists, the majority of whom were both Jewish and anti-Nazi, have remained party members? Martha Stone, a Newark communist who went on to become New Jersey Party secretary, noted the lack of response:

> When the pact took place, it was a very difficult time to accept the position of the Party, and those of us who really didn't accept it, didn't fight back... There was no clear cut opposition ...The Jews that were in the Party were anti-Nazi. You know its inconceivable to me today—how did we get away with that, you know? [136]

These Party Jews were more communist than Jewish. The Party discipline that they accepted outweighed their personal feelings against Nazism. Even those communists who were proud to be Jews and worked in the Yiddish language section of the Party were either uncritical or silent in the face of Stalin's "foreign policy crimes."[137]

For the next twenty months, from the signing of the pact in August 1939 until Nazi Germany's invasion of the Soviet Union in June 1941, Newark communists followed the Party line in denouncing Roosevelt, his foreign policy, and rearmament. They endorsed the Soviet invasions of Finland and Poland, while condemning British and French imperialism. Along with their anti-Nazi rhetoric, they abandoned anti-Nazi front organizations, including the neighborhood and ethnic ones created after Kristallnacht. These organizations quickly disappeared without their communist sponsors. National fronts groups in Newark shared a similar fate. The most successful national front organization, the ALPD, dissolved itself February 1, 1940. Despite evidence to the contrary, its chairman, Dr. Harry F. Ward, protested in his statement of dissolution that the group "was never controlled by Communists."[138] The New Jersey league was already defunct, having closed its Newark office in 1939 after the Loyalists lost the Spanish Civil War.[139]

During 1940, three Newark groups that were part of national organizations were found to be under communist influence. In April, the national board of the German-American League for Culture, following the Communist Party line, appealed to President Roosevelt to observe "the strictest neutrality" toward the war, which was a struggle "of neither the German nation or German-Americans." It soon issued statements against Roosevelt and the New Deal. The communists had captured the Greater New York District of the league a year earlier, as illustrated by a 24-4 vote against a resolution to condemn all forms of political dictatorship including communism.[140] Adolph Friederich refused to bow to pressure from members of the Newark branch to follow the national office's lead. He resigned from the league, stating that many of the group's members, "apparently acting on orders from the other side," had turned against Roosevelt's New Deal and branded the President a "war monger." Friederich charged that the league was now a "leftist group."[141] With the departure of Friederich and several of his adherents, the Newark league disappeared from public view.

The Youth Division of the AJC, including its Newark branch, was forced to disband after supporting the Communist Party line on the Nazi-Soviet Pact and World War II. Against the directives of the AJC, the division affiliated itself with the communist-dominated American Youth Congress. To the chagrin of its parent body, it supported the AYC's positions opposing America's defense program and aid to the Allies. The AJC ordered the youth division to withdraw from the communist-led group and to support the United States Government's policies. The youth division refused to obey the order and permitted the AJC name to be used by the AYC in its propaganda. This left the AJC no choice except to disband its youth affiliate.[142]

The Communist Party also dominated the Newark office of Labor's Non-Partisan League.[143] The league had been an active anti-Nazi force in the late 1930s. Robert Parker was hired as its director in early 1939, after he lost his job with the International Labor Defense, a communist organization that had closed its Newark office.[144] Immediately after the Nazi-Soviet Pact was signed, Parker was called to a meeting with Lena Davis, Newark's Communist Party secretary, and Bill Norman, the New Jersey party secretary. Asked to issue a statement on behalf of his group endorsing the pact, he protested that the league's membership had not yet met to consider the issue. "Party discipline" was invoked and he was ordered to obey the request. He refused, stormed out of the meeting, and lost both his job and his Communist Party membership.[145]

Speakers at the Newark Communist Party's 1940 May Day rally denounced "imperialist" countries and, as per party policy, made no critical references to either Nazi or Fascist actions.[146] The featured speaker, Louis Budenz, praised the Soviet Union, defended its invasions of Finland and Poland, and accused Roosevelt of leading America toward war.[147] Peace—a thinly disguised appeal for no American intervention—became the communists' over-riding issue, first to benefit the Soviet Union's expansionist aims, and second to attract isolationists and pacifists to their cause. To attain this objective the communists set up "peace fronts."

Amelia Moorfield and the Newark chapter of Women's International League for Peace and Freedom (WILPF) became the Newark communist's first "peace front" success. When the war began, Moorfield threw all her energies into WILPF. In the early spring of 1940, an acquaintance of Moorfield's who belonged to the Mother's Group asked her to organize a peace rally for Mother's Day. As this was in keeping with previous WILPF Mother's Day events, Moorfield agreed. She could hardly have known that she was being set-up by the communists. Moorfield lobbied Mayor Meyer Ellenstein to proclaim Mother's Day "Mother's Peace Day." She organized a committee of peace supporters but was unable to get mainstream involvement. The WILPF, the Mother's Group, the Essex Players (a leftist theatrical troop), and the AYC were the only groups agreeing to participate. A peace rally was planned for the Friday before Mothers' Day at Newark City Hall.[148] At the rally 300 people heard speakers urge Americans to work for peace, particularly since World War I did not "make the world safe for democracy." The AYC's vice-chair, Richard Sidon, recommended spending money on schools, hospitals, and jobs rather than on war. Moorfield asked attendees to sign a petition against American entrance into the war, which would be presented to Congress by a group of mothers.[149]

A *Newark Star Ledger* editorial called those attending the meeting "dangerous fifth-columnists." Conceding that many in the audience and perhaps several of the speakers were not communists, the *Ledger* nevertheless opined, "The Communist influences behind the rally are visible except to those who would be blind."[150] At a Catholic War Veterans' event the same day, Rev. Matthew Toohey echoed the *Ledger's* "fifth-column" charge. He went even further, accusing "government officials, educators, and scientists" of being "tools and stooges of the agents of totalitarianism."[151]

A delegation of representatives from the AYC, CIO, and Labor's Non-Partisan League appeared at the newspaper's office to protest the editorial. They were refused a meeting with the editor. A letter writing campaign by the Mother's Group and others succeeded in persuading the paper to print both an AYC rebuttal of the editorial and letters to the editor protesting the paper's position.[152] Newark communists considered the rally a great success. Reporting on Newark activities before the Eleventh Communist Party Congress, Lawrence Mahon remarked on the capacity crowd at City Hall and lauded the Mothers' Group for their dedication to preventing American entry into the war.[153]

Frank Kingdon and Moorfield were on opposite sides of the "great debate." After the war began, Kingdon took a one-year leave of absence from his position as President of Newark University to accept the chairmanship of the New York Chapter of CDA. In that position, he became an ardent interventionist and leading critic of the AFC.[154] Kingdon was forced to resign from Newark University even before his leave of absence expired. He had been under attack by the University's Board of Trustees because of outspoken liberalism and defense of academic freedom.[155] After he left Newark University, Kingdon accepted the paid chairmanship of the Emergency Rescue Committee (ERC) in June 1940, a group he and others founded immediately after the fall of Paris to save "the artists, writers, and spokesmen for liberty who [are] the guardians of the values we cherish."[156] On October 13, 1940 a ship carrying prominent anti-Nazis, including the novelist Franz Werfel and both the brother and son of Nobel Prize winner Thomas Mann, arrived in New York Harbor.[157] Meeting the immigrants at the pier, Kingdon held a press conference at which he announced the founding of the ERC. Two weeks later Kingdon was in Newark with Mann's daughter, Erika, to speak at a forum entitled "Is Democracy Doomed?"[158]

* * *

The outbreak of war created a crisis for America's two major boycott groups. In October 1939 both the Joint Boycott Committee (JBC) and the NSANL held meetings to discuss whether England's naval blockade of Germany obviated the need for the groups to continue. The JBC decided to cease operations, whereas the NSANL opted to continue its existence, but to direct its activities against "Nazi-like and anti-democratic activities" in the United States. Kalb, now chairman of the national board of directors, was influential in issuing a letter to all local and state branches to either adapt to its new policy of fighting domestic Nazism or shut down.[159] The decision to drop the boycott was in total disregard of the wishes of Samuel Untermyer, who wanted his creation to cease operations altogether.[160]

After several months, the JBC reversed its decision because German goods were still entering the country. With reduced financial contributions from the Joint Labor Committee (JLC) and the AJC, it decided to work with a smaller staff but resume the anti-Nazi boycott. Like the NSANL, the JBC also added a new mission—to combat domestic Nazism. When the British blockade was strengthened and America increased security measures to protect its coastlines, the boycott mission became increasingly obsolete. The fight against domestic Nazism was already being addressed by the AJC, which with its greater resources was better equipped for the battle. Thus the JBC became a "dying organization with each passing day."[161]

The New Jersey NSANL's future was threatened by financial problems as well as by the war. The Newark Conference of Jewish Charities again refused to help fund the league when it attempted to get operating funds for the 1939-1940 fiscal year.[162] Within weeks of the war's start, the last employee of the Newark office was terminated. Shortly after, rent arrears forced the NSANL to close its Hill Street office.[163] The national office assumed the New Jersey office's activities, including fundraising.[164]

A small cadre of loyalists still met at Harkavy's law offices to determine how to raise sufficient funds to remain in existence. In early March 1940, Kalb, Alenick, and Harkavy traveled to New York to participate in a national conference at which 300 delegates passed a resolution condemning communists "as blood brothers of the Nazis," the only difference being "the color of their shirts."[165] Later in the month, the three again went to New York, this time for the funeral of Samuel Untermyer.[166] In May, Kalb organized a testimonial dinner for Abraham Harkavy, the popular president, to raise money to cover the group's debts.[167] The event was the last one for the New Jersey NSANL. Kalb and other former leaders now referred all boycott questions to the New York office. Kalb remained on the national board until mid-1941, but no longer took part in day-to-day business. Nathaniel Nathan, a former vice president of the New Jersey group, was its representative on the national executive board for the balance of the year.[168]

* * *

Unlike the NSANL, the Minutemen still had a mission to complete after the outbreak of war. On the evening of the day Germany invaded Poland the Minutemen and a group of Polish Americans from Irvington attacked uniformed Bundists as they left a meeting. Using baseball bats, the attackers sent several Nazis to the hospital.[169] Although weakened, the Bund still posed a "fifth column" threat in Newark. A relatively new nativist and anti-Semitic group inspired by Father Coughlin also posed a challenge to the Minutemen. The Christian Front was gaining adherents in Newark, mainly from anti-British Irish Catholics.

The Christian Front was founded in New York City in July 1938 in response to an article in Father Coughlin's newspaper, *Social Justice,* that called for the creation of a group to combat communist influence and return Christian concepts to America. A series of street-corner meetings in Brooklyn brought young Catholic anti-communists and anti-Semites into the Christian Front fold. Elements within the Catholic press and clergy backed the project, and an organizational meeting was held in Manhattan at the Catholic Church, St.

John the Apostle. Priests and "laymen" in Irish areas of New York recruited early members. Initially there was cooperation with the German-American Bund, but this ceased, on Father Coughlin's urging, after the Nazi-Soviet Pact of August 1939.[170]

The front believed Jews were involved in communism and controlled labor unions and retail establishments. Members were primarily lower-middle and middle-class Irish Americans who resented Jewish financial success.[171] The front's growth resulted from a combination of inter-ethnic tensions, anti-Semitism, and Church endorsement, especially that of Father Coughlin.[172] The front's increasingly anti-Semitic rhetoric encouraged numerous assaults on the New York Jewish community. Street-corner rallies turned into brawls between fronters and Jews. During the last six months of 1939, there were 238 arrests at front meetings. The group also organized boycotts of Jewish-owned stores in Irish neighborhoods, and expanded into Boston, Philadelphia, Pittsburgh, Jersey City, Newark, and elsewhere.[173]

In Newark, the presence of the Minutemen prevented the Christian Front from using street-corner meetings to recruit members. Instead they used bars and social clubs. As in New York, Irish resentment of Jews was a factor in the organization of the Newark group, which was incorporated as the Christian Front of New Jersey in July 1939. By the end of the year, the front claimed 700 New Jersey members, according to William Hammal, an Irvington gas station operator and secretary of the group. The president was Ernest Hawkins, an Irvington bus driver.[174]

The FBI's arrest of eighteen men in New York on the charge of conspiring to overthrow the government made headlines throughout America in January 1940. The conspiracy's leaders were members of the Christian Front, as were thirteen of the conspirators (including ten Irish and three German Americans).[175] The plot included plans for assassinations, a revolution, and a new American government led by fronters and their allies. The outlandishness of the operation demonstrated not only the plotters' lack of reality, but also the depth of their anti-Semitism.[176] The *Jewish Chronicle,* in a front-page editorial, blamed Father Coughlin and his newspaper *Social Justice* for encouraging the front and its planned revolution. The paper claimed that the front "reached into all channels of our political and commercial life."[177] The existence of a Newark branch was not mentioned in either the Jewish or the local press.

Despite the arrests of the New York Eighteen, the Newark front increased both the size and frequency of its meetings. By 1940, the group was meeting every other week at St. Mary's auditorium at the intersection of High and William Streets, one-half block from the Turn Verein. Anti-Semitic and anti-communist speeches were the meetings' main events. Money was raised from contributions and the sale of *Social Justice* and other anti-Semitic publications. Front meetings resembled Bund gatherings, without the uniforms, "heils," and German language. Some Germans did belong to the front, but Coughlin's anti-Bund sentiments precluded any relationship between the two Newark groups.

Nat Arno was well aware of Christian Front activities, and several Minutemen attended meetings at St. Mary's. Arno waited for a well-publicized event that would attract a large crowd. In February 1940, the Newark front ran a dance at Sokol Hall for the benefit of Father Coughlin's radio fund, with about 450 attendees. Arno threatened to break up the gathering if any remarks were made "against this country, President Roosevelt, or the Jews." Over two-dozen police stationed outside the hall prevented an equal number of Minutemen from entering. No speeches were made and the dance ended as scheduled at 1 a.m., without incident. Front president Ernest Hawkins told the press after the event that his organization was pro-American and opposed communism, Nazism, and fascism. He also denied that the group was anti-Semitic and said that any members "uttering words conveying race hatred are thrown out." It was also noted by the press that in addition to the officers guarding Sokol Hall, several Newark Police who belonged to the front were inside dancing.[178]   Newark Policemen were targeted for Front recruitment because the vast majority were Irish—as were the upper echelons of the force—and they were influential in their neighborhoods. Notoriously corrupt, the department was in the midst of a towing scandal involving fifty officers in 1940. At the same time, the death of Michael P. Duffy, Commissioner of Public Safety, in January 1940, caused a stalemate over who would succeed him. Duffy had been a close ally of Zwillman and of Mayor Meyer Ellenstein. Ellenstein wanted to control of the Police Department, and he used the issue of the Christian Front to gain his objective.

A list of policemen in the Front was sent to the FBI office in Newark in mid-April and shortly after a "confidential source" called the two Newark dailies and told them that the FBI was investigating charges that Newark policemen were members of the front. The list sent to the FBI was reported to be in the possession of Police Inspector John A. Brady,[179] at the time an ally of Ellenstein and an enemy of John B. Keenan, the acting public safety director. When reporters questioned Brady about the list he said, "There is nothing to it." However, he had already launched his own investigation "to crack down on Christian Front activities in the police department."[180] The FBI refused comment but later issued a press release claiming that the front had approximately 1,000 members in Newark.[181]

Members of the Newark Police who were in the front issued a statement expressing indignation that their "constitutional rights to join the organization" should be criticized. Over thirty officers admitted Front membership and denied that the movement wanted to overthrow the government. Most said they were willing to be questioned by the FBI. Brady responded by recommending that every officer in the force fill out a questionnaire about membership in the front "or any other subversive group," saying it was necessary to know the extent of front penetration in the police because of the sedition charges against New York fronters and the ongoing FBI investigation.[182]

While the FBI investigation was underway, Mayor Ellenstein assumed supervision of Newark's Police Department, replacing acting director Keenan. Citing poor morale and a lack of discipline, Ellenstein specifically denied that his move was related to the Christian Front investigation.[183] After a meeting with Brady and the Inspector's ally, Acting Chief John Haller, the mayor announced the transfer of fifty-one officers and five sergeants. Officers with preferred positions were sent back to street patrol if they were in disfavor with the new regime. Not coincidentally, most of the known Front members were demoted to lesser assignments.[184]

The mayor attained his main objective—control of the department. He denied that the police shake-up was an anti-Front coup.[185] Some did not take his denial at face value. The *Jewish Chronicle* applauded Ellenstein's efforts to rid the police of front influence.[186] The National NSANL sent a letter to Abe Harkavy asking him to revive the moribund New Jersey league to fight the front and the Ku Klux Klan.[187] The Newark Methodist Council denounced the front for "prostituting" Christianity's name and ideals for base ends. It said the Front's anti-Semitism consisted of "flimsy accusations long ago exposed by responsible investigations."[188]

Ellenstein's chief motivation notwithstanding, the demotions, combined with Brady's anti-front stance, helped weaken police presence in the group. Bad publicity forced the Front to move its meeting place out of downtown Newark to a hall in the heart of the Third Ward. At its next meeting, the 250 members had several unwelcome visitors—two detectives and a patrolman sent to monitor the event by Inspector Brady; reporters from the two Newark dailies; and Nat Arno with a large contingent of Minutemen. Fellow police pointed out traffic officer John C. Corbally as he passed a collection plate for the front. The presence of the press and Arno changed the program's usual tenor; it was devoid of anti-Semitic rhetoric and denounced only communism and the German-American Bund. No violence took place as the crowd filed out of the hall, although it had to pass cursing and threatening Minutemen who lined the street.[189]

The anti-Semitism propagated by Front members had an impact in the Jewish Third Ward. During the two-week front investigation, a gang of youngsters smashed over thirty windows of Jewish-owned stores on Prince Street. Initially the police did not apprehend the culprits. But when Prince Street merchants sent a letter to the Newark Commission protesting police inaction, Ellenstein's man, Deputy Chief Haller, took charge of the investigation and within two days ten boys were arrested. The leader of the gang, a twelve-year-old self-proclaimed "Hitler," told the police that when he gave orders his "men" always obeyed them.[190]

Wth its police component weakened, facing the glare of publicity, and openly threatened by the hostile Minutemen, the Front's influence decreased. Over the next year the group continued to meet and listen to familiar propaganda, but it attracted few new members and lost many original supporters. As America headed toward war, the Front's *raison d'etre* became isolationism and it soon merged its efforts with those of the AFC. In October 1940, anti-Semites—perhaps under Christian Front influence—were the target of a Minuteman operation in Newark. As members of an Orthodox Jewish Congregation that was moving from Hawthorne Avenue to Clinton Place paraded to their new location carrying Torah scrolls, a group of men in their twenties goose-stepped next to the procession shouting, "Heil Hitler! Down with the Jews!" For the next several weeks the men disturbed Saturday services at the synagogue. Their hangout was a garage several doors away where, according to rumor, a printing press used for anti-Semitic literature was located. The hecklers would not have gotten away with their actions under any circumstances, but because Longie Zwillman's mother belonged to the congregation the Minutemen decided that immediate and severe action was necessary. Nat Arno passed word to the Minutemen to come for a battle on Tuesday night, October 1. More than twenty of them arrived armed with baseball bats and rubber-encased steel clubs. The Minutemen stormed the garage and attacked the dozen men inside. When the assault was over, five of the twelve were in the hospital, mainly with head injuries. The Minutemen, except for Jacob Skuratofsky ("Jake Mohawk"), escaped before the police arrived. The Minuteman was seriously injured when he was hit on the head by a friend in the dark garage.[191] Zwillman visited Skuratofsky in the hospital and called in medical specialists from New York to treat him.[192]

* * *

Germany's invasion of Denmark, Norway, Belgium, Holland, and France in April and May received daily headlines in the Newark press. At the same time, a new theme began to appear regularly in the nation's press—the danger of a "fifth column." Nazi victories in Europe made Americans increasingly aware that Germany was a threat to their country. Italy's June entry into the war on the side of Nazi Germany gave Americans another reason to feel threatened.

The *New York Times* claimed that the fall of Europe could be attributed to the existence of "fifth columns." A national poll showed that over 70 percent of Americans believed that the Germans had already set up a "fifth column" in America.[193] Dickstein and Dies competed for headlines in denouncing "fifth column" Bundists, communists, Christian Fronters, and others. In a late May "fireside chat," President Roosevelt warned Americans to be on guard against a "fifth column."[194]

Samuel Dickstein, speaking before the House, blamed a "fifth column" for the defeat of several European countries. He called attention to a 10,000-person Bund rally held in North Bergen to celebrate Hitler's victories, and stated that the Bund was "drilling with rifles more intensely than before" at Camp Nordland.[195] The New Jersey State Police immediately announced that they would put the camp under "closer scrutiny." The Sussex County Prosecutor warned that Nordland was strategically located for a "fifth column" because of its proximity to the Picattiny Arsenal, a munitions depot, and to the zinc mines that supplied the nearby munitions industry. He said that the American Legion and county officials would not tolerate any subversive activities at the camp.[196]

"Fifth column" concerns intensified government activities aimed at the Bund. Essex County Prosecutor William Wachenfeld created a seven-man squad to investigate subversive activities. He said the squad was needed because of numerous complaints of un-American activities his office received from all sections of the county.[197] John Brady increased the Newark police department's radical and alien squad from two to five men in order to combat Nazi, fascist, and communist "fifth column" activity. The unit coordinated its activities with those of the Newark office of the FBI and the police emergency squad in dealing with sabotage. The enlarged squad reexamined its ten-year accumulation of dossiers on communists, fascists, and Nazis to determine potential security threats.[198] Irvington police followed suit by establishing a special bureau to handle cases of subversive or un-American activities and to work with the FBI and the Newark radical and alien squad. In creating the bureau, Public Safety Director Balentine denied the FBI report that Irvington was "a hotbed of Nazism."[199] Balentine may have been motivated by the creation of an undercover committee to "cope with Nazi activities" by representatives of Irvington fraternal and civic groups who wanted to lift the stigma of the "hotbed" epithet.[200]

At a Newark B'Nai Brith meeting, Colonel Mark Kimberling, Superintendent of the New Jersey State Police, urged that a statewide list of all "un-Americans" be compiled and shared with the FBI. New Jersey Congressman J. Parnell Thomas, a member of the Dies Committee, arranged a meeting of police officials, including Kimberling, from New York, New Jersey and Pennsylvania to discuss joint action against "fifth columnists."[201]

By the summer of 1940, most German Americans wanted nothing to do with the Bund. Camp Nordland's fourth season began in June 1940 with a rally of only 500 Bundists. Kuhn's conviction the previous summer, the tense international scene, New Jersey laws against Nazi uniforms, heiling, pictures of Hitler, swastikas and "hate" speech, and "fifth-column" charges all caused German Americans to shun the Bund.[202] At the event—at which no photographs were permitted— August Klapprott and other Bund officials ridiculed the "fifth column" charges. The rally underscored the need to keep the United States out of the war, as England and France "were never friends of America."[203]

The Sussex County Sheriff, with the cooperation of the American Legion, began an investigation of the camp. A preliminary report concluded that the camp violated New Jersey laws prohibiting the wearing of foreign uniforms and insignias and the incitement of racial and religious hatred. Sussex County Assemblyman Alfred Littell introduced a resolution calling on federal, state, and local authorities to investigate Nordland and the Bund. It was speedily passed by both houses of the Legislature. The *Jewish Chronicle* applauded the action and urged the FBI to immediately begin a probe.[204]

William Kunze, August Klapprott, and Matthias Kohler were arrested at a July 4 celebration at Nordland and charged with violating provisions of the state's anti-Nazi laws. The three were held overnight and released the next morning on $1,000 bail each. On the day of the arrests, 500 non-uniformed Bundists gathered at Nordland to hear anti-British speeches, which now shared the spotlight with diatribes against communists and Jews.[205] The New Jersey Division of the American Civil Liberties Union lodged the only protest against the arrests, questioning the constitutionality of the anti-Nazi laws.[206]

A highlight of Nordland's summer season was a Ku Klux Klan rally on August 18 to "test the Americanism of the Bund," according to Rev. Edwin H. Young, grand giant of the New Jersey Realm of the Klan. It was later discovered that the Bund did not charge the Klan a fee for the use of Nordland, imposing only a twenty-five cent parking charge.[207] Of the 1,000 who attended, fewer than 100 were Klansmen. The rally was replete with speeches, initiations, and a cross burning.

The speakers stressed that the Bund and Klan had common missions and both faced "persecution." They declared themselves against conscription and American entry into the war. Young urged a boycott of the song "God Bless America" because its author, Irving Berlin, was a Jew. Arthur Bell, a Grand Dragon of the Klan, drew loud applause when he accused American Jews of trying to push the country into war. Outside, brass-knuckled guards kept more than 1,000 anti-Nazis from storming the camp. The demonstrators unsuccessfully attempted to drown out the speakers.[208] The Klan was, however, a sideshow. The real fireworks came from an internecine battle within the Bund. A busload of twenty-three supporters of the jailed Fritz Kuhn arrived at Nordland and began passing out leaflets attacking the new American Führer, William Kunze, and his ally August Klapprott. Kuhn and Kunze supporters battled it out and nine

Bundists from New York were arrested. Subsequently, Kuhn's backers pressed assault charges against Klapprott and Matthias Kohler.[209]

Nordland was relatively empty the next three Sundays, with only twenty-five to thirty cars arriving each week. One reason was that the Sussex County Sheriff's Department jotted down the license-plate number of every car that came to the camp. Three hundred ten frequent visitors—with the largest number, 119, coming from Essex County—had been identified and their names forwarded to their respective county sheriffs.[210]

In the summer of 1940 Congress passed the "Alien Registration Act," which required aliens over fourteen to appear at a designated post office in the county seat for registration and fingerprinting. The law took effect on August 27, and by October 1 the Newark Post Office had registered 29,300 aliens, or about 80 percent of the Essex County total.[211] This law was more effective against communists than Nazis; The Party lost 7,500 members between June 1940 and January 1941.[212]

The "fifth column" charge had a serious impact in the Newark area, particularly in Irvington. J. Edgar Hoover's office denied rumors that the FBI was investigating Nazi activities in Irvington and spies had already been arrested. A town vigilante group organized by Harry F. Knowles, manager of the Irvington Unemployment Compensation Commission, said it would drive Nazis out of Irvington by force if necessary. He claimed his group had formulated a plan for the "investigation of schools, industrial workers, and 'hyphenated' groups." Knowles said Irvington manufacturers had complained to him that it was difficult to get national defense contracts because of the town's Nazi reputation.[213] The *Jewish Chronicle* criticized the vigilante effort, stating that although the group's intentions were "good" it should not interfere with police business.[214]

German-owned businesses in Irvington were boycotted and painted with anti-Nazi graffiti. Some merchants lost up to 50 percent of their business because of rumors they were Nazi sympathizers. One bakery window was covered with American bunting and a sign stating that the owner was 100 percent American and promising $500 to anyone who could prove he was a Nazi. A nearby German-American bar near sported a sign proclaiming: "God Bless America—We are Proud to be Americans."[215] The German-American Federation for the Preservation of American Ideals was established in Newark to combat the Bund and to "prevent the tide of public opinion from turning against German Americans as it did in 1918." The group complained that people with German accents faced discrimination at employment agencies and German Americans were removing their names from mailing lists of German organizations. The Bund was blamed for these troubles. [216] The Anti-Nazi feeling was so intense that Adolph Friederich, who had not yet resigned his presidency of the anti-Nazi German-American League for Culture, asked Irvington Mayor Herbert Kruttschnitt to help protect innocent people from rumors. [217]

Friederich did not consider his long-time nemesis Dr. Francis Just "innocent." As president of the German-American Societies of Newark, Just was in charge of the annual German Day outing in Singer's Park in Springfield. Friederich predicted that the swastika would, as usual, be displayed and sent a letter to Congressman Fred Hartley,[218] the scheduled speaker, requesting that he not appear. Just, realizing the precariousness of the Bund's position, responded that there would be no swastika, and Hartley replied that he wouldn't appear if there were any Nazi manifestations. Just's friend and fellow Nazi sympathizer Otto Stiefel, the other scheduled speaker, said he would talk on the "need" for American defense measures.[219]

Newark Bund leader Matthias Kohler, who had become increasingly militant as the Bund's cause weakened, insisted that the swastika be displayed on German Day. Just met with National Bundesleiter Wilhelm Kunze in New York and advised him to restrain Kohler in order to preserve what little support the Bund still enjoyed.[220] But Kunze either would not or could not control Kohler. German Day was held without incident. Congressman Hartley inspected the grounds to make sure there were no Nazi emblems on display, but apparently missed the pro-Nazi leaflets that were being distributed. Hartley made a brief address praising the contributions of German Americans to the country and stating his opposition to American involvement in the war. Officials said the crowd of 700 was the smallest in the 12-year history of the event. [221] Kohler raged at Just's decision against the swastika and proposed an alternative slate against Just's candidates at the annual election for officers of the League of German-American Societies. Just's candidates prevailed, ending Bund infiltration of mainline Newark German-American organizations. This was made official in August when Kohler sent a letter of resignation to the league on behalf of the Bund, citing "fundamental" differences between the two organizations.[222] Just issued a public acceptance of the resignation in which he did not mention Nazism, simply stating that "our sympathies were not the same and this was the best way out."[223]

* * *

On July 9, 1940 the "Battle of Britain" began as German bombs fell on London. France had already surrendered to Nazi Germany and the Vichy regime had begun mass arrests of Jewish journalists, attorneys, and merchants. Hitler seemed unstoppable. In an effort to counter this feeling, Roosevelt spoke to the nation, cautioning Americans not to become too impressed by the efficiency of dictatorships. FDR said such impressions would endanger America's democratic ideals and the specific freedoms guaranteed in the Constitution.[224] The "great debate" over intervention intensified.

Newark's first isolationist response to the "Battle of Britain" was a Mosque Theater peace rally of 3,000 held under the aegis of the New Jersey Committee for Peace and Preparedness, at which Father Coughlin's *Social Justice* was sold. Rev. Matthew Toohey spoke against compulsory conscription. Father Edward Lodge Curran, president of the International Catholic Truth Society, urged America to strengthen its defenses so that no "red or brown" tyrant can duplicate "the rape of Poland." Representative Fred Hartley lobbied against supplying Japan with war materials.

Judge John A. Matthews delivered the rally's most controversial speech. He denounced English and American warmongers and advised the audience not "to fall for this bunk about the death of civilization when the British are conquered." The crowd booed at the mention of "perfidious Albion" when Matthews described how England bombed the French fleet at Oran and "slaughtered French sailor boys."[225] The jurist then painted a rosy picture of fascist France. He declared that "Frenchmen today, like Franco, are determined that France should have a corporate state." France would again become, he said "a great stronghold of the Christian way of life" under the "great patriots of France, Petain and Weygand," who, along with Pierre Laval, "will be written in history as the deliverers of France from the slavery and domination of international intrigue as well as from the constant threat of Communism." With these leaders, France was facing a "warless future for generations to come." Matthews, parroting Father Coughlin and other anti-Semites, characterized warmongers as "The international gang, the financiers and intriguers who control the wealth, the credit, and the trade of the world."[226]

Matthews' speech provoked a furious response from Anton Kaufman, publisher of the *Jewish Chronicle*. In a front page editorial "Mr. Matthews' Very Rosy View of Fascism," Kaufman recounted that in addition to the judge's appearance with Coughlin, Matthews had praised Hitler at the 1939 St. Patrick's Day dinner. He wondered how Matthews knew that the French wanted a "corporate state" and the Petain-Weygand-Laval brand of fascism would make that country a stronghold of Christian life.[227]

Other than Kaufman, no other Newark publication or organization—Christian or Jewish—put itself on record against Matthews. Jacob Stacher wrote a letter to the editor of the *Newark News* in which he said that he read Matthews' remarks "with a sickening feeling and despair of ever seeing a realization of the dream of democracy." Stacher wondered what the average American thought about a member of the judiciary stating that France would be better off with a fascist regime than a democracy. He suggested that New Jersey remove Matthews from the bench because of the judge's "doubt as to the efficacy of our democratic processes of government."[228]

Two months after the jurist's speech, both houses of Congress passed by a two-to-one margin the first peacetime draft in American history. All men between the ages of twenty-one and thirty-five were required to register at a draft board. Approximately 16,500,000 men were expected to register and 900,000 be conscripted. Almost $2 billion was added to the defense budget.[229] These measures provoked isolationists, anti-Britishers, and pro-fascists to adopt a last line of defense to prevent America from going to war.

* * *

The America First Committee (AFC) was founded at Yale Law School in late 1940 to counter the U.S.'s increasingly interventionist stance. R. Douglas Stuart, Jr., a third-year law student organized the committee which he modeled after the CDA. Charles Lindbergh addressed 3,000 students at the first meeting at Yale in October. The world-famous aviator gave a two-hour speech in which he attacked Roosevelt for arousing the hostility of dictators and opined that America should make its peace with "the new powers in Europe" because the Germans were sure to win the war. Back home in Chicago, Stuart, with the help of his father, R. Douglas, Sr., the senior vice president of Quaker Oats, recruited corporate leaders from such Chicago-area companies as Sears Roebuck, Quaker Oats, Hormel Meats, and Inland Steel. General Robert Wood Johnson, World War I hero and chairman of the board of Sears Roebuck & Co., became national chairman of the AFC and remained its leader until the group ceased operations after Pearl Harbor. He believed that in order to preserve America's institutions the country had to stay out of war at all costs.[230] Wood was a moderate isolationist who supported some of President Roosevelt's New Deal Policies. However, extremists— Roosevelt haters, Anglophobes, and anti-Semites—also belonged to the AFC.[231]

The AFC attracted such famous Americans as Lindbergh, Henry Ford, Edward Rickenbacker, World War I flying ace and president of Eastern Air Lines, and Chester Bowles, advertising pioneer and executive.[232] Thomas N. McCarter, chairman of Newark's Public Service Corporation, was one of the committee's original board members. He acknowledged his role in December 1940 after a Washington newspaper named him an active member, admitting that he joined after hearing a speech by General Johnson in New York. McCarter claimed that the evils of communism and fascism could be avoided if America remained out of the war.[233] In December 1940, *Time* reported that the AFC had 60,000 members, eleven chapters, and "an organization drive that was going like a house afire."[234]

As American entry into the war came closer, fifth-column fears grew more acute. The fears seemed justified when a huge explosion at the Kenvil, New Jersey Hercules Powder Plant killed forty-seven workers on September 12, 1940. The plant was located near Nordland, and newspapers throughout the country assumed that the Nazis were behind the blast. Three days after the incident, the Sussex County Sheriff and twenty deputies armed with search warrants raided Nordland. They found only armbands with swastikas on them, one rifle with a telescopic lens, and some anti-Semitic literature.[235] Samuel Dickstein attacked Congressman Dies for not acting earlier on information the committee received that the Hercules Powder Plant was a target. Dickstein read into the Congressional Record a list of 100 New Jersey residents and companies that should be investigated because of the explosion.[236]

The Dies Committee sent its investigators to Kenvil. After a two-week probe, the committee scheduled an October 1 hearing at the

Newark Post Office. Congressman J. Parnell Thomas requested Newark hearings on Nazi activities several months before the explosion, and committee investigators were sent to the city to meet with members of the police department's radical and alien squad.[237] The public was eager for information on "fifth-column" Nazi activities, especially about the Hercules tragedy, but the Newark investigation proved disappointing. The two days the committee spent in Newark produced no testimony on the Hercules Powder Plant tragedy. Several witnesses testified on Bund members who worked at other plants with defense contracts. Dies was not present at the hearings, leaving Thomas to garner maximum publicity in his home state. Kunze and Klapprott were the main witnesses, and both noted the steep decline in the Bund's fortunes. Kunze testified that since August 1939 the number of Bund units in the country had decreased from sixty-eight to forty.[238] Klapprott testified that there were only four units in New Jersey, with a total membership of approximately 500. Nordland's revenues had decreased from $40,000 in 1938 to $4,000- $5,000 in 1940. The Newark unit no longer held meetings, and had only "loose members who come up to Camp Nordland." The same was true of the other three New Jersey units.[239]

Two months after the Newark hearings, Dies made a speech advocating immediate discharge of "subversives" in government service or defense industries. Dies, as exaggeration prone as Dickstein, charged that the Newark Bund had 600 members employed in defense industries. Perhaps to prevent panic, The *Newark News,* in a rare journalistic response to a wire story, printed a statement immediately beneath the Dies charges, reporting that although some German Americans from Newark and Irvington had been mentioned in connection with the Bund, "the organization does not have any regularly organized units in either of the two communities."[240] The *Newark News* underestimated Bund activities in Newark, perhaps relying too much on Kunze's and Klapprott's testimony. Jugendschaft, the Bund youth group, continued to meet in the city on a regular basis during 1940. It began publishing a paper, *Wir Sturmer,* in the fall, which was still being published in 1941. Articles in the paper, in both English and German, reported on social and athletic events and praised Hitler's military successes in Western Europe.[241] Bund correspondence indicates an active and successful Jugendschaft recruiting program in Newark until the end of 1940.[242]

A Sussex County Grand Jury convened for the fall term in September and began another probe of the Bund. This resulted in indictments against nine Bundists including Klapprott, Kunze, and Kohler on charges of violating the state law against promotion of race hate. Some of the Nazis were accused of sanctioning hate programs at Nordland against Jews, whereas others faced charges that they made hate speeches. Kohler was quoted as saying, "Our day is coming, we know who you are, all Jews, and we'll get rid of you!" The Bundists were arraigned, pled not guilty, and were held on $1,000 bail each.[243]

All the defendants admitted the facts set forth in the indictment but said they would fight the charge on the grounds that it violated their constitutional right to free speech. They promised to appeal the case to the Supreme Court, if necessary, and made a plea to the public for funds to cover legal costs. The Bund attorney filed a motion with Judge John C. Losey to dismiss the indictments on constitutional grounds. The Judge said he would rule on the motion in January. The American Civil Liberties Union filed a supporting brief urging Losey to dismiss the indictments so the Bundists "may stand as living monuments of proof that this strongest of all democracies can tolerate even expression of loathsome opinions, confident that its people will reject them."[244]

* * *

Newark's Italians received the news of Italy's entrance into World War II with mixed emotions. The most negative response was from Dr. Angelo Bianchi, arguably Newark's most prominent Italian, who resigned from both the Order of the Sons of Italy and the Dante Alighieri Society the next day. He was criticized by both groups for "turning his back on his compatriots."[245] A few Italian Americans attempted to defend Mussolini on the grounds that Great Britain and France had wronged Italy in the past. However, most remained silent.

The October 1940 Columbus Day celebration demonstrated that many in the Italian-American community still supported Mussolini, and that those who dissented from this sentiment did so at their own peril. Dr. Bianchi, chairman of the Columbus Day Committee, tried to avoid the issue of "Il Duce" by focusing the celebration on Italian-American contributions to America. Two other committee members, Nicholas Albano and Themistocles Mancusi-Ungaro, supported

Bianchi. At the final planning meeting it was pointed out that Columbus Day was a legal holiday in America, and "not a holiday for Mussolini."[246]

The three leaders did not speak for many working-class Newark Italians, most of whom refused to take part in the festivities. The lack of participants forced a cancellation of the traditional outdoor parade and rally at the Columbus statue in Washington Park. Instead, the celebration was held in the half-empty Central High School auditorium. In his speech, Albano excoriated the Italian-American community for not supporting the event. Governor A. Harry Moore, who had spoken at Newark's Columbus Day festivities in the past, must have been shocked by the low attendance, but avoided the issue and told those assembled not to worry about the problem of "brother-fighting-brother" since the "United States was not going to war."[247]

* * *

The Nazi-Soviet Pact and the outbreak of World War II completely broke the pattern of the previous six years. Nazi Germany was seen by many as a mortal threat to America by the end of 1940. Public opinion and government actions had decimated the ranks of the German-American Bund nationally and in Newark. Paradoxically, the two groups in Newark that had most opposed foreign and domestic Nazism were now irrelevant. The Newark NSANL had already disbanded, and the Minutemen had fought their last battle against the Bund. The Communist Party, regardless of its motives, had been an anti-Nazi factor since 1933, and particularly from Kristallnacht to the Nazi-Soviet Pact. But the Pact and the subsequent slavish support for Moscow's betrayal of the Allies discredited the American Communist Party to such an extent that it never fully recovered.

At the end of 1940, Jews were also in a different position. They were well integrated into the war preparedness effort and were Newark's—and, for that matter, the country's—only major ethnic group in favor of intervention. The historian Henry Feingold noted that, "direct interventionist posture distinguished Jews from other hyphenated groups like German, Italian, and Irish Americans."[248] However, until Pearl Harbor, despite the growing consensus for intervention, Newark's Jews still had to deal with anti-Semitic forces; the remnants of the German-American Bund and the Christian Front had found a new home with America First.

Notes

1. N.N., 1/31/39, p. 15.
2. J.C., 3/17/39, p. 8.
3. Ibid., 1/7/39, p. 1; 1/14/39, p. 1, 1/21/38, p. 1. The steering committee meeting that made the Committee of 100 permanent was called by Dr. Foulkes and held in Frank Kingdon's office. Others present were Michael Stavitsky, Joseph Kraemer, Dr. Max Danzis, and Mrs. Esther Jameson. Foulkes said an executive committee of thirty, of all religions and races, would soon be appointed.
4. N.N., 2/25/39, p. 3.
5. Ibid., 3/11/39, p. 4.
6. Moorfield's grandson, William Shannon, claims that Moorfield was an informer for the FBI. He remembers being present in his grandmother's house when she was questioned by FBI agents. He recollects that the agents and Amelia were on very friendly terms and that she would give them reports on meetings she attended. Although Shannon could not remember what organization(s) his grandmother reported upon, the American League Against War and Fascism would be a logical choice of interest for the FBI. Interview, William Shannon, 11/7/98
    No information was found on Moorfield in FBI files under a FOIA request.
7. Detzer, Dorothy, *Appointment on the Hill*, New York, 1948, p. 198.
8. Soon after her marriage to Robert Parker, executive director of Newark's International Labor Defense, a communist front, Cox was called to a board meeting of the ACLU and offered a job in New York with the ALPD. This was engineered Reverend Henry Ward, the chairman of the ALPD and a national board member of the ACLU, to remove any communist tint from the ACLU because of Cox's marriage to Parker. Within a few months Cox was transferred to Newark to establish a New Jersey headquarters for the League and to serve as its executive secretary.
9. Cox, Nancy, unpublished manuscript, p. 325.
10. N.N., 1/9/39, p. 6.
11. Those in Newark who backed Franco held a church service to celebrate his victory. Nancy Cox, who had spent the last year working on behalf of the Loyalists, organized a protest at the church against the Francoists which provoked a riot. She was chastised editorially by the *Sunday Call* for calling for civil rights for the "left' but denying them to the pro-Francoists. S.C., 5/14/39, Part III, p.12.
12. Cox, unpublished manuscript, p. 341.
13. WPA New Jersey Writer's Project, Subgroup New Jersey Ethnological Survey, Box 2, Folder 25, "survey of 54 Jewish organizations," undated, p. 1.
14. Cox, unpublished manuscript, pp. 322, 323.
15. Interview, Leo and Lilly Lowenthal, 2/27/98.
16. Klehr, Harvey, *The Heyday of American Communism -The Depression Decade*, New York, 1984, p. 384.
17. WPA, New Jersey Writer's Project, op. cit. pp. 9, 10.
18. S.C., 3/12/39, p. 16.
19. Klehr, *The Heyday of American Communism*, pp. 294-303.
20. N.N., 1/19/39, p. 6.
21. Ibid., 3/2/39, p. 6. Among the speakers at the meeting was Elwood Dean, African-American leader in Newark's branch of the National Negro Congress and member of the Newark Communist Party.
22. Klehr, *The Heyday of American Communism*, p. 383.
23. WPA, op. cit., Box 5, Folder 26, Notes/Data, p. 4.
24. S.C., 3/26/38, Part II, p. 5.
25. WPA, New Jersey Writer's Project, Box 2, Folder 25, "The Jewish People's Committee of Newark," undated.
26. Papers of A. Harry Moore, Vol. 369—1938-1941, Memo from "F.V.S." to Governor, undated.

27.   Klehr, *The Heyday of American Communism*, p. 201. California's Labors Non-Partisan League was likewise controlled by the Communist Party. See Labors Non-Partisan League, FBI file 61-10749, 10/23/40.
28.   According to Jack Gipfel the West Side Neighborhood Committee was a communist front. Interview, Jack Gipfel, 12/17/96.
29.   N.N., 2/24/39, p. 3.
30.   Papers of A. Harry Moore, Vol. 368, 1938-1941, Letters from Procida to Moore, 2/21/39; Moore to Procida, 2/25/39.
31.   N.N., 5 /18/39, p. 9.
32.   Ibid., 4/9/39, p. 17.
33.   Ibid., 4/11/39, p. 6.
34.   S.C., 4/23/39, p. 4.
35.   N.N., 4/3/39, p. 30. The genesis for both the Ukrainian and the Czechoslovakian ad hoc committees in Newark was the 1938-9 discussion in the American Communist Party on the dearth of popular front activities generated by national bureaus for foreign speaking ethnics. See Klehr, op. cit., p. 382.
36.   S.C., 7/2/39, p. 1; N.N., 9/20/38, p. 38.
37.   *New Jersey Herald News*, 3/8/38, p. 1.
38.   National Negro Congress, FBI File 100-1467, Report of 2/1/43, p. 3.
39.   *New Jersey Herald News*, 3/8/38, p. 1; 8/5/39, pp. 1,2.
40.   N.N., 10/28/39, p. 1; 1/23/40, p. 11.
41.   Ibid., 5/26/39, p. 1.
42.   Ibid., 9/30/39, p. 2.
43.   Ibid., 11/18/39, p. 2; 11/30/39, p. 16; 12/5/39, p. 1.
44.   Ibid., 12/5/39, p. 16.
45.   German-American Bund, RG 131, 304A, Box 10, Folder 153, Letter from Philip Hochstein to Camp Nordland, 3/18/39.
46.   N.N., 4/29/40, p. 2.
47.   Ibid., 12/20/39, p. 10; J.C., 5/10/40, p. 1.
48.   N.N., 11/7/39, p. 7.
49.   Ibid., 1/22/40, p. 7. The committee included six churchmen (including Garner and Clarence Bleakney), six academics (including Franz Boaz and Edward Fuhlbruegge), Harold Lett of the Urban League, Simon Doniger, a social worker, and Herman B. Walker, a labor leader. Of the fifteen, at least three were Communist Party members.
50.   N.N., 6/27/39, p. 7; 4/21/39, p. 2.
51.   German American Bund, op. cit., Box 7, Folder 109, "Final Statement- Pro-American Rally-February 20th 1939-Madison Square Garden. The Hudson County unit's quota was 2,000 and it sold over a 1,000. The Bergen and Passaic units together sold 200 tickets.
52.   N.N., 2/21/39, p. 7.
53.   S.C., 2/26/39, p. 1.
54.   Ogden, August Raymond, *The Dies Committee*, Washington, DC, 1945, pp. 101-113.
55.   N.N., 4/3/39, p. 1.
56.   Ibid., 4/6/39, p. 1; 4/8/39, p. 2. The FBI estimate of 285 members in the Newark Bund was substantiated as Kohler's testimony at Kuhn's 1939 trial indicated a membership of 250 to 300.
57.   FBI, Herman Von Busch, File 100-25344, Report from Newark, NJ, 12/31/41, pp. 1-3.
58.   FBI, op. cit., Report from Newark, NJ, 10/9/42, p. 4.
59.   I.H., 4/14/39, p. 4.
60.   J.C., 4/14/39, p. 1.
61.   I.H., 4/7/39, p. 16; Siegel, Alan A, *Out of Our Past, A History of Irvington, New Jersey,* Irvington, NJ, 1974, p. 347.
62.   S.C., 4/16/39, p. 7; N.N., 4/17/39, p. 7. Special guests at the convention were Rev. William Hiram Foulkes, Dr. Samuel Goodman, Rabbi Julius Silberfeld, and Herman B. Walker.

63. N.N., 4/7/39, p. 8.

64. Ibid., 4/13/39, p. 23.

65. Ibid., 3/12/39, p. 14.

66. Ibid., 3/19/39, p. 19; 3/26/39, p. 1.

67. German-American Bund, RG 131, 305 A, Box 2, Handbill announcing meeting, 5/14/39.

68. S.C., 6/18/39, p. 9.

69. N.N., 6/20/39, p. 27; 6/21/39, p. 15.

70. I.H., 6/22/39, p. 1.

71. N.N., 6/24/39, p. 3.

72. Ibid., 6/26/39, p. 19.

73. Interview, Irving Edisis, 4/15/98.

74. Sayers, Michael and Albert E. Kahn, *Sabotage! The Secret War Against America*, New York, 1942, pp. 158, 159, 162.

75. Ibid., pp. 159, 160.

76. American Jewish Committee, YIVO, RG 347.6, Box 20, pp. 1518-1521.

77. Charles Lindbergh became a worldwide hero in May 1927 when he became the first person to fly non-stop across the Atlantic Ocean. From 1935 to 1939 he lived and traveled in Europe, where he made harsh judgments on both the politics and quality of air power in England, France, and the Soviet Union. He visited Germany three times from 1936 to 1938 to gather intelligence on Nazi military aviation developments for the United States Military Attaché in Berlin. Each time he met Herman Goering head of the Nazi airforce. He became enamored of not only Hitlerite air power but also of the German spirit, technical ability, and leadership. He criticized democracy as compared to the Nazi system: "Are we deluding ourselves when we attempt to run governments by counting the number of heads, without a thought of what lies within them?" In 1936 he viewed Germany as a "stabilizing factor" in Europe. In 1937, Lindbergh claimed that although he disliked the fanaticism displayed by the Nazis, he felt in them "a sense of decency and value which in many ways is far ahead of our own." In October 1938 he accepted a medal from Goering "in the name of the Führer."

When war broke out in Europe, Lindbergh urged American non-intervention. He said England and France could not beat Germany. When the Nazis attacked the Soviet Union, he spoke for a Russian defeat and opposed Lend Lease before Congress. All the while he appeared throughout the United States on behalf of groups against American aid to the Allies. His arch-conservative political views and his hatred of Franklin Roosevelt made him an ideal spokesperson for anti-Semitic isolationists. Among those he supported was the "No Foreign War Committee," which cooperated with known anti-Semitic organizations. Lindbergh found his niche with America First in 1940. See, Wayne S. Cole, *Charles Lindbergh and the Battle Against American Intervention in World War II*, New York, 1970, pp. 25-42.

78. American Jewish Committee, op. cit., Box 21, pp. 253, 255.

79. Sayers, *Sabotage*, pp. 161, 164-167.

80. Ibid., p. 161.

81. American Jewish Committee, op. cit., Box, 20, p. 233; Box 21, pp. 1027, 1059, 1340.

82. NSANL, Box 11, Folder 5, "Out-of-Town Membership," undated, circa August 1939.

83. Ibid., Box 11, Folder 5, "Organization Members of the NSANL of New Jersey." Included in the 119 Newark organizations paying dues to the League were unions and tradesmen's associations, 13; KUVs and their ladies auxiliaries, 32; synagogues, 10; welfare—ladies and men's lodges, workers groups, and health related groups, 55; social and cultural, 8; veterans, 1. The average dues paid were $10, and the only group that provided above $30 was the Erste Bershader KUV which gave the League $200.

84. J.C., 4/7/39, p. 1.

85. N.N., 4/17/39, p. 20.

86. Untermyer Papers, Letters, Kalb to Untermyer, 4/15/39; Untermyer to Dubovsky, 4/18/39.

87. NSANL, Box 11, Folder 4, Letters from Kuhn to Kalb and Kuhn to NSANL, 4/21/39.
88. Ibid., Letter from Frederick to Carroll, 6/11/39.
89. Ibid., Letters Frederick to Harriman, 3/8/39, Harriman to Frederick, 3/9/39; Folder 5, Letters Harkavy to Harriman, 7/10/39, Harriman to Harkavy, 7/11/39.
90. Interview, Abraham Harkavy, 1/9/97.
91. Gottlieb, Moshe R., *American Anti-Nazi Resistance, 1933-1941*, New York, 1982, pp. 268, 269.
92. N.N., 7/5/39, p. 28; S.C., 7/9/39, p. 1.
93. N.N., 7/31/39, p. 9.
94. Ibid., 7/15/39, p. 2; S.C., 7/16/39, p. 1.
95. Ogden, *The Dies Committee*, pp. 116-119.
96. Ibid., pp. 123, 124.
97. N.N., 8/18/39, pp. 1, 2.
98. Ogden, *The Dies Committee*, pp. 125, 126.
99. Johnson, Walter, *The Battle Against Isolation, Chicago*, 1944, p. 94. This work is a pro-interventionist account using mainly the Committee to Defend America and the William Allen White archives.
100. N.N., 9/14/39, p. 29. Prinz's prescience can be contrasted with the words delivered on the same day by Rabbi Solomon Foster of Temple B'Nai Jeshurun, who said that the challenge of Germany and Russia would be met by "the revival of spiritual interests by the commingling of religious groups and by the reaffirmation of the truths of religion as the only foundation on which to build a safe and durable civilization."

    Other reactions by Newark's Jewish Community to the war were similar to Prinz's —concern for the fate of Europe's Jews. The United Jewish Appeal (successor to the Newark Conference of Jewish Charities) issued a pamphlet to its employees and lay people involved in the solicitation of funds detailing catastrophic conditions in German-occupied Poland. See, Stavitsky Papers, Clippings 1939, Series I, Box 1-12, The UJA Community Comment, December 1939.
101. N.N., 9/30/39, p. 9.
102. S.C., 1/28/40, Part 4, p. 3. Youth Alyah was supported by Orthodox Jews from Eastern Europe. A perusal of the list of over fifty sponsors of the Ball reveal no Conference of Jewish Charities activists.
103. J.C., 9/22/39, p. 1.
104. Breitman, Richard and Alan M. Kraut, *American Refugee Policy and European Jewry, 1933-1945*, Bloomington, IN, 1987, p. 77. The Intergovernmental Committee on Refugees was created at the Evian Conference in July 1938. This conference was called by the United States for the international community to facilitate and finance emigration from Germany and Austria. Thirty-two nations met and expressed concern about persecution and their hope for eventual resettlement of refugees. However, only the Dominican Republic eventually opened its doors to Jews. All the other nations gave reasons why they could not accommodate an increased number of Jews, some stating that Jews could not assimilate in their countries. See above, pp. 59-62.
105. N.N., 10/23/39, p. 14.
106. Ibid., 6/3/40, p. 8.
107. Two meetings of the Newark Council of the Zionist Organization of America demonstrate the change in emphasis. At the first meeting, two Newark rabbis from influential congregations spoke on problems facing Palestine. Rabbi Louis Levitsky of Newark's Temple Oheb Shalom argued that the spiritual and cultural forces of Zionist ideology were more important than the "physical upbuilding" of Palestine. Rabbi Julius Silberfeld, Rabbi Emeritus of Temple B'Nai Abraham, disputed Levitsky and said that the material upbuilding of Palestine was of vital concern, for without it "spiritual attainments could not be realized." Leo Yanoff, president of the Council was the conciliator and got all to agree that American Jews must provide both financial and moral concern over the future of Palestine.

    Six months later, the Zionist group heard Joseph Kraemer assert that "the Jews of military age in Palestine are eager to protect and defend that country and the Suez Canal from any Fascist army which may try to come through Egypt or Syria."

Kraemer recalled the Jewish Legion from World War I that helped the British conquer Palestine from Turkey. See, N.N., 6/20/40, p. 11; 10/8/40, p. 16.

108. N.N., 12/26/40, p. 26; J.C., 3/14/41, p. 7. Rabbi Meyer Bloomenfeld of Newark's Congregation Beth Samuel, a Zionist activist, organized the Newark branch of the American Federation of Polish Jews.

109. J.C., 9/22/39, p. 1.

110. N.N., 9/14/39, p. 8.

111. Records of the Committee to Defend America by Aiding the Allies, 1940-1942, MC #011 (hereafter cited as Committee to Defend America), Description of Collection, pp. 1-3. Chapters were formed in every state and in most important cities. In addition to a small paid staff, there were over 4,300 volunteers who worked at the Committee's National office in New York City. The group was ran a successful fundraising campaign that paid for operating expenses including print and radio communications to members and the public.

112. Ibid., Box 6, Folder, Executive Committee, List of National Committee Members.

113. Johnson, *The Battle Against Isolation*, p. 147.

114. N.N. , 7/22/40, p. 2.

115. At the same time Kurk assumed the chairmanship, Thomas asked Dante Cetrulo to assume the position. Cetrulo demurred, telling Thomas that he could not be active with the group because he needed a paying job. Several months later, Thomas asked Dr. Eagleton to investigate Kurk since "not much is being done in Newark." Eagleton wrote back that his inquiry into Kurk found "no criticism of his character or habits." Committee to Defend America, op. cit., Letters from Dante Cetrulo to Thomas, 7/26/40; Thomas to Eagleton, 10/9/40; Eagleton to Thomas, 11/20/40.

116. Committee to Defend America, Letter from William A. Lord to Hon. William H. Smathers, 8/21/40; Retired General William A. Lord (President of the Society of the War of 1812), sent letters to the entire New Jersey Congressional delegation.

117. Ibid., Letter from Kurk to Thomas, 9/3/40; Letter from Thomas to Kurk, 9/4/40; Letter from Kurk to Thomas, 10/31/40.

118. Johnson, *The Battle Against Isolation*, p. 147 When Eichelberger and White received an initial check for $3,000, the largest contribution to that point, they didn't know of the Eagletons. Afraid of accepting money from an "improper" source, they investigated the couple before cashing the check. The Committee would not accept donations of $1,000 or more from munitions makers or any "unsocial or improper source."

119. Committee to Defend America, Letter from Eagleton to Thomas, 11/20/40; J.C., 9/20/40, p. 3. The other Jewish members appointed were Jerome L. Kessler, Dr. Henry H. Kessler, Albert Abeles, Mrs. Joseph Reinfeld, and Mrs. Max Kummel.

120. Feingold, Henry L., *The Jewish People in America, A Time for Searching, Entering the Mainstream, 1920-1945,* Baltimore, MD, 1992, pp. 207-209.

121. Carlson, John Roy, *Under Cover*, New York, 1943, p. 56.

122. American Jewish Committee, op. cit., Box 20, 1939, pp. 661, 669.

123. Thomas J. Walsh Papers, RG 5, Box 5, Telegram from Charles E. Coughlin to Bishop Walsh, 7/28/35. The conservatism of the Newark Diocese was demonstrated when a Catholic official was requested to represent the diocese at a YMHA Lyceum panel on religious liberty. Alan Lowenstein, organizer of the series, called an acquaintance at the Associated Catholic Charities, Monsignor Trainor, who told him that the Diocese would supply no one for a Jewish program, and certainly not on the issue of religious freedom. Trainor told Lowenstein to call the Trenton Diocese, which was more liberal. Lowenstein's call was successful, and a Catholic speaker from Trenton traveled to Newark to represent the Catholic Church. Interviews, Alan V. Lowenstein, 6/9/98; 8/22/01.

124. John A. Matthews was described in a 1932 *Newark News* profile as one of the best-known figures in New Jersey public life. The article said that although Matthews was a "brilliant pleader at the bar, a forceful orator and an eloquent after dinner speaker" his real interest was philosophy, and every night he read the works of St. Thomas Aquinas, St. Augustine, Hegel, Kant, and Descartes in his study. Born to a working-class family in Massachusetts, Matthews originally studied for the priesthood, but

changed his mind and became a lawyer. In Newark as his legal career blossomed he became active in Catholic lay groups, particularly in the Holy Name Society. He entered Democratic politics and among his early activities were avid opposition to both women's suffrage and prohibition. After being elected to the New Jersey Legislature, he twice put out trial balloons to run for Governor, in 1927 and in 1933. He was later appointed an Advisory Master, which was then a position similar to a judge, except it was not full-time.

Matthews' oratorical abilities made him a sought after speaker particularly and through such engagements he was able to preach on a favorite topic— clean morals. In 1925 he spoke before Temple B'Nai Abraham on objectionable literature and plays. He asserted that the stage should be clean and that "the Jews could go a long way toward helping to keep it clean." The reaction by the congregation, if any, to this gratuitous advice was not recorded in the article. His later comments about Jews were thus presaged in 1925. See *Newark News* Morgue, File on John A. Matthews.

125. S.L., 3/18/39, pp. 1, 4.
126. N.N., 3/18/39, p. 3.
127. S.L., 3/18/39, p. 1; N.N., 3/18/39, p. 3.
128. Carlson, *Under Cover*, p. 68.
129. N.N., 10/30/39, p. 11.
130. Ibid., 9/1/39, p. 21.
131. Klehr, *The Heyday of American Communism*, pp. 387, 390.
132. CPUSA, Reel 307, Delo 4091: "American Question, a List of Documents," No.1, The Organizational Position of the CPUSA, 1/4/41, p. 1.
133. Klehr, *The Heyday of American Communism*, pp. 400, 409.
134. N.N., 8/24/39, p. 2; 9/22/39, p. 9; 11/6/39, p. 6.
135. Interview, Jack Gipfel, 1/7/97.
136. Interview, Martha Stone, 3/2/98.
137. Buhle, Paul, "Jews and American Communism: The Cultural Question," *Radical History Review*, 23, Spring 1980, p. 25.
138. N.N., 2/2/39, p. 5.
139. Interview, Nancy Cox, 4/8/97.
140. FBI, German-American League for Culture, File # 100-HQ-131905, Report of New York Office, 3/20/44, p. 8; Report of New York Office, 9/19/49, Enclosure—Booklet by Rudolf Brandl, "That Good Old Fool, Uncle Sam," 5/2/40, p. 15.
141. N.N., 7/24/40, p. 18.
142. J.C., 7/5/40, p. 8.
143. Despite communist domination at its Newark office, the state unit of Labor's Non-Partisan League under its leader, Carl Holderman, beat back communist attempts to dictate isolationist and anti-Roosevelt policies at the League's 1940 annual convention. The League endorsed both Roosevelt's defense policies and his intent to run for a third term despite stiff opposition from Communist controlled labor groups. See, CPUSA, Reel 315, Delo 4178, "Documents 11th Congress, CPUSA, May-June 1940," Speech of Larry Main (Lawrence Mahon), 5/31/40, p. 3.
144. The CIO had used the International Labor Defense during its New Jersey organizing drive, but by 1939 started to distance itself from Communist Party backing.
145. Cox, Nancy, unpublished manuscript, pp. 350, 351 Parker's wife, Nancy Cox, was also punished for his breach of discipline. She had been offered a $50 per week job as treasurer of the Jefferson School for Workers, a Marxist school in Manhattan. Lena Davis and Bill Norman had recommended her for the position immediately before the Nazi-Soviet Pact. The first day she reported to work she was told the offer was rescinded because of her husband's action. Cox, op. cit., pp. 351-354.
146. August Klapprott, New Jersey Bund leader, noted the decrease of communist attacks against the Bund since the pact, in an appearance before the October 1940 Dies Committee Hearing in Newark. See, N.N., 10/2/40, p. 2.
147. N.N., 5/2/40, p. 19.
148. Ibid., 5/8/40, p. 17; 5/15/40, p. 18.
149. Ibid., 5/18/40, p. 2.

150. S.L., 5/20/40, p. 7.
151. Ibid., p. 18.
152. Ibid., 5/22/40, p. 11.
153. CPUSA, Reed 315, Delo 4178: "Documents," Party Congress, CPUSA, May-June 1940, "Speech of Larry Main" (Lawrence Mahon), 5/31/40, p. 5.
154. Stenehjem, Michele Flynn, *An American First*, New Rochelle, NY, 1976, pp. 125, 131. This work is sympathetic to America First and is written by the daughter of John T. Flynn, chair of the group's New York Chapter, and a national leader of the movement. It is based mainly on the America First and John T. Flynn archives.

   Luke Garner, the third of Newark's great liberals, stayed away from headlines as he worked as Newark's labor relations director. His professional reputation as a mediator of labor-management disputes increased as he was credited with almost a 100 percent success rate in preventing strikes. He was appointed by Mayor Ellenstein to the Newark Defense Council, which was created in September 1940 to prepare the city if war came. When Ellenstein was defeated for reelection in 1941, Mayor Murphy immediately reorganized the Defense Council, dropping Garner from its membership. See, "Report of the Newark Defense Council 9/30/40—6/30/41."
155. S.L., 4/3/40, p. 2. During Kingdon's leave the Board made a decision based upon economics as well as politics. A $1,000,000 endowment campaign launched by the University of Newark was making little headway, and some trustees blamed the negative publicity resulting from Father Matthew Toohey's charge that the University were a "hotbed of Communism." Their argument that the campaign would only be successful if a conservative administration was installed and all radicals removed from the faculty was adopted by the board. Franklin Conklin, Chairman of the Board of Trustees, told Kingdon of the decision and gave him the opportunity to resign.

   The charge of "Communism" against the University of Newark was personally as well as professionally damaging to Kingdon. His son recalls that during this period, Kingdon stopped going to the Downtown Club (one of Newark's three elite luncheon clubs) because of the "unpleasant atmosphere." See, Interview, John Kingdon, 5/31/98.
156. Kingdon Papers, 1935-1940. The ERC smuggled distinguished anti-Nazis out of Europe who were on a Hitler list of approximately 3,000 to capture and kill. Most of these people escaped from Germany and Austria to France prior to the invasion of that country. They congregated in Marseilles hoping to get passage to America. It was to that city that the ERC dispatched Varian Fry to run the emergency operation.

   After Vichy France agreed to help the Nazis in capturing their enemies, it was almost impossible to sail from Marseilles. The only way they could escape was to be led over the Pyrenees to Portugal from where they would be transported to Lisbon and then boarded on ships to the United States. In its first year, the ERC through the efforts of Varian Fry, brought to America over 600 threatened individuals.
157. N.N., 10/14/40, p. 18; J.C., 10/18/40, p. 1.
158. J.C., 10/25/40, p. 1.
159. NSANL, Box 11, Folder 5, Letter from Harriman to Ross, 9/21/39.
160. Samuel Untermyer Papers, Box 1/2, Folder 1/2, Letter from Edward W. Russell to Dr. Benjamin Dubovsky, 7/5/40.
161. Gottlieb, *American Anti-Nazi Resistance*, pp. 293-296.
162. Executive Committee Meeting, Newark Conference of Jewish Charities, Report on Allocation Committee, 9/22/39.
163. NSANL, Box 11, Folder 5, Letter from Dr. Benjamin Dubovsky to Mr. R. Grant, 2/13/40.
164. Ibid., Box 12, Folder 3, Letters from NSANL national headquarters to Miss Helen Mendelson, 4/18/40 and to Mrs. Goldman, 7/12/40.
165. FBI, Non Sectarian Anti-Nazi League, File # 100-9552, Section 2, Report of 5/29/45, p. 6.
166. J.C., 3/29/40, p. 3.
167. N.N., 3/1/40, p. 13.
168. NSANL, op. cit., Letter from Dubovsky to Nathaniel Nathan, 1/20/41; Letter from Dubovsky to Kalb, 2/3/41.

169. Interview, Shirley Shapiro, 4/27/98 Shirley lived in Irvington on the corner of 16th Ave. and Grove St., in the center of the German-American neighborhood. Parallel to Grove was Myrtle Ave., where a large Polish population lived. Shirley was in her senior year at Irvington High School, when Germans attacked Poland on September 1. That night from her 3rd story porch on 16th Ave. she heard and saw a large disturbance on Grove St. She saw "men with bats and sticks beating up uniformed Bundists. Fighting and screaming went on for one or two hours and then the attackers left. Bodies were laying around. Ambulances and police came after the attackers had left. I later heard that this was a combination of Minutemen and Polish men from the Polish Hall. For weeks afterwards Polish and Jewish women would talk about how their men got together to beat up the Nazis."

170. Bayor, Ronald H., *Neighbors in Conflict, The Irish, Germans, Jews, and Italians of New York City, 1929-1941,* Urbana, 1988, *pp.* 97, 98, 101.

171. Ibid., pp. 29, 62.

172. Ibid., pp. 100, 101.

173. Ibid., pp. 99, 100, 196 note 42, 197 note 54.

174. N.N., 1/27/40, p. 4.

175. Bayor, *Neighbors in Conflict,* pp. 102, 103.

176. The plot included the bombing of Jewish neighborhoods and businesses, and the assassination of Jewish Congressmen. It was hoped that this terrorism would ignite a significant anti-Semitic movement in America, and cause the United States Army to be called in to protect the Jews. This would prove to the population that the Jews controlled the government. The Communists and Jews then would start a revolution to complete this control, and the Fronters would lead a counter revolution to set up a dictatorship and rid America of Jews. See, Bayor, Ibid.

177. J.C., 1/19/40, p. 1.

178. N.N. 2/3/40, p. 4; 4/16/40, p. 2.

179. Brady had been a protegee of Joseph Mann, a Jewish Democratic leader in Newark's Third Ward. Years after Mann's death, Brady was promoted to Captain of the 4th Precinct, and called Jack Gipfel into his office. Gipfel, Mann's nephew, was a young Communist Party worker who under the alias, Jack David, had gained notoriety in the city. Brady told Gipfel that he knew his lineage and that he should take a civil service test so he could get a "nice" office job. Gipfel expressed concern that he could pass the exam. Brady assured him, "We'll see that you pass it!" Gipfel never took the test. Interview, Jack Gipfel, 1/17/97.

180. S.L., 4/16/40, p. 1.

181. N.N., 4/15/40, pp. 1, 2; I.H., 4/18/40, p. 1.

182. N.N., 4/16/40, p. 2; S.L., 4/17/40, pp. 1, 2.

183. NYT, 4/17/40, p. 10.

184. N.N., 4/20/40, pp. 1, 2.

185. John B. Keenan, acting Public Safety Commissioner, charged that Ellenstein had destroyed the Vice Squad and had taken over the Department in response to Keenan's order to "raid everything raidable." N.N., 5/9/40, p. 1.

186. J.C., 4/26/40, p. 1.

187. NSANL, Box 2, Folder 5, Letter from Dubovsky to Harkavy, 4/20/40.

188. J.C., 4/19/40, p. 1.

189. N.N., 5/29/40, p. 14.

190. Ibid., 5/25/40, p. 1.

191. Ibid., 10/2/40, p. 5; J.C., 10/11/40, p. 3.

192. Interview, Faye Skuratofsky, 5/12/1996.

193. Glaser, Martha, "The German-American Bund in New Jersey," New Jersey History, Vol. XCII, N. 1., Spring 1974, p. 43.

194. S.L., 5/27/40, p. 1.

195. N.N., 5/23/40, p. 16.

196. Ibid., 5/24/40, p. 5; 5/25/40, p. 2.

197. Ibid., 9/25/40, p. 30.

198. Ibid., 6/20/40, p. 22.
199. Ibid., 9/3/40, p. 22; I.H., 9/5/40, p. 1.
200. S.C., 7/14/40, p. 1. Nazis had nothing to fear from this "secret" group. The group's first activity was to prevent an advertised "Deutsch Tag." It believed that Irvington Nazis were holding a "tag day" to raise funds. When a delegation of the unit went to the Irvington police for help in preventing the event, they were told that *tag* meant day in German, and that German Day was to be held in Springfield, not Irvington.
201. N.N, 7/5/40, p. 8.
202. Glaser, "The German-American Bund in New Jersey," op. cit.
203. N.N., 6/10/40, p. 2.
204. Ibid., 7/2/40, p. 14; J.C., 7/5/40, p. 1.
205. J.C., 7/5/40, p. 8.
206. Ibid., 7/12/40, p. 4.
207. U.S. Congressional Hearings, Investigation of Un-American Propaganda Activities in the United States, Committee on Un-American Activities House of Representatives, 77th Congress First Session, Vol. 14, p. 8317.
208. J.C., 8/23/40, p. 1.
209. N.N., 8/19/40, p. 1.
210. Ibid., 9/10/40, p. 1.
211. I.H., 8/29/40, p. 4; N.N., 10/1/40, p. 2.
212. CPUSA, Reel 307, Delo 4091: "American Question, a List of Documents," No. 1, The Organizational Position of the CPUSA, 1/4/41, p. 2. The loss of aliens was bemoaned in the document which stated: "Practically all the National bureaus of the CC [Central Committee] and the editorial boards of the national press were nearly depleted of their operational leadership." p. 4.
213. S.C., 9/8/40, p. 1.
214. J.C., 9/13/40, p. 1.
215. N.N., 6/7/40, p. 20; 6/11/40, p. 40; S.C., 6/9/40, p. 16; I.H., 6/13/40, p. 1.
216. S.C., 6/23/40, p 40
217. N.N., 6/10/40, p. 18.
218. Fred Hartley (1903-1969) served as United States Congressman from 1928 to 1948 when he chose not to run again. A conservative Republican, he represented a district including his hometown of Kearny and a large portion of Newark. He is best known for his co-sponsorship of the anti-labor Taft-Hartley Law. He was an active isolationist during the "great debate" and previously had spoken at Bund-sponsored events. His reelection bid in 1942 was opposed by a former supporter, George E. Stringfellow, senior vice president of Thomas A. Edison Industries, who was a Republican stalwart and civic leader. A.W. Hawkes, the 1942 Republican senatorial candidate and a fellow industrialist, asked Stringfellow to give financial aid to Hartley in order to help his own bid for office. Stringfellow, in reply, analyzed the isolationist voting record of the Representative and added:
    In addition to this record, he has done much to discourage our people by his activities with the American First Committee and through his association with the Bund. It might be argued that if Fred isn't re-elected, and I sincerely hope that he is not, a New Dealer will replace him. I can think of a lot of New Dealers, and so can you, who have made a better record, especially in the last two years.
    See, *Newark News* Morgue, Fred Hartley, Letter from George S. Stringfellow to A.W. Hawkes, 6/15/42.
219. N.N., 7/12/40, p. 4.
220. German-American Bund, Box 13, F 217, Letter from Dr. Frances Just to Wilhelm Kunze, 5/9/40.
221. S.L., 7/15/40, p. 1.
222. FBI, Matthias Kohler, File No: HQ 100-9464, Section 1, Letter from Unit Leader to German-American League League, 8/5/40.
223. N.N., 9/10/40, p. 2.
224. J.C., 7/19/40, p. 1.

225. The fleet was to be turned over by Vichy to the Nazis to use against the British.
226. N.N., 7/13/40, p. 3.
227. J.C., 7/19/40, pp. 1, 4.
228. N.N., 7/19/40, p. 6.
229. S.C., 9/15/40, p. 1.
230. Jonas, Manfred, *Isolationism in America 1935-1941*, Ithaca, NY, 1966, p. 92.
231. Ibid., pp. 94, 95, 239, 253, 254.
232. Committee to Defend America, Series 1, Box 7, America First, Confidential Report on America First, 12/40, pp. 1,2,8. This eighteen page document has no attribution, but a predecessor of Fight for Freedom, the Century Group, which often cooperated with the CDA issued a "Detailed Report on America First Committee" on 11/27/40. See, Chadwin, Mark Lincoln, *The Hawks of World War II*, Chapel Hill, 1968, p. 120, footnote 29.
233. N.N., 12/14/40, p. 2. Early in 1941 Chicago and New York newspapers requested both the Committee to Defend America and America First to list their contributors of over $100. The Committee to Defend America complied and issued a detailed report of all such contributors. America First said it would have to first ask permission of the donors before publishing names. After some weeks only half the donors gave such authorization. Thomas N. McCarter was one of the sixty-six allowing his name to be published. See, NYT, 3/12/41, p. 1; N.N., 3/12/41, p. 2.
234. Doenecke, Justus D., *In Danger Undaunted: The Anti-Interventionist Movement of 1940-1941 as Revealed in the Papers of the America First Committee*, Stanford, CA, 1990, p. 12.
235. N.N., 9/16/40, p. 2.
236. Ibid., 9/21/40, p. 1.
237. Ibid., 8/20/40, p. 4, 9/5/40, p. 1.
238. U. S. Congressional Hearings, Investigation of Un-American Propaganda, p. 8256.
239. Ibid., pp. 8302, 8304.
240. N.N., 12/16/40, p. 7.
241. German-American Bund, 304 A, Box 2, *Wir Sturmer*, Newark, 12/40, 1/41 The writing for *Wir Sturmer* was done exclusively by men. The Madchenschaft brought refreshments to the men, were thanked, and then "unceremoniously ushered out." *Wir Sturmer*, 1/41, p. 3.
242. Ibid., Box 10, Folder 145, Letter from Gerhard Spieler to Newark Bund, 11/27/40.
243. N.N., 9/24/40, p. 20; 10/10/40, p. 1; 10/11/40, p. 13; 10/18/40, p. 2; 11/15/40, p. 30.
244. Ibid., 10/19/40, p. 2; 11/28/40, p. 5; S.C., 12/1/40, p. 12. Lucille Milner, nominally Roger Baldwin's secretary, but more importantly an active independent voice within the ACLU (she wrote civil liberties articles for the *New Republic, Harpers,* the *Nation,* and others), was troubled by the decision of the ACLU to defend Klapprott. While admitting the "badness" of the anti-Nazi legislation, she countered this with the fact that the Bundists were out to deny civil rights to a minority group (Jews), to repeal the Bill of Rights, and the 14th and 15th Amendments, "which we are organized to uphold." See ACLU, Reel 189, V 2239, Memo from Milner to Jerome Britchey, Staff Counsel, 12/16/40.
245. N.N., 6/11/40, p. 16; 8/21/40, p. 26.
246. Ibid., 9/13/40, p. 3.
247. S.C., 10/13/40, p. 8.
248. Feingold, *A Time for Searching*, p. 207. Jewish interventionism did not include the espousal of American entry into the war until after Pearl Harbor. Feingold, ibid., p. 209.

9

1941, America Enters the War

President Roosevelt and a majority in Congress took the reins of the anti-Nazi battle as America headed toward war in 1941. Consequently, Newark's anti-Nazi campaign was transformed. By the spring of 1941, the local branch of the Non-Sectarian Anti-Nazi League (NSANL) was defunct; the German-American Bund was too weak to muster meetings in Newark or Irvington; and the Minutemen, with no Bund to fight, had virtually retired from the battlefield. The focus of Newark's Jewish community shifted from the threat of Nazism to war preparedness.

The Newark branch of the Committee to Defend America (CDA), which included much of the city's Protestant elite as well as liberals, labor union leaders, and government officials led the campaign for intervention. Most of Newark's German, Italian, and Irish Americans were against intervention but stayed on the sidelines, realizing that America was headed toward war. Newark's premier liberal trio parted ways over intervention: Amelia Moorfield remained a pacifist, whereas Frank Kingdon and Luke Garner, former pacifists, became ardent interventionists. When Germany attacked the Soviet Union on June 21, 1941 the communists re-assumed their pre Nazi-Soviet Pact stance and switched from isolationism to interventionism. The remnants of Newark's Bund and Christian Front, on the other hand, transferred their allegiance to the America First Committee (AFC), the country's leading isolationist organization.

* * *

While Bund and Christian Front activities were at a minimum, the Minutemen nevertheless remained attentive to any new threat. Arno's

307

role with the Minutemen ended when his draft board called him to
report for a physical in February, 1941. He passed the exam and the
same day was sent for basic training to Fort Dix, New Jersey. Reporters from both Newark dailies were present to capture Arno's last
quip before he left Newark:

> I feel like a lion and am anxious to get going in the army. It won't be easy going from
> Commander of the Minutemen to buck private in the army. What a letdown! [1]

Arno did not forget business before he departed. He met with
Max Feilschuss and turned over command of the group to the "chaplain," authorizing him to solicit contributions, although—as he told the
press—he himself would continue to control "all problems of policy."[2]

* * *

The German-American Bund drew its last breath in 1941, without
help from Arno. Federal, state, and local investigations in 1939 and
1940 had weakened the organization, and by 1941 only the most
diehard Nazis remained—many of them aliens. German Americans
who had joined or sympathized with the Bund in its heyday either
worked with the AFC or kept their views to themselves.

The January 1941 sentencing of nine Bundists found guilty of
inciting "race hatred" to jail terms of from one year to fourteen months
presaged a difficult year for the Bund. Judge John Losey said that
the Bundists were attempting to gain Gentile ascendancy over Jews
despite the Constitution's proclamation that all men were equal. Bund
leaders Gerhard William Kunze, August Klapprott, and Matthias
Kohler were released on bail pending appeal while the others were
held until the Bund raised additional money.[3]

Irvington's public safety director reported that the city was no
longer a "Nazi hotbed." The director of the city's subversive activities squad claimed that he had a list of former Nordland attendees
who lived in Irvington, and that most had dropped out of Bund activities. The squad also had lists of attendees at all "un-American
meetings" held in Irvington.[4]

The Newark Bund ceased activities in Newark and Irvington by
April. A remnant of the group led by Matthias Kohler tried to operate out of Camp Nordland, where August Klapprott maintained his
headquarters. The camp, now under federal, state, and local surveillance, was seen as a security threat and authorities decided it was

time to shut it down. On May 30, Sussex County Sheriff Denton Quick raided Nordland and ordered it closed as a "public nuisance." Accompanied by an FBI agent, eight deputies, and members of the Andover Township Committee, Quick searched the entire camp, confiscating Nazi propaganda and a small amount of ammunition. Klapprott and fifty Bundists were ejected. Paul Huissel of Newark was arrested when he refused to vacate the premises. A diary listing Nazi officials and sympathizers with codes after their names and a road map with markings at reservoirs in the New York watershed were seized. One notation in the diary read: "Lindbergh will take command of the United States when Hitler wins."[5]

The raid on Nordland was quickly followed by a resolution of the New Jersey Legislature revoking the charter of the corporation that owned Nordland. The ACLU protested to New Jersey Governor Charles Edison, but to no avail.[6] Anticipating the legislative initiative, the Bund sold the entire property to 218 sympathizers. Sheriff Quick announced the closing of the property and denied its transfer to the "new" owners. He simultaneously took possession of the camp for the state.

Two of the 218 new owners of the camp filed suit against Quick's action. Judge James F. Fielder threw out the suit, opining that the United States was on the verge of war with Germany and that it must do everything possible to protect itself. He added that many of those who attended Nordland call themselves German Americans, but are "Germans to their souls and are anti-American."[7]

After Nordland's closing, Klapprott moved the New Jersey Bund headquarters to Union City. Mayor Harry Thourot immediately cancelled the liquor license of the bar and adjoining beer garden that served as Bund headquarters on the grounds that it was a nuisance and that the conduct there was "contrary to the principles of our American life." Thourot placed a large sign on the fence surrounding the beer garden that read: "God Bless America. Love America or Leave America."[8]

During the summer of 1941 two German-American anti-Nazi groups whose aims were to demonstrate German-American patriotism and minimize anti-German discrimination were formed in Newark. The first was the Essex-Union-Hudson chapter of the German-American Congress for Democracy. The national group, claiming 15,000 members, had been founded less than a year earlier with the express purpose of teaching Americans the difference between Germans and Nazis.[9] The second anti-Nazi group, Loyal Americans of German Descent, was partially funded by Fight for Freedom,[10] a more militant interventionist group than the CDA. Loyal Americans' New Jersey leader was Carl Holderman, state chairman of Labor's Non-Partisan League[11] and a prominent state official in the Congress of Industrial Organizations (CIO), who later became president of the New Jersey CIO. According to Holderman, workers of German extraction who joined Loyal Americans helped fight "blind discrimination."[12]

Italian Americans were also eager to prove their Americanism in the face of "fifth column" charges. A February, 1941 *Newark Sunday Call* survey found more American flags displayed on Lincoln's Birthday in Italian neighborhoods than anywhere else in the city. The survey determined that the community was split evenly between pro-and anti Mussolini sentiment, with those several generations removed from Italy more likely to reject "Il Duce" than those born there. War discussion was soft-pedaled in favor of avid debates on the upcoming municipal elections, in which several Italian Americans were candidates.[13] In March, in retaliation for the closing of the American consulates in Palmero and Naples and restrictions on the movement of American diplomats in Italy, the United States ordered the closing of Italian consulates in Detroit and Newark. Newark's Italian-American community did not protest.[14]

The Newark YWCA held a panel discussion on job discrimination at its January 1941 annual meeting in response to the high number of complaints from both the Italian and German-American communities. Women of Italian and German extraction told attendees about their experiences with discrimination, and YWCA members determined that there should be more education in Newark schools regarding the patriotism of the two ethnic groups.[15]

As the year unfolded, most Newark Italian-Americans who had been sympathetic to Mussolini became supportive of American defense efforts. The Sons of Italy, the largest Italian-American civic association in Newark and in Essex County, opposed Mussolini. The seventeen lodges in Essex County supported a resolution in August that denounced all "isms"—communism, Nazism, and fascism. They also pledged their resources, devotion, and loyalty to America because "we are for America and America only."[16] That fall's Columbus Day event was indicative of the reduced support for Mussolini in the city. Unlike the previous year's event, all Italian-American groups participated. The celebration was returned to the Columbus monument in Washington Park and the parade was reinstated. The speakers extolled democracy and denounced fascist publications in Italy that had recently claimed that Columbus had made a "mistake" in discovering America.[17]

* * *

Interfaith organizations continued to refute Nazi racial and religious doctrines and to demonstrate the unity of Newarkers of various religions and ethnicities. Rev. William Hiram Foulkes and Rev. Clarence Bleakney worked with these organizations throughout 1941. At a New Year's candle lighting ceremony at Newark's First Presbyterian Church, Rev. Foulkes said,

> I light this candle for some little baby about to be born to some young Jewish mother in one of those unspeakable concentration camps...or unspeakable ghettos. I do so in the memory of the One whose birthday we now celebrate. God have mercy upon us![18]

Less than a week later, at the 150th anniversary celebration of "Old First," Foulkes deplored bigotry and the persecution of European Jews.[19]

The Good Will Commission of New Jersey, which was based in Newark, became the focus of both clerics' efforts in 1941. When President Roosevelt proclaimed the last week of February "Brotherhood Week," the commission decided to sponsor Brotherhood Week in Newark and invite Catholics, Protestants, and Jews to participate. The example of the Good Will Commission inspired Abraham Silverstein, President of the Commencement in Absentia League, to change the name of his group to the League for the Advancement of Good Will. In coordination with the Commission, this new Jewish organization held meetings and symposia with churches and other Christian groups.[20]

Luke Garner spoke before Newark Jewish groups on refugee and civil rights issues throughout the year, even after losing his City Hall job in May when his mentor, Mayor Meyer Ellenstein, was defeated for reelection.[21] Frank Kingdon, now a national figure, divided his time between New York and Washington, making few Newark appearances in 1941.[22] However, the former president of Newark University made news each time he spoke in the city. Kingdon's first speaking engagement of the year in Newark was at an interfaith forum, "Which Way Democracy?" at which he advocated increasing President Roosevelt's power to grant aid to the Allies and promulgate American defense policies. Another panelist, Rabbi Solomon Foster, always a man of caution, said that democracy would best be served by the study of "community problems" rather than by increasing presidential powers. To avoid offending either man, the forum ducked the issue and unanimously passed a resolution calling for a democracy "truly free from intolerance and hostility toward racial and religious groups."[23]

Kingdon co-sponsored a dinner in Newark with the New Jersey Committee for National Sharecroppers Week as part of his fundraising activities for the Emergency Rescue Committee. Norman Thomas, sponsor of the national "Week," was the main speaker. This unlikely combination of causes drew only a hundred people. Kingdon complimented Thomas's courage in dealing with the "practical application of democracy" in support of sharecroppers. Thomas said he shared Kingdon's concern for the "victims of Europe's war."[24]

The Jewish refugee problem continued to attract attention in Newark in 1941, albeit from a different perspective than in the past. Immediate settlement in Palestine was no longer an option because of the war in Europe. The Newark district of the Zionist Organization of America (ZOA) welcomed national speakers to discuss the creation of a Jewish state after the war. To prepare for this eventuality financially and politically, district president, Leo Yanoff, announced a campaign to sign up 2,000 new members,[25] and a plan to expand the ZOA to all of Essex County.[26] The Newark United Palestine Appeal, an agency of the United Jewish Appeal, met at the same time to discuss its vision and make plans for the future. Over 400 heard Rabbi Baruch Braunstein of New York predict that after the war penniless refugees in Europe could prove a "leaven for revolution," leading new governments to work for Palestine as a Jewish homeland. Rabbi Stephen Wise, National Co-Chair of the Appeal, predicted that the war would end in a year and the dominant theme at the "peace table" would be equal rights for all men. He anticipated that one to two million refugees would enter Palestine from Nazi dominated lands.[27]

A truly Christian response to the plight of Jewish refugees came from Dr. Conrad Hoffman, Episcopal national director for missionary activities to the Jews. In a talk before the refugee committee of Newark's Trinity Church, he said what most Jewish leaders were afraid to say. Hoffman called the refugees a Christian problem and urged America to accept the refugees lest Hitler "exterminate all the Jews of Europe." He also denied that refugees would take jobs from Americans. On the contrary, Hoffman stated, the newcomers would create new jobs because they would create new industries in America. [28]

Two Jewish voices not affiliated with the Zionist movement took a position similar to Hoffman's. Joseph Steiner, president of the Emigre Service Bureau of New Jersey, echoed the Episcopalian leader in denying that refugees took jobs from Americans. He decried the fact that since 1940 more Christian refugees than Jewish ones were being allowed to enter America.[29] Rabbi Marius Ranson of Temple Sharey Tefilo called for liberalization of American immigration policy, stating, "It ill behooves a nation of 130 million to accept only 27,000 refugees a year. As President Roosevelt has said, we are all refugees."[30]

April witnessed the Nazi invasions of Greece and Yugoslavia. Robert Minor, acting head of the American Communist Party, excused rather than condemned the Nazi aggression at the 1941 May Day Rally in Newark. He told an audience of 600 that the Tory government of Britain, the French capitalist government, and President Roosevelt were all to blame because they had aided Hitler. Minor warned against letting Britain trap the United States into war. Lawrence Mahon, Essex County Communist Party secretary, said the party was not only against war but also against air raid drills in Newark![31] The author and lecturer Johannes Steele, on the other hand, urged an immediate declaration of war against Germany. Speaking before the Essex County United Jewish Appeal, Steele said it was necessary for the United States to go to war to prevent Hitler's triumph in Europe and the eventual loss of American liberty.[32]

The Minutemen became involved in Newark's Great Debate after the AFC established its Newark office. AFC's anti-Semitic reputation coupled with participation by Bundists and Christian Fronters in the group, brought the Minutemen back into action. At the initial meeting of Newark's AFC in June, 1941, its chairman, Milton Fulle, declared, "Our first duty is to keep America out of foreign wars." Fulle stated that communists, fascists, Nazis, and Bundists were not eligible for membership in the AFC. However, at the AFC's very next meeting, Ernest Hawkins, president of the Newark Christian Front, was one of the speakers. He claimed "the foreign policy of the United States is made in London by Winston Churchill." The 100 attendees gave their biggest cheer of the evening to a comment from the floor hailing Charles Lindbergh as "our leader."[33] By the end of July, the Newark chapter claimed 2,909 members, including former Newark Bund leader Herman Von Busch, who volunteered his services because "if this country is to be saved from ruin and destruction, it can only be done by fearless American men." Von Busch claimed that those wearing the AFC button "are being sneered and stared at." His offer of assistance was accepted.[34]

At the August AFC meeting, fifty participants signed a petition requesting national chairman General Robert E. Wood to "organize and support a march on Washington as the only way to keep our country out of war." The Newark chapter promised its unequivocal support and predicted that a march of millions would "recapture Washington for the American people." The national office replied that such a march had been discussed many times, but since it had the potential to destroy the organization, it would only be held as a last resort.[35] John T. Flynn, New York City AFC chairman, had already rejected demands for a Washington march because "a large mass of people in already overcrowded Washington might easily become disorderly and bring discredit to the AFC movement."[36]

Chicago and New York newspapers requested that the AFC and the CDA list contributors of over one hundred dollars. The CDA complied, whereas the AFC said it would have to first ask the donors' permission before publishing names. After some weeks it released a list of only half its contributors, without any dollar amounts. Thomas N. McCarter, Chairman of Newark's Public Service Electric and Gas, was one of the sixty-six who allowed his name to be published.[37]

* * *

Hitler's June, 1941 invasion of the Soviet Union was a watershed for European Jewry, and caused the collapse of the Nazi-Soviet Pact. During the summer, mass killings of Jews in Bialystock and Minsk by advancing Nazi forces were reported in the Newark Jewish press.[38] They were followed by news of the deportation of German Jews to Poland and the mass slaughter of Polish Jews.[39] In September, Hitler specifically targeted Jews when he said that Germany was not only fighting for its own existence, "but for the existence of all Europe against Jewish capitalism and bolshevism."[40]

The invasion of the Soviet Union forced another about face for the American Communist Party.[41] It reverted to its pre-pact denunciations of Nazism, support for Roosevelt, and united-front strategy.

Party affiliates in Newark sought to ally with the Newark CDA. This created a subplot in the Great Debate—a struggle between communists and non-communists over who would lead the Newark interventionists.

American Youth Congress (AYC) members began attending CDA meetings in the summer.[42] The Congress had lost much of its support, including that of First Lady, Eleanor Roosevelt, after it backed the Nazi Soviet Pact and the Soviet invasion of Poland and the Baltic countries in 1939.[43] Following the invasion of the Soviet Union, the AYC sought to recoup its credibility by taking a vigorous interventionist stance. Members of the Newark CDA were split over AYC participation because of the youth group's communist reputation. However, the committee decided to accept AYC aid because it had failed to attract other youth groups. By the end of the summer, Newark Communist party members were also attending CDA meetings.

Communists were not the AFC's only enemies in Newark. Minutemen attended its meetings and observed Bundist and Christian Front participation. Despite their anti-Roosevelt and anti-British invective, AFC speakers were careful not to mention the word "Jew," employing instead the time-tested innuendos of "international conspirators" and "banking interests." The meetings were held in downtown Newark with police protection.

The police, however, were not the Minutemen's main deterrent. Rather, it was indecision on how to deal with the AFC, a group supported by prominent business leaders, congressmen, and America's best-known hero, Charles Lindbergh. This foe was vastly different from the Friends of the New Germany, the Bund, the Silver Shirts, and the Christian Front.

Charles Lindbergh delivered his infamous speech "Who Are the War Agitators" at an AFC rally in Des Moines, Iowa on September 11, 1941. He cited the Roosevelt administration, the British, and the Jews as the three groups pushing the country toward war,[44] arguing that "the greatest danger to this country lies in their [the Jews] large ownership and influence in our motion picture industry, our press, our radio, and our government." He threatened that in the advent of war American Jews would be "among the first to feel its consequences."[45] Ninety-three percent of the nation's press denounced the speech. Lindbergh's characterization of powerful Jews as advocates of intervention was incorrect. Those Jews closest to Roosevelt dealt primarily with domestic affairs and were afraid to take a position in the Great Debate.[46]

Fellow isolationist and AFC leader Senator Gerald P. Nye of North Dakota defended Lindbergh. Nye accused Jews of seeking to drag America into war to avenge Hitler's persecution of their co-religionists. New York Senator Robert Wagner denounced Lindbergh and Nye for using "Hitler's well-known, well-worn tactics of weakening his prospective victims from within by inciting racial animosities."[47]

The response in Newark was immediate. At a City Hall CDA meeting, business, labor, and religious leaders denounced Lindbergh and Nye.[48] Carl Holderman condemned Nye and Lindbergh for their "smug warnings to the Jews to withdraw from public life." Holderman recalled that the same warnings had been issued to Jews during the Nazi rise to power in Germany. He also warned that the AFC's next step would be to create a political movement as "a logical development for those who, knowingly or not, follow in Hitler's path."[49] The *Newark Star Ledger* chastised Nye for singling out Jews. The paper said, "Nye and Lindbergh preach a peculiar doctrine for a Christian civilization when they imply that none but Jews have a grievance against Adolph Hitler. They should not judge the good people of other races who inhabit this country by the coldness of their own souls."[50]

Thomas N. McCarter resigned from the AFC to protest the Lindbergh speech, stating "it is a time for tolerance; not for intolerance." The organization asked McCarter not to publicize his action, since it would be "eagerly seized upon by a hostile press."[51] McCarter agreed and said nothing for over a month. However, with the AFC presence in Newark attracting increasing publicity, he issued a press release that he had resigned from the group after its "activities developed and became better known." When asked by the press to elaborate, McCarter refused comment.[52]

Most America Firsters agreed with Lindbergh's speech; 90 percent of the letters members sent to the Chicago national office were supportive. American Firsters speaking in New York received their most favorable crowd responses of the year immediately after Des Moines.[53] Several days after Lindbergh's remarks, Newark's AFC announced a September 23 rally at the Mosque Theater featuring Senator Nye. This was to be the AFC's first rally in the city. The fourteen-member committee appointed to organize the rally included

Ernest Hawkins, Newark's Christian Front leader, and nine German Americans.[54]

The CDA met at City Hall to plan a response. This was the opportunity the AYC and the communists had been waiting for, and they packed the meeting. Over 150 participants unanimously agreed on a counter-rally at the Mosque one week after the AFC's. Committee president Diran Kurk appointed a ten-person organizing committee, which included Rabbi Joachim Prinz and Newark Mayor Vincent Murphy, but no AYC members or communists. There was general opposition to an AYC motion to picket the AFC rally. A compromise was reached that allowed individual groups to picket but only under their own banners.[55]

National AYC chairman Jack McMichael, an ordained Methodist minister and chairman of the National Intercollegiate Christian Youth Council the college division of the YM&YWCA[56] arrived in Newark after the CDA meeting at City Hall hoping to convince the CDA to authorize a Newark youth division under AYC leadership, thus creating a "popular front."[57] CDA maintained youth and college divisions, most of which were in the northeast.[58] New Jersey had two relatively inactive college branches, one at Seton Hall College and another at the New Jersey College for Women (now part of Rutgers University).[59] There were no youth branches in New Jersey when McMichael arrived.

Longie Zwillman also used the AFC rally to demonstrate his strength. He called several of his lieutenants, including Max Feilshuss, and instructed them to have a large force at the rally but not to use violence. Rumors of a Minuteman action reached Police Chief John F. Harris, who gave orders to protect the rally because "there may be a disturbance," promising to deploy twenty detectives from the alien and radical squad and a large contingent of patrolman.[60]

Interest in the rally was piqued by Fight for Freedom's (FFF)[61] large ad in the *Newark News* on the day it was to take place. In challenging Sen. Nye's isolationist and racist views, the ad declared: "We demand that you stop spreading disunity by mouthing Hitler's doctrines of racial prejudice."[62]

The Minutemen began to assemble in front of the Mosque one hour before the rally. Following instructions, the men carried no weapons or picket signs. Asked about the Minuteman presence, Max Feilschuss told a reporter they were there to "listen and look things over."[63]

While the CDA picketed, the Minutemen eyeballed the American Firsters. Police cleared a path between the latter two groups so that attendees could enter unmolested. Jack McMichael led scores of men, women, and teens carrying homemade banners and signs urging aid to Britain and blasting the isolationists with such insults as, "Rattlesnakes Lindbergh, Nye, Goebbels, Wheeler" and "Senator Nye Hitler thanks you for your services." Several America Firsters carried signs proclaiming "Nye or Die."[64] Over 120 Newark police tried to maintain order. By 8PM approximately 3,000 people—equally divided between men and women—filled the Mosque, while outside another 1,500 listened to the speeches from loud speakers, their cheering and booing matching the reactions inside.[65] The anti-AFC pickets tried to drown out their adversaries. The hundred Minutemen, however, were silent as they listened intently for anti-Semitic comments.

Seton Hall professor James F. O'Connell presided. He said that his opinions were not to be construed as those of the college.[66] O'Connell claimed that democracy was facing a crisis, not from foreign countries, but from within. He accused certain interests in the country, "either through conviction or through ulterior motives, of bringing us closer and closer to disaster." He urged the crowd to flood the president and Congress with mail opposing American entry into the war. The highlight of the evening, however, was Nye's speech. He excoriated President Roosevelt's policy of "hunting trouble" by trying to bring America into war in violation of the Constitution and against the will "of the great majority of American people. It shall have to be everlastingly recorded that there never was a better time for peace than now," he said. Nye declared that neither he nor Lindbergh had "an anti-Semitic hair in his head." On several occasions, police had to remove hecklers.[67]

The AFC speakers were very careful to avoid overtly anti-Semitic statements. However, when Roosevelt's name was mentioned "wild hisses" erupted, whereas when Hitler's was spoken there was no response. The next day's *Star Ledger* editorial said:

> The audience stamped itself and the speakers unmistakably. Hisses for our chosen President and respect for the Nazi lunatic who has plunged the world into chaos! And not a word of rebuke from the eminent gentlemen on the platform! [68]

When the event ended, the audience filed out without incident. The Minutemen, the picketers, and the America Firsters went home with different impressions of the rally. The America Firsters were elated about the overflow crowd and still abuzz over Nye's speech. The AYC pickets were satisfied that their voices had been heard. The only dissatisfied participants were the Minutemen. They had obeyed orders and caused no fuss but were confused as to what their response to the AFC should be. They waited for further developments.

***

Newark newspapers carried frontpage coverage of the rally, featuring pictures of picketers identified as CDA members. Kurk was furious because some of the banners had the Committee's name on them, contrary to the compromise they had worked out. They could not control the communists, a fact soon known at CDA New York headquarters.[69] Frances Thomas wrote Frank Kingdon in Washington asking for advice. She told him that a Newark dentist, Dr. Isadore Weinman, suggested that a good leader, such as Rev. Lester Clee, the moderate minister of Newark's Second Presbyterian Church and former Republican candidate for governor, would attract an "excellent group of people" who could rid the CDA of communist influence.[70] Weinman spoke with Clee and Beatrice Winser, Director of the Newark Library and a close friend of Frank Kingdon, about eliminating Kurk and forcing the communist groups to "gracefully" withdraw from the organization.[71] Whether due to Weinman's efforts or disillusion, Kurk announced he would resign at the end of October. There was to be no "graceful" withdrawal of communists from the Committee.

Communists and the AYC packed the CDA's next meeting on October 30. The first order of business was Kurk's resignation. Since Clee had not decided whether to take the chairmanship, a motion was made to hold another meeting to choose Kurk's successor. The communist forces defeated the motion and nominated Joseph Marzell, an AYC veteran. In the absence of another candidate, Marzell was elected temporary chairman.[72] Marzell, an AYC leader in the mid-1930s, was McMichael's hand-picked choice. The new leader's first order of business was to entertain a motion to establish the Newark Youth Committee to Aid the Allies. The motion passed with little opposition. The Mosque rally was postponed until December 11 to give the new leadership time to get speakers and organize the event.[73] Jack McMichael now controlled Newark's major interventionist organization.[74]

When Marzell informed Frances Thomas of his election, her response was to begin searching for a more appropriate chairman and

to attempt widening the Newark group's base to counter its communist tilt. She and Weinman tried to convince both Clee and Dr. Wells
Eagleton to head the group, but both refused. The situation was so
serious that CDA's national chairman, Clark Eichelberger, wrote Msgr.
John Delaney of Newark's St. Patrick's Cathedral to ask him to be
honorary chairman of the Newark branch. Delaney refused. Thomas fared no better in her attempt to expand the Committee's base.
She sent out several letters asking her New York contacts for lists of
anti-fascist Italians in Newark who would work with the chapter, but
received no satisfactory responses.[75]

November 11, Armistice Day, witnessed the first organized effort
of the Newark Youth Committee to Aid the Allies. The holiday was
tailor-made for another confrontation between interventionists and
isolationists over a bill before Congress to amend the Neutrality Act
in order to permit America to give unrestricted aid to Britain. The
AFC announced its second Mosque Theater rally would take place
on Armistice Day evening. William H. "Alfalfa Bill" Murray, former
governor of Oklahoma, Representative Fred A. Hartley, Jr.,[76] and
Professor James J. O'Connell were to be the speakers.[77]

McMichael announced a CDA youth committee rally for the same
evening at Newark City Hall. He asserted that American youth "can
outdo the Nazi regimented robot in war as in peace."[78] McMichael
and David Hirschhorn, president of the Newark branch of the Cardozo
Club, an interventionist group,[79] set to work organizing the rally. He
asked city officials, particularly those in civil defense, to help legiti-
mize his group and attract more members. McMichael knew his actions had alienated most pre-June 1941 CDA members, but he hoped
a successful rally would win back some of the disaffected.

The AFC's Armistice Day rally at the Mosque drew 1,500 people.
Murray was not as great an attraction as Sen. Nye, and the AFC had
lost ground to the interventionists during the previous two months.
The sixty Newark police present had little to do since there were no
hecklers inside the theater or protestors outside. The Minutemen did
not show up. Professor O'Connell opened the rally and claimed that
the recent sinking of American cargo ships was the fault not of Nazi
aggression but of Roosevelt's purposeful policy to "incite us, the
people, to a state of war." The audience passed a resolution urging
all congressmen to vote against revision of the Neutrality Act. The
next speaker, Rep. Hartley, said that the President was moving the
country closer to war by "control of the press, radio, and movies,"

and the only way of expressing opposition was through the AFC. He asserted that there was no use in "fighting a dictator 3,000 miles away when we have set up one at home." Hartley also accused the Roosevelt administration of harboring communists in key positions. "Alfalfa Bill" Murray, a seventy-four-year-old westerner with a thick drawl, bushy eyebrows, and a flowing mustache, spoke seated on a chair. He outdid Hartley with an anti-Roosevelt tirade that denounced the president as an aspiring Stalin. Murray predicted that FDR would never leave the White House on his own, and it would take a second American revolution to "return the country to the people."[80]

The meeting of the Newark Youth CDA was held one block away at City Hall. A group of 250, mainly high school and college age, heard David Hirschhorn blast AFC's call for an immediate negotiated peace with Hitler, which "would result in world slavery." McMichael said the AFC was anti-Semitic and should rename itself "Nazis First." The rally ended with a resolution calling for repeal of the Neutrality Act and all-out aid for the Allies (Britain and the Soviet Union); a Congressional investigation of the "true nature and affiliations" of the AFC; expulsion of all Nazi agents from the United States; and support of Roosevelt's defense program and foreign policy. The CDA also pledged support for civilian defense. Harold John Adonis [81] of the Newark Defense Council asked everyone in the audience to register with his organization.[82]

The rally's rhetoric, along with the participation of known Newark communists, disturbed moderate and liberal elements in the Newark CDA. Non-communist AFL and CIO leaders left the group and organized the United Labor Committee to Help Defeat Hitlerism. They announced an anti-Hitler rally at the Mosque for December 4, one week before the Newark CDA's Mosque event.[83] Other moderates and liberals, unwilling to risk the publicity that an attempt to wrest control of their group from McMichael would generate, founded the Essex County Chapter of the CDA and within two weeks had over a hundred members.

Six days before Pearl Harbor, thirty people came to the inaugural meeting of the Essex CDA and selected Robert E. Moore, a Newark industrialist, chairman and Dr. Wells Eagleton and Judge Richard Hartshorne honorary chairmen. Hartshorne said the group's prime purpose was "to attain a public unity behind the actions of our elected representatives." In a slap at McMichael, Hartshorne criticized efforts to become involved in issues "wherein we have no actual knowledge." Eagleton, describing Newark as one of the most metropolitan cities in the country, urged Newarkers to unite behind the United States government. The group voted to stage "the biggest rally in the history of the city" at the Mosque Theater on January 7, and predicted an overflow crowd of "all nationalities and creeds to fill the streets of Newark."[84] There were now three Mosque rallies planned by Newark interventionists, all aimed, at least in part, at the AFC.

At the end of November, the AFC held what was to be its final event in Newark at Ukrainian Hall. This venue was chosen to gain support for non-intervention from Newark's Ukrainian population, which was for the most part anti-Soviet. Professor James F. O'Connell was the featured speaker and said that claims Hitler was seeking to conquer the world were "so much baloney." In opposing aid to the Soviet Union, then at war with Nazi Germany, O'Connell stated that such aid would bolster an anti-Catholic government.[85]

* * *

Pearl Harbor put an end to the Great Debate and led to the demise of its major participants. AFC dissolved on December 11, its leaders proclaiming that history would vindicate them.[86] The CDA acknowledged that its work had come to an end, but briefly became part of Citizens for Victory, a group formed to promote peace after the Allied victory.[87]

Pearl Harbor also terminated the German-American Bund. Three days earlier, the Nazis had celebrated the New Jersey Supreme Court's reversal of the convictions of nine Bund leaders accused of violating the state's 1935 anti-Nazi laws. The Court ruled that the legislation was unconstitutional because it violated the right of free speech.[88] The Bund's celebration, however, was short lived; the day after the Japanese attack, President Roosevelt declared that non-citizen Germans, Italians, and Japanese were enemy aliens. FDR authorized the Attorney General to arrest those aliens he believed dangerous to the nation's peace and security. The Newark FBI office immediately arrested seven Bundists, six of them from Irvington.[89]

The outbreak of war caused the Essex County CDA to move up the date of its rally. New Jersey Governor Charles Edison agreed to be the main speaker and guest of honor. To get maximum public participation, the CDA added fifty-two prominent citizens to its list of sponsors.[90] The rally's themes were state unity in prosecuting the war and the need to combine state and local civil defense efforts. The AYC was to have no role in the rally and the group soon disintegrated. McMichael returned to New York.

The *Newark Star Ledger* urged readers to attend the rally to show their support for the defense effort. It praised the CDA for performing "a priceless patriotic service in paving the way for the lend lease program [without which] our country would today be fighting the Axis powers alone on two oceans."[91]

The Mosque rally attracted over 2,500 people. Governor Edison warned that disunity could destroy America more certainly than the Axis powers. He said that New Jersey's diverse population had been a prime target of Mussolini's and Hitler's agents, but those born abroad or with close ties to foreign lands "have very generally scorned the messengers of disunity." Clark M.Eichelberger, national CDA director, urged Americans to be mindful of what they were fighting for, not merely what they were fighting against. Befitting their roles as anti-Nazi clergy, Msgr. James F. Kelley of Seton Hall gave the invocation; Rabbi Joachim Prinz of Temple B'Nai Abraham led the audience in the 23rd Psalm; and Rev. William Hiram Foulkes of First Presbyterian Church delivered the benediction.[92]

* * *

What would have occurred in Newark had the United States remained out of the war longer, or not entered at all?

Would the AFC have become more powerful? Would it have become the basis for a third party? Or would it have transformed itself into a proto-Nazi organization? And how would the Minutemen and the rest of Newark Jewry have reacted to these changes?

What would have been the outcome of the ideological split in CDA?

Would the "good will" efforts of the city's liberal Protestants and Jews have expanded beyond their small base to attract others, especially Catholics?

These difficult questions aside, it is important to note that by the end of 1941 three of the four largest ethnic groups in Newark—German, Italian, and Irish—were anti interventionist. Afraid, however, of being accused of dual or even foreign loyalty, German and Italian Americans no longer articulated pro-Hitler or pro-Mussolini sentiments at the end of 1941. Irish Americans, on the other hand, operated from a stronger position, as their Americanism was taken for granted. Hatred of the English and communism fueled their anti- interventionism.

Jews were the only major Newark ethnic group in favor of intervention. Even as Hitler overran Europe, intervention was not a majority position in the city.[93] Without support for intervention from the Protestant elite and organized labor, Jews would have encountered increasing hostility.

Newark's anti-Nazis, particularly the Minutemen and the NSANL, never thought about their place in history. Nevertheless, they can proudly face the tribunal of historical judgment. The city's Jews owe a debt of gratitude to Nat Arno, Dr. S.William Kalb, and their supporters. Longie Zwillman deserves kudos for having created and backed the Minutemen.

Others acted against Nazism in Newark, but none made it a priority. The Conference of Jewish Charities was active in aiding refugees from Hitler's persecution, helping them resettle either in the Newark area or Palestine. It also provided relief to Jews living under Nazi domination in Europe. However, as was the case in other American Jewish communities, the Newark Conference took no unified action against foreign or domestic Nazism. The Conference's leader, Michael Stavitsky, personally participated in anti-Nazi activities, but his executive board, dominated by wealthy German Jews, eschewed this approach.

The elitist American Jewish Committee, one of three national Jewish defense organizations, took no part in Newark's anti-Nazi movement. Newark B'Nai Brith's Ezekiel Lodge had a mixed record: Until 1937, it participated in anti-Nazi events and endorsed the anti-Nazi boycott. Afterward, other than a denunciation of Kristallnacht, the lodge took no initiatives in the anti-Nazi struggle. The American Jewish Congress became active in Newark and Essex County mainly in response to Nazism. However, it took Kalb's prodding for the Congress to support the boycott.

Zionist organizations, particularly the Newark branch of the Zionist Organization of America (ZOA), were more concerned with finding refuge for European Jews in Palestine than with either the anti-Nazi boycott or domestic Nazism.[94] A month before Pearl Harbor, Zionists demanded that Britain fulfill its 1917 pledge to facilitate a Jewish homeland in Palestine and urged the British Government to permit Jews in Palestine to form an army.[95]

More active in anti-Nazism were the scores of Jewish charitable, social, and benevolent institutions known as KUVs, and the other fraternal organizations of Newark's Eastern European Jews. Their members lived near the action, and they opposed Nazism through participation in Kalb's boycott campaign and support for the Minutemen.

Other groups responded either inconsistently or ineffectively. The indefatigable liberal trio of Amelia Moorfield, Luke Garner, and Frank Kingdon failed to sway Christian public opinion in Newark against Nazism. Kingdon and Garner worked their liberal agendas at their own peril. Kingdon lost his college presidency and Garner his pulpit because of ideological differences with the conservative boards for which they worked.

The city's socialists were pacifists, but they took part in some anti-Nazi events because of the threat to peace the Nazis posed. Until 1939, they devoted most of their energies to labor, civil rights, and civil liberties issues. With the increasing military preparedness of the United States and the outbreak of World War II in Europe, pacifism dominated Norman Thomas's agenda. Newark's socialists followed suit, although none went to the lengths their leader did in supporting the AFC.[96]

The anti-Nazism of Newark's communists was opportunistic. From May, 1933, when they led the first anti-Nazi demonstration in the Newark area, to the August, 1939 Nazi Soviet Pact, Newark's communists used their considerable organizational and propagandistic skills in the battle against Hitler. After the pact, the American Communist Party abandoned its anti-Nazism and instead attacked President Roosevelt's alleged support of French and English imperialism. Only when Germany invaded the Soviet Union in June 1941 did the communists revert to their previous anti-Nazism.

Kalb and Arno were Newark's most consistent and fervent anti-Nazis. The collaboration of a boycott group and a street army made Newark's anti-Nazi struggle unique in America. Kalb's boycott movement recruited those who wanted to act against Nazism. He educated the KUVs and other Jewish social welfare and benevolent organizations and inspired them to take an active role in the boycott. Through his leadership roles in Newark's Jewish War Veterans and the AJC he attracted middle-class Jews for the battle. Combining all the city's boycott forces, Kalb organized the Newark division of the NSANL, which effectively waged the anti-Nazi campaign for five years. The boycott, Joseph Tenenbaum said:

> proved the power and ability of a 'helpless' people, as consumers in general, to fight for the redress of an injustice committed by a big power, and its readiness to 'boycott' for the sake of freedom. [97]

Kalb's anti-Nazi efforts reached beyond the boycott. He organized and participated in events to educate the public on the evils of German and domestic Nazism. Because of his friendship and collaboration with Nat Arno, Newark's two most militant anti-Nazi groups, the NSANL and the Minutemen, coordinated activities whenever possible. His public relations skills guaranteed a constant stream of publicity for anti-Nazi activities. His "boycott violators" handbills served as a prototype for other organizations affiliated with the NSANL.

Kalb, like many Newark professionals, joined organizations to make contacts and gain patients. His leadership talents made him a success and he could have continued to build his medical practice. However, he spent nearly seven years serving the boycott movement, often neglecting his practice and his family's financial security. Moreover, he often put himself in physical danger by taking part in Minutemen actions.

Nat Arno risked both his life and freedom to lead the Minutemen for over eight years. The anti-Nazi group's fighting prowess resonated with Newark's working class Jews. The Minutemen prevented Nazis and other anti-Semites from controlling the streets of Newark and Irvington, countering the danger posed to Jews by the Friends of the New Germany and its successor, the German American Bund.

Often scorned by the Jewish establishment, the Minutemen were seldom acknowledged in the *Jewish Chronicle*, the unofficial weekly of the organized Jewish community. They were actively opposed by the ACLU, which consistently filed suits on behalf of the Friends and the Bund. Condemned by the city's major newspaper, the *Newark News*, the Minutemen were said to foment "mob rule." Despite their notoriety, the Minutemen were heroes to the majority of Newark's first and second generation Eastern European Jews.

When Arno began his Minutemen activities, he was twenty-five, with a credible boxing career behind him. Other boxers soon joined the anti-Nazi group, and, like Arno, Zwillman's criminal organization. Many young Jews were eager to fight the Nazis, at least partly because they looked up to Arno. Even today, men in their seventies and eighties who grew up in the area of the Third Ward have praise for him. A former Minuteman, Alex Portnoff, said of Arno, "He made us proud to be Jews!"[98]

* * *

The anti-Nazi struggle changed Newark. Ethnic tensions were understandably exacerbated. The once friendly relations between the city's Jews and its German Americans became hostile. Relations between Jews and Irish, which had never been good, deteriorated even further, whereas Jews and Italians managed to stay on good terms because local Italian leaders spoke out against Mussolini's racial laws.

The Protestant elite, which had attempted to remain neutral in the early days of Hitler's rule, was forced to take a position after Germany attacked Great Britain. Thereafter they became vocal Nazi critics. The only Newarkers to stay out of the anti-Nazi struggle were African Americans. Shunned by all groups, they remained on the sidelines.

With America's entry into World War II, ethnic disputes were put aside as thousands of Newarkers fought and worked together to defend their country. Bolstered by defense contracts, Newark's industry boomed. Once again African Americans flocked to Newark to fill wartime jobs. The stage was set for Newark's next ethnic conflict.

Notes

1. N.N., 2/12/41, p. 2; S.L., 2/22/41, p. 3.
2. S.L., 2/22/41, p. 3.
3. N.N., 1/31/41, p. 1.
4. N.N., 6/1/41, p 15; S.C., 10/19/41, p17
5. N.N.., 5/31/41
6. NJA, Papers Charles Edison Volume 92—1941-1944, Letter from John Hayes Holmes to Edison, 6/4/41. Months later Zionist leader Joseph Kraemer wrote to Edison commending the revocation. Letter from Joseph Kraemer to Edison, 10/7/41.
7. J.C., 6/6/41, p. 1; N.N., 6/10/41, p. 1; 7/21/41, p. 1.
8. N.N., 7/18/41, p. 40. The City Hall Tavern in Union City continued to act as Bund headquarters until an FBI raid in April 1942 interrupted Klapprott and thirty others in the midst of a Hitler birthday celebration. Firearms, short wave radio sets, and German money were seized. See Glaser, "The German-American Bund in New Jersey," p. 45.
9. N.N., 8/12/41, p. 21 It was founded by two officials of the German-American League for Culture, Dr. Frank Bohn and Gerhart H. Seger. At the Newark meeting, Seger said the only way for Germany to regain liberty was at the expense of a military defeat. The members pledged to spread anti-Nazi propaganda in Northern New Jersey.
10. Chadwin, Mark Lincoln, The Hawks of World War II, Chapel Hill, 1968, p. 187.
11. The state chapter of Labor's Non-Partisan League, under Holderman, unlike the Newark branch was not under communist domination.
12. N.N., 7/27/41, p. 5. Holderman, a German-American, urged every fellow American of German extraction "to stand up and be counted as a leader in the fight for freedom." They would do this by joining the organization and by displaying the letter "V" on lapels, in store windows, and on correspondence, thus demonstrating that "the heritage of humane German culture has not been destroyed."
13. S.C., 2/16/41, p. 10.

14. Ibid., 3/6/41, p. 1. Giulio Pascucci-Righi, the Italian vice consul in Newark was "shocked" by the move and denied making any pro-Mussolini statements (not that he was accused of this).

15. N.N., 1/31/41, p. 20.

16. Ibid., 8/15/42, p. 7.

17. Ibid., 10/13/41, p. 4; 10/14/41, p. 6.

18. J.C., 1/3/41, p. 1.

19. Ibid., 1/10/41, p. 1.

20. Ibid., 2/7/41, p. 1. Not directly related to the Commission, but also promoting inter-faith relations, the Essex County Division of the Interfaith Committee for Aid to the Democracies was established by the AJC to assist in efforts for British war relief. The Interfaith Committee, a national group, was organized to obtain maximum Catholic, Protestant, and Jewish support for England, and to explain to Americans the issues involved in that country's struggle against totalitarianism. Charles Handler, president of the Essex Chapter of the Congress, said affiliates would run fundraisers to aid the Allies. See N.N., 3/5/41, p. 4.

21. A slate led by Commissioner Joseph Byrne challenged Mayor Meyer Ellenstein and his two allies on the City Commission. Byrne made headlines when he charged that Longie Zwillman and his mob were the "real backers" of the Ellenstein ticket. He added: "This city is dominated by a gang that has destroyed everything it has ever touched." Ellenstein was also attacked for disbanding a special crime squad that had the temerity of raiding the operations of two Zwillman associates.

    The mayor was already weakened by two years of controversy over the "land scandal." Ellenstein and his ally, Commissioner Pierce Franklin, were indicted along with friends and political appointees of the Mayor's on charges involving the purchase and sale of property at Newark Airport. Although all defendants were acquitted months before the election, Ellenstein and Franklin were unable to overcome the effects of over two years of negative press and the public's perception of corruption in Newark and were not reelected to office. Zwillman temporarily lost patronage and contract opportunities in Newark, but still had much of the police hierarchy on his payroll to protect his illegal business.

    Ellenstein was involved in a fierce battle for re-election in May 1941, and Garner, a well-known advocate of the Mayor, was an asset to his campaign. When Ellenstein was defeated, a majority of the new Commission voted to abolish the Labor Relations Board as punishment for Garner's support of the former Mayor.

22. Garner Papers, "Date Book, 1941" Among his talks were nine to Jewish groups, six to educational institutions, and five to social service groups.

23. Kingdon Papers, S.L., 2/20/41.

24. S.L., 3/1/41; J.C., 3/14/41, p. 5.

25. N.N., 2/4/41, p. 22.

26. J.C., 3/7/41, p. 1; 3/14/41, p. 1. This effort was also sponsored by the Order of the Sons of Zion, Hadassah, Jewish National Fund, Labor Zionists, and Mizrachi. Representatives of these and other Zionist groups organized the Zionist Council of Essex County, electing Harry Pine of the Sons of Zion as the President and Yanoff, vice president.

27. N.N., 3/17/41, p. 6. The group also voted a resolution endorsing the United Jewish Appeal as the sole fund-raising arm for raising overseas relief.

28. Ibid., 3/24/41, p. 17.

29. Ibid., 10/9/41, p. 8.

30. Ibid., 10/25/41, p. 20.

31. Ibid. , 5/2/41, p. 25.

32. Ibid., 5/6/41, p. 4. Michael A. Stavitsky, Samuel I. Kessler, and Joseph Siegler leaders of the Jewish Community also spoke at the event. None addressed Steele's remarks.

33. Ibid., 6/3/41, p. 16; 7/16/41, p. 17.

34. America First, Box 15, letter from Herman Von Busch to the American First Committee, 7/25/41; Letter from John S. Broeksmit, Jr. to H.V. Busch, 7/25/41.

35. Ibid., Petition of Newark Chapter to General Wood, 8/28/41; Postcard from Newark Chapter to General Wood, 9/2/41; Letter from Harry C. Schnibbe to Newark Chapter, 9/10/41 Analysis of the fifty petition names discloses thirty-eight with German surnames; six with Italian; three with Irish; three unidentifiable. Also, nineteen signers were from Newark; sixteen from the rest of Essex; fifteen from the rest of New Jersey.

36. Stenehjem, Michele Flynn, *An America First, John T. Flynn and the America First Committee*, New Rochelle, NY, 1976, p. 63.

37. NYT, 3/12/41, p. 1; N.N., 3/12/41, p. 2.

38. J.C., 7/25/41, p. 14; 8/15/41, p. 20.

39. N.N., 10/30/41, p. 17, 11/6/41, p. 4, 11/7/41, p. 20.

40. Ibid., 9/12/41, p. 2.

41. Communists, used to rapid changes in the Party line, outdid themselves on Sunday afternoon June 22, 1941, at Harlem's Golden Gate Ballroom, where Adam Clayton Powell, Sr., Dorothy Parker and others were addressing a Fight for Freedom Rally. As the audience filed in for the event, pickets carrying signs with communist slogans such as "imperialist warmongers" berated them. When the event ended, the demonstrators, who usually remained to accost the audience, were gone. While the rally was in progress, the pickets learned that the Nazis had invaded the Soviet Union. See Chadwin, The Hawks of World War II, p. 242.

42. For a discussion of the early days of the AYC and Eleanor Roosevelt's support of the group, see Robert Cohen, *When the Old Left Was Young,* New York, 1993, pp. 188-195.

43. Lewy, Guenter, *The Cause That Failed, Communism in American Political Life*, New York, 1990, p. 32.

44. Stenehjem, *An America First*, p. 136.

45. Chadwin, *The Hawks of World War II*, p. 210.

46. Feingold, Henry L., *The Jewish People in America, Vol. 4*, A Time For Searching, Baltimore, 1992, p. 208.

47. S.L., 9/21/41, p. 11.

48. I.H., 9/18/41, p. 3. The Committee to Defend America requested UJA to send a representative to the meeting, and the president of UJA, Samuel Kessler, appointed Michael Stavitsky to attend. See, Federation Board of Directors Minutes, 9/9/41; Letter from Anna Morgenroth for Committee to "Dear Friends," 9/3/41.

49. N.N.,9/20/41, p. 2.

50. S.L.., 9/22/41, p. 14.

51. America First Committee, Box 163, Letter from Thomas N. McCarter to General Wood, 9/29/41; Letter from America First to Thomas N. McCarter, 10/4/41. Allan Lowenstein, a young attorney during this period, remembers McCarter as "very conservative" but not anti-Semitic. Lowenstein was offered the job as Assistant General Counsel to Public Service Co. by McCarter in 1939, when almost no Jews were officers in public utilities. Interview, Alan Lowenstein, 12/21/00.

52. N.N., 11/7/41, p. 2.

53. Stenehjem, *An America First*, p. 137. The attitude towards anti-Semitism by the AFC was paradoxical. Despite a leadership that mainly eschewed anti-Semitism, the support of anti-Semites was both present and indirectly welcomed in the AFC. Works by Stenehjem, Cole, Jonas, and Doenecke describe anti-Semites within the leadership and membership of AFC but basically defend the organization against anti-Semitic charges by pointing out that General Johnson nationally and John T. Flynn in New York were not themselves anti-Semites and tried to oust anti-Semites from positions of leadership in the group. However, the popularity within AFC ranks of Lindbergh's anti-Semitic Des Moines speech, the failure of the AFC to denounce the speech, General Wood's letter to Coughlin's Social Justice that its followers were welcome in AFC (see Bayor, Ronald, Neighbors in Conflict: The Irish, Germans, Jews, and Italians of New York City, 1929-1941, Urbana, 1988, p. 114), the non-critical view of Hitler by AFC members (such as in Newark), all point to anti-Semitism as being deeply intertwined with the ethos of the isolationist group.

54.   S.C., 9/14/41, p. 24. The committee consisted of Mary M. Henninger, Florence M. Siegfried, E.J. Kussmaul, Fred W. Phelps, Florence C. Riley, Mrs. Valentine Miller, Thomas Ritt, Olga Schultheis, Albert Siegfried, Frank A. Gegauff, Samuel Ragonesi, Louis DeVisia, and Ernest C. Hawkins.

55.   N.N., 9/20/41, p. 2; S.L., 9/21/41, p. 2.

56.   Klehr, Harvey, *The Heyday of American Communism, The Depression Decade*, New York, 1984, p. 321. According to Klehr, McMichael was a fellow-traveler who denied Communist Party membership. Robert Cohen labels McMichael "an ally of the Communist Party." See, Cohen, op. cit., p. 259.

57.   The Newark Committee to Defend America was not the only local interventionist group which Communists tried to infiltrate. Fight for Freedom's (FFF) local chapters in the District of Columbia and in Boston were also subjects of such infiltration. The American Student Union, a Communist front, provided pickets for the Boston FFF chapter. Chadwin, op. cit., 247.

58.   The Committee to Defend America began organizing youth groups on campuses in many cities beginning in June 1941. Newark was not one of them. See Johnson, Walter, *The Battle Against Isolation*, Chicago, 1944, pp. 76, 77.

59.   Committee to Defend America, Series 3, Box 28, "College Division Chapter Notebook." Neither branch was particularly active, and no New Jersey students attended a national convention of the college division in April 1941 at Union College in Schenectady, New York. See above, Proceedings of colleges in defense of democracy, 4/25-4/27/41.

60.   S. L., 9/21/41, p. 2.

61.   The FFF, founded in March 1941, favored immediate American armed intervention in Europe rather than "all aid to the Allies short of war," the position taken by the Committee to Defend America. This difference did not prevent the two groups from cooperating with each other, both to swing American public opinion toward more aid to the Allies and to oppose America First. Many prominent Americans supported FFF while at the same time actively aiding the Committee to Defend America. However, since the FFF never achieved the stature of the Committee and had started their efforts much later, its internal staff discouraged cooperation between the two groups. National Executive Director Liddon Graham discouraged efforts of FFF chapters in Princeton and Bergen County from merging with their Committee to Defend America counterparts without offering a valid reason for his actions.

      FFF had no branch in Newark, but it operated a state headquarters in Trenton and branches in other New Jersey cities, including a seventy-member group in the Newark suburb of Montclair. See, Fight for Freedom (FFF), Box 45, File "Missouri- New Jersey."

62.   N.N., 9/23/41, p. 14.

63.   Ibid., 9/24/41, p. 12.

64.   Ibid., p. 1.

65.   An American First official at the rally claimed 4,200 in the Mosque and 2,500 outside. See America First, Box 15, Letter from Florence M. Seifried to General Robert E. Wood, 9/28/41.

66.   O'Connell was correct since his conspiratorial interpretation of events was not shared by Msgr. James Kelley, President of Seton Hall. Kelley, who had studied abroad, was more liberal than most Catholic Clergymen. He introduced a mandatory course on Americanism at the college in 1938 because he had delivered "so many speeches on the evils of Nazism and Communism." See, James Kelley, *Memoirs of Msgr. ("Doc") Kelley*, Locust, New Jersey, 1987, p. 284

      Kelley was close to many Jews according to his memoir. A surprising friend not mentioned in his work is Nat Arno. The Monsignor attended Arno's wedding in 1945 and delivered a blessing to the couple. See Interview, Anne Arno, 8/6/97.

67.   N.N., 9/24/41, pp. 1, 12; S.L., 9/24/41, pp. 1, 6.

68.   S.L., 9/25/41, p. 14 The more conservative *Newark News* editorialized on the rally by congratulating Newarkers for eschewing disorder and recognizing the fundamental right to dissent from government policy. See, N.N., 9/24/41, p. 10.

69. Fight for Freedom was apparently more aware than the Committee to Defend America of the attempts of communists and their allies to gain influence in their organizations. In the Summer of 1941, the FFF created a New York City umbrella of pro-interventionist youth groups, including its own unit, the New York Youth Committee to Defend America, and the small but active Cardozo Club. It then issued a pamphlet addressed to the new group which warned about the dangers of working with "fronts" and their members. The AYC was specifically prohibited from participating in the group's activities in order to "prevent [communist] infiltration and perversion of these new organizations." See, Fight for Freedom, MC #025, Box 37, Folder "Youth Division," "Info, Clearing House for Youth Groups," Vol. I, No. I, n.d.

70. Committee to Defend America, op. cit., Series 3, Box 21, Letter from Frances Thomas to Dr. Frank Kingdon, 10/10/41.

71. Ibid., Letter from Isidore Weinman to Frances Thomas, 10/21/41.

72. N.N., 10/31/41, p. 10. To avoid a split in the group, the communists agreed that the new chairman would be "temporary" until a full slate of officers was installed.

73. Ibid.

74. In little over a month, McMichael would be out of Newark permanently.

75. Committee to Defend America, op. cit., Series 3, Box 21, Letters from Joseph Marzell to Frances Thomas, 11/1/41; Rev. Lester Clee to Dr. Isidore Weinman, 11/11/41; Msgr. John Delaney to Craig Eichelberger, 11/17/41; Frances Thomas to Dr. Max Ascoli, 11/15/41; A. Tarchiano to Frances Thomas, 11/21/41. Tarchiano, secretary of the New York Mazzini Society, told Thomas that "the majority of Italian nationals [in Newark] are either indifferent, fascist, or anarchist." However, he did recommend two people who "might be useful for democratic propaganda" in Newark, Michele Russomanno ("a liberal democrat") and Gaspare Nicotri ("a Socialist").

76. For Hartley, see p. 305 n218.

77. N.N., 11/5/41, p. 7.

78. Ibid., 11/6/41, p. 3.

79. The Cardozo Club was established in New York City in 1939 as a youth group to fight against the German-American Bund, the Christian Front, and other anti-Semitic groups. It worked with the New York Youth Division of the Committee to Defend America to support maximum aid for the Allies.

80. N.N., 11/12/41, p. 4; S.L., 11/12/41, pp. 1, 6.

81. Harold John Adonis, after being appointed to various municipal positions, was named Executive Clerk to New Jersey Governor Alfred E. Driscoll in 1946. He was charged in 1950 with accepting $228,000 from gangster Willie Moretti to protect the Bergen County gambling syndicate. He fled to Holland but was arrested two years later and extradited back to New Jersey. In 1955, after refusing for two years to identify the recipients of the pay-off, he was tried, convicted, and sentenced to five years in jail for income tax evasion. A public relations expert, poet, bon vivant, and self-proclaimed political reformer, Adonis was one of New Jersey's more colorful political figures. *Newark News* Morgue, Harold John Adonis.

82. N.N., 11/12/41, p. 4.

83. Ibid., 11/14/41, p. 10. The leaders of the United Labor Committee included Jacob C. Baer, president of the Essex Trades Council of the AFL, Newark mayor, Vincent Murphy, secretary of the New Jersey Federation of Labor, Peter Yablonsky, president of the Painter's Union, AFL, and William Ross, president of the Greater Newark Industrial Council, CIO.

84. S.L., 12/2/41, p. 7; N.N., 12/2/41, p. 16.

85. N.N., 11/27/41, p. 24.

86. Stenehjem, *An America First*, p. 118.

87. Committee to Defend America, Introduction to MC #11, p. 3. In January, the Committee helped form the Citizens for Victory to plan for peace after the war. Citizens for Victory suspended activities in October 1942 because of lack of interest.

88. N.N., 12/5/41, p. 1.

89. Ibid., 12/9/41, p. 1; I. H., 12/11/41, p. 14.

90.   S.L., 12/17/41, p. 17. Among the fifty-two sponsors were nine Jews and one African American, Herbert H. Tate.

91.   Ibid., 12/16/41, pp. 13, 14. Honorary chairmen for the rally included such familiar names as Dr. Wells P. Eagleton, Samuel I. Kessler, Ralph E. Lum, Peter A. Cavicchia, and Judge Daniel Brennan. See N.N., 12/17/41, p. 17.

92.   N.N., 12/18/41, p. 28; S.L., 12/18/41, p. 3.

93.   Polish and Czechoslovakian Newarkers were also pro-interventionist given the invasions of their countries by the Nazis.

94.   Interviews, Joe Lerner, 5/16/97 and Judge Leo Yanoff, 2/12/98. Lerner, already involved in the local branch of the Zionist Organization of America, was later to become one of its national leaders. He claims that in the pre-war period the ZOA was exclusively interested in Palestine to the exclusion of anti-Nazi activities. Lerner's long-time colleague in the ZOA, Judge Leo Yanoff, also points out the lack of anti-Nazi activities by the ZOA, explaining, "We didn't believe in the Nazi threat."

95.   S. C., 11/2/41, p. 14; N. N., 11/3/41, p. 13; 11/4/41, p. 4.

96.   Some Socialist Party members were dissatisfied with Norman Thomas's opposition to Lend-Lease and to the extension of the draft. Even more were opposed to his speech at a rally at Madison Square Garden in May, 1940. See, Shannon, David A., The Socialist Party of America: A History, New York, 1955, p. 256.

97.   Tenenbaum, Joseph, "The Anti-Nazi Boycott Movement in the United States," Yad Vashem Studies III, 1959, pp. 158, 159.

98.   Interview, Alex Portnoff, 6/25/96.

Afterword

Drafted in 1941, Nat Arno saw action with the 29th Infantry and was wounded during the Normandy invasion. Not long after his return to Newark in 1945, he was married. Following the birth of the Arno's first child, Longie Zwillman got Nat work as a liquor salesman, a job he held for several years. Despite his apparent domesticity, old habits came back to haunt him and in April 1947, Arno was indicted—along with a Newark police detective—for extortion. Arno was aquitted in October 1948, but immediately reindicted for false swearing. His plea of *non vult* (no defense) resulted in a probation term.

Within a month, he was called to a meeting with Zwillman at Public Service Tobacco Company in Hillside New Jersey. Longie told Nat that his Newark days were over and that he had to relocate to California. Zwillman warned Arno that under the probation terms, if he got into trouble in California, he would be extradited back to New Jersey and sent to jail. Nat left Newark for California in February 1949.

After a difficult adjustment period, Arno starting working in the furniture industry, which he remained in until illness forced him to retire in 1970. He became a model citizen—a family man and a dedicated volunteer for the Disabled American Veterans (DAV). He became commander of the Hollywood Chapter of the DAV, regularly visiting veterans at the DAV Hospital and soliciting employers to hire disabled veterans. Arno was also active with Temple Beth Torah in Hollywood, appearing in fundraising productions portraying Damon Runyonesque characters.

Arno jeopardized his freedom only once. When he heard that the American Nazi Party was staging a rally in downtown Los Angeles, he gathered a group of veterans to protest. When one of the speakers made anti-Semitic statements, Arno rushed the platform and threw him to the ground. He was arrested but released without being charged, thereby avoiding extradition to Newark.

Nat visited Newark several times before Longie Zwillman's 1953 suicide. The last time they saw each other they embraced, and Longie told his "commander" how proud he was that Arno had turned his life around. Unfortunately for Longie, what he did for Arno he could not do for himself. Arno died in 1972, survived by his wife and two sons.

Some men's deeds outlive them but others outlive their deeds. Dr. S. William Kalb, who died ten days short of his ninety-fifth birthday, belonged to the latter group. By the time he died, his anti-Nazi work had long been forgotten by his community, and even by some in his family.

Kalb had served in World War I and, although over-age, wanted to enlist in 1941. His wife protested and, according to his daughters, this provoked a serious fight that Mrs. Kalb eventually won. Kalb did, however, realize his desire to participate in the war effort when he became the doctor for hundreds of Newark defense plant workers. After the war ended, he abandoned his general practice and began specializing in "diet medicine." Everyday, scores of overweight patients, most of them women, came to his Clinton Place office.

When Kalb retired from practice in 1962, he again became a volunteer worker. He was elected president of the Essex County Medical Society and worked for many years with the Future Physicians of America. Kalb helped organize high school Future Physicians Clubs and served as the Essex County coordinator for the group. During the 1960s, Kalb was as an advisor on weight reduction for both the Food and Drug Administration and the Federal Trade Commission.

In 1965, Kalb came out of retirement to treat civilians in Vietnam in a program co-sponsored by the People-to-People Health Foundation and the American Medical Society. To prepare himself for this new challenge, he worked in Newark Beth Israel Hospital's emergency room for eight weeks. He spent three months in Vietnam, traveling with a translator from village to village, treating patients. Upon returning to the United States, Kalb reassumed his work with the Future Physicians of America, which he continued until the early 1980s.

Kalb died in 1992, survived by his two daughters.

Both Frank Kingdon and Luke Garner were in their forties when America entered World War II and both used their prodigious talents to help the American war effort. However, their subsequent careers could not have been more different: Luke Garner became successful in private industry, while Frank Kingdon became a victim of Cold War politics.

The war years proved to be the highpoint of Frank Kingdon's career. He was hired as a spokesman for the American war effort by the United States Office of Emergency Management in early 1942. Kingdon was subjected to an extensive FBI investigation that found that he was neither a communist nor a fellow traveler. Indeed, the FBI reported "the applicant has been heard to make fiery speeches condemning the Communist Party." In mid-1942, he became a news commentator on radio station WMCA. In January 1943, the station announced that Kingdon would host a weekday program on which he would "interpret news of the world in terms of democratic achievements." WMCA heralded the program as "a milestone in liberal education by radio." Simultaneously, Kingdon was hired by radio station WOR to review the week's events on Sunday morning. His programs attracted a wide audience and he became a celebrity. His first book, *Jacob's Ladder,* an autobiography, was published in May 1943.

In August 1944, Kingdon was featured in a laudatory article in the *New York Post.* It reported, however, that his liberal views were not popular with conservatives and that the House Un-American Committee (the Dies Committee) was characterizing Kingdon as a communist tool. (Kingdon had incurred the wrath of the committee as early as 1940 when he signed a petition that appeared in the *New York Times* calling for the committee's dissolution.) Despite the Dies Committee's attempts to smear him, he was awarded the Newspaper Guild's "Page One Award" for his war efforts on radio and for outstanding liberal commentary. Kingdon was by now so famous that his next book, *That Man in the White House*, written to help Roosevelt's 1944 re-election campaign, sold over 100,000 copies.

By 1947, Kingdon's liberal commentaries were under continuous attack by conservative veterans' groups, as well as by the Dies Committee. Although his broadcasts enjoyed high ratings, by the spring he had lost so many sponsors that both stations fired him. The Dies Committee exulted, releasing a statement that "red fronts" had not fared as well on the airwaves since Kingdon's departure.

In the summer of 1947, Kingdon embarked on a new career as an editorial page columnist for the *New York Post.* He soon was awarded his own column, "To be Frank," which ran until 1952. One of his first columns was responsible for his undoing. In an August 1947 column, he criticized President Truman and FBI director J. Edgar Hoover for their roles in the establishment of loyalty boards. Kingdon opined that the boards, which had the power to fire federal employees for disloyalty, were unconstitutional. Hoover was personally offended by the attack and sent Kingdon a letter accusing him of undermining public confidence in the FBI. He also reminded Kingdon that it was the FBI that had cleared him for his job in the Office of Emergency Management. Kingdon would not back down, responding that loyalty boards were an assault on civil liberties. For the rest of his *Post* career, Kingdon was under FBI surveillance.

Dissatisfied with what he perceived as Truman's assault on civil liberties, Kingdon became associated with Henry Wallace's Progressive Party. Kingdon's son John remembers riding in a limousine to a 1948 Wallace rally in Philadelphia with his father, the Broadway actor Alfred Drake, Paul Robeson, and another Wallace supporter of the time, Ronald Reagan. In 1948, Kingdon once again sought a United States Senate seat, this time going so far as to file petitions in the Democratic primary. He withdrew from the race in March, however, charging that the party was boss-ridden. Two months later he denounced Henry Wallace and the Progressive Party for kowtowing to Moscow. *The Daily Worker* in turn denounced Kingdon for "red-baiting."

Dolly Schiff, the *Post's* owner and publisher, supported Kingdon's column until 1952, when she fired him because of mounting McCarthyite pressure. According to his daughter Trudi, Kingdon's life took a dramatic turn for the worse after his firing. Age fifty-seven and blacklisted, he was unable to find work in any of the news media. Kingdon's granddaughter Jill, who lived with him the last five years of his life, said that after being blacklisted the Jewish community took care of him.

Kingdon was an early supporter of the State of Israel. Because of his fame, he was a much in demand speaker and often spoke at United Jewish Appeal events. In December 1948, the Joint Distribution Committee asked Kingdon to go to Germany to visit refugee camps in the American zone. The State Department obviously did not agree with the Committee on its choice of representative. It refused him a visa, stating that he had been a "notorious fellow traveler, if not a party member." Whether or not Jewish groups knew of his problems with the FBI and the State Department, he continued to speak before them through the 1950s and into the early 1960s, an eloquent proponent of Israel who was able to convince his audiences to contribute money to the new state.

He spent most of the last twenty years of his life at the New School and the Stephen Wise Free Synagogue lecturing on politics and current events. He also wrote salesmen's motivational materials and did ghost writing for public figures. The last FBI report on Kingdon in 1963 related to his membership on the "Committee of 100" in support of the NAACP Legal Defense and Educational Fund. An investigator claimed he could find no current employment for Kingdon.

Kingdon is not forgotten. Those who visited the exhibit on Varian Fry and the Emergency Relief Committee, which traveled nationwide during the mid-1990s, heard a recorded recreation of an excerpt from the speech Kingdon delivered to open the organization's first meeting in 1940. In Philip Roth's 1969 novel *Portnoy's Complaint*, the twelve-year-old Alex Portnoy exults when he gets to shake Kingdon's hand at a labor rally at Newark's Mosque Theater. Portnoy exclaims that Frank Kingdon is "the renowned columnist whom I read every day in *PM*." The Frank Kingdon Lecture Hall can be found in the New School University's 12th Street Building in Manhattan. A plaque reads, "In honor of an inspiring and beloved teacher."

Frank Kingdon died in 1972, survived by six children.

Like Kingdon, Luke Garner was active in liberal and communist front groups in the 1930s. As late as August 1940, an FBI report stated that Garner was "a person with Communistic tendencies." Unlike Kingdon, however, by the time World War II started, the only activist group that Garner belonged to was the Newark Urban League. When the United States entered World War II, Garner, who had worked with the Newark Labor Relations Board, became a regional manager of the National Labor Relations Board in New York. During the war he traveled throughout New Jersey, New York, and New England settling labor management disputes, particularly in the defense industries.

When the war ended, Garner was recruited to work for a large labor relations firm, Stevenson, Jordan, and Harrison. He later became a partner in another labor relations firm, Case and Company. Other than in private discussions with friends, he kept his political opinions to himself. According to his son David, Garner "never rocked the boat" during his public and private labor relations career. In fact, David claims his father was at the height of his career during the McCarthy era and into the 1960s. During the latter period, Garner was earning in excess of $60,000 a year.

Like Kingdon, Garner's private network of friends was Jewish. The Jewish couples the Garners met in the 1930s remained their lifelong friends. This group was active with Garner in New York Ethical Culture affairs but never formally joined the movement. In 1962 Garner moved from Newark to West Orange, where he remained the rest of his life.

Garner retired from Case and Company in 1971, but retained a few private clients on a part-time basis. A few years later, perhaps to gain a pension from the Universalist Church—he was three years short in service to qualify—he became pastor of a small Universalist Church in Orange, New Jersey. While delivering a Sunday sermon in 1975, Garner suffered a severe stroke from which he never fully recovered. He died in 1979, a month short of his eightieth birthday, survived by three sons.

Amelia Moorfield, Newark's third great liberal of the 1930s, was despondent after Pearl Harbor and America's entry into World War II. Her struggle for peace had been in vain. At sixty-six, she would never again be in the limelight; her important roles in Newark's suffrage and peace movements were behind her. During the war, the activities of New Jersey's Women's International League for Peace and Democracy (WILPF) were minimal. At the first wartime meeting of the Essex WILPF in February 1942, Moorfield stressed cooperation with the Newark Inter-Racial Council. The unit's next meeting was not until March 1945 and had only five attendees, Moorfield among them. Her chief interest was again Newark's African Americans, who she claimed were being discriminated against in Newark's war industries.

During and after the war, Moorfield was active in church work and some women's clubs. Her health deteriorated after the war and she spent much time in hospitals and nursing homes. Most of her friends were dead or incapacitated and she increasingly depended on her daughter, Hannah.

Amelia Moorfield died in February 1950, survived by her daughter and one grandson. She was profiled forty-seven years after her death in *Past and Promise: The Lives of New Jersey Women*.

Nancy Cox was located in 1998, living in Santa Barbara, California. Her Newark days were still fresh in her mind, perhaps the most vivid memories in her long and active life. She was still protesting against what she perceived as social injustices. A member of the Society of Friends, once a week Nancy and her husband stood silently in front of the Santa Barbara Art Museum carrying signs that called for the abolishment of capital punishment.

Nancy left Newark in 1939, at the age of twenty-five, never to return. For the next twenty years she was constantly in motion, relocating ten times. She remained an ardent leftist, taking jobs with the Massachusetts and National Councils for American-Soviet Friendship, organizing for the Union of Social Service Workers, and assisting Corliss Lamont. Interspersed with these positions were careers in farming, real estate sales, poodle breeding (in Greenwich Village), tapestry weaving, and sculpting.

In 1959, Nancy began studying Quakerism and for the rest of her life remained active in the movement. Many of her subsequent activities centered around Quaker social services and education. She served as assistant director of the Quaker Berea Institute in Philadelphia, where she taught and developed curricula. She became a board member of the Philadelphia NAACP and was appointed to the Philadelphia Human Relations Committee. In the 1960s, she moved to Providence, Rhode Island where she worked as a program coordinator for one of the city's community action programs, "Self-Help, Inc."

During the 1970s, Nancy spent much of the time nursing her father and sculpting. In 1977, she ran into Russell Hollister, whom she had first met at Antioch College in the early 1930s. They were soon married, the fourth time for her. My 1998 interview with her inspired Nancy to write a memoir, *My Story, 1934-1939*. Nancy died in 2001, survived by her husband.

Newark's "Führer," Herman Von Busch, suffered during the war, but by its end he was able to resume a normal life. On December 31, 1941, a warrant was issued for his arrest on the grounds that he was an enemy alien. It was not served, however, because it was discovered that Von Busch was an American citizen. The Department of Justice subsequently instituted denaturalization proceedings to revoke his citizenship. During fall 1942 the proceedings, the War Department had Von Busch fired from Public Service. As part of the denaturalization proceedings, the FBI questioned his friends, family, co-workers, neighbors, and former Bund members. Executives of his long-time employer, Newark Public Service Electric and Gas, attested to his Americanism. However, the FBI noted that the CIO's Light Workers Organizing Committee, which represented Public Service employees, had complained that Von Busch was a Nazi and asked for his removal from the company. Von Busch claimed in an FBI interview that he was a patriotic American who was active in the Red Cross and spent $3 every week on United States War Bonds. The case dragged on until July 1944, when Federal Judge William F. Smith dismissed the complaint. No treasonable activities had been discovered. The FBI closed the Newark Führer's file in August 1945.

Von Busch was rehired by Public Service soon after the federal charges were dropped and he remained there until his retirement in the early 1950s. Still popular with a certain stratum of Newark and Irvington German-Americans, Von Busch began a new career as the manager of Schwabenhalle. He remained at this job and in his Newark house until his death in 1968.

Bibliography

Books, Journals, Periodicals

Adler, Selig and Thomas E. Connolly. *The History of the Jewish Community of Buffalo.* Philadelphia: The Jewish Publication Society of America, 1960.

Allan, Douglas. *Building Careers.* Newark, NJ: The Lowden Publishers, 1934.

Bayor, Ronald H. *Neighbors in Conflict: The Irish, Germans, Jews, and Italians of New York City, 1929-1941.* Urbana: University of Illinois Press, 1988.

Bell, Leland V. *In Hitler's Shadow: The Anatomy of American Nazism.* Port Washington, NY: Kennikat Press, 1973.

Belth, Nathan C. *A Promise to Keep, A Narrative of the American Encounter with Anti-Semitism.* New York: Times Books, 1979.

Bodner, Allen. *When Boxing was a Jewish Sport.* Westport, CT: Praeger, 1997.

Boxerman, Burton Alan. "Rise of Anti-Semitism in St. Louis, 1933-1945." *YIVO Annual,* XIV (1969), pp. 251-269.

Berman, Susan. *Easy Street.* New York: Dial Press, 1981.

Breitman, Richard and Alan M. Kraut. *American Refugee Policy and European Jewry, 1933-1945.* Bloomington: Indiana University Press, 1987.

Brinkley, Alan. *The End of Reform: New Deal Liberalism in Recession and War.* New York: Alfred A. Knopf, 1995.

Buhle, Paul. "Jews and American Communism: The Cultural Question." *Radical History Review,* 23, Spring 1980, pp. 9-33.

Canedy, Susan. *America's Nazis: A Democratic Dilemma.* Menlo Park, CA: Markgraf Publications, 1990.

Chadwin, Mark Lincoln. *The Hawks of World War II.* Chapel Hill: University of North Carolina Press, 1968.

Cohen, Robert. *When the Old Left Was Young.* New York: Oxford University Press, 1993.

Cole, Wayne S. *Charles A. Lindbergh and the Battle Against American Intervention in World War II.* New York: Harcourt Brace Jovanovich, 1974.

Cox- Hollister, Nancy. *My Life.* Unpublished manuscript, undated, 360 pages.

—. *My Story.* Santa Barbara, CA: Self-published, 2001.

Cunningham, John T. *Newark.* Newark: The New Jersey Historical Society, 1988.

Cutler, Irving. *The Jews of Chicago.* Urbana: University of Illinois Press, 1996.

Detzer, Dorothy. *Appointment on the Hill.* New York: Henry Holt & Company, 1948.

Diamond, Sander A. *The Nazi Movement in the United States, 1924-1941.* Ithaca, NY: Cornell University Press, 1974.

Doenecke, Justus D. *In Danger Undaunted: the Anti-Intervention Movement of 1940-1941 as Revealed in the Papers of the America First Committee.* Stanford, CA: Hoover Institution Press, 1990.

Eisenberg, Dennis, Uri Dan, and Eli Landau. *Meyer Lansky, Mogul of the Mob.* New York: Paddington Press, 1979.

Endleman, Judith E. *The Jewish Community of Indianapolis.* Bloomington: Indiana University Press, 1984.

Feingold, Henry L. *A Time for Searching: Entering the Mainstream, 1920-1945* (Vol. IV, The Jewish People in America). Baltimore, MD: The Johns Hopkins University Press, 1992.

Friedman Murray, ed. *Jewish Life in Philadelphia, 1830-1940.* Philadelphia: ISHI Publications, 1983.

Fry, Varian. *Surrender on Demand.* Boulder, CO: Johnson Books, 1997.

Frye, Alton. *Nazi Germany and the American Hemisphere, 1933-1941.* New Haven, CT: Yale University Press, 1967.

Gartner, Lloyd P. *History of the Jews of Cleveland.* Cleveland, OH: Western Reserve Historical Society, 1978.

Glaser, Martha. " The German-American Bund in New Jersey." *New Jersey History,* XCII, (Spring 1974), pp. 33-49.

Goodman, Walter. *The Committee: The Extraordinary Career of the House Committee on Un-American Activities.* New York: Farrar Strauss, 1968.

Gordon, Rabbi Albert I. *Jews in Transition.* Minneapolis: University of Minnesota Press, 1949.

Gordon, Felice D. *After Winning: The Legacy of the New Jersey Suffragists, 1920-1947.* New Brunswick, NJ: Rutgers University Press, 1986.

Gottlieb, Moshe R. "In the Shadow of War: The American Anti-Nazi Boycott Movement in 1939-1941." *American Jewish Historical Quarterly* 62 (2), December 1972, pp. 146-161.

—.   "Boycott, Rescue, and Ransom: The Threefold Dilemma of American Jewry in 1938-1939," *Yivo Annual XV,* 1974, pp. 235-279.

—.   *American Anti-Nazi Resistance, 1933-1941.* New York: Ktav Publishing House, 1982.

Grover, Warren. "In Search of Jennie Caputo." *New Jersey Italian Tribune,* 5/18/00, 8/17/00.

—. *Relief in Newark, 1929-1933.* M.A.Thesis, New York University, 1961.

Hanighen, Frank C. " Foreign Political Movements in the United States." *Foreign Affairs,* Vol.16, No. I (October 1937), pp. 1-20.

Helmreich, William B. *The Enduring Community: The Jews of Newark and MetroWest.* New Brunswick, NJ: Transaction Publishers, 1999.

Hilberg, Raul. *The Destruction of the European Jews,* Vol. 1. New York: Holmes & Meier, 1985.

Jackson, Kenneth T. and Barbara. "The Black Experience in Newark: The Growth of the Ghetto, 1870-1970." In William C. Wright, ed., *New Jersey Since 1860: New Findings and Interpretations,* pp. 36-59. Trenton: New Jersey Historical Commission, 1972

Johnson, Walter. *The Battle Against Isolation.* Chicago: University of Chicago Press, 1944.

Jonas, Manfred. *Isolationism in America, 1935-1941.* Ithaca, NY: Cornell University Press, 1966.

Journal of Industry & Finance, New Jersey, Vols. 10-13, December 1935-May 1939.

Kelley, James. *Memoirs of Msgr.(Doc) Kelley.* Locust, NJ: Self-published, 1987.

Kingdon, Frank. *Jacob's Ladder.* New York: L.B. Fischer, 1943.

—. *Inside the Golden Door: A Personal Report on American Institutions and Men Observed Through Fifty Years After Immigration.* Unpublished manuscript, 289 pages, circa 1962.

Klehr, Harvey. *The Heyday of American Communism: The Depression Decade.* New York: Basic Books, 1984.

Klinger, Maurice, A. Abbot Rosen. and Dr. Walter Zand. "Jewish Defense Agencies." In *History of Chicago's Jewry, 1911-1961*, pp. 175-178. Chicago: Sentinel Publishing Co., 1961.

Knobloch, Evelyn Katherine. *The Nazi Bund Movement in Metropolitan New York.* M.A. Thesis, Columbia University.

Laqueur, Walter. A History of Zionism. New York: Schocken Books, 1972

Levitt, Cyril H. and William Shaffir. *The Riot at Christie Pits.* Toronto: Lester & Orpen Dennys, 1987.

Lewy, Guenter. *The Cause that Failed: Communism in American Political Life.* New York: Oxford University Press, 1990.

Lipstadt, Deborah E. *Beyond Belief: The American Press and the Coming of the Holocaust, 1933-1945.* New York: Free Press, 1986.

Lookstein, Haskel. *Were We Our Brothers' Keepers? The Public Response of American Jews to the Holocaust, 1938-1944.* New York: Hartmore House, 1985.

Lowenstein, Alan V. *Alan V. Lowenstein: New Jersey Lawyer and Community Leader.* New Brunswick: New Jersey Institute for Continuing Legal Education, 2001.

Mandell, Richard D. *The Nazi Olympics.* New York: Macmillan, 1971.

Mendes-Flohr, Paul and Jehuda Reinharz, eds. *The Jew in the Modern World—A Documentary History.* New York: Oxford University Press, 1995.

New Jersey Legislature, *Report of the New Jersey State Temporary Commission on the Condition of the Urban Colored Population.* Trenton, 1939.

Newsweek. "Longie Zwillman: Big Businessman and/or Gangster," Vol. 38, No. 9 (August 27, 1951), pp. 23-27.

Ogden, August Raymond. *The Dies Committee: A Study of the Special House Committee for the Investigation of Un-American Activities, 1938-1944,* Washington, DC: Catholic University of America Press, 1945.

Oshinsky, David, M., Richard P. McCormick and Daniel Horn. *The Case of the Nazi Professor.* New Brunswick, NJ: Rutgers University Press, 1989.

Price, Clement Alexander, ed. *Freedom Not Far Distant: A Documentary History of Afro-Americans in New Jersey.* Newark: New Jersey Historical Society, 1980.

—. "The Beleaguered City as a Promised Land: Blacks in Newark, 1917-1947." In William C. Wright, ed., *Urban New Jersey Since 1870,* pp. 10-45. Trenton: New Jersey Historical Commission, 1975.

—.*The Afro-American Community of Newark, 1917-1947: A Social History.* PHD Dissertation, Rutgers University, 1975.

Public Service Electric and Gas. "*Public Service News,*" 4/15/30. Public Service Electric and Gas. "*Public Service News,*" 4/15/30.

Raphael, Marc Lee. *Jews and Judaism in a Midwestern Community: Columbus Ohio, 1840-1975.* Columbus: Ohio Historical Society, 1975.

Remak, Joachim. "Friends of the New Germany: The Bund and German-American Relations." *Journal of Modern History,* XXIX, (1957), pp. 38-41.

Rockaway, Robert A. *But-He Was Good to His Mother: The Lives and Crimes of Jewish Gangsters.* Jerusalem: Gefen Publishing, 1993.

Rogge, John O. *The Official German Report on Nazi Penetration, 1924-1942: Pan-Arabism 1939-Today.* New York: Thomas Yoseloff, 1961.

Salvemini, Gaetano. *Italian Fascist Activities in the United States.* New York: Center for Migration Studies, 1977.

Sarna, Jonathan D. and Nancy H. Klein. *The Jews of Cincinnati.* Cincinnati: Hebrew Union College, 1989.

Sayers, Michael and Albert E. Kahn. *Sabotage! The Secret War Against America.* New York: Harper & Brothers Publishers, 1942.

Shannon, David A. *The Socialist Party of America: A History.* New York: Macmillan Company, 1955.

Shapiro, Edward. S. "The Jews of New Jersey," *The New Jersey Ethnic Experience.* Barbara Cunningham, ed., Union City: Wm. H. Wise & Co., 1977, pp. 294-313.

Siegel, Alan A. *Out of Our Past: A History of Irvington, New Jersey.* Irvington, NJ: Irvington Centennial Committee, 1974.

—. *Smile, A Picture History of Olympic Park, 1887-1965.* New Brunswick, NJ: Rutgers University Press, 1995.

Slater, Robert. *Great Jews in Sports.* Middle Village, NY: Jonathan David Publishers, 1983.

Sorin, Gerald. "Mutual Contempt, Mutual Benefit: The Strained Encounter Between German and Eastern European Jews in America, 1880-1920," *American Jewish History,* LXXXI, (Autumn, 1993), pp. 34-59.

Soyer, Daniel. *Jewish Immigrant Associations and American Identity in New York, 1880-1939.* Cambridge, MA: Harvard University Press, 1997.

Stellhorn, Paul. *Depression and Decline: Newark, New Jersey: 1929-1941.* PHD. Dissertation, Rutgers University, 1982.

—. "Champion of the City: Reflections on the Political Career of Meyer C. Ellenstein." Unpublished manuscript based upon a paper delivered before the Jewish Historical Society of MetroWest, June 9, 1997.

Stenehjem, Michele Flynn. *An American First: John T. Flynn and the America First Committee.* New Rochelle, NY: Arlington House, 1976.

Strong, Donald. *Organized AntiSemitism in America.* Washington, DC: American Council on Foreign Affairs, 1941.

Stuart, Mark A. *Gangster # 2: Longy Zwillman.* Secaucus, NJ: Lyle Stuart, 1985.

Swichkow, Louis J. and Lloyd Gartner. *The History of the Jews of Milwaulkee.* Philadelphia: Jewish Publication Society of America, 1963.

Teller, Judd, *Scapegoat of Revolution.* New York: Charles Scribner's Sons, 1954.

—.*Strangers and Natives, The Evolution of the American Jew from 1921 to the Present.* New York: Delacorte Press, 1968.

Tenenbaum, Joseph. The Anti-Nazi Boycott Movement in the United States. *Yad Vashem Studies* III, (1959), pp. 141-159.

Urofsky, Melvin I. *A Voice That Spoke for Justice: The Life and times of Stephen S. Wise.* Albany: State University of New York Press, 1982.

U.S. Bureau of the Census. *Fifteenth Census of the United States: 1930, New Jersey Abstract,* New Jersey Division, Newark Public Library, n.d.

—. *Sixteenth Census of the United States: 1940,* Population, Vol. II, Part 4, Washington, DC,1943.

U.S. Congressional Committee Hearings, A Subcommittee of the Special Committee on Un-American Activities, 73rd Congress, 2nd Session, Confidential Committee Print, at Newark, N.J., May 26, 1934.

—.Hearing No. 73-N.J.-1

U.S. Congressional Hearings, Investigation of Un-American Propaganda Activities in the United States, Committee on Un-American Activities House of Representatives, 77th Congress, First Session, Vol. 14.

Urquhart, Frank John. *A History of the City of Newark, Vols. I, II.* New York: Lewis Historical Publishing Co., 1913.

Valparaiso University, *"The Record,"* 1921.

Vecoli, Rudolph J. *The People of New Jersey*. Princeton: D. Van Nostrand Company, Inc., 1965.

Velie, Lester. "From Rags to Riches." *Collier's*, Vol. 128, No. 9 (September 1, 1951), pp. 28-29, 48-50.

Vorspan, Max and Lloyd P. Gartner. *History of the Jews of Los Angeles*. Philadelphia: Jewish Publication Society, 1970.

Walker, Samuel. *In Defense of American Liberties: A History of the ACLU*. New York: Oxford University Press, 1990.

Weinstein, Allen and Alexander Vassiliev. *The Haunted Wood: Soviet Espionage in America—the Stalin Era*. New York: Random House, 1999.

Women's Project of New Jersey, Inc. *Past and Promise: Lives of New Jersey Women*. Syracuse: Syracuse University Press, 1997.

Manuscript Collections

Abramowitz, Sidney (Nat Arno), Freedom of Information Act (FOIA), File 60-1501-3203, Federal Bureau of Investigation, Department of Justice.

ACLU Papers, Manuscript Collection 001, Seeley G. Mudd Manuscript Library, Princeton University.

America First Committee, Hoover Institution Archives, Palo Alto, California.

American Jewish Committee, Meetings of the Executive Committee, 1933-1940, American Jewish Committee Library, New York.

American Jewish Committee, Morris Waldman Archives, Record Group 347.6, YIVO, New York.

American Jewish Congress, Record Group 77, American Jewish Historical Society, New York.

Louis Bamberger Biographical File, Jewish Historical Society of MetroWest (JHSMW), Whippany, New Jersey.

Temple B'Nai Jeshurun Collection, Record Group 15-98, JHSMW.

Papers of J. (Jacob) X. Cohen, Record Group 111, Steven Wise Free Synagogue Archive, New York

Committee to Defend America by Aiding the Allies, Manuscript Collection 011, Seeley G. Mudd Manuscript Library, Princeton, New Jersey.

Conference of Jewish Charities of Newark, JHSMW.
    Board of Director's Minutes, Record Group 1, S1.
    Director of Social Plannings Agencies and Subject Files, Record Group 2, SG6, S1.
    Executive Committee Minutes, Record Group 1, SG1.
    Executive Director's Agency Files, Record Group 2, SG6.
    National Agencies File, Record Group 2, SG4.

Communist Party of the USA (CPUSA) Records, Reels 225, 255, 260, 269, 270,280, 281, 297, 300, 302-304, 306, 307, 315, Library of Congress.

Contemporary, Archives and Manuscript Collection of the New Jersey Division, Newark Public Library.

Reminiscences of Samuel Dickstein, Oral History Project, Columbia University Rare Book and Manuscript Library.

Samuel Dickstein Papers, Record Group 8, American Jewish Archives, Cincinnati, OH.

Papers of Charles Edison, New Jersey State Archives.

Federation of Women's Clubs, New Jersey, Archives and Manuscripts Collection of the New Jersey Division, Newark Public Library.

Fight for Freedom, Manuscript Collection 025, Seeley G. Mudd Manuscript Library, Princeton, NJ.

Papers of Rabbi Solomon Foster, Record Group 1350, New Jersey Historical Society.

J. George Fredman Collection, National Museum of American Jewish Military History, Washington, DC.

Hamilton L. Garner, FOIA, File 190-HQ-1296108, Federal Bureau of Investigation, U.S. Department of Justice.

Rev. Lucius Hamilton Garner Papers, Author's Possession, West Orange, NJ.

Rev. Lucius Hamilton Garner, bMS 900/16, bMS 1446/68, Andover-Harvard Theological Library, Cambridge, MA.

Records of the German-American Bund, Record Group 131, National Archives.

German-American League for Culture, FOIA, File 100-HQ-131905, Federal Bureau of Investigation, U.S. Department of Justice.

Dr. Abraham Grossman Papers, Record Group 286, YIVO, New York.

Arthur Garfield Hayes Papers, Manuscript Collection 72, Seeley G. Mudd Manuscript Library, Princeton University.

Israel Sick Benefits Society (KUV) Records, Record Group 30, JHSMW.

Jewish Agency for Palestine, American Section, Record Group 5, Central Zionist Archive, Jerusalem.

Records of the Joint Boycott Council, Special Collections, New York Public Library.

Junior League of Newark, Inc., Archives and Manuscripts Collection of the New Jersey Division, Newark Public Library.

Dr. S. William Kalb Biographical File, JHSMW.

Dr. S. William Kalb Interview, William Wiener Oral History Library of the American Jewish Committee, Jewish Division, New York Public Library.

Papers of Dr. S. William Kalb, Record Group 10-99, JHSMW.

James F. Kelley Papers, Record Group 2.11, Walsh Library Special Collections Center, Seton Hall University.

Frank Kingdon, FOIA, File 77-15553, Federal Bureau of Investigation, U.S. Department of Justice.

Frank Kingdon Papers, John Kingdon, Melbourne Florida, Jill Kingdon, Vero Beach, FL.

Frank Kingdon Scrapbook, Archives and Manuscripts Collections of the New Jersey Division, Newark Public Library.

Matthias Kohler, FOIA, File 100-9464, Federal Bureau of Investigation, U.S. Department of Justice.

Labor's Non-Partisan League, FOIA, File 61-10749, Federal Bureau of Investigation, U.S. Department of Justice.

Papers of A. Harry Moore, New Jersey State Archives.

Amelia Moorfield, Record Group1051, New Jersey Historical Society.

National Council of Jewish Women-Essex County Section, Livingston, NJ.

National Council of Jewish Women-Newark Section, Archives and Manuscripts Collection of the New Jersey Division, Newark Public Library.

Nazism, Record Group 307, American Jewish Archives, Cincinnati, OH.

Newark Business and Professional Women's Club, Special Collections and University Archives, Rutgers University.

Newark City Directory, 1933-1941, City of Newark Archives.

Newark Clergy Folder, Archives and Manuscripts Collection of the New Jersey Division, Newark Public Library.

Newark College of Arts and Science, University of Newark Office Records, 1934-1936, Special Collections and University Archives, Rutgers University.

Newark Defense Council, Archives and Manuscripts Collection of the New Jersey Division, Newark Public Library.

Newark Interracial Council, Archives and Manuscripts Collection of the New Jersey Division, Newark Public Library.

Newark Municipal Court Records, 1933, City of Newark Archive.

National Negro Congress, FOIA, File 100-1467, Federal Bureau of Investigation, U.S. Department of Justice.

Non-Sectarian Anti-Nazi League, FOIA, Files 100-9552, HQ60-1817, Federal Bureau of Investigation, U.S. Department of Justice.

Non-Sectarian Anti-Nazi League, Columbia University Rare Book and Manuscript Library.

Peoples Mandate, Record Group 109, Peace Collection, Swarthmore College.

Rabbi Eli Pilchik Collection, Record Group 40-99, JHSMW.

Rabbi Julius Silberfeld Biographical File, JHSMW.

Michael Aaron Stavitsky Biographical File, JHSMW.

Papers of Michael Aaron Stavitsky, JHSMW.

Joseph Tenenbaum Papers, Record Group 283, YIVO, New York.

Records of the U. S. House of Representatives, 73rd Congress, Committee Papers, Special Committee on Un-American Activities and Nazi Propaganda, Record Group 233, National Archives.

Daily Reports of the United States Secret Service, 1933-1936, National Archives.

Samuel Untermyer Papers, Record Group 251, American Jewish Archives, Cincinnati, OH.

Herman Von Busch, FOIA, File 100-25344, Federal Bureau of Investigation, U.S. Department of Justice.

Thomas Walsh Papers, Record Group 5, Walsh Library Special Collections Center, Seton Hall University.

Women's International League for Peace and Freedom, Record Group 43, Peace Collection, Swarthmore College.

Women's International League for Peace and Freedom-Essex County Group, New Jersey Branch, Author's Possession, West Orange, NJ.

WPA New Jersey Writers' Project, New Jersey Ethnological Survey, New Jersey State Archives.

Abner Zwillman, FOIA, Files 92-3105, 62-360-85, Federal Bureau of Investigation, U.S. Department of Justice.

Abner Zwillman Biographical File, JHSMW.

Newspapers

Dana College Chronicle	1934
Der Tog	1933
Elizabeth Daily Journal	1938
Forward	1933
Irvington Herald	1933-1941
Jewish Chronicle	1933-1941
New Jersey Herald News	1938
Newark Evening News	1933-1941
Newark Evening News Morgue	1920-1951
Newark Herald News	1938
Newark Ledger	1936-1937
Newark Star Eagle	1933-1939
Newark Star Ledger	1940-1941

Newark Sunday Call	1933-1941
New York Daily Mirror	1933
New York Evening Journal	1933
New York Journal	1933
New York Herald Tribune	1933
New York Times	1933-1941
New York Daily Mirror	1933
New York Evening Journal	1933
New York Journal	1933
New York Herald Tribune	1933
New York Times	1933-1941

Interviews

Jerry Alenick (phone), 6/12/97
Anne Arnold (Arno), 8/7/97, 8/8/97
Vivian Mintz Barnert, 11/15/99
Gertrude Behrle, 5/9/98
Jerry Ben-Asher, 5/16/98
Irving Berlin, 1/17/97
Dr. Arthur Bernstein, 9/16/96
Bernard Castellane, 1/10/97
Frank Davis, 5/16/96
Jill Kingdon Dempsey, 12/17/98
Dr. Samuel Diener, 3/9/98
Irving Edisis (phone), 4/15/98
Dr. Harvey Einhorn, 2/19/98
Pat Kalb Einhorn, 1/12/97
Dr. Ben Epstein (deceased), 6/19/98
Herman Fast, 1/10/97
Al Fisher, 6/16/98
Shirley Flax, 2/13/98
Lucille Freeman, 6/6/97
Eleanor Friedman (deceased), 4/7/99
David Garner (deceased), 6/27/98
Fradleigh Garner, 7/16/98
Dr. Peter Garner, 6/27/98
Charlotte Gelb, 4/19/98
Martin Gen, 11/13/97
Jack Gipfel, 1/7/96, 1/17/96, 12/24/96, 1/2/97
Itzig Goldstein (deceased), 6/14/96
Abe Greene, 4/20/00
Fred Haber, 9/20/96
Leon Haber, 9/20/96
Dave Halper (deceased), 6/3/96
Abraham Harkavy (deceased), 1/9/97, 1/11/97
Dotty Hinkes, 5/24/96
Nancy Cox Hollister (deceased), 4/17/98, 4/18/98
Martin Horowitz, 9/24/97
Paul Josloff (deceased), 6/4/96

Richard Kessler, 2/11/99
John Kingdon, (deceased) 5/31/98
Dr. Milton Konvitz, 2/15/00
Phil Konvitz, 11/21/96
Daniel Kraemer, 8/4/98
Louis Kraemer, 8/4/98
Joe Lerner, 5/16/97
Lowenstein, Alan V., 9/20/96, 6/9/98
Leo and Lilly Lowenthal, 2/27/98
Murray Manders, 4/6/97
Bernard Margolis, 8/12/98
Seymour Markowitz (deceased), 10/17/96
Grace Milgram (deceased), 4/14/98
Dr. Bella Kussy Milmed (deceased), 2/14/98, 2/15/98
Dave Muskat, 1/12/97
Joe "Yuss" Pisano (deceased), 4/12/97
Alex Portnoff, 6/25/96, 1/11/97
Hoxie Rabinowitz, 1/12/97
Barbara Rachlin, 2/23/98
Walter Rayelt (deceased), 6/4/96
Gertrude Rieger, 2/20/98
Milton Ritz (phone), 4/5/98
Hon. Peter Rodino, 6/26/98
Anne Schreiber, 5/7/98
Schwarz, Saul (deceased), 9/7/98
William Shannon, 11/7/98
Shirley Shapiro, 4/28/98
Fay Skuratofsky (deceased), 5/12/96
Steve Slott, 4/7/99
Phil Small, 4/8/98
Saul Stettin, 2/18/98
Martha Stone, 3/2/98
Heshey Weiner (deceased), 6/29/96
Ida Weiner, 7/6/98
Rose Abramowitz Yannick (deceased), 8/7/98
Judge Leo Yanoff, 2/12/98.

Index

á Kempis Society, 241
Abarbanel, Albert, 108n68
Abeles, Albert, 301n119
Abramowitz, Sidney. *See* **Arno, Nat**
Abramson, Alexander, 258
academic freedom, 108n70, 160
ACLU. *See* American Civil Liberties Union
Addams, Jane, 148
Adonis, Harold John, 321, 331n81
Adonis, Joe, 44
AFC. *See* America First Committee
AFF (American Fellowship Forum), 265–267
AFL. *See* American Federation of Labor
African Americans: American Communist Party and, 144, 162, 239; anti-Nazi activism, 327; Community Forum, 155; Community Forum and Institute, 173n118; Depression and, 143; discrimination against, 22, 143, 240–241, 249n111, 258; "Don't Buy Where You Don't Work" campaign, 239; Garner and, Luke, 155–156; housing, 258; infant mortality, 239; Italy's invasion of Ethiopia, 162; Jews, relations with, 239, 241; Kristallnacht and, 239, 249n110; liberalism and, 142, 146; most influential liberal among, 143; municipal workers, 239; Newark Community Chest, 22; population of, 3, 143; press coverage, 240–241; Roosevelt, support for, Franklin Delano, 143; Southern influx, 21–22, 327; teachers, 239; Third Ward, 6, 21–22, 239, 246n7, 258; unions, 249n111; welfare cases, 143
agents provocateurs, 7, 81
Agfa Film, 247n47
AJC. *See* American Jewish Congress

ALAWF. *See* American League Against War and Fascism
Albano, Nicholas, 295–296
Alenick, Michael: Bund's Schwabenhalle rally (Oct. 27, 1938), 234; Camp Nordland, 225–226; German-American Bund, 267; Israel KUV, 216; Italian anti-Jewish laws, 227; Kalb and, 221; Non-Sectarian Anti-Nazi League, 218–219, 281
Alexander, Walter G., 173n118, 245
Alien Registration Act (1940), 289
Alien Registration Bill (1939), 260
ALPD. *See* American League for Peace and Democracy
Amalgamated Clothing Workers of America, 114
America First Committee (AFC): anti-Semitism and, 321, 329n53; Armistice Day rally (Nov. 11, 1941), 320–321; avoidance of "Jew," 315; Christian Front and, 285, 313; dissolution, 322; famous Americans attracted to, 293; forerunners, 266; founding, 292; German-American Bund and, 313; Lindbergh and, 292, 315–316; Minutemen and, 315, 317–320, 323; Mosque Theater rally (Sept. 23, 1941), 316–319, 330n68; Nazism and, 1; Newark chapter membership, 314; non-interventionism and, 307, 313, 315–316; request to publish membership list, 306n233, 314
American Christian Conference on Palestine, 165
American Civil Liberties Union (ACLU): among liberal organizations, 145; Anti-Nazi Act (1935), 88–90; anti-Nazi activism and, 88–90; Bergel academic freedom case, 108n70; Camp Nordland arrests, 288; Camp

351

190, 194, 219; cult of personality, 177–178; Ford Motors, 176; Frei Korps member, 175; Friends of the New Germany, 176; German-American Bund, 175, 202, 209, 210, 226; Gissibl and, 176; HUAC hearings (Aug. 16, 1939), 269; Kalb and, 268; Klapprott and, 288–289; Kohler and, 259; Kunze and, 176, 288–289; military service, 175; Nazi Party membership, 176; publicist, 189; strategy of Nazifying German-Americans, 194

Kummel, Max, Mrs., 301n119

Kunze, Gerhard William: American Führer, 288; arrests, 288; Bund's Hackensack rally (1937), 202–203; Bund's New Milford meeting (1938), 232–233; German Day (1940), 290; Hercules Powder Plant tragedy, 294; indictments, 295; Kuhn and, 176, 288–289; sentencing, 308

Kurk, Diran, 272–273, 301n115, 317, 319

KUVs (sick and benefit societies): anti-Nazi activism, 324; anti-Nazi boycott, 116, 120, 133, 185, 187, 218; arrangements with doctors, 116; defined, 116; Erste Bershader KUV, 18, 63, 116, 120, 187, 217; Israel KUV, 18, 116, 120, 187, 216, 217; Israel Verein, 218; purpose, 14, 26n17; Rzezower KUV, 217

L. Bamberger & Co., 120–124, 130–131, 187, 241

Labor's Non-Partisan League: anti-Nazi activism, 256–257; Bund's Schwabenhalle rally (Oct. 27, 1938), 234, 235; communists and, 256, 278, 302n143, 327n11; Congress of Industrial Organizations, 256; founding, 144; leaders, 233–234, 278, 310; Lerner and, 144; purpose, 310; WILPF's Mother's Peace Day (1940), 279

Laddey, John V., 63

LaGuardia, Fiorello, 15, 189–190, 227, 260

Lamont, Corliss, 339

Landon, Alf, 142

landsmanshaftn. See KUVs

Lang, Leo, 13

Lansky, Meyer, 9n3, 44, 54

Lasser, Aaron, 120, 173n118

Laurel Gardens, 45, 50

Laval, Pierre, 291–292

Lazarus, Betty, 188

League of Industrial Democracy (LID), 248n74

League of Women Voters (LWV), 148, 149

Lehlbach, Frederick R., 12

Lehman, Herbert, 90

Leipzig, Max, 25

Leiter, N. P., 118

Leonard, Benny, 49

Lerner, Jack, 144, 233–234

Lett, Harold, 108n68, 143, 241, 298n49

Levine, Benny, 49, 50, 52

Levine, Gertrude, 125

Levitsky, Louis, 300n107

Lewis, John L., 144, 189

Leyden, Joseph, 202

liberalism/liberals, 138–170; African Americans and, 142, 146; American Civil Liberties Union's place in, 145; American Communist Party and, 3, 144, 276; anti-Bund coalition, 230–231; anti-Nazi activism, 3, 139, 169–170, 174; Business and Professional Women's Club, 147, 149–150; educators and, 170n15; failure to promote anti-Nazism, reasons for, 139; Garner and, Luke, 138, 152, 153; issues addressed by, 141, 146; Kingdon and, Frank, 138, 152, 153; Moorfield and, Amelia, 138; New Deal, 141–142; pacifists and, 138; personifications, 138–139; Socialist Party and, 144; Spanknoebel's denunciation of, 28; women's organizations, 146–147, 151

Liberator, 84

LID (League of Industrial Democracy), 248n74

Lieberman, Louis, 222–223

Lindbergh, Charles: America First Committee, 292, 315–316; anti-Semitism, 299n77, 315–316; called future commander of US, 309; candidacy for president, 266; Germany and, 292, 299n77; Goering and, 299n77; war agitators speech, 315–316

Linden (New Jersey), 92–93